INCLUDING ADOLESCENTS WITH DISABILITIES IN GENERAL EDUCATION CLASSROOMS

INCLUDING ADOLESCENTS WITH DISABILITIES IN GENERAL EDUCATION CLASSROOMS

TOM E. C. SMITH
University of Arkansas

BARBARA C. GARTIN
University of Arkansas

NIKKI L. MURDICK
St. Louis University

PEARSON

Boston   Columbus   Indianapolis   New York   San Francisco   Upper Saddle River
Amsterdam   Cape Town   Dubai   London   Madrid   Milan   Munich   Paris   Montreal   Toronto
Delhi   Mexico City   São Paulo   Sydney   Hong Kong   Seoul   Singapore   Taipei   Tokyo

KH

Vice President and Editorial Director:
  Jeffery W. Johnston
Executive Editor and Publisher:
  Stephen D. Dragin
Editorial Assistant: Jamie Bushell
Vice President, Director of Marketing:
  Margaret Waples
Marketing Manager: Wesley Sellinger
Senior Managing Editor: Pamela D. Bennett
Senior Project Manager: Sheryl Glicker Langner
Senior Operations Supervisor: Matthew
  Ottenweller

Senior Art Director: Diane C. Lorenzo
Cover Designer: Kellyn E. Donnelly
Cover Image: SuperStock
Full-Service Project Management: S4Carlisle
  Publishing Services
Composition: S4Carlisle Publishing
  Services
Printer/Binder: Edwards Brothers
Cover Printer: Lehigh-Phoenix
  Color/Hagerstown
Text Font: Adobe Garamond Pro
  Regular

Credits and acknowledgments for material borrowed from other sources and reproduced, with permission, in this textbook appear on the appropriate page within the text.

Every effort has been made to provide accurate and current Internet information in this book. However, the Internet and information posted on it are constantly changing, so it is inevitable that some of the Internet addresses listed in this textbook will change.

Photo Credits: Anthony Magnacca/Merrill, pp. 2, 116, 164, 212, 266; Katelyn Metzger/Merrill, pp. 22, 234; George Dodson/PH College, p. 44; Michael Newman/PhotoEdit Inc., p. 72; Maria B. Vonada/Merrill, p. 92; Liz Moore/Merrill, p. 142; Prentice Hall School Division, p. 184; Robin Nelson/PhotoEdit Inc., p. 292; Laura Bolesta/Merrill, p. 314

Library of Congress Cataloging-in-Publication Data

Smith, Tom E. C.
  Including adolescents with disabilities in general education classrooms / Tom E. C. Smith, Barbara C. Gartin, Nikki L. Murdick.—1st ed.
    p. cm.
  ISBN-13: 978-0-13-501496-7
  ISBN-10: 0-13-501496-4
  1. Youth with disabilities—Education (Secondary)—United States. 2. Inclusive education—United States. I. Title.
  LC4031.S66 2012
  371.9'046--dc22

                              2011011757

10 9 8 7 6 5 4 3 2 1

PEARSON

ISBN-10:   0-13-501496-4
ISBN-13: 978-0-13-501496-7

3/6/10

Dedicated to

Debi, Ed,

and

Mike

PREFACE

Students with disabilities are receiving a better, more appropriate education in public schools than ever before. Since the passage of Public Law 94-142, the Education for All Handicapped Children Act of 1973, public schools have expanded the quality of services for this group of students to unparalleled levels. This law, which has been amended numerous times and is now called the Individuals with Disabilities Education Act (IDEA), has resulted in more students being identified as having disabilities and receiving services in inclusive settings with their nondisabled peers. In addition to IDEA, Section 504 of the Rehabilitation Act of 1973 and the Americans with Disabilities Act (ADA) have resulted in expanded services for students with disabilities in public schools.

While IDEA, Section 504, and the ADA have resulted in a tremendous expansion of appropriate services for students with disabilities, the primary gain has occurred at the elementary level. There continues to be large numbers of students with disabilities in middle school and high school whose educational programs are less than optimal. In elementary classrooms, teachers are typically prepared to teach students at varying developmental levels because their students often display widely different levels of development. Since elementary teachers primarily teach students basic skills, they are able to modify their instructional strategies and make accommodations without making significant changes to their teaching methods or course content. On the other hand, secondary teachers have primarily been prepared to teach subject matter content such as English, math, history, foreign languages, and science. They are often less knowledgeable about individual developmental differences than teachers in elementary grades, and are therefore unaware of strategies and instructional techniques that may be needed by students with disabilities. Many also assume that students are capable of success in their classrooms or they would not have been included. Unfortunately, the result too often is that without supports, many of these students experience great difficulties in content-based classes and are often unsuccessful. Middle and high school teachers, therefore, must develop an understanding of how to make accommodations and modifications to meet the needs of this group of students.

There is no doubt that students with disabilities in middle school and high school can be successful. However, in order for them to overcome the manifestations of their disability which impede their learning, teachers need to have an understanding of individual learning differences and different research-based techniques that can result in student learning and success. There are numerous strategies and techniques that are easy for teachers and other school personnel to use; many simply need to be instructed in how to use these strategies.

This text provides an overview of disabilities experienced by middle and high school students, and ways teachers can help them overcome their learning difficulties. Specific strategies, such as differentiated instruction, cooperative teaching, strategies instruction, and using peer-assisted learning are presented throughout the text, with examples on how to implement these strategies in daily instruction. Chapter opening questions help guide students through their reading by serving as advanced organizers.

The book is organized into two major sections. The first section, chapters 1–4, covers educational services for adolescents with disabilities. It provides an overview of adolescent development, different disabilities that can impact adolescents, and special education services available for this group of students. Also included is information on the legal bases for providing special education services and information on how to collaborate with families to meet the needs of this group of students. This section sets the stage for specific information on including students with disabilities in middle and secondary classrooms.

The second section, chapters 5–14, provides in-depth information on appropriate educational programs and strategies for students with disabilities in middle and secondary schools. Specific areas included are classroom management, coteaching, differentiated instruction, and strategies instruction. Additional chapters provide information and strategies for teaching specific content to students with disabilities, including literacy, math, science, self-determination, and social skills. Throughout each chapter, tables and figures are provided to help organize content. Several chapters also include scenarios related to the content of the chapter to provide real-life examples of how to implement different teaching methods.

This text provides students who are preparing to be middle and high school teachers with the knowledge and skills they need to successfully include students with disabilities in their classrooms. Many students identified as having disabilities are very capable of achieving success. It is incumbent on teachers, educational leaders, and other school staff to work with students and their families to assist them in achieving this success.

ACKNOWLEDGMENTS

We would like to acknowledge several individuals who were instrumental in the successful completion of this text. First and foremost, we want to thank all middle and high school teachers, administrators, and other school staff who make significant efforts each day to facilitate the success of students with disabilities. It is through their efforts that many students succeed as adolescents and later as adults in our society. Secondly, we want to thank our colleagues who picked up some of our job duties while we were engaged in researching and writing the book.

We also want to thank our families, including our adult children, who are permanent reminders of the importance of appropriate educational opportunities, and to our partners in life—Debi, Ed, and Mike—who provided support throughout the research and writing process. Our personal and professional lives would not be nearly as complete without the contributions these special individuals make every day. And finally we need to thank the reviewers who made significant contributions to the book with their constructive criticisms and great suggestions. These individuals include Greg Conderman, Northern Illinois University; Emily Bouck, Purdue University; Frances Butler, Weber State University; Melissa Jones, Northern Kentucky University; Maribeth Montgomery Kasik, Governors State University; Donna Kearns, University of Central Oklahoma; Gholam Kibna, Delaware State University; Keith Lenz, University of Kansas; Robbie Ludy, Buena Vista University; Mary Milleret Ring, University of South Dakota; Lynne Snyder, Berrien Regional Education Service Agency; Brenda-Jean Tyler, Radford University; Johanna Westby, Minot State University; and Lynn Zubov, Winston-Salem State University.

As always, this project would not have come to a successful conclusion without the great support from our editorial and publishing team at Pearson Education. This includes Ann Davis, our initial editor; Steve Dragin, who took over toward the end of the project; and Jamie Bushell, editorial assistant.

BRIEF CONTENTS

CONTENTS

Chapter 3

The Special Education Process in Middle and Secondary Schools   44

Chapter 4
Transition Programming for Adolescents with Disabilities   72

Chapter 5

School/Family Collaboration in a Middle/Secondary Inclusive Classroom   92

Chapter 6

Classroom Management and Adolescents with Disabilities   116

Chapter 12

Strategies for Teaching Social Skills to Adolescents with Disabilities   266

Chapter 13

Strategies for Teaching Self-Determination Skills to Adolescents with Disabilities   292

Chapter 14
Vocational/Technical Education for Adolescents with Disabilities   314

INCLUDING ADOLESCENTS WITH DISABILITIES IN GENERAL EDUCATION CLASSROOMS

1

Adolescents with Disabilities

Study Questions

1. How are adolescents unique?

2. How are secondary schools designed to meet these unique needs of adolescent students?

3. What types of disabilities might secondary students in your classroom exhibit?

4. Why is it essential for future secondary teachers to be prepared to address the diverse educational needs of students in their classrooms?

TYPES OF DEVELOPMENT

Educators agree that secondary schools, both middle level and high school, significantly differ in organization and academic and social demands from elementary schools. These differences are a result of not only the focus of the school and the curriculum but also of the characteristics of the students—that is, adolescents. So, who are these adolescents, and why is school organized differently for them?

Students in secondary schools comprise a diverse group labeled adolescents. Adolescence is a specific transitional period between childhood and adulthood beginning somewhere between ages 10 and 13 years and ending in the late teens or early 20s. During this period, adolescents move through developmental changes physically, cognitively, and emotionally. Lerner and Johns (2009) reported that "the period of adolescence is marked by conflicting feelings about (1) freedom and independence versus security and dependence, (2) rapid physical changes, (3) developing sexuality, (4) peer pressure, and (5) self-consciousness. Many of the characteristics of adolescence can affect the processes of learning" (p. 286). While all adolescents undergo these changes, they occur at different rates for different individuals.

Developmental psychologists have identified specific characteristics evident in younger adolescents compared to older adolescents, which are not the result of genetics or cultural differences (Kellough & Kellough, 2008). In 1987, the California Middle Grades Task Force organized the characteristics of *young* adolescents into five developmental groups: intellectual, physical, emotional/psychological, social, and moral/ethical. Below is a brief discussion of each of these characteristics. Table 1.1 provides a list of web resources related to adolescent development.

Intellectual Development

Intellectually, adolescents tend to be egocentric—that is, they believe their individual problems, experiences, feelings, and thoughts are unique. It is important for teachers to understand that at this stage in their life, adolescents often consider academic goals and intellectual pursuits as secondary to social and peer relationship concerns. Thus, adolescents may be willing to learn but only if they consider the information useful for their real-life situations. In addition, adolescents prefer to learn materials when a more active learning style is used, especially one that includes peer interaction. At the same time, adolescents are intensely curious about the world around them. They are experiencing intellectual changes as their ability to think moves from the concrete to the abstract level of thought. In addition, adolescents begin to understand the process of metacognition and develop knowledge of how learning occurs for them. "Adolescents can think in terms of what might be true, rather than just in terms of what they see in a

TABLE 1.1 ● Adolescent Stages of Development Web Resources

Child Development Institute

www.childdevelopmentinfo.com/development/teens_stages.shtml

American Academy of Child & Adolescent Psychiatry: Facts for Families

www.aacap.org/

Centers for Disease Control and Prevention

www.cdc.gov/ncbddd/child/earlyadolescence.htm

concrete situation. Since they can imagine an infinite variety of possibilities, they are capable of hypothetical reasoning. They are able to think in broader terms about moral issues and about plans for their own future" (Papalia & Olds, 1992, p. 324).

Physical Development

The most noticeable change in adolescents occurs in their rapid, physical development. During this period of adolescence the adolescent growth spurt occurs. This growth spurt accompanies a change in physical appearance resulting from the development of secondary sex characteristics and subsequent sexual maturity. These physical changes occur at different rates in boys and girls, but both change in their physical characteristics during the adolescent period. Because of these changes, many adolescents are physically awkward, show posture problems, and have body parts that mature at different rates resulting sometimes in an odd and gangly appearance. Unfortunately, this occurs just as they become excessively concerned with their physical appearance. It is often during this time that adolescents are confronted with opportunities for sexual activity when they may not be physically, or emotionally, mature.

Emotional/Psychological Development

When describing adolescents, most teachers refer to the intense emotional and psychological changes that occur during this period. There continues to be a great deal of argument over whether adolescence is truly a time of "storm and stress" as G. Stanley Hall proposed or whether this emotional roller-coaster type of behavior is not normal for all adolescents as Margaret Mead has suggested (Papalia & Olds, 1992). Regardless, most teachers and parents note that younger adolescents tend to be sensitive to criticism and easily take offense at comments made by peers and family. Adolescents have a tendency to display inconsistent behaviors, moodiness, and often self-consciousness. These emotional changes are often a result of the physical and hormonal changes that occur during this time.

Social Development

Accompanying emotional changes are changes in social development, especially the increasing importance of peer relationships. Many parents as well as teachers note that adolescents are very loyal to their chosen peer group and use these peers as a source of support as opposed to their family or teachers. Loyalty to peers can manifest itself in rebellion toward parents, cruelty or insensitivity to those not in a chosen group, or behaviors that challenge authority figures such as teachers, coaches, or police officers. Throughout this turbulent emotional time, though, adolescents still "want to know and feel that significant adults, including parents and teachers, love and accept them" (Kellough & Kellough, 2008, p. 23).

Moral/Ethical Development

The final component of adolescent development is in the areas of morality and ethics. Adolescents begin to question concepts related to the meaning of life, religious beliefs, and other ethical issues. These students also are very idealistic and expect teachers, parents, and others to exhibit fairness in their behaviors. This characteristic, when merged with their need to confront authority figures, can result in controversy in the classroom as students compare what is said with the actions of those around them. Teachers also need to remember that young adolescents ask many "unanswerable questions about the meaning of life; not expecting absolute answers but being turned off by trivial adult responses" (Kellough & Kellough, 2008, p. 24).

Teachers should take advantage of this attitude and encourage the development of morality and ethics through real-life scenarios and use discussions to determine the "right" and "wrong" of different responses. Students' development of taking responsibility for their behaviors and for questions about the "fairness" of these behaviors can be one of the more difficult areas for teachers to address.

As adolescents progress toward maturity, their characteristics change. By high school age, many older adolescents have moved past their childhood years; most have completed the physical, cognitive, emotional, and social changes of early adolescence. As a result, high school age students begin to focus on their future goals. This means that high school age adolescents are generally less egocentric, more independent, more confident, and less easily discouraged when compared to younger adolescents (Duplass, 2006). Still, most high school age adolescents are idealistic, anxious about their physical appearance, less indifferent to adults, and more concerned with their future (Duplass, 2006).

ADOLESCENTS WITH DISABILITIES

Adolescents with disabilities experience the same developmental changes as their peers without disabilities, and these changes may be compounded by the characteristics of the individual disability and the type and complexity of the demands of a secondary school classroom (Raymond, 2008). In addition, issues related to possible bias in testing and identifying students from culturally and linguistically diverse backgrounds have resulted in continued concerns about the overidentification of students of color and its impact on the specialized programming and classroom placement of students (Sattler, 2001; Venn, 2007). However, despite disability and diversity, the majority of adolescents with mild disabilities will be educated in the general education program at both the middle and high school levels.

Of the more than 6 million students with disabilities who receive services in federally supported special education programs, nearly one-third are between the ages of 14 and 17. The severity of disability exhibited by this group of students, as well as the extent of its impact on an individual student's ability to learn, vary considerably, both across and within particular disability classifications (Swanson, 2008). In general, many of these students have difficulties in achieving academic success because of inappropriate school behaviors and difficulties with a variety of tasks. Table 1.2 provides a list of web resources related to adolescents with disabilities. Common characteristics of this group that negatively impact schools include (Olson, Platt, & Dieker, 2008; Raymond, 2008):

TABLE 1.2 ● Adolescents with Disabilities Web Resources

CanChild (Centers for Child Disability Research)

transitions.canchild.ca/en/ltResources/keepingcurrent.asp

Adolescents and Youth with Disabilities: Issues and Challenges

www.aifo.it/english/resources/online/apdrj/apdrj204/adolescent.pdf

National Center on Secondary Education and Transition

www.ncset.org/

National Dissemination Center for Children with Disabilities

www.nichcy.org

- Attending to school-related tasks
- Remembering information
- Monitoring their own behaviors (metacognition)
- Lacking effective study skills
- Establishing unsatisfactory personal relationships
- Having a poor self-concept

Many adolescents with disabilities experience significant difficulties in school. In fact, a large number of secondary special education students do not successfully complete high school. During the 2005–2006 school year, only 56.5% of students with disabilities received a regular high school diploma. Another 15.3% received a certificate of attendance. While these data reflect a significant improvement over a 10-year period, they still reflect a large number of secondary students with disabilities whose needs are not being adequately met (National Center for Educational Statistics, 2008). Table 1.3 reveals the number of students with disabilities, ages 14–21, who exited schools between 1996 and 2006.

Just as adolescents have unique characteristics, each disability also results in different issues. In middle and secondary programs, adolescents with mild disabilities are generally in one of the four major classifications of mild intellectual disabilities, learning disabilities, mild emotional/behavior disorders, and less severe forms of autism, especially Asperger's syndrome. The four categories of disabilities sometimes are called high-incidence disabilities because they occur more frequently in the student population.

TABLE 1.3 ● Number and Percentage of Students with Disabilities, Ages 14–21, Exiting School by Exit Status

Exit Status	1996–97	1997–98	1998–99	1999–2000	2000–01	2001–02	2002–03	2003–04	2004–05	2005–06
Total, number	308,538	323,093	318,386	348,385	362,065	370,106	373,916	392,663	393,579	396,857
Total, percentage	100.0	100.0	100.0	100.0	100.0	100.0	100.0	100.0	100.0	100.0
Graduated with diploma	43.1	45.5	46.8	46.5	48.0	51.4	52.5	54.5	54.6	56.5
Received a certificate of attendance[1]	9.0	9.0	9.0	9.2	9.0	9.3	12.5	13.0	15.3	15.3
Reached maximum age[2]	0.9	0.9	1.0	1.5	1.4	1.0	1.0	1.0	1.3	1.4
Died	0.5	0.5	0.5	0.5	0.5	0.5	0.5	0.5	0.5	0.5
Dropped out[3]	46.4	44.0	42.6	42.3	41.2	37.8	33.6	31.1	28.3	26.2

Note: Data are from a cumulative 12-month reporting period. Detail may not sum to totals because of rounding. Estimates include students from the United States and other jurisdictions including American Samoa, Guam, Northern Marianas, Puerto Rico, Virgin Islands, and Bureau of India Education (BIE) schools.

[1]Students who exited an educational program and received a certificate of completion, modified diploma, or some similar document. This includes students who received a high school diploma, but did not meet the same standards for graduation as those for students without disabilities.
[2]Students may exit special education services by reaching the maximum age beginning at age 18, depending on state law or practice or order of any court.
[3]Defined as the total who were enrolled at some point in the reporting year, were not enrolled at the end of the reporting year, and did not exit for any of the other reasons described. For the purpose of calculating dropout rates, the Office of Special Education Programs (OSEP) counts as dropouts students who moved and were not known to continue.

Source: U.S. Department of Education, Office of Special Education Programs (OSEP), Data Analysis System (DANS), *Children with Disabilities Exiting Special Education, 2005-06* (OMB #1820-0521). Retrieved November 28, 2007, from https://www.ideadata.org/arc_toc8.asp#partbEX.

Intellectual Disability

Intellectual disability, formerly known as mental retardation, is one of the oldest categories of disability served in public schools. Individuals with this disability have issues with cognitive or intellectual functioning. Both the definition and the terminology for this category of disability have changed over the past three decades. Although the term *intellectual disabilities* is changing to the term *mental retardation*, the Individuals with Disabilities Education Improvement Act of 2004 (IDEA), label of mental retardation is still used to identify adolescents with intellectual disability for special education services. The IDEA 2004 definition states, "mental retardation means significant subaverage general intellectual functioning, existing concurrently with deficits in adaptive behavior and manifested during the developmental period, that adversely affects a child's educational performance" (20 U.S.C. 1400 §602.30). This disability category is subdivided into levels according to severity, with students at the mild and moderate levels being found most often within middle and secondary classrooms. In fact, 85% of all individuals identified with intellectual disability are within the mild and moderate levels.

According to the definition of intellectual disabilities used by the American Association on Intellectual and Developmental Disabilities (AAIDD), the first identification criterion requires that the individual will have "subaverage general intellectual functioning." Intellectual functioning is identified by the use of a standardized individual intelligence test from which an intelligence quotient (IQ) score is derived. Those individuals having the label of mild intellectual disabilities would have an IQ score between approximately 55 and 70 while those with moderate intellectual disabilities would have an IQ score between approximately 35 and 55 (AAIDD, 2007).

However, an IQ score alone is not sufficient to result in a label of intellectual disabilities; the individual must also have deficits in adaptive behavior. Adaptive behavior is defined by the AAIDD as "the collection of conceptual, social, and practical skills that have been learned by people in order to function in their daily lives" (2007, p. 5). In addition, the intellectual delay must have occurred within the developmental period from birth to age 18. In order to be eligible for special education services under IDEA as a child with intellectual disabilities, the exhibited characteristics must also negatively affect the individual's chances of educational success. Table 1.4 provides a list of web resources related to adolescents with intellectual disabilities.

The intellectual and adaptive behavior characteristics inherent in intellectual disabilities often have a significant impact on success in academic areas. For example, consider the story of Michael, a 14-year-old in the eighth grade. Michael has both a significant cognitive delay as noted by his Wechsler Intelligence Scale for Children (WISC) IQ score of 64 and his stated deficits in social skills. He also lacks self-confidence. Thus, his achievement test scores range from the 9th to the 14th percentile, indicating that he may have significant difficulties in the academic arena.

TABLE 1.4 ● Adolescents with Intellectual Disabilities Web Resources

American Academy of Child & Adolescent Psychiatry: Facts for Families

www.aacap.org/

Division on Autism and Developmental Disabilities

www.dddcec.org/

American Association on Intellectual and Developmental Disabilities

www.aaidd.org/

SIDE BAR

1.1   The Story of Michael

Michael is 14 years old and is presently in the eighth grade. He was diagnosed with intellectual disabilities when he was 4 years old. Michael was placed in a preschool program for 2 years prior to entering an elementary school. He has received special education services his entire school period, ranging from full-time placement in a self-contained classroom to his current placement—2 hours of resource room each day and inclusive placement in math, English, social studies, and physical science. His resource room time is spent on assisting him with his inclusive classes. Michael has deficits in social skills and lacks self-confidence. Recent test scores revealed the following:

Wechsler Intelligence Scale for Children
(average score ranges from 85 to 115 with
a standard deviation of 15)

Full-scale IQ	64
Performance IQ	76
Verbal IQ	60

Woodcock-Johnson Achievement Test Scores
(percentile ranks)

Oral language	13th percentile
Broad reading	9th percentile
Broad math	11th percentile
Broad written expression	10th percentile
Math calculation	14th percentile
Written expression	9th percentile

One of the most significant areas impacting adolescents with intellectual disabilities is delayed cognitive development. Intellectual disabilities result in students having difficulties learning new skills, and learning occurs at a slower rate than found among students without disabilities. According to Bryant, Smith, and Bryant (2008), "learning new skills, storing and retrieving information (memory), and transferring knowledge to either new situations or slightly different skills are challenges" (p. 71). These students can and do learn academic materials, but it occurs at a slower rate than their peers. Also for learning to occur, teachers may need to rely on direct instruction of the requisite information along with the use of concrete examples to enhance understanding and memory.

When teaching adolescents with intellectual disabilities, it is important to remember that language difficulties are frequently present. These difficulties may occur in the area of expressing language, understanding language, or both. Language difficulties only exacerbate the issues of teaching content when combined with issues in cognition and memory. Indeed, with adolescents who have intellectual disabilities, the ability to use language is often significantly below age level, especially in fluency and conceptual understanding. Thus, the use of extensive oral directions, teacher lectures, and whole class discussions may pose problems for these students and revisions in the organization and delivery of instruction may be required.

Another frequent characteristic of students with intellectual disabilities is social skill deficits. This frequently results in difficulty in developing friendships and successful peer relationships—two areas that have a major impact on the basic adolescent need for peer acceptance. Therefore, teachers need to review their classroom environments and prepare activities and opportunities for students with intellectual delays to participate in groups with their peers. If possible, role-playing activities that emphasize appropriate language and social skills in specific situations that are relevant to your class could be used. Regardless of what specific steps teachers take, the important thing to remember is that social skills and social relationships need to be addressed for this population of students. The number of students with intellectual disabilities who exit school each year with a regular diploma is approximately 37% (National Center for Education Statistics, 2008). Table 1.5 provides information for the high school exit status for each category of disability.

TABLE 1.5 ● Number and Percentage of Students, Ages 14–21, Exiting School by Age and Disability Category

Age and Type of Disability	Total Exiting Special Education	Graduated with Diploma	Received a Certificate of Attendance[1]	Reached Maximum Age[2]	Died	Dropped Out[3]
Total	396,857	56.5	15.3	1.4	0.5	26.2
Age						
14	5,935	1.6	0.4	0.0	5.5	92.5
15	11,067	0.7	0.5	0.0	3.4	95.5
16	27,713	17.4	2.2	0.0	1.4	79.0
17	142,510	66.3	12.3	0.0	0.3	21.1
18	141,364	64.9	17.7	0.5	0.2	16.6
19	42,605	55.6	23.1	0.9	0.4	20.0
20	15,397	42.8	27.7	9.6	0.6	19.3
21	10,266	27.0	34.5	27.6	0.6	10.3
Disability						
Specific learning disability	236,135	61.6	12.5	0.5	0.3	25.1
Mental retardation	46,588	36.7	35.5	4.6	0.8	22.3
Emotional disturbance	47,519	43.4	9.9	1.2	0.5	44.9
Speech or language impairment	8,923	67.3	9.2	0.5	0.2	22.7
Multiple disabilities	8,251	43.8	25.6	8.3	3.6	18.7
Other health impairment	32,274	63.4	11.7	0.6	0.9	23.4
Hearing impairment[4]	4,674	68.7	16.5	1.2	0.3	13.4
Orthopedic impairment	3,455	61.7	19.2	3.8	3.6	11.7
Visual impairment	1,766	72.1	13.9	1.6	1.1	11.4
Autism	4,876	57.1	26.6	6.7	0.5	9.1
Deaf-blindness	150	65.3	14.0	8.7	3.3	8.7
Traumatic brain injury	2,246	65.0	16.5	2.9	0.8	14.8

Note: Data are from a cumulative 12-month reporting period. Detail may not sum to totals because of rounding. Estimates include students from the United States and other jurisdictions including American Samoa, Guam, Northern Marianas, Puerto Rico, Virgin Islands, and Bureau of Indian Education (BIE) schools.

[1]Students who exited an educational program and received a certificate of completion, modified diploma, or some similar document. This includes students who received a high school diploma, but did not meet the same standards for graduation as those for students without disabilities.

[2]Students may exit special education services by reaching the maximum age beginning at age 18, depending on state law or practice or order of any court.

[3]Defined as the total who were enrolled at some point in the reporting year, were not enrolled at the end of the reporting year, and did not exit for any of the other reasons described. For the purpose of calculating dropout rates, the Office of Special Education Programs (OSEP) counts as dropouts students who moved and were not known to continue.

[4]Includes deaf and hard-of-hearing.

Source: U.S. Department of Education, Office of Special Education Programs (OSEP), Data Analysis System (DANS), Children with Disabilities Exiting Special Education, 2005–06 (OMB #1820-0521). Retrieved November 28, 2007, from https://www.ideadata.org/arc_toc8.asp#partbEX.

Learning Disabilities

The most common category of disabilities identified in students at the middle and secondary level is learning disabilities, a general term describing a heterogeneous group of learning problems. Table 1.6 lists websites related to adolescents with learning disabilities. In the 1960s, Samuel Kirk used the term *learning disability* as a means of categorizing those children who did not meet the criteria for intellectual disabilities but for unknown reasons were not successful in school. Many of these children, who were not eligible to be classified as having intellectual disabilities, received appropriate services and often experienced significant learning difficulties in general education classrooms.

The U.S. Department of Education (2007) estimates that children with learning disabilities account for approximately 54% of all students served under IDEA. The IDEA 2004 definition of specific learning disability is:

> A disorder in one or more of the basic psychological processes involved in understanding or in using language, spoken or written, which may manifest itself in an imperfect ability to listen, speak, read, write, spell, or to do mathematical calculations. Such term includes such conditions as perceptual disabilities, brain injury, minimal brain dysfunction, dyslexia, and developmental aphasia. Such term does not include a learning problem that is primarily the result of visual, hearing, or motor disabilities, of intellectual disabilities, of emotional disturbance, or of environmental, cultural, or economic disadvantage. (20 U.S.C. 1400 § 602.30)

Adolescents with learning disabilities may exhibit one or more of several characteristics. Table 1.7 lists many of these characteristics. Of all characteristics exhibited by students with learning disabilities, issues related to language seem to be the predominant characteristic associated with this disability. As a result of this common deficit area, students typically do not perform academically as well as expected, based on their ability level. In fact, a general way of describing students with learning disabilities is that these are students who do not achieve at their expected level, without any specific explanation. For example, consider the story of

---

TABLE 1.6 ● Adolescents with Learning Disabilities Web Resources

Learning Disabilities Research & Training Center

http://people.rit.edu/easi/easisem/ldnoelbw.htm

LD Online

www.ldonline.com

American Academy of Child & Adolescent Psychiatry: Facts for Families

www.aacap.org/

Focus Adolescent Services

www.focusas.com/LearningDisabilities.html

TABLE 1.7 ● Characteristics of Students with Learning Disabilities

- Attention deficits
- Hyperactivity
- Academic deficits
- Sensorimotor deficits
- Social skills deficits
- Self-determination deficits

SIDE BAR

1.2   The Story of Sophia

Sophia is 12 years old and is in the sixth grade. She was diagnosed with learning disabilities and possible ADHD when she was in the second grade. She has average intelligence but has significant problems in the areas of reading and written expression. In addition, her attention span tends to be extremely brief, making it difficult for her to concentrate on any learning task for an extended period. She is very outgoing and has good social skills. She is also self-confident and aware of her disabilities. The most recent evaluation resulted in the following test scores.

Woodcock-Johnson Achievement Test Scores
(percentile ranks)

Oral language	53rd percentile
Broad reading	21st percentile
Broad math	64th percentile
Broad written expression	15th percentile
Math calculation	69th percentile
Written expression	18th percentile

Wechsler Intelligence Scale for Children
(average score ranges from 85 to 115 with a standard deviation of 15)

Full-scale IQ	106
Verbal IQ	115
Performance IQ	93

Sophia, a 12-year-old, who is in the sixth grade. Sophia has an average IQ score (106) based on the WISC but has good social skills and is self-confident. Her disability manifests itself by her lower than expected scores in the academic areas of reading and written expression. She scores on the Woodcock-Johnson Achievement Tests in the 21st percentile in reading and in the 15th percentile in written expression. Thus, Sophia continues to have difficulty in the inclusive classroom.

The majority of adolescents identified as learning disabled have either difficulty or inability decoding new words, they read very slowly and in a labored manner, or they lack effective strategies for fluent reading. This results in major problems acquiring information in the content areas through reading. Since reading is an essential component of academic success at the middle and high school levels, adolescents with learning disabilities experience major problems in content areas. Teachers in middle and secondary classrooms, therefore, must be prepared to modify the written and reading assignments to support those students with reading difficulties. For example, teachers may need to provide both written and oral directions for assignments, provide students with taped copies of textbooks, provide extended time for students to complete lengthy reading assignments, and even reduce amounts of reading on homework assignments.

In conjunction with reading difficulties, many adolescents with learning disabilities have difficulties with several other components of language, including grammar, spelling, handwriting, and written expression. These difficulties often result in students' misunderstanding of language in both its written and spoken formats. Since language and reading play a significant role in educational activities at the secondary level, adolescents with learning disabilities will have problems in being successful when these skills are required. To provide opportunities for students with these problems to be successful, adaptations to written assignments should be considered. These could include (1) allowing spelling and grammar checkers on computers,

(2) peer editing, (3) extended time for completion of written work, (4) extended time for tests, and (5) modifications to homework assignments. For many of these students, it is often not an inability to learn or a reduced rate of learning that impedes their educational success, but their difficulty with the use and understanding of language.

In addition to students with learning disabilities having difficulties with language-based subject areas, some may have problems in mathematics that may be unrelated to the issue of reading or decoding language. These mathematics issues may include a delay or inability to learn basic facts and rules, a lack of understanding of the required procedures for completing mathematical formulas, and a delay or lack of understanding of the basic, requisite mathematical concepts. Many researchers are unsure whether this mathematics learning disability is a result of cognitive issues with learning the "language" of mathematics or whether it involves the same issues that are involved in learning to read. As a result, math teachers need to ensure that lesson directions are clear and provided in both oral and written format, and that direct instruction is used to teach the language of mathematics as well as mathematics concepts.

Cognitive issues related to the areas of thinking and reasoning also are characteristics of adolescents with learning disabilities. For instance, the ability to reason abstractly, which should be present by the time adolescence has begun, may be delayed or absent and as a result, these adolescents may have difficulties with organizing their thinking and drawing conclusions from materials, regardless of the method of presentation (either visual or auditory). In addition, they may lack effective strategies for solving problems, whether the problems are academic or social. These cognitive issues relate to the delay in developing metacognition, or the knowledge about one's own learning and understanding. Thus, adolescents with learning disabilities may have difficulty learning how to study effectively, how to self-monitor their own behavior, and how to self-regulate their time. As a result, teachers may need to specifically introduce appropriate ways for students to organize materials, and provide specific direction and training in effective problem-solving strategies, study skills, and test-taking strategies.

In addition to the difficulties encountered in academic areas, adolescents with learning disabilities often encounter both attention and memory difficulties that may impact on their success in learning. A significant number of adolescents with learning disabilities report problems with sustaining attention and with using both long- and short-term memory. Like Sophia, this problem with attention results in many adolescents with learning disabilities also having the label of attention deficit hyperactivity disorder (ADHD). While ADHD is not a specific category delineated in the IDEA 2004, it is a characteristic of many adolescents with disabilities. For teachers, it is important that procedures for "getting" student attention before beginning a lesson be instituted. In addition, students should be provided with cues or strategies to assist them in retaining information, such as the use of semantic maps or keywords.

For adolescents with learning disabilities, the social and emotional changes that affect them may be overwhelming. These students may have difficulties with low self-esteem, imperfect self-awareness, and flawed self-perception. Often, social and academic difficulties undermine self-confidence that can result in anxiety, depression, or acting-out behaviors. Unfortunately, these behaviors may interfere with classroom success, as well as the academic success of individual students.

Behavioral/Emotional Disorders

One of the most difficult student groups for teachers to work with are adolescents with behavioral or emotional disorders. This category of disabilities is difficult to define and identify because (1) behavior occurs on an age and situational continuum, (2) emotions and behaviors are difficult to assess, and (3) culture provides significant variation as to what constitutes an unacceptable behavior. On top of these issues, many adolescents experience a variety of behavioral and emotional issues as part of the typical developmental period. The definition of emotional disturbance accepted by educators is provided in IDEA 2004. (Note: The legislation does not address or define behavior disorders, only emotional disturbance.) According to IDEA 2004, the term *emotional disturbance* means:

i. …a condition exhibiting one or more of the following characteristics over a long period of time and to a marked degree that adversely affects a child's educational performance:

a. An inability to learn that cannot be explained by intellectual, sensory, or health factors.

b. An inability to build or maintain satisfactory interpersonal relationships with peers and teachers.

c. Inappropriate types of behavior or feelings under normal circumstances.

d. A general pervasive mood of unhappiness or depression.

e. A tendency to develop physical symptoms or fears associated with personal or school problems.

ii. The term includes schizophrenia. The term does not apply to children who are socially maladjusted, unless it is determined that they have an emotional disturbance. [20 U.S.C. §300.7(c)(4)]

Students with behavioral and/or emotional disorders may or may not have concurrent cognitive/intellectual concerns. In many if not most instances, the individual's behavior is the factor hampering success in the classroom. In fact, behavior is a significant identifying factor in the decision as to whether the individual has a behavioral disorder or a learning disability. Table 1.8 lists websites related to adolescents with behavior disorders.

During adolescence, the social arena is one of the most important areas of development for individuals. This is a time when friendships and social activities become critically important. Unfortunately, for students with emotional and behavioral disorders, social behaviors are a significant issue. Most of these students have immature or inappropriate social skills at a time when social skills are an important factor for success in the school environment and acceptance among peers. This lack of appropriate social skills may manifest itself in inappropriate classroom behaviors, such as acting out in class, not responding appropriately to discipline from teachers, and seemingly being oblivious to class and school rules. In addition, some students, when faced with social situations in which they feel uncomfortable or with disciplinary actions by teachers, may exhibit aggressive behaviors, which could result in harm to their peers and the adults.

TABLE 1.8 ● Adolescents with Behavioral/Emotional Disorders Web Resources

---

National Mental Health Information Center

www.mentalhealth.samhsa.gov/publications/allpubs/CA…/default.asp

Medline Plus

www.nlm.nih.gov/medlineplus/childbehaviordisorders.html

Council for Children with Behavioral Disorders

www.ccbd.net/

Guidebook for Caregivers of Children and Adolescents with Severe Emotional Disorders

www.naminh.org/parent-guidebook

These behavioral issues impact the student's academic behaviors at a time when subject-specific content and independent learning are being emphasized. Unfortunately, most students with emotional and behavioral disorders are at least 2 years below grade level in reading, mathematics, spelling, and writing. They often exhibit immature metacognitive skills, reduced memory skills, and deficits in attention. All of these issues tend to strengthen the probability that such students will become school dropouts. See Table 1.5 to determine the rate of dropouts for students with emotional and behavioral disorders.

Autism Spectrum Disorders: Autism and Asperger's Syndrome

Over the past 10 years the prevalence of students identified as having autism spectrum disorders (ASD) has skyrocketed. Students with ASD, especially mild forms such as Asperger's syndrome (AS), are increasingly being included in middle and secondary classrooms. According to IDEA 2004:

    i. Autism means a developmental disability significantly affecting verbal and nonverbal communication and social interaction, generally evident before age 3, that adversely affects a child's educational performance. Other characteristics often associated with autism are engagement in repetitive activities and stereotyped movements, resistance to environmental change or change in daily routines, and unusual responses to sensory experiences. The term does not apply if a child's educational performance is adversely affected primarily because the child has an emotional disturbance, as defined in paragraph (b)(4) of this section.

    ii. A child who manifests the characteristics of "autism" after age 3 could be diagnosed as having "autism" if the criteria in paragraph (c)(1)(i) of this section are satisfied [34 C.F.R. §300.7(c)(1)]

Many teachers do not understand that the definition of autism includes students who have characteristics ranging from mild to severe on the autism continuum, known as the autism spectrum. Although the differences among those labeled as being within the autism spectrum can be minimal, teachers often believe that all students with autism have severe disabilities. For those students identified as having mild autism and/or AS, this may not be the case. In fact, many of these students may be extremely intelligent but possess behavioral and psychological characteristics that hamper their ability to succeed in a middle or secondary classroom. Table 1.9 lists web resources related to adolescents with ASD.

For example, consider the story of Robert, an 18-year-old who is a 12th grader with Asperger's syndrome. Robert has an IQ score on the WISC of 110 and has high achievement scores on the Woodcock-Johnson Achievement Tests, ranging from the 54th to the 89th percentile. However, he has poor social skills, has difficulty interacting with peers, and lacks self-confidence. As a result, even though he is capable of academic success, his deficits in social skills, peer relationships, and self-confidence result in frustrations that frequently turn into behavioral problems, thus making it very difficult for him to be successful in his academic classes.

TABLE 1.9 ● Adolescents with Autism Spectrum Disorders (ASD) Web Resources

National Association of Parents with Children in Special Education

www.napcse.org/exceptionalchildren/traumaticbraininjury.php

Asperger's Disorder Homepage

www.aspergers.com

Autism Speaks

www.autismspeaks.org

SIDE BAR

1.3   The Story of Robert

Robert is 18 years old and in the 12th grade. He was diagnosed with Asperger's syndrome when he was in the third grade. He attends general education classes with his age peers and is considered to be "fully included" in all of his classes. In addition, he receives some indirect special education services from a special education teacher who comes into his classes periodically to assist him with various assignments. Robert is very bright and wants to attend college with a major in mathematics. Robert's measured IQ score is likely less than his true intellectual capacity, as depicted by his very high achievement scores. Robert has poor social skills and difficulties interacting with other students; possibly as a result, he lacks self-confidence. Recent test scores revealed the following:

Woodcock-Johnson Achievement Test Scores (percentile ranks)

Oral language	73rd percentile
Broad reading	81st percentile
Broad math	84th percentile
Broad written expression	64th percentile
Math calculation	89th percentile
Written expression	54th percentile

Wechsler Intelligence Scale for Children (average score ranges from 85 to 115 with a standard deviation of 15)

Full-scale IQ	110
Verbal IQ	117
Performance IQ	112

Educational concerns for adolescents with autism spectrum disorders fall into three areas: communication skills, social competence, and behavior issues. Communication skills are of increasing importance at the middle and secondary levels, both for academic and social reasons. Although students with mild autism or Asperger's most often have the ability to communicate verbally, they may still have some difficulties with the use of conversational skills (especially the use of idioms), the understanding of inferential language, and the use and understanding of nonverbal communication support skills. Since a more complex use of language is expected at the secondary level, the difficulty with communication may result in problems within the school environment. As a result, teachers need to provide opportunities for students to learn and practice conversational skills and provide direct instruction in nonverbal communication.

A second facet of the language/communication skills issue relates to the impact of language on students' social competence. Since being able to understand verbal and nonverbal language is essential for social competence, deficits in these skills areas could result in social difficulties. As social skills become increasingly important in the life of adolescents, students who are not socially competent become more isolated. Students with mild autism and/or Asperger's syndrome may become frustrated with their difficulty with communication skills and social skills which in turn may increase their stress and anxiety levels. Unfortunately, this stress and anxiety, coupled with not understanding the "rules" of the classroom, could result in behavioral outbursts.

Low-Incidence Categories

Although the majority of students with disabilities included in middle and high school classes represent high-incidence categories discussed above, teachers may also encounter students classified as having low-incidence disability categories. Low-incidence disability categories are those

TABLE 1.10 ● Examples of Low-Incidence Disabilities and Their Characteristics

Disability	Predominant Characteristics
Hearing impairment	Difficulty understanding spoken speech
Visual impairment	Difficulty seeing and understanding visual objects
Traumatic brain injury	Acquired injury to the brain resulting in cognitive, behavioral, and emotional problems
Cerebral palsy	Disorder of movement or posture caused by brain damage
Spina bifida	Congenital neural tube disorder resulting in lower limb paralysis

that occur less frequently in the student population, and may include sensory impairments, severe disabilities, or physical and other health impairments. Table 1.10 provides examples of low-incidence disabilities and some of their predominant characteristics.

Among the low-incidence disabilities, teachers are more likely to encounter students with physical or other health impairments in their classrooms. IDEA 2004 defines physical, or orthopedic impairments, as:

a severe orthopedic impairment that adversely affects a child's educational performance. The term includes impairments caused by congenital anomaly, impairments caused by disease (e.g., poliomyelitis, bone tuberculosis, etc.), and impairments from other causes (e.g., cerebral palsy, amputations, and fractures or burns that cause contractures). (34 C.F.R. 300.8(c)(8)

IDEA 2004 defines other health impairment as:

Having limited strength, vitality, or alertness, including a heightened alertness to environmental stimuli, that results in limited alertness with respect to the education environment, that—

i. Is due to chronic or acute health problems such as asthma, attention deficit disorder or attention deficit hyperactivity disorder, diabetes, epilepsy, a heart condition, hemophilia, lead poisoning, leukemia, nephritis, rheumatic fever, sickle cell anemia, Tourette syndrome, and
ii. Adversely affects a child's educational performance. (34 C.F.R. 300.8(c)(9)

Of these students with physical and other health impairments, those with cerebral palsy or traumatic brain injury will usually be included in the general education program. Following will be a brief review of these two areas of disability and their impact on the success of the individual student in the secondary classroom.

Cerebral Palsy

One of the most well-known categories of physical impairment is that of cerebral palsy (CP). According to Pellegrino (2007), "cerebral palsy is a disorder of movement and posture that is caused by a nonprogressive abnormality of the immature brain" (p. 388). Cerebral palsy can result from damage to the brain that occurs prenatally (before birth), perinatally (during birth), or postnatally (after birth). Cerebral palsy affects individuals differently depending on the site of the brain abnormality, which results in several different types of CP. The four most predominant types of CP include spasticity, athetosis, ataxia, and rigidity. Spasticity accounts for approximately 50% to 60% of all cases of cerebral palsy and results in involuntary muscle contractions. Athetosis results in the individual having constant, uncontrollable movements. Difficulty with balance results from ataxia, and rigidity is a severe form of spasticity. Web resources related to cerebral palsy are listed in Table 1.11.

TABLE 1.11 ● Adolescents with Cerebral Palsy Web Resources

Massachusetts General Hospital for Children

www.mgh.harvard.edu/adolescenthealth/cerebralpalsy

Cerebral Palsy International Research Foundation

www.cpirf.org

Disabled World

www.disabled-world.com/health/neurology/cerebral-palsy/

In the classroom, children with cerebral palsy exhibit significant motor problems, generalized physical weakness, and lack of muscle coordination. Some other disabilities that frequently accompany the physical problems include "intellectual disability, visual impairments, hearing impairments, speech-language disorders, seizures, feeding and growth abnormalities, and behavior/emotional disorders" (Pellegrino, 2007, p. 395).

Students with cerebral palsy may use orthotic devices such as braces or splints as well as positioning devices to assist with maintenance of their physical abilities. A physical therapist (PT) or an occupational therapist (OT) may be working with the student and with you, as the teacher, to ensure the student's access to the classroom. This person will provide you with information and support in selecting adaptive equipment that can be used to organize your classroom for the student's physical access and to compensate for his or her lack of motor coordination. Examples of adaptive equipment include various forms of crutches, walkers, wheelchairs, special seat cushions, and chair supports.

The complexity of this disability as well as the wide range of functional abilities of students with cerebral palsy requires that teachers become aware of the individual student's areas of strength as well as areas of need. In the story of Lachesa, a 16-year-old in the 10th grade, she has both physical and cognitive concerns, which impact her educational success. Lachesa uses a wheelchair because of lower limb spasticity and has some upper limb involvement that results in difficulty with writing and other fine motor activities. Lachesa has an IQ score of 82 that is within the low average range and achievement scores that range from the 9th to the 29th percentile with the lowest area being written expression.

Because of the complexity of this condition, students with cerebral palsy often require teachers to use specific material modifications, special adaptations, equipment, therapies, and/ or instruction that are necessary for students to have success in school. Classroom teachers may need to work with support personnel—such as communication specialists, occupational or physical therapists, and possibly special educators—to identify ways to assist students with physical access and educational opportunities.

Traumatic Brain Injury

Traumatic brain injury can occur at any point in a person's life. However, adolescence is one of the most significant times for brain injury to occur because adolescence is "when peer approval, impulsivity, and a sense of immortality increase risk-taking behaviors" (Michaud, Duhaime, Wade, Rabin, & Jones, 2007, p. 462). Injuries to the brain can be the result of falls, sports accidents, motor vehicle accidents, child abuse, or gunshot wounds. Because of the significant numbers of students with this disability, a specific category was included in IDEA 2004 to address traumatic brain injury (TBI). TBI means:

An acquired injury to the brain caused by an external physical force, resulting in total or partial functional disability or psychosocial impairment, or both, that adversely affects a child's

SIDE BAR

1.4 The Story of Lachesa

Lachesa is 16 years old and in the 10th grade. She was diagnosed at birth as having cerebral palsy. She has lower limb spasticity and is immobile without the use of a wheelchair. She also has some involvement with her upper extremities, making it difficult for her to write. Lachesa also has mild learning problems, although not classified as having a learning disability. She would like to attend a vocational/technical school after completing high school and focus on learning how to be an office assistant. Her social skills are good, but she lacks self-confidence. Recent test scores revealed the following:

Wechsler Intelligence Scale for Children (average score ranges from 85 to 115 with a standard deviation of 15)

Full-scale IQ	82
Verbal IQ	81
Performance IQ	84

Woodcock-Johnson Achievement Test Scores (percentile ranks)

Oral language	24th percentile
Broad reading	29th percentile
Broad math	23rd percentile
Broad written expression	9th percentile
Math calculation	21st percentile
Written expression	16th percentile

educational performance. Traumatic brain injury applies to open or closed head injuries resulting in impairments in one or more areas, such as cognition; language; memory; attention; reasoning; abstract thinking; judgment; problem-solving; sensory, perceptual, and motor abilities; psychosocial behavior; physical functions; information processing; and speech. Traumatic brain injury does not apply to brain injuries that are congenital or degenerative, or to brain injuries induced by birth trauma. [34 C.F.R. 300.8(c)(8)(12)]

As noted in the definition, there are two forms of TBI: closed and open head injury. Closed head injury is a generalized head injury that does not include any form of penetration of the brain itself; open head injury is a localized head injury that does include penetration of the skull and results in injury to specific areas of the brain. The type of head injury depends on whether the injury is the result of an impact or inertial forces (Michaud et al., 2007). Impact injuries result from the head striking a surface such as from a fall or a car accident or when something such as a moving object strikes the head. The impact may result in skull fractures, brain contusions, hemorrhages, or hematomas. According to Garguilo (2006), this type of injury often results in diffuse damage—that is, damage that may be mild or severe and occurs throughout the brain. Inertial force injuries, on the other hand, are the result of the brain moving violently back and forth or side to side inside the skull. This is sometimes referred to as a contrecoup injury that can tear nerve fibers or blood vessels and result in hematomas and/or swelling of the brain causing significant damage (Garguilo, 2006). Web resources related to TBI are listed in Table 1.12.

School personnel must be aware of the significant educational issues students with TBI often must face. The most common characteristics relate to physical changes, which often include seizures, poor coordination, weakness, fatigue, headaches, spasticity or paralysis, as well as problems

TABLE 1.12 ● Adolescents with Traumatic Brain Injury (TBI) Web Resources

Medline Plus

www.ncbi.nlm.nih.gov/pubmed/18674403

Centers for Disease Control and Prevention

www.cdc.gov/ncbddd/dd/ddmr.htm

Child Research Net

www.childresearch.net/RESOURCE/NEWS

with vision, hearing, and perception (Michaud et al., 2007). Additionally, cognitive changes and subsequent problems in the areas of attention, memory, reasoning, and judgment also impact students' educational status. Many of these students also display problems with language, especially in the area of understanding or using oral or written language (Garguilo, 2006; Michaud et al., 2007). TBI can also impact the social, emotional, and behavioral characteristics. These changes can result in a lack of motivation for school, poor self-monitoring skills, the inability to interpret social cues, lack of inhibition, and poor anger control (Garguilo, 2006; Michaud et al., 2007).

Obviously, the numerous changes impacting students with TBI require extensive teacher supports. In order to effectively work with this group of students, teachers must promote a safe and healthy environment for their students, as well as monitor their health and provide appropriate interventions if necessary (Heller, Forney, Alberto, Schwartzman, & Goeckel, 2000). Changes affecting students with TBI are difficult for the individual student, family members, the student's friends and schoolmates, and classroom teachers who all knew the student before the injury. As with other students with disabilities, teachers need to consider material modifications, special classroom adaptations, adapted equipment, therapies, and/or adapted instruction if this group of students will be successful.

Adolescents, in general, face many different problems as they transition from childhood to adulthood. These include issues related to physical and emotional changes. Unfortunately, having disabilities only compounds these problems. Teachers and other school personnel must be prepared to address these needs through modifications, accommodations, and other programmatic interventions. Since the majority of students with disabilities are included in general classrooms, it is imperative for school personnel to promote the social and educational assimilation of these students with their nondisabled peers.

SUMMARY

Teachers at the middle and secondary levels should be prepared to address the educational, social, and behavioral issues that often result from students' disabilities. With the increased numbers of students being included in general education at the middle and secondary levels, it is essential that teachers be prepared to adapt and/or modify their curriculum, instructional practices, communication and social demands, and assessment procedures to enhance the success of all students in the classroom.

Adolescence is a turbulent developmental period for many individuals. Making the transition from childhood

to adulthood is often difficult because of the significant changes that occur physically and emotionally. This period, described as between the ages of 10–13 and early 20s, is the time when boys grow up to be men and girls grow up to be women. In addition to getting used to a changing body, this group of individuals begins to think and act differently. For the first time in most of their lives, what their peers think about them is more important than their parents' views.

When adolescents experience disabilities, the problems of adolescence are only compounded. When it is critical for students to believe that they are "cool" and accepted by their peers, characteristics associated with disabilities make it extremely difficult. Indeed, many adolescents with disabilities display behavioral problems due to the frustration and low self-concepts associated with their disabilities. The federal government, through the Individuals with Disabilities Education Act, has mandated that students who meet specific criteria are provided a free appropriate public education in the least restrictive environment. This means that students with disabilities should be educated with their nondisabled peers, in general education classrooms, when possible. The result is that general classroom teachers are now responsible for the academic success of students with disabilities. Groups typically found in general classrooms include those classified as having learning disabilities, mild intellectual disabilities, emotional problems, mild autism, and physical and health issues.

ACTIVITIES

1. Identify a parent of an adolescent with a disability who is willing to talk with you. Ask the parent what he or she hopes will happen when the student graduates or leaves high school. What does the parent want for the student in terms of work, daily activities, living situation, free time, and love life? What can the school do to help these ideals happen? As a teacher, how might this information impact your curriculum development?

2. Identify an adolescent with a disability who is willing to talk with you. Ask the student what he or she hopes will happen upon graduation from high school. What are the student's ideals beyond high school in terms of work, daily activities, living situation, free time, and love life? What can the school do to help this happen? How might this information impact your instruction of this student?

3. Identify differences and similarities between the student with a disability and the parents of a student with a disability. As a teacher, how do you plan curriculum and instruction to meet the needs of both student and parents?

REFERENCES

American Association on Intellectual and Developmental Disabilities (AAIDD). (2007). *User's guide: Intellectual disabilities: Definition, classification, and systems of support* (10th ed.). Washington, DC: Author.

Bryant, D. P., Smith, D. D., & Bryant, B. R. (2008). *Teaching students with special needs in inclusive classrooms.* Upper Saddle River, NJ: Allyn & Bacon/Pearson.

California Middle Grade Task Force. (1987). *Caught in the middle: Educational reform for young adolescents in California public schools.* Sacramento: California State Department of Education.

Duplass, J. A. (2006). *Middle and high school teaching: Methods, standards, and best practices.* Boston: Houghton Mifflin.

Garguilo, R. M. (2006). *Special education in contemporary society* (2nd ed.). Belmont, CA: Thomson Wadsworth.

Heller, K. W., Forney, P. E., Alberto, P. A., Schwartzman, M. N., & Goeckel, T. M. (2000). *Meeting physical and health needs of children with disabilities: Teaching student participation and management.* Belmont, CA: Wadsworth/Thomson Learning.

Individuals with Disabilities Education Improvement Act of 2004. 20 U.S.C. §1400 et seq.

Individuals with Disabilities Education Improvement Act of 2004. 34 C.F.R. §300 et seq.

Kellough, R. D., & Kellough, N. G. (2008). *Teaching young adolescents: Methods and resources for middle grades teaching.* Upper Saddle River, NJ: Merrill/Pearson.

Lerner, J., & Johns, B. (2009). *Learning disabilities and related mild disabilities: Characteristics, teaching strategies, and new directions.* Boston: Houghton Mifflin Harcourt.

Michaud, L. J., Duhaime, A. C., Wade, S. L., Rabin, J. P., Jones, D. O., & Lazar, M. F. (2007). Traumatic brain injury. In M. L. Batshaw, L. Pellegrino, & N. J. Roizen (Eds.), *Children with disabilities* (6th ed., pp. 461–476). Baltimore: Paul H. Brookes.

National Center for Education Statistics. (2008). *The condition of education 2000–2010.* Retrieved from http://necs.ed.gov/pubs2008/2008031.pdf

Olson, J. L., Platt, J. C., & Dieker, L. A. (2008). *Teaching children and adolescents with special needs* (5th ed.). Upper Saddle River, NJ: Merrill/Pearson.

Papalia, D. E., & Olds, S. W. (1992). *Human development* (5th ed.). New York: McGraw-Hill.

Pellegrino, L. (2007). Cerebral palsy. In M. L. Batshaw, L. Pellegrino, & N. J. Roizen (Eds.), *Children with disabilities* (6th ed., pp. 387–408). Baltimore: Paul H. Brookes.

Raymond, E. B. (2008). *Learners with mild disabilities: A characteristics approach.* Upper Saddle River, NJ: Allyn & Bacon/Pearson.

Sattler, J. (2001). *Assessment of children: Cognitive applications* (4th ed.). San Diego, CA: Author.

Swanson, C. B. (2008). *Special education in America: The state of students with disabilities in the nation's high schools.* Bethesda, MD: Editorial Projects in Education Research Center. Retrieved from www.edweek.org/rc

U.S. Department of Education. (2007). *Twenty-ninth annual report to Congress on the implementation of the Individuals with Disabilities Education Improvement Act.* Washington, DC: Government Printing Office.

Venn, J. J. (2007). *Assessing students with special needs* (4th ed.). Upper Saddle River, NJ: Merrill/Pearson.

Services for Adolescents with Disabilities in Middle and Secondary Schools

Study Questions

1. What law mandates services for students with disabilities in public schools?

2. What are some of the challenges those in secondary schools face today?

3. What does the term *inclusion* mean?

4. What are some advantages and disadvantages of inclusion?

5. What are the major requirements of IDEA?

INTRODUCTION

Appropriate educational services for students with disabilities have expanded dramatically because Public Law 94-142 was implemented in 1978. The passage of this law, later reauthorized as the Individuals with Disabilities Education Act (IDEA), directly led to the (1) increased numbers of students receiving special education services; (2) increased numbers of students included in general education classrooms; and (3) increased funding for special education services (Smith, Polloway, Patton, & Dowdy, 2012). Despite the wide-ranging benefits of this legislation, services for students with disabilities at the secondary level were not its primary focus. The initial focus targeted children with disabilities in primary grades, often leaving older students with disabilities to fend for themselves. This followed the same pattern as the development of public schools in the United States: early emphasis on educating younger children in basic academic skills, with attention to older students coming later.

Public education in the United States has a long history, dating from colonial America. Our founding fathers recognized early on the importance of having an educated citizenry. Indeed, one of the foundations of the new democracy was an educated populace; Thomas Jefferson believed that citizens had to be educated in order to support this new form of government called democracy (Ornstein & Hunkins, 2009).

SECONDARY PUBLIC EDUCATION

Education in the United States originally focused on elementary schools during the colonial period. The Latin grammar school became an option for secondary education during this time; however, it was primarily for upper-class boys who needed preparation for college. During the early 1800s, the academy, championed by Benjamin Franklin, began replacing these schools. The schools had three different tracks: college preparation, similar to Latin grammar schools; a general curriculum for students not going on to college; and a normal track, primarily for girls who wanted to be elementary teachers (Johnson, Musial, Hall, Gollnick, & Dupuis, 2008). While most academies were private, publicly supported high schools quickly emerged following a Kalamazoo, Michigan, court case in 1874, which recognized the legality of districts levying taxes for establishing and supporting high schools.

Organization of Secondary Education

By the 1920s, most high schools included grades 9–12 and had four curricular options: college preparatory, commercial/business, vocational, and general. Junior high schools began appearing during the 1920s and 1930s as a transitional period between elementary school and high school, generally including grades 7 and 8, and occasionally grade 9. In the 1960s, the middle school began to emerge as an organizational option, typically including grades 6–8, again as a transition from elementary school to high school (Ornstein & Levine, 2008).

Purpose of Secondary Schools

In 1918, the Commission on the Reorganization of Secondary Education published the "Cardinal Principles of Secondary Education" (Ornstein & Levine, 2008). These principles included:

- *Health:* Provide health instruction and a program of physical activities; cooperate with home and community in promoting health.

- *Command of fundamental processes:* Develop fundamental thought processes to meet the needs of modern life.
- *Worthy home membership:* Develop qualities that make the individual a worthy member of a family.
- *Vocation:* Equip students to earn a living, service society well through a vocation, and achieve personal development through that vocation.
- *Civic education:* Foster qualities that help a person play a part in the community and understand international problems.
- *Worthy use of leisure:* Equip people to find recreation of body, mind, and spirit that will enrich their personalities.
- *Ethical character:* Develop ethical character both through instructional methods and social contacts among students and teachers.

While other reports have modified the purposes or goals of secondary education, they have all been oriented to a comprehensive model, one that could meet the needs of a diverse student population (Johnson et al., 2008).

Secondary School Curricula

American secondary education continues to be based on the idea of a comprehensive high school. This model "was a reaction to specialized high schools that cared for specific segments of the student population" (Oliva, 2005, p. 284), which was the model used in Europe and early colonial secondary schools. Today, the purpose of the comprehensive high school is to provide a wide range of different opportunities for students from diverse backgrounds to play, learn, and work together; and to promote democracy (Oliva, 2005). In this model, students are prepared for college and postsecondary education, vocational and technical education, and vocational opportunities.

While most secondary schools continue to follow the comprehensive model, there are efforts underway to radically change high schools. The Nation at Risk report, issued in the early 1980s, called for more rigor in public education, especially in the areas of math and science. Most recently, the No Child Left Behind legislation has had a significant impact on public schools by requiring that all students have high-quality teachers and that the academic achievement of all students, including those with disabilities, reach prescribed levels (Simpson, LaCava, & Graner, 2004).

While reform efforts come and go, it is unlikely that secondary schools will change significantly over the next several years. They will undoubtedly continue to be comprehensive in nature, providing at least minimal educational opportunities for students from very diverse backgrounds in a wide range of areas. Unlike secondary schools in some countries, in the United States these schools are open for all students, including those with disabilities.

Diversity in Secondary Schools

The diversity found among secondary schools, similar to the diversity of the population in the United States, has increased dramatically over the past 25 years. Diversity of language, race, culture, and religion are not the only factors resulting in more diverse schools. Another very important factor is the ability levels of students in classrooms. Students today come to middle and high schools with an incredible diversity of ability. With the advent of including students with disabilities in public schools and in general education classrooms has come significantly more diverse classrooms related to learning. This learning diversity creates a need for differentiated instruction; teachers can no longer expect all of their students to be capable of achieving at the same level in the same way (Tomlinson, 2007). "When students in a classroom present extreme variance in their learning abilities, some form of individualized instruction and planning is essential" (Gartin & Murdick, 2008, p. 175). Differentiated instruction is a way of meeting this challenge.

Challenges in Secondary Schools

Including students with disabilities in secondary schools and recognizing the increasing diversity of students create numerous challenges for both special education and general education teachers. In addition to these challenges are numerous other issues that result in even more challenges to address. For the most part, these challenges mirror those found in society: substance abuse, violence in schools, increased accountability standards, high dropout rates, and limited parental involvement. While all of these challenges impact students with disabilities, high dropout rates and increased accountability seem to have had the most recent impact on this group of students and the service delivery system attempting to provide an appropriate education for them.

High Dropout Rate.   One of the biggest problems facing secondary schools continues to be school dropout rates. Dropping out of school is problematic not only for the individual student, but also for the school system, community, and society at large; it is a "complex social problem for which there is no simple solution" (Christle, Jolivette, & Nelson, 2007, p. 334). Students who do not complete high school can expect significant challenges as adults.

While the dropout rate has remained virtually unchanged over the past 30 years, the impact remains devastating for those who do not complete high school (Christle et al., 2007). One of the greatest negative impacts of dropping out of school is financial instability. The U.S. Census Bureau Standard (2003) reported that 56% of high school dropouts were unemployed. The potential income of individuals who do not complete high school is significantly below that of individuals who are high school graduates. The Alabama Cooperative Extension System (2000) estimated that high school dropouts earn approximately 45% less than individuals who either complete high school or complete a GED.

In analyzing numerous studies related to school dropouts, Cobb, Sample, Alwell, and Johns (2007) found one overriding factor—feelings of social alienation resulting from lack of competence in social skills and how to use social skills. In another study, Reschly and Christenson (2006) noted that variables impacting a student's dropping out of school fall into three areas: (1) student variables, such as homework completion and behavior; (2) family variables, including motivational support and monitoring activities; and (3) school variables, including caring teachers and orderly school environments.

Preventing students from dropping out of school is a major challenge for school personnel, but the benefits for students and society require schools to make an effort to reduce dropouts (Cobb et al., 2006). To address the high school dropout problem, school staff should consider school demographics, classroom environments and instruction, administrative issues, staff issues, and student characteristics to determine if changes could positively impact this issue. Without addressing all of these factors, a comprehensive program for dealing with school dropouts will not be achieved.

In 2002, President George W. Bush signed the No Child Left Behind (NCLB) Act of 2001. This law authorized more than $26 billion for K–12 public education in an effort to increase student achievement and hold schools more accountable for student performance.

Along with the significant increase in federal funding came numerous requirements, including the following (Morrison, 2006, p. 339):

- Schools must administer annual state tests in reading and math for every child in grades 3 through 8. Schools whose scores fail to improve 2 years in a row could receive more federal aid. If scores still fail to improve, low-income students can receive funding for tutoring or transportation to another public school. A school in which scores do not improve over 6 years could be restaffed.
- Schools must raise all students' reading and math proficiency in the next 12 years. Schools must also close gaps in scores between wealthy and poor students and white and minority students.
- States must ensure within 4 years that all teachers are qualified to teach in their subject areas. States could require teachers to pass subject tests or major in their fields in college.

Teaching in Secondary Schools

Unlike elementary teachers who typically teach all subjects to students, at the secondary level teachers specialize in content areas. Most states license secondary teachers to teach only specific content areas, for example, science, math, English, or history. Some states even require more specialization, such as chemistry, biology, and physics for science and Spanish and French for foreign language. As a result of secondary teachers focusing so much on subject matter, they are often less likely to address the developmental needs of students. Elementary teachers, because they provide instruction in basic academic skills to students with wide-ranging developmental readiness, may be more inclined to address individual learning needs than secondary teachers. This could have a negative impact on secondary students with disabilities.

SPECIAL EDUCATION SERVICES IN SECONDARY SCHOOLS

Although secondary schools in the United States have long been associated with a comprehensive model, and some schools provided special education services prior to the passage of the IDEA, it has only been in the last 25 years that appropriate services for secondary students with disabilities have been implemented on a widespread basis (Smith et al., 2012). As noted, educational services for students with disabilities were initially focused on students in elementary grades. In fact, extensive special education programs for secondary students with disabilities did not emerge until the late 1970s. Many school districts had elementary special education programs but did not provide any specialized programming for students with disabilities in secondary schools. The result was that many students with disabilities did not complete high school because they needed support and instructional programs that were not present. Without necessary supports, secondary students with disabilities could not be successful academically. The result for many of these students was dropping out of school, often unprepared for vocational success or independent living success.

Once special education services for students with disabilities began to grow, the number of students increased dramatically. According to the 27th Annual Report to Congress on the Implementation of IDEA (2008), in 1990–1991, 4.7 million students received special education services; this number increased to 6.7 million in 2005–2006. At the secondary level, 1.5 million students, ages 14 and older, were served in special education programs in 1994; 2.9 million students, ages 12–17, were served in 2003.

Traditional Services for Adolescents with Disabilities in Middle and Secondary Schools

As noted, services for students with disabilities in secondary schools did not expand until the 1980s. Prior to the expansion of services at the secondary level, and the mandate to educate students with disabilities in the least restrictive environment, traditional special education programs available at the secondary level were provided in self-contained classrooms. In this model, the special education teacher taught the same group of students most of each day, similar to how lower elementary grade teachers work with their classrooms.

While not currently considered an appropriate model, there are some advantages to the special class model at the secondary level, including: (1) educational programs are provided by teachers specifically trained to teach students with disabilities; (2) students are more likely to be grouped according to their ability levels; and (3) student progress can be more easily monitored. There are also some inherent disadvantages in serving students with disabilities in self-contained settings. These include (Smith et al., 2012):

- Students are isolated from their age peers for instructional and social activities.
- There are limited appropriate role models.
- Teachers may have limited knowledge of some subject areas.
- Students are considered to belong to the special group, not the majority group.

Although these disadvantages to the self-controlled model are significant, before more inclusive services were offered, this approach was considered a major step forward. Prior to these services, most students with disabilities at the secondary level received no services.

Current Programming Models

Secondary students with disabilities are a very heterogeneous group. Some have the cognitive abilities, and desire, to achieve success in postsecondary educational programs, while others may need ongoing supports in the community just to be minimally successful. At the elementary level, most students, including those with disabilities, are working on the development and improvement of basic academic skills. Regardless of their likely futures, all students need to develop the highest level of these basic skills as possible.

This is different at the secondary level; programs for adolescents with disabilities must be tied more specifically to their futures. Students with the skills and desire to attend postsecondary educational programs need programming to best prepare them for those opportunities; other students may need assistance in developing skills for independent living and successful employment. Therefore, for secondary students with disabilities, individualization based on future needs is critical. Smith and Dowdy (1988) referred to this as future-based intervention—educational programming based on the future needs of students. Regardless of its title, understanding what this group of students will need to be successful after school is critical in developing appropriate educational programs.

In order for secondary schools to implement a comprehensive educational program for students with disabilities, educators must focus on a variety of different areas (Mercer & Pullen, 2009). Zigmond (1993) suggests two different tracks for students with learning disabilities at the secondary level. In track 1, students with plans on attending postsecondary educational programs focus on academic preparation, whereas in track 2, students are more engaged in activities that would prepare them for entering the workforce. Figure 2.1 depicts these two tracks. Polloway, Patton, Epstein, and Smith (1993) identify four primary variables contributing to curricular decisions. These include student variables, parent variables, general classroom variables, and special education variables. Table 2.1 summarizes the four curricular areas.

Track #1—Less but Very Special Special Education

- Students are assigned to regular classrooms for math, content subjects required for graduation, and elective courses.
- One special education teacher is assigned as a support or consulting teacher to work with regular classroom teachers.
- Additional special education teachers are responsible for English/reading classes, survival skills class, and supervised study hall.
- Students interact regularly with counselor for transition planning.
- Required graduation courses are spaced evenly throughout the high school years.

Track #2—More Special Education

- All basic skills are taught by a special education teacher; instruction in basic skills linked to transition planning.
- Required content subjects are cotaught by special education teachers.
- Vocational education is provided in inclusive classrooms and coordinated with transition planning.
- All ninth-grade students take a class on survival skills.
- Students' schedules reflect light academic load in ninth grade.

FIGURE 2.1 ● Curricular Tracks for Secondary Students with Learning Disabilities

Source: From "Rethinking Secondary School Programs for Students With Learning Disabilities, by N. Zigmond, 1993, in *Educating Students With Mild Disabilities.* Edited by E. L. Meyen, G. A. Vergason, and R. J. Whelan. Denver, CO: Love.

Resource Room Model.   With the mandate to provide educational services for students with disabilities in the least restrictive environment came the resource room model as the predominant way of providing services to this group of students. The resource room model is based on students with disabilities receiving some of their instruction in general education classrooms and other services in resource rooms. Resource rooms are locations where special education teachers provide instruction to students during the day when they are pulled out of their general classroom. The amount of time spent in resource rooms is directly related to the needs of students and is determined on an individual basis. Advantages of the resource room model include (Smith et al., 2012):

- Students are considered a part of the total school population because they are in general education settings part of the day.
- Instruction is provided by several teachers, including content class teachers and the special education teacher.
- Instruction is provided by teachers who specialize in particular content (e.g., history teacher, biology teacher).
- Special education teachers are assimilated into the school by working closely with general classroom teachers.

Although considered a positive move away from the self-contained model, there are some disadvantages to the resource room approach. For example, students have to come and go between general education classrooms and the resource room, which can be disruptive and result in the student missing some important information or content. Some students may be ostracized because of their going to the resource room. Also, if the resource room teacher and general classroom teacher do not communicate effectively, a great deal of confusion from different strategies and teaching approaches may exist (Smith et al., 2012). The resource room

TABLE 2.1 ● Four Variables Related to Secondary Curricula

1. Student variables
   - Cognitive-intellectual level
   - Academic skills preparedness
   - Academic achievement as determined by tests
   - Academic achievement as determined by class grades
   - Grade placement
   - Motivation and responsibility
   - Social interactions with peers and adults
   - Behavioral self-control
2. Family variables
   - Short- and long-term parental expectations
   - Degree of support provided (e.g., financial, emotional, academic)
   - Parental values toward education
   - Cultural influence (e.g., language, values)
3. General education variables
   - Teacher and nondisabled student acceptance of diversity (classroom climate)
   - Administrative support for integrated education
   - Availability of curricular variance
   - Accommodative capacity of the classroom
   - Flexibility of daily class schedules and units earned toward graduation
   - Options for vocational programs
4. Special education variables
   - Size of caseload
   - Availability of paraprofessionals or tutors
   - Access to curricular materials
   - Focus of teacher's training
   - Consultative and materials support available
   - Related services available to students

Source: From "Comprehensive Curriculum for Students With Mild Disabilities," by E. A. Polloway,
J. R. Patton, M. H. Epstein, and T. E. C. Smith, 1993, in *Educating Students With Mild Disabilities*,
p. 264. Edited by E. L. Meyen, G. A. Vergason, and R. J. Whelan. Denver, CO: Love.

approach to serving students with disabilities, at both the elementary and secondary levels, remains the primary special education service model.

Work-Study Programs.   One of the early approaches to providing services to students with disabilities in secondary settings was the work-study program. As a result of students not being considered capable of many academic programs, emphasis was placed on a vocationally oriented program. These programs provided an opportunity for students to work part time in the community and receive credit toward high school completion. The programs included job- and career-related skill training, as well as supervised on-the-job experiences (Sabornie & deBettencourt, 2009). Some schools even allowed students to earn a work-study diploma based partly on their work in the community (Salend, 2008). The program was very effective in schools where a strong relationship existed between the school and rehabilitation agency. However, without the ongoing support of other state and community agencies, work-study programs suffered demise.

INCLUSION OF STUDENTS WITH DISABILITIES IN SECONDARY SCHOOLS

Regardless of the problems that many secondary students with disabilities face in general education classrooms, current legislative trends, namely IDEA, have resulted in significant increases in their inclusion in general education classrooms (Fontana, Scruggs, & Mastropieri, 2007). The most recent Annual Report to Congress on the Implementation of IDEA (2008) reported that during the 2003 school year, more than 1.2 million students with disabilities, ages 12–17, were outside their regular classroom less than 21% of the time, meaning that they were in their regular classroom 80% or more of the time. This accounts for approximately 44% of all secondary students served in special education. Another 966,000 were outside the general education classroom between 21% and 60% of the time, with only 604,478 students served in general education classrooms less than 40% of the time. This compares to 36.8%, 36%, and 27%, respectively, in 1994. Therefore, in 10 years there has been a 20% increase in the percentage of students with disabilities educated in general education classrooms at least 80% of the time. It is safe to say that inclusion is being implemented at a rapid pace in secondary schools.

The Inclusion Movement

The education of students with disabilities has followed a progression starting with no services to the current model of including students in general education classrooms. Figure 2.2 depicts the steps along the way. Students with disabilities were traditionally excluded from public schools until the latter half of the 20th century. When finally enrolled, they were primarily educated in separate, segregated programs. Public Law 94-142, passed in 1975, required school districts to serve students with disabilities in the least restrictive environment. In other words, students with disabilities were to be educated with their nondisabled peers as much as possible. The result of this requirement was the mainstreaming movement.

Mainstreaming was based on the assumption that students with disabilities belonged in special classrooms and should be placed in general classrooms when possible. While this resulted in many students with disabilities spending time with their nondisabled peers, often this was only in physical education, music, lunch room, or other similar nonacademic classes. This trend gave way in the 1990s to inclusion. While on the surface mainstreaming and inclusion may look alike, with the resource room being the primary location for special services, there is one very big difference—mainstreaming assumes that students with disabilities should be educated in special education settings, with their peers with disabilities, until they become ready to be included in general classrooms. Inclusion on the other hand, assumes that students

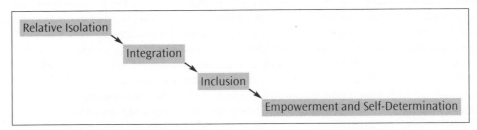

FIGURE 2.2 ● Historical Changes in Education for Students with Disabilities

Source: From E. A. Polloway, J. D. Smith, J. R. Patton, and T. E. C. Smith, 1996, in *Education and Training in Mental Retardation and Developmental Disabilities, 31,* p. 9. Used with permission.

with disabilities belong with their nondisabled, chronological age peers and should be removed from this setting and placed in a resource room only when necessary to provide appropriate education (Smith et al., 2012). Table 2.2 depicts the major differences between mainstreaming and inclusion.

Rationale Supporting Inclusion

The rationale behind inclusion began being voiced in the 1980s and 1990s. Inclusion actually began to take hold as a movement in the 1970s, following an article by Lloyd Dunn (1968) who questioned the efficacy of special class placements for students with mental retardation. After citing research that indicated that students with mental retardation in self-contained classrooms performed about as well as students with mental retardation in general classrooms, professionals and parents began questioning the entire notion of separate services.

One result of Dunn's article was the Regular Education Initiative. This initiative, which gained momentum in the 1980s, effectively questioned the need for a dual system of education,

TABLE 2.2 ● Differences Between Mainstreaming and Inclusion

Traditional Models	Inclusive Models
1. Some students do not "fit" in general education classrooms.	1. All students "fit" in general education classrooms.
2. The teacher is the instructional leader.	2. Collaborative teams share leadership responsibilities.
3. Students learn from teachers and teachers solve the problems.	3. Students and teachers learn from each other and solve problems together.
4. Students are purposely grouped by similar ability.	4. Students are purposely grouped by differing abilities.
5. Instruction is geared toward middle-achieving students.	5. Instruction is geared to match students at all levels of achievement.
6. Grade-level placement is considered synonymous with curricular content.	6. Grade-level placement and individual curricular options among members of the classroom.
7. Instruction is often passive, competitive, didactic, and/or teacher-directed.	7. Instruction is active, creative, and collaborative among members of the class.
8. Most instructional supports are provided outside the classroom.	8. Most instructional supports are provided within the classroom.
9. Students who do not "fit in" are excluded from general classes and/or activities.	9. Activities are designed to include students though participation levels may vary.
10. The classroom teacher assumes ownership for the education of general education students, and special education staff assume ownership for the education of students with special needs.	10. The classroom teacher, special educators, related service staff, and families assume shared ownership for educating all students.
11. Students are evaluated by common standards.	11. Students are evaluated by individually appropriate standards.
12. Students' success is achieved by common standards.	12. The system of education is considered successful when it strives to meet each student's needs. Students' success is achieved when both individual and group goals are met.

Source: Adapted from "Problem-Solving Methods to Facilitate Inclusive Education," by M. F. Giangreco, C. J. Cloniger, R. E. Dennis, and S. W. Edelman, 1991, in *Creativity and Collaborative Learning: A Practical Guide to Empowering Students and Teachers.* Edited by J. S. Thousand, R. A. Villa, and A. I. Nevin. Baltimore: Brookes.

one for "regular" students and one for students served in special education programs. In 1984, an article by Stainback and Stainback pointed out several reasons to support the regular education initiative and do away with the dual system of regular and special education. For example, they pointed out that (1) the dual system assumes two distinct group of students, "special" and "regular," when, in fact, there are not two distinct groups; and (2) all children could benefit from individualized programs. The regular education initiative evolved into the inclusion movement in the early 1990s.

Unfortunately, the first focus of inclusion was initially referred to as full inclusion. Supported by The Association for the Severely Handicapped (TASH) and the Association for Retarded Citizens (now referred to as The Arc), this model called for the full-time inclusion of students with disabilities—regardless of the severity of the disability—in general education classrooms. Advocates of this model effectively called for the elimination of a variety of placement options noting that the least restrictive environment for all students was the general education classroom (Kavale & Forness, 2000).

Although the motives underlying support for this movement were genuine, the reality of fully including all students with disabilities received a great deal of criticism from many professionals and some parent groups. Rather than including all students with disabilities, on a full-time basis, most professionals advocated a more moderate approach, or responsible inclusion (Smith & Dowdy, 1998). Under this model, students with disabilities are considered to "belong" in general education classrooms; however, it is appropriate to remove students with disabilities when they need to receive services unavailable in the general education classroom. Thus, the resource room model, which became the predominant service approach during the mainstreaming movement, continues to be the physical placement where students with disabilities receive most of their special education.

Advantages and Disadvantages of Inclusion

The rationale for inclusion is sound; however, there are advantages and disadvantages with any educational model. Some obvious advantages include (Smith et al., 2012):

- More opportunities to interact with nondisabled peers
- Positive academic and social outcomes for students with disabilities
- Positive academic and social outcomes for students without disabilities
- Access to the general curriculum
- Better utilization of instructional resources

Several studies have focused on the efficacy of inclusion. In one study, Rea, McLaughlin, and Walther-Thomas (2002) compared the outcomes for middle school students with learning disabilities in inclusive and pullout programs. They found that students with learning disabilities included in general classrooms did the following:

- Achieved better course grades than those in pullout programs in language arts, mathematics, science, and social studies
- Scored higher on the Iowa Test of Basic Skills than those in pullout programs in language and mathematics
- Performed as well as those in pullout programs on state proficiency tests in reading, writing, and mathematics
- Had the same behavioral infractions as those in pullout programs
- Attended more days than those in pullout programs

While research has shown support for inclusion, there are still some disadvantages to the model. These include (Smith et al., 2012):

1. General education teachers and administrators may not have been extensively involved in preparing for inclusion.
2. Teacher and administrator preparation programs have not changed to focus on an inclusion model.
3. While supportive, empirical studies on the impact of inclusion are limited.

Parent and Teacher Support for Inclusion

Studies on teacher and parental support for inclusion have been mostly positive (Smith et al., 2012). In Idol's (2006) program evaluation of four secondary schools implementing inclusion, she found the following:

- All principals were very supportive of inclusion.
- Teachers viewed administrators as supportive of inclusion.
- Teachers viewed themselves as skilled in adapting instruction and modifying instruction for students with disabilities.
- Most teachers were very supportive of students with disabilities.
- Most teachers were either willing to try or very much in favor of including students with disabilities.
- Very few teachers felt that students with disabilities should be educated in separate classes; and none in special schools.
- Most students felt that students without disabilities were either not impacted or were positively impacted by the presence of students with disabilities in their classes.

Not all studies of teacher attitudes toward inclusion have been positive. In a recent study of inclusive teachers' attitudes of their students with disabilities, Cook, Cameron, and Tankersley (2007) found that while teachers had higher concern for and provided more instructional support for this group, they also exhibited ratings of rejection for the group. The conclusion was that students' inappropriate behaviors may have resulted in this increased level of rejection.

While policy makers have apparently determined that the inclusion of students with disabilities will be the model used to educate this group of students, the degree of inclusion must be determined on an individual basis, contingent on the needs of students. Placement decisions should never be made based on the philosophy of inclusion, but the needs of each student (Smith & Hilton, 1994). For example, Bouck (2007) pointed out several issues facing students with mild mental retardation in inclusive secondary schools. It may not be in the best interest of students with cognitive impairments to include them in some secondary classes, while they may be included very successfully in other classes. Placing students inappropriately in inclusive classes can be detrimental to students with and without disabilities and presents an unfair situation to the general classroom teacher.

Regardless of the positive or negative attitudes teachers hold toward the inclusion of students with disabilities, there are numerous issues facing teachers that create difficulties for them to successfully include this group of students. These include teachers being under increased pressures to teach all students, including those with disabilities, and to ensure that all students pass high stakes tests (Sabornie & deBettencourt, 2009). Teaching in today's secondary schools is very demanding. With the additional demands of federal legislation to have all students performing at proficiency levels, and with the continuing increase in diversity, teaching is a more difficult challenge than ever before.

LEGAL BASIS FOR SPECIAL EDUCATION SERVICES

While there is a strong legal basis for many aspects of public education, the growth of special education has been largely shaped by legal issues. State and federal legislation, as well as litigation, have all had a significant impact on special education services. In fact, without the legal bases for special education, it is unlikely services for this group of students would be nearly as available as they are. While several laws have impacted special education at the secondary level, IDEA has by far been the most influential of these laws.

Individuals with Disabilities Education Act

The passage of the Individuals with Disabilities Education Act (IDEA), originally as Public Law 94-142 (Education for All Handicapped Children Act) in 1975, was a critical moment in the history of special education. Prior to the passage of this law, many students with disabilities were totally excluded from public schools. In fact, Congress reported that 1 million of the 8 million children with disabilities recognized in 1975 were totally excluded from public education, with another 3 million considered underserved.

Public Law 94-142 was the culmination of significant efforts on the part of disability advocacy groups. In fact, advocacy groups, the civil rights movement, and state and federal legislation all laid the foundation for the passage of this law. IDEA requires schools to provide students with disabilities a free appropriate public education in the least restrictive environment. This means that it is the local public school's responsibility to provide, at no cost to the parents, appropriate educational services for children with disabilities. A major provision of the law is that these services must be provided in the least restrictive environment—with nondisabled peers as much as possible. Major provisions are summarized in Table 2.3 and briefly described below.

Eligibility.   Students who are eligible for special education services under IDEA must meet the qualifications for 1 of 10 disability categories. These specific disabilities included in the law are (IDEA 2004, PL 108-446, Sec. 602[3][A][I]):

- Intellectual disabilities
- Specific learning disabilities
- Hearing impairment (including deafness)
- Visual impairment (including blindness)
- Serious emotional disturbance
- Orthopedic impairment
- Other health impairments
- Multiple disabilities
- Autism
- Traumatic brain injury
- Speech or language impairments

Assessment.   Once a student has been referred for special education services, a comprehensive, nondiscriminatory assessment of the student must be conducted. This assessment provides information to assist the school in determining (1) if the student is eligible for services and (2) what services need to be provided to ensure the student is receiving a free appropriate public education (FAPE).

Individualized Educational Program.   If the student is determined to be eligible for special education services, then a committee must develop an individualized educational program

**TABLE 2.3 ● ** Major Provisions of IDEA

Provision	Description
Least restrictive environment	Children with disabilities are educated with nondisabled peers as much as possible.
Individualized educational program	All children served in special education must have an individually designed educational program.
Due process rights	Children and their parents must be involved in decisions about special education.
Due process hearing	Parents and schools can request an impartial hearing if there is a conflict over special education services.
Nondiscriminatory assessment	Students must be given a comprehensive assessment that is fair for all students.
Related services	Schools must provide related services, such as physical therapy, counseling, and transportation, if needed.
Free appropriate public education	The primary requirement of IDEA is the provision of a free appropriate public education to all school-age children with disabilities.
Mediation/resolution	Parents have a right, if they choose, to mediation or a resolution session to resolve differences with the school. Using mediation should not deny or delay a parent's request for a due-process hearing.
Transfer of rights	When the student reaches the age of majority, as defined by the state, the school shall notify both the parents and the student and transfer all rights of the parents to the child.
Discipline	A child with a disability cannot be expelled or suspended for 10 or more cumulative days in a school year without a manifest determination as to whether or not the child's disability is related to the inappropriate behavior.
State assessments	Children with disabilities must be included in district-wide and statewide assessment programs with appropriate accommodations. Alternative assessment programs must be developed for children who cannot participate in district-wide or statewide assessment programs.
Transition	Transition planning and programming must begin when students with disabilities reach age 16.

Source: From T. E. C. Smith, E. A. Polloway, J. R. Patton, and C. A. Dowdy, 2012, *Teaching Students With Special Needs in Inclusive Settings,* 6th ed., p. 10. Boston: Allyn & Bacon/Pearson Education. Used with permission.

(IEP). This IEP is an individually tailored program designed to meet the unique needs of students in special education programs. The IEP must include (1) current functioning levels; (2) annual goals; (3) how progress toward goals will be measured; (4) services to be provided; (5) explanation of extent, if any, the student will be removed from the general education classroom; and (6) statement of any accommodations needed for high stakes assessments.

Least Restrictive Environment.   After developing the IEP, the school committee must determine the appropriate placement for the student. The IDEA requires students with disabilities to receive their education in the least restrictive environment. In other words, students with disabilities should be educated with their nondisabled peers as much as possible. IDEA 2004 (PL 108-446, Sec 614[d]) states:

> To the maximum extent appropriate, children with disabilities, including children in public and private institutions or other care facilities, are educated with children who are not disabled and that special classes, separate schooling, or other removal of children with disabilities from the regular education environment occurs only when the nature or severity of the disability is such that education in regular classes with the use of supplementary aids and services cannot be achieved satisfactorily.

Transition.   While all components of IDEA impact secondary students with disabilities, the one element that only deals with secondary schools is the requirement that schools facilitate the transition of students from public schools to postsecondary environments. While there were some transition programs in place prior to the 1990 reauthorization of IDEA, there were no specific transition requirements in IDEA. However, after numerous follow-up studies found that students with disabilities were not faring well after exiting high school, Congress included requirements for transition in the 1990 reauthorization of IDEA. Transition requirements have been included in each subsequent reauthorization of IDEA. IDEA 2004, the most recent reauthorization, continued with specific language related to transition. The act states that transition services means a "coordinated set of activities" for students, with the following goals (Kochhar-Bryant & Greene, 2009, pp. 122–123; IDEA 2004, Sec 602):

- It is designed within a result-oriented process, which promotes movement from school to postschool activities, including postsecondary education, career-technical training, integrated employment (including supported employment), continuing and adult education, adult services, independent living, or community participation.
- It is based upon the individual student's strengths, taking into account the student's preferences and interests.
- It includes instruction, related services, community experiences, the development of employment and other postschool adult living objectives, and when appropriate, acquisition of daily living skills and functional-vocational evaluation.

The law requires schools to include a statement of "appropriate measurable postsecondary goals based on age appropriate transition assessments related to training, education, employment, and independent living skills" (IDEA, 2004, Sec 614) in students' IEPs that become effective when the student is 16 years old. This statement must be updated annually (Kochhar-Bryant & Greene, 2009). Once transition planning is part of a student's IEP, the student must be present during the IEP process.

Section 504 and the ADA

Section 504 and the Americans with Disabilities Act (ADA) are both considered civil rights legislation. Both of these laws focus on the prevention of discrimination against otherwise qualified individuals with disabilities. While virtually the same in their requirements, Section 504 only applies to entities that receive federal funding whereas the ADA applies to all other entities, except churches and private clubs.

One of the key differences between Section 504 and the ADA, and IDEA, is the definition of disability and therefore eligibility. As noted, eligibility for IDEA requires that individuals have a specific category of disabilities resulting in their needing special education. There are no specific categories of disabilities required for eligibility under 504 and the ADA. Rather, in order to qualify for protections and services under the laws, an individual must only have any physical or mental impairment that substantially limits a major life activity. This means that an individual must have a physical or mental impairment (none specified) that results in the individual not being able to perform a major life activity (e.g., walking, talking, seeing, hearing, learning, working, performing manual tasks) as well as an average individual can perform that major life activity.

Also, IDEA only applies to individuals aged birth to 22; Section 504 and the ADA are laws that apply to individuals during their entire life span, birth to death. This means that while IDEA only applies to individuals with disabilities and public schools (P–12), Section 504 and the ADA apply to individuals of all ages and in all aspects of life, including education and training (P–12 and postsecondary), employment, and accessing public accommodations such as places of lodging, restaurants, retail establishments, and service centers.

Students eligible for services under Section 504 typically have disabilities that result in more minor academic problems than those served under IDEA. If students with disabilities needed special education services then they would likely be eligible for special education. Because most students eligible under Section 504 do not need special education, teachers only need to provide accommodations or modifications that are generally easy to implement. For example, preferential seating, providing a note-taker, or allowing the student to have extra time on tests are the kinds of accommodations these students usually require.

With the expanded definition of disabilities found in Section 504 and the ADA, there are some students eligible under these laws who are not eligible under IDEA; however, all students eligible under IDEA also meet the eligibility criteria of Section 504 and the ADA. So, the provisions of these two laws apply to all IDEA-eligible students.

Litigation and Special Education

There has been a great deal of litigation impacting services to students with disabilities. Indeed, had it not been for some early court cases it is unlikely that special education services for students with disabilities would be nearly as widespread today as they are. Some of the early court cases impacting special education are described in Table 2.4. In addition to these cases, there continue to be multiple cases every year clarifying issues related to special education programs. The following summarizes a few early cases dealing with students with disabilities.

TABLE 2.4 ● Early Court Cases Impacting Special Education Services

Case	Key Issue	Ruling
SUPREME COURT CASES		
Board of Education of the Hendrick Hudson Central School District v. Rowley (1982)	FAPE	• Schools would be considered to have met the FAPE provision of IDEA if the IEP, developed through the act's procedures, is reasonably calculated to enable the child to receive educational benefits.
Irving Independent School District v. Tatro (1984)	Related services	• Health services must be necessary to assist the student to benefit from special education, and the service must be performed by a nonphysician, to be considered a related service.
Burlington School Committee of the Town of Burlington v. Department of Education of Massachusetts (1985)	Tuition reimbursement	• Parents who unilaterally place their children with disabilities in a private school are entitled to reimbursement for tuition and living expenses if a court finds that the public school's proposed IEP was inappropriate.
Honig v. Doe (1988)	Discipline	• Schools must abide by the stay-put provision (during administrative or court proceedings, the student must remain in his or her present placement). • Students cannot be excluded unilaterally for misbehavior that is related to their disability. • Exclusions over 10 days constitute a change of placement.
Florence County School District Four v. Carter (1993)	Tuition reimbursement	• Parents can be reimbursed for private school tuition if the public school failed to offer an appropriate education and if the private school offered an appropriate education. • Private schools do not have to be on a state-approved list for a court to order reimbursement.

(continued)

TABLE 2.4 ● (continued)

Case	Key Issue	Ruling
Zobrest v. Catalina Foothills School District (1993)	Establishment clause and services in parochial schools	• The establishment clause of the U.S. constitution does not bar interpreter services to a student with a disability unilaterally placed by his or her parents in a parochial school. • The services must be provided in a religiously neutral manner, and IDEA funds must not fund their way into a parochial school's coffers.
Cedar Rapids Community School District v. Garrett F. (1999)	Related services	• Health services deemed necessary for a qualified child with a disability by the IEP team must be provided as long as a nonphysician can perform the services.

LOWER COURT CASES

Case	Key Issue	Ruling
• *Timothy W. v. Rouchester. New Hamphure School District (1989)*	Zero reject	• FAPE must be available to all qualified students with disablties, without exception. • School cannot use a student's ability to benefit educationally as a condition of eligibility for special education services.
• *Daniel R. R. v. State board Education (1989)*	Least restrictive environment	• To determine whether a school has adhered to the LRE mandate of the IDEA, a court must ask (a) if education in the regular classroom with supplementary aids and services can be achived satisfactorily, and (b) if a student is placed in a more restrictive setting, whether the student is integrated to the maximum extent appropriate.
• *Hartman v. Loudovn County Board of Education (1997)*		• The IDEA's mainstreaming provision is a presumption, not an inflexible mandate. • Mainstreaming is not required when (a) a student with a disability would not receive benefit from such placement; (b) any marginal benefits would be significantly outweighed by benefits that could feasibly be obtained in a separate setting; and (c) the student's presence is a disruptive force.
• *Armstrong v. Kline (1979)*	Extended school year	• Students with disabilities are entitled to extended school year services if necessary to receive a FAPE.
• *K. R. v. Anderson Community School Corporation (1996)*	Private schools	• If a public school has offered a FAPE to a student with disabilities unilaterally placed in a private school by his or her parents, the school has no further obligation.
• *S-1 v. Turlington (1981)*	Discipline	• A manifest determination is necessary before expulsion for students with disabilities; disciplinary exclusions are subject to IDEA procedural safeguards; and cessation of services is prohibited.
• *Spielberg v. Henrico Public School (1988)*	Placement	• The school determination to change a student's placement prior to developing an IEP violates a parent's right to participate in its development and therefore violates the IDEA.

Note: FAPE = free, appropriate public education; LRE = least restrictive environment: IDEA = Individuals with Disabilities Education Act; IEP = Individualized Education Program.

Source: From "Reflections on the 25th Anniversary of the Individuals with Disabilities Education Act," by A. Katsiyanis, M. L. Yell, and R. Bradley, 2001. *Remedial and Special Education, 22,* pp. 328–329. Used with permission.

GOALS FOR ADOLESCENTS WITH DISABILITIES IN MIDDLE AND SECONDARY SCHOOLS

The goals for students in secondary schools revolve around three areas: (1) preparation for post-secondary education and training; (2) preparation for a vocational career; and (3) preparation for independent living. The same goals apply for students with disabilities. While some students with disabilities may not be capable of postsecondary educational and training opportunities, others are very capable. For example, students with learning disabilities often have above average cognitive abilities and should be encouraged to pursue postsecondary educational opportunities; an emphasis in their program should be on preparing them for these postsecondary opportunities. For others, the goals focus on preparation for life after formal schooling, including vocational competence.

ISSUES FACING SECONDARY SPECIAL EDUCATION

Dropping Out of School

As previously noted, the rate of high school dropout is a problem for all students, but significantly more of an issue for students with disabilities. During the 2004–2005 school year, only 56.5% of students aged 14–21 received a regular high school diploma; another 15% received a certificate of attendance (Digest of Education Statistics, 2008). Not completing high school with a regular high school diploma has a life-long economic impact on the individual and community. For students with disabilities, dropping out of school can be even more problematic than for nondisabled students. Students with disabilities are less likely to gain employment, less likely to complete a GED, and less likely to attempt postsecondary education or training, compared to students without disabilities (Reschly & Christenson, 2006).

Increasing Accountability

Over the past 10 years, accountability of students and schools has become a major policy emphasis at federal and state levels. Indeed, IDEA 1997 and 2004, and No Child Left Behind, require that all students, including most of those with disabilities, perform at grade level on various measures (Cox, Herner, Demczyk, & Nieberding, 2006). Both of these acts apply a standards-based reform to students with disabilities (Stodden, Galloway, & Stodden, 2003).

While standards-based reforms for students with disabilities attempt to increase access to the general curriculum, increase achievement levels, and provide more rigor, there are also some negative consequences from these efforts. These include increasing dropout rates, use of test scores for inappropriate purposes, and altering inclusive placements to avoid lowering school performance (Quenemoen, Lehr, Thurlow, & Massanari, 2001).

With accountability becoming more of a policy issue for all of public education, the impact of high school exit exams and diploma options on secondary students with disabilities has become a major issue. Erickson, Kleinhammer-Tramill, and Thurlow (2007) found that many more students with disabilities exit high school with nontraditional exit certificates than nondisabled students. While nontraditional exit certificates provide students with disabilities who complete their high school curriculum with a document of completion, there are concerns about this form of recognition. For example, students without a traditional high school diploma are less likely to be employed or accepted into some form of postsecondary educational or preparation program than students with traditional high school diplomas.

Another issue related to increased accountability standards is high stakes testing and students with disabilities. With the movement toward increased standards and accountability has come an increase in the development of statewide assessment systems. These statewide assessments are indeed mandated by the No Child Left Behind legislation with school districts having to show the annual yearly progress of their students. While the intent of the standards-based educational reform movement is to improve the education of all students, the process of using high stakes testing to determine the performance of students with disabilities is problematic. In the 2001–2002 school year, 20 states used minimum-competency testing as a requirement for high school graduation (Digest of Education Statistics, 2007).

One result of the high stakes testing is the provision of testing accommodations and modifications for students with disabilities. While measuring a student's educational progress is important, it is equally important to give students with disabilities an equal opportunity to be successful. Modifications and accommodations are designed to do just that—give students an equal opportunity while maintaining the integrity of the tests.

Bolt and Thurlow (2004) reviewed research on typical testing accommodations and found that accommodations are provided without a great deal of consistency or uniformity. Indeed, they concluded that even with widespread increase in testing accommodations provided, "very little research has been conducted to demonstrate whether accommodations allow for appropriate assessment" (p. 148).

Some students with disabilities, those deemed to be severely disabled, can be assessed using alternative assessment strategies. "Alternative assessment has the potential to enhance expectations for students with significant cognitive disabilities and to increase consideration of this population's needs in setting state and district policy" (Browder & Spooner, 2003, p. 58). Most students with mild disabilities can be assessed using the same assessments with accommodations.

One means of assuring accountability for schools is through the mandate in No Child Left Behind which required schools to have "highly qualified" teachers by the end of the 2005–2006 school year (Simpson et al., 2004). As a result, teachers have to be licensed to teach in the subject area they are teaching. This has caused some difficulty in special education due to the significant teacher shortage in this area. Also, because secondary teachers, including secondary special education teachers, teach specific subject areas, ensuring that special education teachers have a teaching license in a content area has caused difficulty in some school districts. As noted by Simpson and colleagues (2004), "the requirement that special education teachers, already overburdened with paperwork and stress, be dually certified might prove to the tipping point that will at the least, negatively impact the hiring and retaining of an already dwindling supply of personnel" (p. 72).

Frequently, educational reform efforts are less than successful. This is also true for reform efforts for students with disabilities. Stodden et al. (2003, p. 21) suggest that the following needs to occur if current reform efforts are to be successful:

- State content standards for general and special education must be carefully aligned with curriculum and assessments. Significant input from those who will administer these measures, and those who should benefit from them, is necessary to emphasize manageable workloads for all and to foster better motivation to meet goals.
- The need for change must be accepted and acted on at the local level. All changes, from policy to school restructuring, must be based on valid research and locally determined objectives and timelines. The input of students with disabilities, parents, general and special educators, administrators, postsecondary personnel, and employers must be used to foster participation, affiliation, and responsibility to the whole school community.

Role of Teachers

With the increased level of inclusion, and the increased level of accountability by focusing on student outcomes, secondary special education teachers find themselves having to be involved in more and more activities. Wasburn-Moses (2005) surveyed more than 300 secondary special education teachers who taught children with learning disabilities and found that they are involved in myriad activities. Findings were as follows:

- 60.7% teach reading daily
- 48.2% teach writing daily
- 52.9% teach study skills daily
- 56% teach math daily
- 37.2% teach social studies daily
- 33.5% teach science daily
- 67% made adaptations or accommodations for students daily

In addition to the above teaching areas, 80.1% of respondents indicated that they completed paperwork daily; 71.7% work with general education teachers daily; and more than 50% work with administrators daily. Wasburn-Moses concluded that "if special education programs do require teachers to be jacks of all trades, they will indeed be masters of none" (2005, p. 157).

One thing secondary special education teachers have had to do is learn new roles. Coteaching has become a common approach in inclusive classrooms. Successful coteaching requires both the special education teacher and the general classroom teacher to assume different roles than they are accustomed (Rice, Drame, Owens, & Frattura, 2007).

SUMMARY

Education in the United States began in colonial times and primarily focused on elementary schools. The focus on educational programs for secondary students did not emerge until the late 1800s, and did not fully reach its potential until mandatory attendance laws were passed in the early 20th century. Special education services followed a similar track—services for elementary students were the initial focus with services for secondary students following.

Services for students with disabilities were initially segregated in self-contained programs, but gave way to initial efforts to include these students in general education classrooms—a model called mainstreaming. Most recently, the predominant service model for this group of students is inclusion. While similar to mainstreaming, inclusion differs in that it is based on the assumption that students with disabilities belong with their nondisabled, chronological age peers, whereas mainstreaming assumes that these students belong in special education until they are ready for inclusion.

Current services for students with disabilities in inclusive settings did not happen quickly; they were the result of several factors that evolved over the last 25 years. Although several factors were instrumental in this evolution, the primary force was federal legislation. Public Law 94-142, reauthorized as the Individuals with Disabilities Education Act (IDEA), had the greatest impact on the development of special education services. The IDEA requires that schools provide a free appropriate public education to all students with disabilities. This requires schools to (1) identify students; (2) conduct a comprehensive assessment of students; (3) develop and implement an individualized educational program (IEP); and (4) serve students in the least restrictive environment.

Several issues can create difficulties in serving secondary students with disabilities. These include the high dropout rate of these students and the increased accountability that resulted from the No Child Left Behind (1992) legislation. Although these factors have resulted in challenges, school districts have implemented several responses to address the issues.

ACTIVITIES

1. Interview five secondary classroom teachers and ask them to share their feelings about inclusion. Have each teacher provide self-perceptions of advantages and disadvantages for students with disabilities and students without disabilities in general education classrooms. Finally, summarize these five teacher interviews and draw your own conclusions about the support inclusion has in secondary schools.

2. Interview five students in secondary classrooms to find out their ideas on inclusion. Make sure to ask them how they feel when students with disabilities are included in their classes; whether the inclusion of students presents a distraction; and if having students with disabilities in their classrooms has made them more or less tolerant about learning diversity.

3. Observe in a secondary classroom for half a day and try to determine which students, if any, have disabilities. After your observations, list the characteristics of students you think have disabilities and why this makes you think they are eligible for special education services.

REFERENCES

Alabama Cooperative Extension System. (2000). Does earning a high school diploma pay dividends? *The Workplace, 1*(2), 1.

Bolt, S. E., & Thurlow, M. L. (2004). Five of the most frequently allowed testing accommodations in state policy. *Remedial and Special Education, 25,* 141–152.

Bouck, E. C. (2007). Lost in translation? Educating secondary students with mild mental impairment. *Journal of Disability Policy Studies, 18,* 79–97.

Browder, D., & Spooner, F. (2003). Understanding the purpose and process of alternate assessment. In D. L. Ryndak & S. Alper (Eds.), *Curriculum and instruction for students with significant disabilities in inclusive settings* (pp. 521–72). Boston: Allyn & Bacon.

Christle, C. A., Jolivette, K., & Nelson, C. M. (2007). School characteristics related to high school dropout rates. *Remedial and Special Education, 28,* 325–339.

Cobb, R., Sample, P. L., Alwell, M., & Johns, N. R. (2007). Cognitive-behavioral interventions, dropout, and youth with disabilities. *Remedial and Special Education, 27,* 259–275.

Cook, B. G., Cameron, D. L., & Tankersley, M. (2007). Inclusive teachers' attitudinal ratings of their students with disabilities. *Journal of Special Education, 40,* 230–238.

Cox, M. L., Herner, J. G., Demczyk, M. J., & Nieberding, J. J. (2006). Provision of testing accommodations for students with disabilities on statewide assessments. *Remedial and Special Education, 27,* 346–354.

Digest of Educational Statistics. (2008). Condition of Education. Washington, DC: U.S. Department of Education.

Digest of Education Statistics. (2007). Condition of Education. Washington, DC: U.S. Department of Education.

Dunn, L. (1968). Special education for the mentally retarded—Is much of it justified? *Exceptional Children, 35,* 5–22.

Erickson, A. S. G., Kleinhammer-Tramill, J., & Thurlow, M. L. (2007). An analysis of the relationship between high school exit exams and diploma options and the impact on students with disabilities. *Journal of Disability Policy Studies, 18,* 117–128.

Fontana, J. L., Scruggs, T., & Mastropieri, M. A. (2007). Mnemonic strategy instruction in inclusive secondary social studies classes. *Remedial and Special Education, 28,* 345–355.

Gartin, B. C., & Murdick, N. L. (2008). Meeting the needs of all students through instructional design. In H. P. Parette & G. R. Peterson-Karlan (Eds.), *Research-based practices in developmental disabilities* (2nd ed., pp. 171–178). Austin, TX: Pro-Ed.

Idol, L. (2006). Toward inclusion of special education students in general education. *Remedial and Special Education, 27,* 77–94.

Individuals with Disabilities Education Act (2004). Washington, DC: U.S. Department of Education.

Johnson, J. A., Musial, D., Hall, G. E., Gollnick, D. M., & Dupuis, V. L. (2008). *Foundations of American education* (14th ed). Boston: Allyn & Bacon.

Kavale, K. A., & Forness, S. R. (2000). History, rhetoric, and reality: Analysis of the inclusion debate. *Remedial and Special Education, 21,* 279–296.

Kochhar-Bryant, C. A., & Greene, G. (2009). *Pathways to successful transition for youth with disabilities.* Upper Saddle River, NJ: Merrill/Pearson.

Mercer, C. D., & Pullen, P. C. (2009). *Students with learning disabilities* (6th ed.). Upper Saddle River, NJ: Pearson.

Morrison, G. S. (2006). *Teaching in America* (4th ed.). Boston: Allyn & Bacon.

Oliva, P. F. (2005). *Developing the curriculum* (6th ed.). Upper Saddle River, NJ: Pearson Education.

Ornstein, A. C., & Hunkins, F. P. (2009). *Curriculum: Foundations, principles, and issues* (5th ed.). Boston: Allyn & Bacon.

Ornstein, A. C., & Levine, D. U. (2008). *Foundations of education* (10th ed.). Boston: Houghton Mifflin Company.

Quenemoen, R. F., Lehr, C. A., Thurlow, M. L., & Massanari, C. B. (2001). *Students with disabilities in standards-based assessment and accountability systems: Emerging issues, strategies, and recommendations.* Discussion paper at the National Capacity Building Institute, Honolulu, HI.

Polloway, E. A., Patton, J. R., Epstein, M. H., & Smith, T. E. C. (1993). Comprehensive curriculum for students with mild handicaps. *Focus on Exceptional Children, 21,* 1–12.

Polloway, E. A., Smith, J. D., Patton, J. R., & Smith, T. E. C. (1996). Historical changes in mental retardation and developmental disabilities. *Education and Training in Mental Retardation and Developmental Disabilities, 31,* 3–12.

Rea, P. J., McLaughlin, V. L., & Walther-Thomas, C. (2002). Outcomes for students with learning disabilities in inclusive and pullout programs. *Exceptional Children, 68,* 203–222.

Reschly, A. L., & Christenson, S. L. (2006). Prediction of dropout among students with mild disabilities. *Remedial and Special Education, 27,* 276–292.

Rice, N., Drame, E., Owens, L., & Frattura, E. M. (2007). Co-instructing at the secondary level: Strategies for success. *Teaching Exceptional Children, 39,* 12–18.

Sabornie, E. J., & deBettencourt, L. U. (2009). *Teaching students with mild and high-incidence disabilities at the secondary level.* Upper Saddle River, NJ: Merrill/Pearson.

Salend, S. J. (2008). *Creating inclusive classrooms: Effective and reflective practices* (6th ed.). Upper Saddle River, NJ: Merrill/Pearson.

Simpson, R. L., LaCava, P. G., & Graner, P. S. (2004). The no child left behind act: Challenges and implicatins for educators. *Intervention in School and Clinic, 40,* 67–76.

Smith, T. E. C., & Dowdy, C. A. (1998). Educating young children with disabilities using responsible inclusion. *Child Education, 74,* 317–320.

Smith, T. E. C., & Hilton, A. (1994). Program design for students with mental retardation. *Education and Training in Mental Retardation, 29,* 3–9.

Smith, T. E. C., Polloway, E. A., Patton, J. R., & Dowdy, C. A. (2012). *Teaching students with special needs in inclusive settings* (6th ed.). Upper Saddle River, NJ: Allyn & Bacon/Pearson.

Stainback, W., & Stainback, S. (1984). A rationale for the merger of special and regular education. *Exceptional Children, 54,* 104–111.

Stodden, R. A., Galloway, L. M., & Stodden, N. J. (2003). Secondary school curricula issues: Impact on postsecondary students with disabilities. *Exceptional Children, 70,* 9–25.

Tomlinson, C. A. (2007). Challenging expectations: Case studies of high-potential, culturally diverse young children. *Gifted Child Quarterly, 41,* 5–18.

U.S. Census Bureau. (2003). Statistical abstract. Washington, DC: Author.

Wasburn-Moses, L. (2005). Roles and responsibilities of secondary special education teachers in an age of reform. *Remedial and Special Education, 26,* 151–158.

Zigmond, N. (1993). Rethinking secondary school programs for students with learning disabilities. In E. L. Meyen, G. A. Vergason, & R. J. Whelan (Eds.), *Educating students with mild disabilities.* Denver, CO: Love.

The Special Education Process in Middle and Secondary Schools

Study Questions

1. What are the steps in the special education process?

2. What are the roles general classroom teachers play in each of the steps in the special education process?

3. Describe the different types of assessments and give strengths and weaknesses of each.

4. What are the components of the IEP?

5. What are due process rights?

INTRODUCTION

The special education process for students in middle and secondary schools is similar to that for students in elementary grades. Namely, students must be referred for services; students must be evaluated and periodically reevaluated to determine if they meet eligibility requirements and to determine what special interventions they may need; individual educational programs must be developed, implemented, and reviewed; and students and their families must be afforded due process rights. Steps in the special education process are mandated by the Individuals with Disabilities Education Act (IDEA). Without this structure, it is highly unlikely that all students with disabilities would receive an appropriate education. The special education process helps to ensure that every student with a disability will receive the mandated free appropriate public education (FAPE), in whatever state the student resides. The provisions of IDEA ensure similar opportunities for services for all students in all states.

IDEA provides details for specific actions related to the identification and the provision of services for students with disabilities. Much of the information in this chapter is taken from the final regulations for IDEA 2004, which provides mandated actions throughout the special education process. Figure 3.1 depicts the steps in the special education process. In addition to these steps, schools must afford due process rights to students and their parents. This means that parents and students have specific rights associated with each step in the process.

At the secondary level, many students have already been identified and provided services in special education in elementary schools. For these students, the IEP process primarily focuses on the annual development and implementation of the IEP, the annual review of the student's IEP, periodic reevaluation of the student, and the provision of due process rights. While these are the primary actions taken by secondary school personnel, they still must be knowledgeable about the entire special education process, beginning with the initial referral of students for special education services.

REFERRAL

The first step in the special education process is referral. Although not mandated by IDEA, many states either require or recommend prereferral efforts aimed at preventing students from going through the special education process. If these prereferral interventions are successful then there is no need to continue with the special education process. IDEA 2004 also suggests that schools might choose to use a response to intervention (RTI) model. Using this model, students are provided various interventions before they are evaluated for special education services to determine if the needs of the student can be met without special education supports. If preferral or RTI is not successful, then students must be referred for special education services to initiate the process. Referrals often occur during the elementary years, with most occurring during the primary grades when the academic needs of students may become obvious for the first time (Smith, Polloway, Patton, & Dowdy, 2012). As a result, it is vital that primary teachers remain aware of issues that might result in students being eligible for special education services.

Even though most students are referred during the primary grades, others may need a referral for special education services at the secondary level for one of the following reasons: Some students may not manifest their disability until later grades; some students may not need special education services until their middle and high school years; or other students were simply not referred for services at the elementary level. For example, a student with a learning

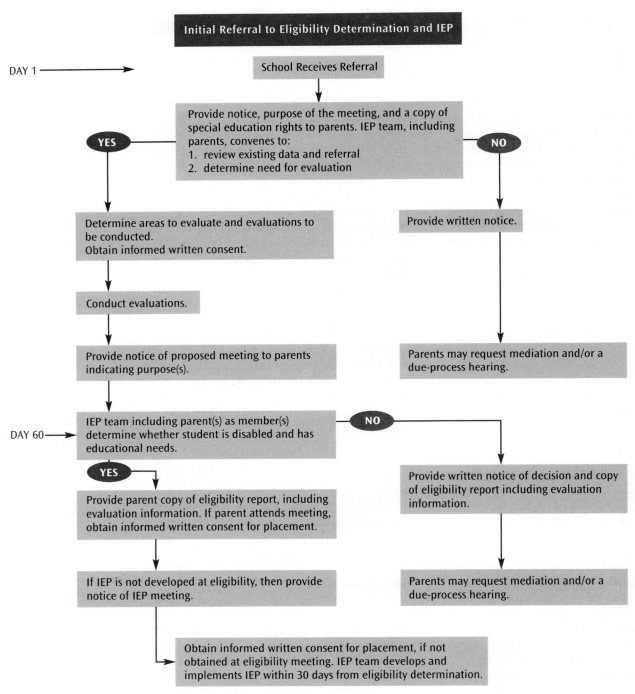

Initial Referral to Eligibility Determination and IEP

DAY 1 ——→ School Receives Referral

Provide notice, purpose of the meeting, and a copy of special education rights to parents. IEP team, including parents, convenes to:
1. review existing data and referral
2. determine need for evaluation

YES

NO

Determine areas to evaluate and evaluations to be conducted.
Obtain informed written consent.

Provide written notice.

Conduct evaluations.

Provide notice of proposed meeting to parents indicating purpose(s).

Parents may request mediation and/or a due-process hearing.

DAY 60 ——→ IEP team including parent(s) as member(s) determine whether student is disabled and has educational needs.

NO

YES

Provide parent copy of eligibility report, including evaluation information. If parent attends meeting, obtain informed written consent for placement.

Provide written notice of decision and copy of eligibility report including evaluation information.

If IEP is not developed at eligibility, then provide notice of IEP meeting.

Parents may request mediation and/or a due-process hearing.

Obtain informed written consent for placement, if not obtained at eligibility meeting. IEP team develops and implements IEP within 30 days from eligibility determination.

FIGURE 3.1 ● The Special Education Process

Note: The 2004 reauthorization of IDEA allows schools to pursue evaluation through due process if parents deny permission. Schools are not allowed to pursue due process if the parents deny consent for services.
Source: From T. E. C. Smith, E. A. .Polloway, J. R. Patton, and C. A. Dowdy, 2012, *Teaching Students With Special Needs in Inclusive Settings* (6th ed.) p. 103. Boston: Allyn & Bacon.

disability may not have significant deficits in achievement until middle or high school when the demands of reading become more critical. Other students may not develop their disability until their adolescent years, such as a student having an orthopedic impairment due to an automobile accident.

Regardless of why some students may need an initial referral for special education services in middle and high schools, it may be up to secondary teachers to initiate the referral process, or at a minimum, know what steps are required if a parent makes a referral for special education services. Therefore, all teachers and staff at all levels need to be aware of the special education process so that they will understand when and how to refer students, and what actions to take if students are referred by others.

In addition to teachers and other school staff making initial referrals for special education services, parents can and often do make these referrals (Yell & Drasgow, 2007). Regardless of who initiates the referral, or at what level, once the referral has been made the special education process begins. IDEA is clear in that it is the school's responsibility to make an initial referral for special education services if the child is suspected of being eligible for such services, regardless of grade level. Once a referral has been made, school personnel consider whether they believe the child would be eligible for special education services.

Behaviors Suggesting Referral

Numerous behaviors and characteristics that are displayed by students could result in a referral for special education services. Some of the major indicators include:

- Not achieving at the level of age-peers
- Difficulties maintaining appropriate levels of behavior
- Serious social skill deficits
- Overly active
- Difficulty maintaining attention
- Limited ability to do what other similarly aged children can do
- Speech-language deficits
- Suspected health issues

These are definitely not all of the characteristics that could lead to a referral, but a few of the more obvious ones. If a teacher suspects a child would be eligible based on these or other characteristics, then the teacher must initiate the process.

Legal Requirements

Under IDEA, "school districts have an affirmative duty under the Child Find requirements . . . to identify, locate, and assess all children with disabilities residing within the district's jurisdiction who (a) have disabilities and need special education as a result or (b) are suspected of having a disability and need special education services" (IDEA 2004, U.S.C. 1412[a]). Schools cannot deny a child appropriate services simply because the parent did not make a referral. Parents may or may not be aware of IDEA, or the types of disabilities covered under the act; therefore, although parents have a right to make a referral, the legal obligation rests with the school.

School districts have forms for each step of the special education process, beginning with the referral. The referral form usually includes general information about the student, as well as the reason for the referral. Figure 3.2 depicts a sample referral form with one of the student cases followed throughout the text. All teachers in secondary schools need to know how to access, complete, and submit a referral form.

Referral Form

ABC Public School System

Student's Name: <u>Sophia Jones</u>   Date of Birth: <u>2/9/98</u>
Grade: <u>6th grade</u>   Teacher: <u>Ms. Daugherty</u>
Date of Referral: <u>10/23/2010</u>
Person Making Referral: <u>Gena Daugherty</u>

Parents' Names: <u>Frank and Amanda Jones</u>

Address: <u>312 E. Lafayette, Bridgewater, New Jersey 07614</u>

Home Phone: <u>555–9010</u>   Work Phone: <u>556–7384</u>

Primary Language of the Home: <u>English</u>

Reason for Referral: Sophia has been experiencing significant difficulties in all of her content classes that require reading and written expression. Her reading skills appear to be several grades below 6th grade, and she has extremely poor written language skills. She tries very hard but gets frustrated while engaging in reading assignments. Her grades are declining weekly, and she is beginning to have some behavior problems.

Have parents been informed of the reason for this referral? <u>YES</u> If no, why?

Prereferral Interventions in General Classrooms (describe):

Additional Information:
1. Attach copies of relevant evaluations or test scores
2. Has student ever repeated a grade?
3. Attach copies of work samples
4. Attach copies of current grades
5. Has student received any other services? <u>No</u> If yes, explain:

6. Does student wear glasses? <u>No</u>; Hearing aid? <u>No</u>
7. Does student have a known health problem? <u>No</u> If yes, explain:

8. Does student take regular medication? <u>No</u> If yes, explain:

FIGURE 3.2 ● Sample Referral Form

Referral Meeting

Once the referral has been made, a committee is formed to consider whether it believes the child would be eligible for special education. This committee is composed of school personnel who have knowledge of the child and who are in a position to offer information that would help the team determine if further assessment for special education is warranted. IDEA does not specify who is included on the referral team, but obvious participants would include (1) the child's teacher(s); (2) special education personnel; (3) someone representing the building administration; and (4) the child's parents (or guardians), should they wish to attend. At the referral meeting, school personnel should provide parents a copy of their legal rights, and explain these rights so that parents understand.

Simply referring the child does not mean the child will be determined eligible for special education services, only that a belief exists that the child could be eligible. The referral committee makes the decision on whether to move to the next step in the process— formal assessment—based on information provided from the child's teacher, other school personnel who know the child, and the child's parents. The referral committee could make any one of the following recommendations:

- Formal assessment to determine eligibility for special education services
- Modifications or accommodations in the general education classroom
- No changes in current services

Teacher's Role in the Referral Process

Middle and high school teachers should participate in the referral process in one of two ways. First, teachers may initiate the referral process. If a student is in a classroom and displays some of the characteristics described above, which leads the teacher to believe that the student might be eligible for special education services, then the teacher should initiate a formal referral. Second, general classroom teachers should also participate in the referral conference to determine if the special education process should move forward. At this meeting, teachers provide anecdotal evidence and any other relevant information to assist team members in making the determination of whether to evaluate or not.

Response to Intervention

Response to intervention (RTI) is a process that has recently become an option for determining eligibility for students for special education services as well as interventions that might enable a student to perform at a more optimal level. While not a new model, IDEA 2004 notes that schools can use an RTI model in lieu of a discrepancy model, primarily for the identification of students with learning disabilities (Berkeley, Bender, Peaster, & Saunders, 2009). RTI follows an approach that does not look at student failures as simply a problem within the student; rather its focus is to determine what other educational approaches might be effective and therefore alleviate the need for special education services (Hardcastle & Justice, 2006). It is unlikely that an RTI model will be used extensively at the secondary level because most students with disabilities are identified during their elementary school years; however, there may be a few cases where RTI is used.

There are several ways that RTI can be used to develop successful interventions or identify students with disabilities. McCook (2006) identifies two different RTI models. The protocol model implements a specific intervention model; the problem-solving model identifies issues experienced by the student, and provides interventions based on the specific needs of the student. Both models focus on developing successful intervention strategies that result in a student making progress and therefore not needing further referral for special education services. These interventions should be research-based, meaning that they have been found to be successful ways to effectively deal with behavior or learning problems. Finally, McCook (2006) noted that a combination of the protocol and problem-solving model can be used. In this model a group of interventions are identified and a problem-solving process is used to determine which intervention would most likely be successful.

ASSESSMENT

If the referral conference results in a decision that the child is likely eligible for special education services, then a comprehensive evaluation must be conducted. The purpose of the evaluation is to determine if the child is eligible for special education services, and if so, information necessary to develop an individualized educational program (IEP) for the student.

Legal Requirements

Prior to conducting the initial evaluation, the school district must notify the parents of its desire to conduct an assessment, and receive written consent from the parents to conduct the evaluation (Yell & Drasgow, 2007). This notice, as well as other required notices, must be provided in the native language of the home—a critical due process requirement. If parents refuse to give consent for the evaluation, then the school cannot conduct the evaluation unless it gains consent through a due process hearing. Parental consent for the initial evaluation is not consent for providing special education services, but only consent for the evaluation.

Once consent is obtained, schools can conduct their initial evaluation to determine if the child is eligible for special education services, and what services are required to ensure that the child receives an appropriate education. IDEA 2004 requires school personnel, when conducting the evaluation, to do the following:

- Use a variety of assessment tools and strategies to gather relevant functional, developmental, and academic information about the child, including information provided by the parent, that may assist in determining whether the child is a child with a disability, as defined in IDEA, and the content of the child's IEP.
- Not use any single measure or assessment as the sole criterion for determining eligibility.
- Use technically sound assessment instruments.
- Conduct the evaluation within 60 days of receiving parental consent for the evaluation.

IDEA specifically prohibits discriminatory assessment. In the 1970s, professionals began to realize that some tests were biased against individuals who had not had similar experiences as the norm group. In other words, some of the tests used to identify students with disabilities were determined to be invalid for that group of students. Beginning with the predecessor to IDEA, Public Law 94-142, schools were mandated to use nondiscriminatory assessment techniques. Prior to the passage of this law most professionals were unaware of the biased nature of some tests.

With the continuing increase in the numbers of students from minority groups, nondiscriminatory assessment becomes more challenging. While culture-free tests do not exist, school personnel can take steps to lessen the impact of discriminatory practices. IDEA 2004 specifically requires schools to ensure that assessment and other evaluation materials are:

1. Selected and administered so as not to be discriminatory on a racial or cultural basis
2. Provided and administered in the language and form most likely to yield accurate information unless not feasible to do so
3. Used for purposes for which the assessments are valid and reliable
4. Administered by trained and knowledgeable personnel
5. Administered in accordance with instructions provided by the producer of such assessments

While not guaranteeing a fair assessment, implementing these steps should reduce discrimination in testing. School personnel should rely on their professional judgment as a useful source of information when making assessment decisions.

Types of Assessment

While IDEA does not require specific tests or types of assessment, it does require that students are determined to be classified as a student with a disability before they receive special education services. IDEA defines "a student with a disability" as a student with mental retardation, learning disabilities, serious emotional disturbance, traumatic brain injury, autism, other health impairment, orthopedic impairment, hearing impairment (including deafness), visual impairment (including blindness), speech-language impairment, deaf-blindness, or multiple disabilities, who needs special education and related services. In order to have sufficient information to determine if a child meets the above definition, norm-referenced tests are frequently necessary.

Norm-Referenced Tests

Norm-referenced assessments enable a student to be compared to a representative, norm sample. This provides information about how a child is performing, compared to his or her chronological age peers. IQ tests and achievement tests are typically norm-referenced. Knowing where a child performs, compared to the normative group, can give school personnel a good understanding of the child's overall ability levels. This type of test is frequently used as a basis for determining a disability category, as well as academic needs.

While hundreds of norm-referenced tests are used in schools, some of the most frequently used tests include the following:

- Stanford-Binet IQ Test
- Wechsler IQ Tests
- Woodcock-Johnson Achievement Test
- Wechsler Individual Achievement Test
- Test of Written Language
- Key Math Diagnostic Test
- Gray Oral Reading Test

While norm-referenced test information can be very compelling, the tests carry certain limitations and problems. Teachers and other consumers of assessment information need to be aware of these issues when considering results for particular students. One of the major concerns about norm-referenced tests is their bias. As noted by Chamberlain (2005), this could take several forms, including content bias, construct bias, limited tests available in different languages, limited opportunity to learn content, and not reflecting the backgrounds of students from some cultural groups. Table 3.1 describes some of these problems and others associated with norm-referenced tests. Even with these weaknesses, norm-referenced tests can provide valuable information when determining if a child is eligible for special education and the specific needs of the child. Teachers and other decision makers simply need to be aware of some of their limitations.

Criterion-Referenced Tests

Criterion-referenced tests provide an opportunity to compare a student's performance to a mastery level in a particular area. These tests do not allow a comparison of a student with a norm group, but rather focus on the knowledge and ability of a particular student. Unlike norm-referenced tests, most criterion-referenced tests are developed by teachers to determine specific skills that students possess (Smith et al., 2012). For example, before beginning a math lesson, teachers might need to know if students have the requisite skills necessary to understand the current math content. A criterion-referenced test on these areas could help teachers understand this.

TABLE 3.1 ● Problems with Norm-Referenced Testing

- *Content bias*—When some students, because of their cultural backgrounds, may not have had an opportunity to learn some content on a test or the content reflects values different from the student's cultural group.
- *Construct bias*—Some tests do not measure what they purport to measure. For example, no one really knows how to measure intelligence, but IQ tests are used as measures of that construct daily.
- *Lack of tests in different languages*—Other than Spanish, no other languages represented on norm-referenced tests are used in the United States. Using translators often change what is being tested.
- *Lack of opportunity to learn content or lack of exposure to the testing situation*—If instruction has not been provided over the content being tested, students should not be expected to know the answers.
- *Norm-referenced tests rely on the melting-pot theory of the typical U.S. student*—Norm-referenced tests must reflect the backgrounds of specific cultures, which most tests do not.

Source: From "Recognizing and Responding to Cultural Differences in the Education of Culturally and Linguistically Diverse Learners," by S. P. Chamberlain, 2005, *Intervention in School and Clinic, 40,* pp. 195–211.

Curriculum-Based Measures. A means of measuring a student's progress within a specific curriculum is called curriculum-based measurement. This form of assessment, a type of criterion-referenced test, is simple, inexpensive, and valid. Examples could include the number of math problems answered correctly in 2 minutes; or the number of correctly spelled words written, correct punctuation, and correct writing sequence in a brief writing assignment (Hessler & Konrad, 2008).

Curriculum-based measures can easily be used to describe current functioning levels and learning objectives because the measures are taken directly from the learning content. Progress monitoring can occur by periodically reviewing the student's success with the content measured by the curriculum-based measure (McMaster, Du, & Petursdottir, 2009). This information can also be easily graphed, presenting a visual display of a student's progress toward IEP goals.

Other Forms of Assessment

In addition to norm-referenced tests and criterion-referenced tests, other forms of assessment can generate very useful information about a student. These include interviews, observations, authentic assessment, portfolio assessment, and ecological assessment. Table 3.2 briefly describes these types of assessments.

SELECTING TYPES OF ASSESSMENTS

The IDEA requires schools to conduct an assessment of each child in order to determine the student's eligibility for special education services, and to determine the nature of those services. However, it does not specify the types of assessments that should be used. When determining which assessments will be used, schools should match the purposes and types of assessment procedures. For example, when screening a large number of students to determine if any need more intensive assessment, screening instruments specifically designed for screening purposes would be better than individual, diagnostic tests (Taylor, 2009). If assessing a child to determine eligibility for IDEA services because of mental retardation, a norm-referenced IQ test would be required. Table 3.3 describes criteria that should be used when considering which assessments are appropriate for different purposes.

TABLE 3.2 ● Additional Forms of Assessment

Type of Assessment	Description
Observations	Observations can be formal or informal; can provide substantive information about how a student performs or behaves in a particular situation or setting. Must be aware of possible observer bias. Presence of observer can alter behaviors.
Interviews	Interview can be of the student or third party, such as parent or teacher. Can be used to collect information about specific issues, such as how a student solves a problem, or more general issues. Students may give more information in an interview setting than other avenues.
Authentic assessment	This is a performance assessment where students must apply knowledge or skills in a real-life situation or a simulated situation. Similar to performance assessment, with the difference being the assessment is conducted in a real-life setting.
Portfolio assessment	An assessment of products or other evidence presented by the student. Assesses a compilation of student's work. Can be used as an alternative means of assessing students with more severe disabilities.
Ecological assessment	This assessment uses direct observations in real-life settings, such as a community setting or employment setting. Provides opportunity to observe issues and determine interventions that could be helpful to the student.

Source: From R. L. Taylor, 2009, *Assessment of Exceptional Students* (8th ed.). Upper Saddle River, NJ: Merrill/Pearson.

TABLE 3.3 ● Test Selection Considerations

Purpose	Type	
	Formal	Informal
1. Initial identification (screening).	Screening and readiness tests; achievement tests.	Criterion-referenced tests; observation; curriculum-based assessment.
2. Determination and evaluation of teaching programs and strategies.	Depends on area of need.	Criterion-referenced tests; error analysis; curriculum-based assessment; portfolios.
3. Determination of current performance level and educational need.	Achievement or diagnostic academic tests; other tests (depending on area of need).	Criterion-referenced tests; observation; curriculum-based assessment.
4. Decisions about eligibility and program placement.	Intelligence, achievement, adaptive-behavior and classroom-behavior measures.	Observation and criterion-referenced tests, used to supplement formal testing.
5. Development of IEPs (goals, objective, teaching strategies).	Commercially prepared inventories and criterion-referenced tests.	Criterion-referenced tests; observation; error analysis; portfolios.
6. Evaluation of IEPs.	Some norm-referenced tests.	Criterion-referenced tests; observation; portfolios.

Source: From R. L. Taylor, 2009, *Assessment of Exceptional Students* (8th ed., p. 47). Upper Saddle River, NJ: Pearson. Used with permission.

TEACHER'S ROLE IN THE ASSESSMENT PROCESS

At the secondary level, general classroom teachers have several roles related to assessment. These include (1) collecting informal assessment information; (2) participating in assessment conferences; (3) understanding assessment information; and (4) monitoring progress. Teachers are in a key position to observe the student daily to determine strengths, weaknesses, and other information that could be useful in determining the student's eligibility, current functioning levels, annual goals, and the student's progress after programs have been developed and implemented.

This informal assessment information can provide very useful information when the assessment committee makes its determination on eligibility and develops the IEP. Not only should the teacher make this information available to the team, but the teacher should also participate in the assessment and IEP meetings. Providing insight into the way the student learns can be invaluable to the other team members. This informal assessment information can also be used in progress monitoring, to determine if elements of the IEP are beneficial for the student. Finally, the general classroom teacher needs to have a basic understanding of assessment practices and be able to interpret assessment results. This requires a general knowledge of different types of assessment instruments and information generated from these instruments.

Another key role for teachers is as consumers of assessment information. Teachers need to have an understanding of what types of assessments were used for students, and what the results mean to their daily instructional process. Knowing that a child has a particular disability, for example, might not be useful for secondary teachers. However, knowing specific strengths and weaknesses of the student, the student's preferred learning styles, and specific information that the student knows and does not know, could be extremely useful in planning and implementing daily learning activities.

Smith, Polloway, Patton, & Dowdy (2008, p. 129) listed the following ways general classroom teachers can be involved in the assessment process:

- *Ask questions about the assessment process.* Special education teachers and school psychologists should be committed to clarifying the nature of the assessments used and the interpretation of the results.
- *Encourage family participation in school activities* so parents can know their input is valued and school personnel can develop a better understanding of their values and differences. If communication is not effective, special education teachers may offer the necessary support during a conference.
- *Provide input.* Formal test data should not be allowed to contradict observations in the classroom about a student's ability, achievement, and learning patterns. A valid diagnostic picture should bring together multiple sources of data, including learning journals, curriculum-based measures, and portfolio assessment from the general education classroom.
- *Observe assessment procedures.* If time and facilities are available (e.g., a one-way mirror), observing the testing process can be educational and enhance your ability to take part in decision making.
- *Consider issues of possible bias.* Because formal assessments are often administered by an individual relatively unknown to the child (e.g., a psychologist), inadvertent bias factors between examiner and examinee may be more likely to creep into the results. Discuss assessment results with other staff to lessen possible bias.
- *Avoid viewing assessment as a means of confirming a set of observations or conclusions* about a student's difficulties. Assessment is exploratory and may not lead to expected results. Too often, after a student is judged not eligible for special services, various parties feel

resentment toward the assessment process. However, the key commitment should be to elicit useful information to help the student, not to arrive at a foregone eligibility decision that may please the student, parent, or teacher.

DETERMINING ELIGIBILITY

After the initial evaluation is completed, a team composed of qualified professionals and the parents (or guardians) determine if the student is eligible for special education services under IDEA. In order to be eligible, the student must meet the definition of disability, which means being classified with one of the prescribed disabilities and needing special education.

Most state departments of education provide guidance on specific criteria for IDEA disability groups. IDEA provides a definition of each disability, but generally leaves specific eligibility criteria for states to determine. The one exception is the area of learning disabilities, where IDEA adds several provisions to the definition that are required before a student can be classified as having a learning disability.

Following the determination of the disability, the team must determine if the student needs special education. While criteria for determining the disability are provided, few if any criteria are provided in IDEA or state guidelines for determining if a child needs special education. This is typically a professional judgment made by the team after considering all of the assessment data generated in the initial evaluation.

Special education is defined in IDEA as specially designed instruction, at no cost to the parents, to meet the unique needs of a child with a disability. This includes instruction conducted in the classroom, in the home, in hospitals and institutions, and in other settings, as well as instruction in physical education. Special education includes speech-language pathology services, travel training for students with vision difficulties, and vocational education.

INDIVIDUALIZED EDUCATIONAL PROGRAMMING

If the team determines that a student is eligible for IDEA services, and parents give consent for services, then an IEP must be developed within 30 days of this decision. All students with disabilities served under IDEA must have an IEP, which is defined as a written plan, often multiple pages long, for each child with a disability that is developed, reviewed, and revised in accordance with prescribed procedures. The IEP is the basis for instructional planning for students with disabilities and should include three planning standards: (1) the involvement of the student in developing the IEP; (2) student's progress in the general education curriculum; and (3) student's functional instructional needs that impact student progress (Knowlton, 2008). A student's IEP drives the day-to-day instructional program of the student. It lays out the framework for interventions that provide the student with a free appropriate public education.

Legal Requirements

Once consent is secured, the IEP team and others, as appropriate, shall develop the IEP. The IDEA has several specific criteria for the development of the IEP, including membership on the

IEP committee, procedure for developing the IEP, and specific components of the IEP. The law requires the IEP team to (IDEA, 2004):

(A) review existing evaluation data on the child, including
    i. evaluations and information provided by the parents of the child;
    ii. current classroom-based, local, or State assessments, and classroom-based observations; and
    iii. observations by teachers and related services providers; and
(B) on the basis of that review, and input from the child's parents, identify what additional data, if any, are needed to determine
    i. whether the child is a child with a disability . . . and the educational needs of the child, or, in case of a reevaluation of a child, whether the child continues to have such a disability and such educational needs;
    ii. the present levels of academic achievement and related developmental needs of the child;
    iii. whether the child needs special education and related services, or in the case of a reevaluation of a child, whether the child continues to need special education and related services; and
    iv. whether any additions or modifications to the special education and related services are needed to enable the child to meet the measurable annual goals set out in the individualized education program of the child and to participate, as appropriate, in the general education curriculum.

THE IEP PROCESS

IEP Participants

One of the most important components of the IEP is the selection of members for the IEP team. This is critical because "the task of designing (and, subsequently, reviewing and revising) an appropriate educational program for a student with a disability falls to the IEP team" (Lake & Norlin, 2007, p. 1). The IDEA specifies membership on the IEP team by stating that each team must include (34 CFR 300.321[a]):

1. The parents of the child;
2. Not less than one regular education teacher of the child (if the child is, or may be, participating in the regular education environment);
3. Not less than one special education teacher, or where appropriate, not less than one special education provider of such child;
4. A representative of the local educational agency who – (i) is qualified to provide, or supervise the provision of, specially designed instruction to meet the unique needs of children with disabilities; (ii) is knowledgeable about the general education curriculum; and (iii) is knowledgeable about the availability of resources of the local educational agency;
5. An individual who can interpret the instructional implications of evaluation results, who may be a member of the team described in paragraphs (a)(2) through (a)(6) of this section;
6. At the discretion of the parent or the agency, other individuals who have knowledge or special expertise regarding the child, including related services personnel as appropriate; and
7. whenever appropriate, the child with a disability.

As noted, IDEA allows for other individuals to participate in the IEP development if needed. If students have unique needs, such as a serious psychiatric disorder or health issues, it might be appropriate to have professionals skilled in psychiatry and health interventions present on the team.

Components of the IEP

Each IEP must contain specific components. The IDEA specifies these to include (IDEA, 2004):

1. A statement of the child's present levels of academic achievement and functional performance.
2. A statement of measurable annual goals, including academic and functional goals.
3. A description of how the child's progress toward meeting the annual goals . . . will be measured and when periodic reports on the progress the child is making toward meeting the annual goals . . . will be provided.
4. A statement of the special education and related services and supplementary aids and services . . . to be provided to the child . . . and a statement of program modifications or supports that will be provided for the child.
5. An explanation of the extent, if any, to which the child will not participate with nondisabled children in the regular class . . .
6. A statement of any individual appropriate accommodations that are necessary to measure the academic achievement and functional performance of the child on State and district-wide assessments . . .
7. The projected date for the beginning of the services and modifications described in sub-clause (VI) and the anticipated frequency, location, and duration of those services and modifications.

In addition to these components, a transition component must be included in the child's IEP that will be in effect on the child's 16th birthday.

Actions during Each Step

Determining Current Functioning Level.   The first step in the IEP process is to develop the section dealing with the student's current academic achievement and functional performance. The purpose of this process is "to describe the problems that interfere with the student's education so that (a) annual goals can be developed, (b) special education services can be determined, and (c) a student's progress can be measured" (Yell & Drasgow, 2007). This is a critical component of the IEP. "If the statement of present levels of academic achievement and functional performance does not consider the unique needs of the student, then the entire IEP likely will be deficient" (Lake & Norlin, 2007, p. 40).

Assessment data gathered during the initial evaluation, as well as other information that might be helpful in describing the student's current functioning level, is used for this step. It is imperative that the team adequately describe the student's current functioning levels because this is used as the basis for establishing annual goals and the services that are required to assist a student in achieving the annual goals. The accompanying sidebar provides a current functioning statement for Sophia and Michael.

Determining Measurable Annual Goals.   After determining current functioning levels of the student, the IEP team sets measurable annual goals. These should be (1) specific, (2) measurable, (3) attainable, (4) routines-based, and (5) tied to a functional priority (Jung & Guskey, 2007). If the IEP does not contain well-written, measurable goals, then the provision of a program that meets the needs of the student will unlikely be provided (Lake & Norlin, 2007).

The ability to measure whether the goals have been achieved is a critical element of the IEP. The only way to determine if the services provided to the student have been successful is to measure the completion of the annual goal. When developing annual goals, team members should consider the student's strengths and weaknesses, current functioning levels, past academic achievement, student preferences, priority of needs, and time frame for achieving the goals (Lake & Norlin, 2007). It stands to reason that goals are derived from the student's current functioning level. The team reviews what the student is currently capable of doing, his or her capabilities, and from there, determines what would be reasonable annual goals.

SIDE BAR

3.1 Sophia's Current Functioning Level

Sophia has average intelligence, somewhat stronger in verbal areas than performance areas. Her reading ability is approximately two grade levels below sixth grade, and she is at least two grade levels below sixth grade in her writing skills. Sophia has a hard time maintaining her attention to tasks that require reading or writing. She makes careless mistakes in writing, and needs to improve her punctuation. She continues to have a positive attitude and is very popular among her peers. Although she is self-confident, she is beginning to get frustrated with her difficulties in reading.

Michael's Current Functioning Level

Michael is performing at the fourth-grade level on most of his work. His performance IQ is higher than his verbal IQ, but he is experiencing significant difficulties in reading, math, and written expression. He currently reads on a fourth-grade level. Michael has difficulties with social skills; he has very few friendships among nondisabled students. He lacks self-confidence and needs to become more self-determined.

In order to be measurable, goals should include information pertaining to (Knowlton, 2008, p. 222):

- The time period in which the goal should be achieved
- Specific behavior(s) to be observed and measured
- Conditions when the behavior will occur
- Level at which the behavior is to occur

By stating that the goals should be measurable means that there is a way to actually measure whether the goals are achieved. The following depicts goal statements that are not measurable and goal statements that are measurable for Sophia and Michael.

Goals that are not measurable

- Sophia will improve her reading ability.
- Sophia will be able to write an essay.
- Michael will make more friends.
- Michael will improve his math calculation skills.

Goals that are measurable

- By the end of the year, Sophia will read orally, on grade level, at a rate of 100 words per minute, with 85% accuracy in decoding and 90% accuracy in comprehension.
- By the end of the year, Sophia will write a two- to three-page essay, when given a prompt, within a 50-minute period, with a maximum of five punctuation and five spelling errors.
- Michael will eat lunch with a lunch buddy three times each week without any behavioral problems by the end of the school year.
- When given 25 math problems at his grade level, Michael will calculate the problems with 90% accurately within a 40-minute period.

In addition to being measurable, goals should also be meaningful. This means that goals should relate to the student's needs, strengths, and circumstances identified in the current levels of functioning (Knowlton, 2008). Goals that are not meaningful distract teachers from focusing on the needs of the student, as identified through the assessment process. In order to be meaningful, goals should focus on the needs of the student in subsequent settings. For example, if a student is in middle school and has reading difficulties, a reasonable goal would be for the student to develop sufficient reading skills to enable the student to be successful in high school content classes. For students nearing the end of their high school years, a meaningful goal would be one tied to their success in employment or an independent living situation.

BEHAVIOR INTERVENTION PLANNING

For students with behavior problems, school personnel must incorporate behavior intervention planning into their IEP. IDEA 2004 requires that the IEP team consider the use of positive behavioral interventions and supports for students whose behavior impedes their learning or the learning of others. Research has shown that by focusing on rewarding appropriate behavior proactively, teachers can "address and prevent challenging forms of behavior by enhancing the capacity of schools, teachers, families, and communities through skills building, the design of effective learning environments, and preventive and proactive evidence-based intervention practices" (Wheeler & Richey, 2008, p. 257).

Legal Requirements

IDEA requires schools to "develop a behavior intervention plan, as part of the IEP, to address how district personnel will deal with a student's challenging, disruptive, or otherwise unacceptable behaviors" (Lake & Norlin, 2007, p. 70). As part of the development procedure, schools must conduct a functional behavior assessment, which is a multistep procedure where structured interviews with teachers, parents, and sometimes students, along with observations, are used to determine under what circumstances inappropriate behaviors occur (Wheeler & Richey, 2008).

Functions of behavior can generally be grouped into four general areas (Barnhill, 2005):

1. To receive attention from others
2. To gain a preferred item or activity
3. To escape from an unpleasant academic or social demand
4. To meet sensory needs

Once the functional behavior assessment and analysis have been conducted and the function determined, then interventions can be planned to address the particular function. Figure 3.3 provides the steps in the functional assessment/intervention process.

---

1. Identify the problem behavior.
2. Describe the problem behavior.
3. Collect baseline data and academic information.
4. Describe the environment and setting demands.
5. Complete a functional assessment form and/or behavior rating scales.
6. Conduct a direct observation.
7. Develop a hypothesis.
8. Hypothesis testing (experimental manipulation).
9. Write a behavioral intervention plan (BIP).
10. Implement BIP.
11. Collect intervention behavioral data.
12. Conduct a follow-up meeting and revise plan as needed.

FIGURE 3.3 ● Steps in Functional Assessment Process

Source: From "Functional Behavioral Assessment in Schools," by G. P. Barnhill, 2005, *Intervention in School and Clinic, 40,* p. 139. Used with permission.

A well-developed behavior intervention plan, based on a functional behavior assessment, is imperative for students whose behaviors impede their academic success. Without this plan, school personnel have a very difficult time designing and implementing appropriate interventions to diminish the impact of the behavior problems. In fact, interventions that are not based on functional assessments could result in worsening behaviors (Barnhill, 2005).

TRANSITION PLANNING

During the 1980s, researchers discovered that many young adults with disabilities, who had been served for several years in special education programs prior to their exiting the school, were experiencing significant difficulties in employment, independent living, and social inclusion. Studies also showed that many students with disabilities were exiting public school programs without a diploma or other official recognition of school completion. The result of these follow-up studies was the mandate that transition planning become a part of the IEP process for secondary students. As a result, school personnel in secondary schools are now concerned about the postschool futures of students with disabilities and how to better prepare this group of students for life after high school.

Legal Requirements

The IDEA regulations state the following related to the child's IEP and transition planning. Beginning no later than the first IEP to be in effect when the child is 16, and updated annually thereafter (IDEA, 2004):

  (aa) appropriate measurable postsecondary goals based upon age appropriate transition assessments related to training, education, employment, and, where appropriate, independent living skills;

  (bb) the transition services (including courses of study) needed to assist the child in reaching those goals; and

  (cc) beginning not later than 1 year before the child reaches the age of majority under State law, a statement that the child has been informed of the child's rights under this title, if any, that will transfer to the child on reaching the age of majority under section 615(m)

Students are required by law to be involved in their transition planning. Using a student-centered approach requires that individuals involved with developing and implementing the student's plan focus on the needs of the student. This should include not only the student's academic and social needs, but also the student's interests and preferences (Zager, Brown, Stenhjem, & Maloney, 2008). Many special education professionals have long advocated for student involvement in their IEP development. The requirements now in IDEA related to transition planning make this mandatory.

When developing transition IEPs, teams should consider each of the following questions to ensure a quality plan (Steere & Cavaiuolo, 2002, p. 58):

1. Does the student take an active role in the transition IEP planning process?
2. Do all team members have a clear understanding of the student's strengths, interests, abilities, and support needs?
3. Has the team clearly defined desired postschool outcomes in areas such as the following:
   • Employment?
   • Postsecondary education or training?
   • Postsecondary living arrangements?
   • Participation in the community?
   • Other aspects of adult life?

4. If not, has the team clearly defined action steps for gathering information or providing the student with additional experiences, with appropriate time lines and responsibilities?
5. Are annual goals and short-term objectives clearly leading toward the attainment of future postschool outcomes?
6. Are annual goals and short-term objectives clear enough to guide the teaching process?
7. Do members of the team have positive and optimistic attitudes about the student's abilities to achieve the state's outcomes?
8. Does the team clarify or revise the student's outcomes as the student gains information and experiences?

Steere and Cavaiuolo (2002) recognize several challenges that IEP teams must meet during the transition planning process. One of the most prevalent is the vagueness of goals, objectives, and outcomes. While transition plans cannot be so specific that they leave out possible postschool outcomes, they must be specific enough to ensure that appropriate support personnel are available to provide assistance after the student leaves high school. It would be inappropriate to state that the goal is for the student to be a successful adult; transition goals should focus on specific adult outcomes. For example, a good transition goal would be that the student successfully completes the first semester of college with a GPA of at least 2.5.

Along with some goals being too vague are some that are unrealistic. When transition goals are being developed, the IEP team wants to ensure that it does not overly limit a student's possibilities while being realistic about the likelihood of goals. Goals must be realistic to maximize the effects of any intervention efforts. For example, it would be unrealistic to state as a transition goal that a student with cognitive limitations successfully graduate from medical school. It might be appropriate to state that this student acquire an employment opportunity in a medical support field.

As with many situations in special education, Steere and Cavaiuolo (2002) point out that many transition goals and outcomes expect too little from students. In fact, one of the weaknesses of special education is the limited expectations held for many students with disabilities by special education teachers (Smith et al., 2012). When developing transition plans for students, a strong balance must be achieved between expectations and limitations—both must be realistic and challenging.

IDEA does not require an action plan as part of transition planning; however, if the transition plan includes a series of specific actions, it is more likely that the plan will be successful. Some of these actions could include investigating desired careers or postsecondary educational options (Steere & Cavaiuolo, 2002). The responsibility for carrying out the action plan would be the student's, with some supervision and oversight from school staff and family members. Figure 3.4 shows an example of a transition plan.

Transfer of Rights

As part of the transition planning process, schools are required by IDEA to transfer legal rights of parents to the students when they reach the age of majority under state law. All rights accorded to the parents under IDEA are transferred to the child upon reaching the age of majority. Individuals generally secure their legal rights as adults upon reaching the age of majority. While this is defined on a state-by-state basis, most states use the chronological age of 18 as the age of majority. IDEA recognizes this age of transfer for the general population and requires schools to ensure the same benefit for students with disabilities.

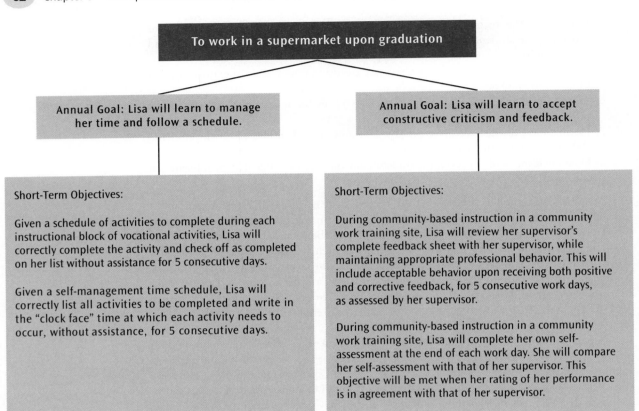

FIGURE 3.4 ● Transition Plan

Source: From "Connecting Outcomes, Goals, and Objectives in Transition Planning," by D. E. Steere and D. Cavaiuolo, 2002, *Teaching Exceptional Children, 34,* p. 56. Used with permission.

Legal Requirements.   IDEA 2004 requires the transfer of parental rights to the student unless the student has been determined to be incompetent under state law. In so doing, IDEA requires the local school district to provide any notice required by IDEA to both the child and the parents; and transfer all rights afforded under IDEA to parents to the student. When this transfer occurs, the school district must notify both parents and the child of the transfer of rights. If the student upon reaching the age of majority is determined not to have the ability to provide informed consent, even though the student has not been determined to be incompetent, parents or another party must be appointed by the state to represent the educational interests of the child.

In order for a successful transfer of these rights, schools need to ensure that students are capable of making informed consent, and understand the rights that have been transferred. Close communication between the school and parents is critical in order to successfully make this transfer. IDEA requires that 1 year before the student reaches the state's age of majority, the student's IEP must include a statement indicating that the student has been informed of the rights that will be transferred upon the age of majority (Kochhar-Bryant & Greene, 2009).

FACILITATING IEP PARTICIPATION

The IDEA mandates the involvement of parents in their child's IEP; it also mandates that students themselves be involved in the IEP process when transition planning becomes a requirement. Also, as a result of the increased number of students with disabilities included in general classrooms, IDEA now mandates the involvement of general education teachers in most IEP procedures. Unfortunately, simply mandating involvement does not guarantee involvement. In fact, parents and students often are somewhat uninvolved in the IEP process (Smith, Gartin, Murdick, & Hilton, 2006), and many general education teachers are not actively involved. School personnel must make a strong effort to increase the amount and level of involvement of parents, students, and general education personnel in this process. The involvement of these groups makes it more likely that an appropriate IEP will be developed and implemented effectively.

Facilitating Parental Involvement

Regardless of meeting specific requirements of IDEA related to the IEP process, securing parental involvement in the IEP process can be difficult. This is often the case, whether the process involves an IEP for younger children, transition planning, or behavior intervention planning. Often parents are simply intimidated by the entire process. They may feel as if it's them against the entire school, rather than as a member of a team with the goal of creating the best possible intervention program for their child.

Although not an option, some school personnel may prefer not to involve parents. They may feel like they can develop and implement the program better if they do not have to deal with parents. Reasons for this attitude include the following (Smith et al., 2008, p. 136):

- School personnel thought that they knew best what actions should be taken regarding a child with a disability.
- School personnel thought that parents would only complicate attempts to provide appropriate services.
- School personnel encountered difficulties in soliciting and securing the involvement of parents.
- School personnel routinely excluded children with disabilities from all services in public schools.

It is critical that school personnel facilitate parental involvement in the IEP process. Having parental input in the development of the IEP and support in carrying out the provisions of the IEP are vital if students are to receive FAPE. Parents are in a unique role in the IEP process. They have intimate, important knowledge that school personnel may not have about the child. They have more opportunities to understand the child's likes and dislikes, behaviors, and family needs (Lytle & Bordin, 2001).

Some things that schools can do to encourage parental involvement in the IEP process include (Lytle & Bordin, 2001, p. 44):

- Send information home before the IEP meeting.
- Deal with difficult or controversial items before the meeting during an informal time with the parents.
- Try to reduce the number of people at the meeting unless parents prefer to have everyone there.
- Be aware of nonverbal communication. Send positive messages during meetings by displaying friendly smiles and open, forward postures rather than looking bored, sitting with arms folded, and leaning back in a chair.

TABLE 3.4 ● Tips for Facilitating Parental Involvement in the IEP Process

- Always consider parents as equal partners in the process.
- Take time to establish a trusting relationship.
- Encourage parents to bring extended family members or advocates.
- Schedule meetings at a time and place convenient to parents.
- Send information home to parents, in an understandable format, prior to the meeting.
- Ensure that interpreters are present if English is not the primary language of the home.
- Say positive things about the student.
- Be positive in the meeting.
- Display positive body language.
- Be friendly.
- Do not use jargon that might be difficult for parents to understand.
- Always ask parents if they understand but not in a patronizing way.
- Summarize previous meetings before beginning.
- Set objectives for the meeting at the beginning.
- Summarize the meeting at the end.

Other tips to facilitate parent–teacher collaboration in the special education process are included in Table 3.4.

Facilitating Student Involvement

As noted, students must be included in the IEP process when transition planning begins, no later than the IEP in place when the child reaches 16 years of age. Prior to IDEA mandating this involvement, students were typically not included in the process. While this is the mandatory time to include students in the IEP process, schools should consider including them at earlier times. Some middle and high school students can be involved even before the transition phase of their IEP is an issue.

While it is important for students to be involved in the IEP process, it is unlikely that this involvement will be meaningful without preparation. Studies have shown that even when students attend they are frequently not actively involved in the process (Martin, Marshall, & Sale, 2004); students will need assistance in learning how to be active participants (Arndt, Konrad, & Test, 2006). This involvement can play an important role in the student's becoming self-determined. Specific strategies for increasing self-determination among students with disabilities are provided in Chapter 13.

Torgerson, Miner, and Shen (2004) described a training program for assisting students to learn how to become involved in the IEP process. The program, including four training sessions, includes a session on helping students learn about themselves, steps in participating in an IEP meeting, social skills needed to be successful in an IEP meeting, and participating in a simulated IEP meeting.

Teacher's Role in the IEP Process

Increasingly, general classroom teachers must play a larger role in the entire IEP process. While always a good idea, the fact that most students with disabilities are included at least a portion of each day in general education classrooms makes it even more important. Now, it is not only a good idea but a legal mandate. IDEA 2004 states:

"A regular education teacher of a child with a disability, as a member of the IEP Team, must, to the extent appropriate, participate in the development of the IEP of the child, including the determination of (i) appropriate positive behavioral interventions and supports and other strategies for the child; and (ii) supplementary aids and services, program modifications, and support for school personnel consistent with (34 CFR) 300.320(a)(4)."

Teachers must be involved in order to have a thorough understanding of the needs of the student. Teachers also need to be involved so that they know specific interventions that they may be responsible for implementing. For example, IEPs should include changes that can be made in how material is presented in the general education classroom.

Tips for Teachers.   As a result of best practices and legal mandates, secondary teachers will be involved in writing and implementing IEPs. Unfortunately, many secondary teachers have not been prepared to be active team members. They have unlikely had any preparation in how to develop annual goals based on students' current functioning levels and unique needs. Kamens (2004) identified several important aspects to remember when participating in writing IEPs. These should help secondary teachers during the process.

1. Goals are broader than objectives and should be written when considering the student's strengths and weaknesses.
2. Goals and objectives should be measurable.
3. Goals and objectives should be created after consideration of the student's needs and current functioning level.
4. Emphasize the positive abilities of the student, not negative areas.
5. Organize information so that it can be easily understood.
6. Take advantage of the student's strengths.

While all of these points should be remembered when serving on IEP committees, one of the most important things to remember is to advocate not only for the student but also for yourself. Teachers need to remember that they will be responsible for implementing the plan; they may not decide on their own which parts of the IEP to implement and which ones to ignore. Therefore, teachers need to speak up at these committee meetings and make their desires known. While the plan is designed to meet the individual needs of the student, teachers must be willing to indicate what can be accomplished in reality.

LEAST RESTRICTIVE ENVIRONMENT

The IDEA requires that schools provide services to students with disabilities in the least restrictive environment. This means that students with disabilities should be educated with children without disabilities as much as possible. This requirement promotes increased access to the general education classrooms for students with disabilities (Rueda, Gallego, & Moll, 2000), more involvement with general education teachers, and more social opportunities with students without disabilities. The least restrictive environment mandate is the foundation for inclusion—including students with disabilities in general education settings as much as possible while continuing to provide them with an appropriate educational program (Smith et al., 2012).

Legal Requirements

The IDEA regulations state that each public agency must ensure that:

i. to the maximum extent appropriate, children with disabilities, including children in public or private institutions or other care facilities, are educated with children who are non-disabled; and

ii. Special classes, separate schooling or other removal of children with disabilities from the regular educational environment occurs only if the nature or severity of the disability is such that education in regular classes with the use of supplementary aids and services cannot be achieved satisfactorily.

Continuum of Placement Options

In order to implement the least restrictive environment mandate, schools must have a continuum of placement options available for students. The availability of placement options along this continuum will ensure that students are indeed placed in the *least* restrictive setting. In addition to the general education classroom, schools must offer the following placement options: special class, special school, home instruction, and instruction in hospitals and institutions (IDEA 2004, 34 CFR 300.114[a][2]). Figure 3.5 depicts a continuum of placement options.

In determining the least restrictive environment for a student, the IEP team must consider the needs of the child. An overall philosophy of inclusion should never trump the needs of students in determining appropriate placement (Smith & Hilton, 1996). Determining the appropriate placement for a student is often difficult and contentious. Because including students with disabilities with their nondisabled peers in the general education classroom is the preferred placement, the team should always begin with the assumption that the student should be in that placement and determine if the provision of aids and services would enable the student to be placed in that setting. If with the provision of these supports it is the team's decision that an appropriate education cannot be provided, then the team should consider the next, more restrictive option until an appropriate placement is determined. Other factors that should be taken into consideration when making the decision for the least restrictive environment include (Lake & Norlin, 2007, p. 78):

- Category and significance of the child's disability
- Availability of special education and related services
- Configuration of the service delivery system
- Availability of space
- Administrative convenience

Rueda and colleagues (2000) argue for another factor to be considered in determining least restrictive setting for a student. Using a sociocultural approach, they support viewing the least restrictive environment for a child as "an interaction of individual characteristics with the features of specific activity settings, rather than a placement in a physical setting" (p. 77). In other words, social relationships are important and should be a consideration when determining the least restrictive environment for a particular child.

Least restrictive	Full-time general classroom with or without assistance
	Part-time general classroom/part-time resource room
	Self-contained special education classroom
	Special school
	Home-bound services
Most restrictive	Residential/hospital facility

FIGURE 3.5 ● Continuum of Placement Options

DUE PROCESS

The IDEA requires schools to provide students with a free appropriate public education, meaning an education that is individually designed to be delivered to each child in the least restrictive environment for that child. As previously described, this requires numerous steps to ensure that each child receives FAPE. In addition to providing students with FAPE, schools must address due process requirements. Due process requirements can be defined as legal rights of students with disabilities and their families. Schools must adhere to the basic requirements related to due process.

Legal Requirements

The IDEA requires schools to provide numerous due process rights to parents and students. These include the right to:

- Examine records
- Secure an independent evaluation
- Be notified before actions are taken with the student
- Consent
- Receive a due process hearing, mediation, and resolution

Table 3.5 describes each of these due process rights. Schools must be vigilant in ensuring that due process rights are afforded to students with disabilities and their families. No longer can schools make decisions about students with disabilities without involving parents. A fundamental requirement of the law is ensuring due process.

TABLE 3.5 ● Due Process Rights

Requirement	Explanation	Reference
Opportunity to examine records	Parents have a right to inspect and review all educational records.	300.501
Independent evaluation	Parents have a right to obtain an independent evaluation of their child at their expense or the school's expense. The school pays only if it agrees to the evaluation or if it is required by a hearing officer.	300.502
Prior notice, parental consent	Schools must provide written notice to parents before the school initiates or changes the identification, evaluation, or placement of a child. Consent must be obtained before conducting the evaluation and before initial placement.	300.503 300.505
Contents of notice	Parental notice must provide a description of the proposed actions in the written native language of the home. If the communication is not written, oral notification must be given. The notice must be understandable to the parents.	300.504
Impartial due-process hearing, mediation, resolution	A parent or school may initiate a due-process hearing, engage in mediation, or a resolution session to resolve a dispute.	300.507

Source: From *IDEA 2004*, Washington, DC U.S. Government Printing Office.

ROLE OF SPECIAL EDUCATION AND CLASSROOM TEACHERS IN THE SPECIAL EDUCATION PROCESS

School personnel are directly involved in the entire special education process, beginning with referral all the way through implementing IEPs and assessing the results of interventions. As the system for educating students with disabilities continues to move more toward an inclusive model, secondary classroom teachers and special education teachers will become more involved in a collaborative system. They must work together to effectively implement the intent of IDEA. An inclusive educational approach that involves a pure dual system of education—regular and special—no longer exists. Rather, the inclusion movement has dissolved, to some extent, the boundaries separating these two traditional educational programs. Furthermore, it is likely that the line between these two programs will continue to erode.

Hoover and Patton (2008) refer to the emerging service model as a multitiered instructional system, where all students, including those with disabilities and other different learning needs, are educated in a system where the individual student's response to instruction is the foundation for instructional and diagnostic decisions. In this system, the roles of special education teachers and general education teachers merge into a more collaborative model.

There are several reasons for this transition, but the most likely reason is the increasing diversity found in public schools. No longer do secondary teachers have students who represent a homogenous set of characteristics. Indeed, the current and future population of students in secondary schools continues to become more diverse. Language, culture, race, religion, and ability are increasingly different among secondary students. As a result, the educational system must make significant changes to meet the needs of this growing diverse population.

One of these important changes is in the way special education is delivered to students with disabilities. The growing levels of inclusion of this group of students mandate that *all* teachers work together more, to effectively teach all students. The multitiered system suggested by Hoover and Patton (2008) supports this model. In a multitiered system, three levels of instruction are provided for all students, based on their individual instructional needs. The system, therefore, provides appropriate instruction for the entire student population based on needs, not whether a student is eligible for special education, English second language (ESL) services, or any other support model. The three levels include (1) high-quality core instruction in a challenging curriculum in general education; (2) high-quality targeted supplemental instruction which includes targeted and focused intervention to supplement the core instruction; and (3) high-quality intensive intervention, which includes more specialized interventions to meet significant needs.

Within a multitiered system, the roles of teachers must change. Special education teachers must become even more collaborative with general education teachers. Hoover and Patton (2008) suggest five roles for special education teachers in this system. Indeed, general secondary teachers would have to work within the same roles. These include engaging in data-driven decision making; implementing evidence-based interventions; differentiating instruction; implementing socioemotional and behavioral supports; and collaborating. Table 3.6 describes subskills associated with each of these roles.

Regardless of the model used, the role of secondary classroom teachers and special education teachers must change. Coteaching, collaboration, teaching in a multitiered system, and other ways of working together must be used. Students with disabilities, as well as those with other diverse needs, demand that all secondary teachers work together to meet their challenging needs.

TABLE 3.6 ● Special Educator Roles and Associated Subskills in Multitiered Instruction

Role	Subskills
Data-driven decision maker	Curriculum based measurement Strategies for effective decision-making Data analysis Multiple monitoring strategies Basic skills assessment Functional skills assessment Special education eligibility Process/criteria
Implement evidence-based intervention	Knowledge of core disciplines Higher order thinking skills Evidence-based instructional strategies Task analysis/direct instruction Programmed instruction Impact of culture and language on learning Determining difference versus disability Functional living and transition skills Mastery learning
Implement socioemotional and behaviorist supports	Classroom management Behavior management Applied behavioral analysis Targeted behavioral supports Social skills instruction Self-management skills instruction Impact of culture and language on behavior Social emotional development Functional behavioral assessment Positive behavioral supports
Differentiate instruction	Accommodations and modifications Differentiation strategies Second language acquisition Culturally relevant instruction Sheltered instruction Study skills and learning strategies Student peer-tutoring models Targeted academic learning time (time, task focus, intensity) Scheduling strategies Alternative curriculum and materials Adapting to address Functional living abilities
Collaborator	Communication skills Coteaching/team processes Consulting/coaching Change strategies Parent–school–community partnerships Cultural/linguistic diversity and collaboration Working with parents on individualized education program (IEP) and disability-related issues Knowledge/understanding of the Individuals With Disabilities Education Improvement Act Amendments of 2004 (IDEA) Knowledge of district special education referral and assessment process

Note: The various subskills were generated from discussions found in the following sources: data-driven decision making, Vaughn and Fuchs (2003) and Hoover and Patton (2005); evidence-based interventions, Moran and Malott (2004); socioemotional and behavioral supports, Crone and Horner (2003); differentiation, Hoover and Patton (2005); collaboration, Idol (2002) and Hoover and Patton (2005).

SUMMARY

An important special education process is required for all students served under the Individuals with Disabilities Education Act (IDEA). The special education process is the structure required under IDEA to ensure that all students receive a free appropriate public education. Referral is the first step in the process. Although most students are initially referred for special education services in elementary grades, secondary teachers need to be aware of the process because some students are not in special education until middle and high schools.

After a student has been referred, if the referral team has reason to believe that the child would be eligible for special education services, with parental consent, the team conducts an evaluation. The evaluation has two purposes: (1) determine if the student is eligible for special education services, and (2) determine the needs of the student so an IEP can be developed. If the assessment results in a decision that the child is eligible, then an IEP team is assembled to develop an individualized educational program.

IDEA prescribes not only the membership of the IEP team, but also the contents of the IEP. The IEP team consists of general and special education teachers, someone qualified to interpret assessment data, someone representing the administration, parents, and others as determined necessary by the team. Each IEP must include information about the student's current functioning level, annual goals, services provided by the school, evaluation procedures, and an explanation concerning why the student will not be fully included in general education classes.

Once the IEP is developed, the team must determine the least restrictive environment for the student. Based on the student's needs and capabilities, schools are required to include students with disabilities with their nondisabled peers, when possible. In doing so, they must have available a continuum of placement options, ranging from full-time inclusion in general education classrooms to residential treatment. The team determines which placement is most appropriate for the student.

Although parents, students, and general classroom teachers are all mandated to participate in the development and implementation of IEPs, they often do not. Regardless of the reasons, it is imperative that school personnel do everything they can to facilitate participation. There are several actions a school can take to gain this participation.

Finally, parents and students with disabilities are afforded specific due process rights under IDEA. These include the right to notice, consent, independent evaluation, and due process hearing. School personnel must ensure that parents are afforded these rights, which are critical in being in full compliance with IDEA.

ACTIVITIES

1. Ask for copies of special education forms used in a secondary school. Review these forms and list the ones required when students are referred for special education, evaluated for special education, and when a decision is made regarding their eligibility. Discuss how you think the forms could be streamlined to reduce paperwork.

2. Interview a special education teacher to determine his or her feelings about the special education process. Make sure to ask the teacher about the steps needed to reduce some of the administrative burden placed on teachers and school officials by the process. Ask the special education teacher what characteristics result in general classroom teachers being good teachers for students with disabilities.

3. Interview the parents of three different students with disabilities to determine what they know about the requirement to transfer majority rights to their child when the student reaches majority age. Find out their feelings of having these rights transferred to the student.

REFERENCES

Arndt, S. A., Konrad, M., & Test, D. W. (2006). Effects of the *self-directed IEP* on student participation in planning meetings. *Remedial and Special Education, 27*, 194–207.

Barnhill, G. P. (2005). Functional behavioral assessment in schools. *Intervention in School and Clinic, 40*, 131–142.

Berkeley, S., Bender, W. N., Peaster, L. G., & Saunders, L. (2009). Implementation of response to intervention: A snapshot of progress. *Journal of Learning Disabilities, 42*, 85–92.

Chamberlain, S. P. (2005). Recognizing and responding to cultural differences in the education of culturally and linguistically diverse learners. *Intervention in School and Clinic, 40*, 195–211.

Hardcastle, B., & Justice, K. (2006). *RTI and the classroom teacher: A guide for fostering teacher buy-in and supporting the intervention process.* Horsham, PA: LRP Publications.

Hessler, T., & Konrad, M. (2008). Using curriculum-based measurement to drive IEPs and instruction in written expression. *Teaching Exceptional Children, 41*, 28–37.

Hoover, J. J., & Patton, J. R. (2008). The role of special educators in a multitiered instructional system. *Intervention in School and Clinic, 43*, 195–202.

Individuals with Disabilities Education Act (2004). Washington, DC: Government Printing Office.

Jung, L. A., & Guskey, T. R. (2007). Standards-based grading and reporting. *Teaching Exceptional Children, 40*, 48–53.

Kamens, M. W. (2004). Learning to write IEPs: A personalized, reflective approach for preservice teachers. *Intervention in School and Clinic, 40*, 76–80.

Knowlton, E. (2008). Instructional planning for students with developmental disabilities. In H. P. Parette & G. R. Peterson-Karlan (Eds.), *Research-based practices in developmental disabilities* (2nd ed., pp. 31–40). Austin, TX: Pro-Ed.

Kochhar-Bryant, C. A., & Greene, G. (2009). *Pathways to successful transition for youth with disabilities* (2nd ed.). Upper Saddle River, NJ: Merrill/Pearson.

Lake, S. E., & Norlin, J. W. (2007). *IEPS that succeed: Developing legally compliant programs.* Horsham, PA: LRP Publications.

Lytle, R. K., & Bordin, J. (2001). Enhancing the IEP team: Strategies for parents and professionals. *Teaching Exceptional Children, 33*, 40–44.

Martin, J. E., Marshall, L. H., & Sale, P. (2004). A 3-year study of middle, junior high, and high school IEP meetings. *Exceptional Children, 70*, 285–297.

McCook, J. E. (2006). *The RTI guide: Developing and implementing a model in your schools.* Horsham, PA: LRP Publications.

McMaster, K. L., Du, X., & Petursdottir, A. (2009). Technical features of curriculum-based measures for beginning writers. *Journal of Learning Disabilities, 42*, 41–59.

Rueda, R., Gallego, M. A., & Moll, L. C. (2000). The least restrictive environment: A place or a context? *Remedial and Special Education, 21*, 70–77.

Smith, T. E. C., Gartin, B. G., Murdick, N. L., & Hilton, A. (2006). *Families and children with special needs: Professional and family partnerships.* Upper Saddle River, NJ: Merrill/Pearson.

Smith, T. E. C., & Hilton, A. (1996). Program design for students with mental retardation. *Education and Training in Mental Retardation and Developmental Disabilities, 29*, 3–8.

Smith, T. E. C., Polloway, E. A., Patton, J. R., & Dowdy, C. A. (2008). *Teaching students with special needs in inclusive settings* (5th ed). Boston: Allyn & Bacon.

Smith, T. E. C., Polloway, E. A., Patton, J. R., & Dowdy, C. A. (2012). *Teaching students with special needs in inclusive settings* (6th ed). Upper Saddle River, NJ: Pearson.

Steere, D. E., & Cavaiuolo, D. (2002). Connecting outcomes, goals, and objectives in transition planning. *Teaching Exceptional Children, 34*, 54–59.

Taylor, R. L. (2009). *Assessment of exceptional students* (8th ed.). Upper Saddle River, NJ: Merrill/Pearson.

Torgerson, C. W., Miner, C. A., & Shen, H. (2004). Developing student competence in self-directed IEPs. *Intervention in School and Clinic, 39*, 162–167.

Wheeler, J. J., & Richey, D. D. (2008). Behavior support strategies for learners with developmental disabilities. In H. P. Parette & G. R. Peterson-Karlan (Eds.), *Research-based practices in developmental disabilities* (2nd ed., pp. 253–268). Austin, TX: Pro-Ed.

Yell, M. L., & Drasgow, E. (2007). The Individuals with Disabilities Education Improvement Act of 2004 and the 2006 regulations. *Assessment for Effective Intervention, 32*, 194–201.

Zager, D., Brown, J., Stenhjem, P. H., & Maloney, A. (2008). Transition practices for persons with developmental disabilities. In H. P. Parette & G. R. Peterson-Karlan (Eds.), *Research-based practices in developmental disabilities* (2nd ed., pp. 309–328). Austin, TX: Pro-Ed.

Transition Programming for Adolescents with Disabilities

Study Questions

1. What are the responsibilities of middle and secondary educators when planning transitions for students with disabilities?

2. What is the general educator's responsibility in providing transition curriculum? Give examples of aligning general education curriculum with transition curriculum.

3. What are the components of a transition assessment and how are they assessed?

4. Who are the members of a transition planning team?

5. What changes occur in transition planning when a student with disabilities reaches the age of majority?

INTRODUCTION

Transition refers to times when changes occur in the lives of individuals and "specifically, transition relates to movement from one situation or setting to another" (Bos & Vaughn, 2006, p. 430). These transitions occur throughout the life of all individuals, regardless of any disabilities they may have. Transitions occur in both a horizontal and a vertical manner. Horizontal transitions are those that occur to individuals in their unique situations—that is, changes in family structure, illness, death, and the like. Thus, horizontal transitions are person-specific and nondevelopmental. Vertical transitions, on the other hand, are those that occur in the lives of most individuals (Smith, Gartin, Murdick, & Hilton, 2006). They are considered to be age or developmentally based and are not specific to a particular individual.

VERTICAL TRANSITIONS

Adolescents encounter vertical transitions at least three times during their years in secondary schools. These include transitions from:

- Elementary to middle school
- Middle school to high school
- High school to postsecondary school environments, such as postsecondary education or vocational settings

All adolescents deal with these transitions, with some having more difficulties than others. For students with disabilities these transitions are generally more challenging. Not only do they deal with the events surrounding the transition, but also the compounding issues related to the disability.

Transitions Within Secondary School

The movement of students from elementary school to middle school is one of the most neglected of the developmental transitions. Teachers who are preparing students with disabilities to enter middle school as well as those teachers who are receiving these students must be aware of the changes that are present in the adolescent and the educational structure (Rosenberg, O'Shea, & O'Shea, 2006). For students to be successful in the transition from elementary school to middle school, receiving teachers must identify the skills required in the "new" environment in the middle school. These include academic skills and social skills that are essential for success. If students do not have the skills, receiving teachers should implement academic skills or social skills training in the areas of deficiency.

The transition process is the same for each new situation, including when students are again transitioning from middle school to high school. Both middle and high school settings have unique features that make each one different from the elementary school setting and different from each other. Teachers at each level must identify and address these differences if the transitions of students with disabilities are to be seamless and successful.

SIDE BAR

4.1   The Story of Michael

Remember Michael who is 14 years old and presently in the eighth grade. He will soon be transitioning to his local high school. Currently he receives two periods of resource room and four periods of inclusion classes in math, English, social studies, and physical science. His resource room time is spent on assisting him with assignments and materials from his general education classes. His academic achievement is significantly below his age-peers and his parents and teachers are concerned that he will drop farther behind when he goes to high school. He is socially immature and has poor social skills. Needless to say, he lacks self-confidence and isolates himself in his inclusion classes.

The IEP team includes the parents, special education teacher, math teacher, English teacher, school counselor, and assistant principal. During a meeting, the parents expressed their concerns over Michael's poor academic progress and the teachers responded that Michael worked up to their expectations, and was a quiet, conscientious student who was no trouble in the classroom. The special education teacher expressed concerns that Michael had not selected a vocational goal as of yet. She felt that if Michael had a vision of what life would be like after graduation, then the classes and content might become more important to him. Also, a vocational goal would provide direction in course selection when he entered high school. The counselor agreed to assist Michael in some career awareness activities including vocational aptitude and vocational preference assessments. The team agreed to meet again at the end of the semester and to include Michael so that he could assist in making his IEP and begin the transition plan process.

Some of the major differences between elementary schools and secondary schools include (Duplass, 2006):

- Larger student populations at secondary schools
- Greater academic demands
- Increased levels of homework
- More emphasis on reading for content
- Increased need for self-regulation
- Increased importance of social skills

For students who have intellectual disabilities, learning disabilities, emotional/behavioral disorders, or mild autism/Asperger's syndrome, these differences may result in tremendous stress, anxiety, and possible academic failure. Thus, teachers at both levels (whether sending or receiving the students) need to prepare their students by orienting them to the structural and organizational changes inherent in the new situation. One of the most essential responsibilities of teachers is to equip students with skills necessary for them to experience academic success when they transition into a new environment. These skills include different classroom rules, procedures, and expectations; new methods for appropriately obtaining teachers' attention; and different ways for making requests. In addition, teachers need to identify academic skills that will be required in the new situation, which are likely more complex. Some of these include note-taking, test-taking, using reference materials, using computers, and reading for content. Students need to have skills in self-management, and self-regulation in areas such as organizational strategies, scheduling, and time management. Some students will need direct instruction in ways to organize their materials, schedule their study time, and manage their time, both during and after school.

Because social and emotional skill development is very important at this age, teachers need to prepare students emotionally and socially for the differences in the requirements of the new educational arena. For example, students may need assistance in making and maintaining friendships, initiating conversations, getting along with classmates, cooperating with others in groups, and respecting the rights of others. In addition, there are individual behaviors that students must understand that are essential for success. Some of these include:

- Accepting feedback and criticism appropriately
- Disagreeing with adults and peers in a nonconfrontational manner
- Giving compliments and feedback when working with peers
- Taking turns in conversations
- Having the willingness to compromise and accept others' views

Although teachers often assume that students have mastered these skills prior to their entering secondary schools, this is frequently not the case for many students with disabilities. In these situations, teachers need to address these skills in classrooms, either through direct instruction or modeling in real-life situations.

Transition Out of School

The third transition occurs as students move from secondary schools into postsecondary environments. One of the goals of secondary education is to ensure that students leave school capable of achieving success in postsecondary educational settings; participating in their career or vocational choices; and living independently in the community (Deshler & Schumaker, 2006; Rosenberg et al., 2006). For many secondary students, this transition from school to postsecondary environments is problematic; for others it is seamless and easily accomplished. However, many students with disabilities experience major problems during this transition period (Schloss, Schloss, & Schloss, 2007).

A major difference between transition from secondary schools and earlier transitions is that students with disabilities are no longer served under the legal mandate of IDEA (Neece, Kraemer, & Blacher, 2009). After leaving school, students with disabilities may be eligible for protections under the Americans with Disability Act (ADA) and the Rehabilitation Act. Whereas IDEA is considered a system of entitlement, the ADA and Rehabilitation Act are

SIDE BAR

4.2   The Story of Robert

As previously discussed, Robert is a student who was diagnosed with Asperger's syndrome in third grade. He is now in the 12th grade with the goal of attending college and studying mathematics. He knows that his achievement scores in written expression are at the 54th and 64th percentiles and that his classroom grades on writing assignments reflect these scores. He and the team know that he has average intelligence so all agree that one of the goals is for Robert to address the issue of "written expression."

His 12th-grade English teacher agrees to help. The teacher will meet with Robert before giving him an assignment to show him examples of good college writing, focusing on the one item addressed in the next writing assignment. The teacher will provide feedback following each assignment. The English teacher feels that identifying a single assignment focus and using multiple writing assignments will enable Robert to make progress toward his goal of attending college. To nourish Robert's interest in writing, the teacher also encourages Robert to choose topics that interest him. The teacher also introduces writing to different audiences and proposes that Robert write different types of products. Simultaneously the teacher provides extra feedback to Robert concerning his classroom assignments so that he can see the application of his new knowledge within the traditional classroom setting.

known as "a system of eligibility" (Neece et al., 2009). Because of this legal change, as well as changes related to the student's special learning needs, academics paired with vocational experiences are necessary to successfully accomplish this transition from school to postsecondary training or employment (Hendricks & Wehman, 2009). Teachers in secondary schools should be involved in this transition through participation on the IEP team in the development of the student's transition plan. The transition plan should guide programming aimed at helping students achieve success during this final transition period.

STUDENT-CENTERED PLANNING

Because transition planning is critical for the success of students after they exit the public school system, they should be involved in the process. Student-centered, or student-focused, planning is a strategy often used when working with students with disabilities and their families during this final transition period. This planning strategy focuses on the students' hopes, dreams, and plans for their life. The goal of the strategy is to involve and empower students in the development and implementation of their IEP, including goal setting, accommodation selection, and program assessment. The use of student-centered planning often results in student-led IEP meetings/conferences, greater student ownership of goals, and student-selected educational supports and services. In Table 4.1, Bassett and Lehmann (2002) propose a students' bill of rights to support the student role of major stakeholder in meetings related to their educational program. If students are indeed included in their IEP development, they must have rights that are equal to others on the IEP team. Having them attend meetings without being able to execute these rights results in the process not being *student-centered*.

In student-centered meetings, it is essential that teachers, parents, and other service providers accept changes in attitudes, actions, and roles. The focus should become one of listening to students. By listening, the team provides support that allows for students to express their goals or dreams. Students' expression of goals gives direction for team members to discuss any barriers that may impede their achievement. This can lead to a discussion of ways to collaborate to achieve the students' goals. This model results in a significant change in the dynamics of planning. In this model, students become responsible for their choice of goals instead of just responding to teacher- or parent-constructed goals. According to Bassett and Lehmann (2002), "The essence of student-focused conferencing and planning strategies is to listen to an

TABLE 4.1 ● Students' Bill of Rights

- Students are entitled to participate in all aspects of the planning process.
- Students are entitled to have parents, friends, advocates, and concerned educators in all decisions that affect their lives.
- Students are entitled to be involved in all decisions that affect their lives.
- Students are entitled to integrated, heterogeneous settings responsive to different learning styles.
- Students are entitled to equal educational opportunities.
- Students are entitled to planning for quality life experiences in all facets of their lives, including vocational, educational, social, emotional, recreations, and residential areas.
- Students and families are entitled to be supported in giving directions to planning across the students' life spans.

Source: From D. S. Bassett and J. Lehmann, 2002, *Student-Focused Conferencing and Planning.* Austin, TX: Pro-Ed.

SIDE BAR

4.3   The Story of Lachesa

We previously learned that Lachesa is 16 years old and in the 10th grade. She was diagnosed at birth as having cerebral palsy with lower limb spasticity and uses a wheelchair. She also has some involvement with her upper extremities and has difficulty with handwriting. She is social and well-liked by her age-peers. Her vocational goal is "office assistant." She plans to attend a vocational school upon graduation. After graduation she hopes to have an apartment and a full social life.

Attending the IEP meeting were Lachesa, her parents, special education teacher, the office careers teacher, and the assistant principal. In the IEP meeting, Lachesa's parents questioned the appropriateness of her vocational goal. Because of their concerns, Lachesa was assigned as an office helper for one period daily to answer the phone, take messages, make copies, and run errands as needed.

Her classes are the standard education program for 10th graders who are planning to graduate and pursue postsecondary training. She is also enrolled in a word-processing/computer class. The IEP/transition team agreed that this was an appropriate prevocational curriculum for her to pursue. Additionally, her parents and the school counselor would assist Lachesa in locating information on vocational schools in the area and arrange for her to visit schools of her choice. Her parents are also going to begin teaching housekeeping skills and cooking to Lachesa. Because of the height of the wheelchair, the family plans to begin with the preparation of foods which can be done on the kitchen table. Later they will include the final sets of cooking on the stovetop or in the oven. Perhaps a family and consumer science class can be added to her class schedule next year as an elective.

individual student, to assist the student in developing a workable plan to achieve goals, and to work together to implement the desired course of action" (p. 6).

When general education teachers participate in student-centered conferences, they should work with the students to set goals and objectives that can be addressed in their classrooms. The teachers' responsibilities will be to infuse real-life topics into the existing curricula, modify the curriculum to reflect the level of functioning of the students, and use presentation and assessment strategies that match the students' learning styles. For example, when teaching a civics, or citizenship, class, it might be appropriate to include components that provide opportunities to teach students about their legal rights, voting responsibilities, and relationship to the government (local, state, and federal). For students with mild cognitive disabilities or with social skills issues, additional information may need to be included that many other students would already know. For example, if the curriculum includes landscaping it might be appropriate to provide information focused on yard maintenance and opportunities for site training for students with disabilities. In vocational classes, a section on cooking that could incorporate math application might be a focus, as well as reading and learning kitchen vocabulary and basic cooking skills that apply to any kitchen. Vocationally the cooking class might lead to employment as a kitchen helper, cook aide, or dishwasher.

TRANSITION CURRICULUM

In order for students, especially those with disabilities, to successfully complete the transitions noted above, it is essential that their future goals be a part of the educational programming. Members of each student's team may be asked to consider the following questions:

- Do the student's future goals include postsecondary education, vocational training, or employment?
- Does the student plan to live independently in the community?

- What will the student's social life be like?
- What will his or her responsibility be in terms of housekeeping, laundry, and other household chores?
- Who will be responsible for bills and bill paying?

The answers to these questions will provide a basis for the team to assist the student in preparing for postschool adult life.

When considering students' futures, one must consider the five domains of adult life: (1) employment and/or education, (2) home and family, (3) leisure pursuits and community involvement, (4) physical and emotional health, and (5) personal responsibility and relationships (Cronin, Patton, & Wood, 2005). Unfortunately, the No Child Left Behind legislation and the resulting state and federal accountability standards have made it increasingly difficult for teachers to include the essential transition content components in their classes as well as address any individualized transition needs of students with disabilities. Nevertheless, all teachers need to address the needs of all students in their classes and consider how to incorporate content related to students' transition goals. As Flexer, Baer, Luft, and Simmons (2008) state, "[T]he importance of high school programs and transition activities directly relates to the degree to which they provide learning and experiences that will move students toward or clarify their transition goals" (p. vii). Table 4.2 provides web resources related to transition, and transition planning.

Postsecondary Education Goal

The goal for many secondary school students, including those with disabilities, is to transition into postsecondary education upon completion of high school. This transition goal may take the form of admission to a community college program, college or university program, or some other form of postsecondary education, such as an adult basic education program or skill-training program. When deciding which type of postsecondary program to consider, students, with the assistance of their families and school personnel, should consider academic and social abilities and their relationship to future vocational plans. These goals may have to be modified depending on the requirements of the educational experience and the skills possessed by students.

TABLE 4.2 ● Information on Transition and Transition Planning

Transition and Transition Planning	Web Resources
Division on Career Development & Transition (DCDT)	http://www.dcdt.org/
National Center on Secondary Education and Transition (NCSET)	http://www.ncset.org/
National Collaborative on Workforce and Disability for Youth (NCWD/Youth)	http://www.ncwd-youth.info/
Office of Disability Employment	http://www.dol.gov/odep/
Institute on Community Integration	http://www.ici.umn.edu/
National Secondary Transition Technical Assistance Center (NSTTAC)	http://www.nsttac.org/

Vocational Goal

Employment is a goal for most individuals in our society; it allows individuals to be self-sufficient and enjoy independent lifestyles. As a result, many students with disabilities choose to enter vocational training when they transition from secondary school to better prepare themselves for various vocations. Vocational training opportunities are varied and may occur in several different settings, including vocational technical centers, apprenticeship programs, rehabilitation facilities, community-based programs, work training centers, or sheltered workshops. When reviewing future vocational options for students, team members should consider the type of employment where the student would most likely achieve success (e.g., competitive employment, supported employment, sheltered employment, or volunteer work). Also, team members should consider the advantages and disadvantages of each type of employment to identify which would be the best fit to achieve the student's vocational goal included in his or her transition plan.

Postsecondary Independent Living Goal

In addition to postsecondary education and employment, students should also develop a vision of their adult life as members of their community. In order to accomplish this, the student's team members need to answer a number of questions before setting the community goals. For example, what type of living arrangements would be best for this student and what skills are needed in order to live successfully in the chosen environment? In addition, what are the community participation options and what are the wishes of the student for participating in the community?

For students planning to live independently, essential educational training addressing social skills, independent living skills, and academic skills may be required. Schloss et al. (2007) described the basic skills that students need to live successfully in the community. These include how to:

- Budget and manage their finances
- Choose an appropriate living space
- Care for the chosen living space
- Identify required medical services
- Access medical services and use available transportation options
- Learn and use social skills appropriate for the workplace
- Know one's legal rights
- Self-advocate

Students with disabilities will need to learn the skills necessary to support their participation in the community. For many students, this begins with their learning how to identify opportunities for community participation. Community participation opportunities may include specialized recreation or social activities, sports or social clubs, community center programs, parks and recreation programs, hobby clubs, independent activities, and church or other community groups. While in school, students with disabilities may need to learn some basic recreational skills. Those who have such skills might participate in school-related activities, then transition into similar activities in the community. Another option might be for them to participate in community activities while still attending secondary school.

Due to the current emphasis on academic accountability, transition topics may not be included in the general education curriculum in many secondary schools. However, when students with disabilities are included in secondary general education classrooms, teachers need to address their transition needs. Since all students are required to have access to the general curriculum, addressing their transition needs is in addition to the general curriculum and goes beyond information and training provided in the past by the career education teacher, counselor, and vocational education teacher.

LEGAL REQUIREMENTS FOR TRANSITION OF STUDENTS WITH DISABILITIES

The 1990 reauthorization of the Individuals with Disabilities Education Act included for the first time a focus on the transition needs of students from secondary schools. IDEA 2004 redefined transition services as:

. . . a coordinated set of activities for a child with a disability that—

1. Is designed to be within a results-oriented process, that is focused on improving the academic and functional achievement of the child with a disability to facilitate the child's movement from school to post-school activities, including postsecondary education, vocational education, integrated employment (including supported employment), continuing and adult education, adult services, independent living, or community participation;
2. Is based on the individual child's needs, taking into account the child's strengths, preferences, and interests; and includes—
   (i) Instruction;
   (ii) Related services;
   (iii) Community experiences;
   (iv) The development of employment and other post-school adult living objectives; and
   (v) If appropriate, acquisition of daily living skills and provision of a functional vocational evaluation. [34 C.F.R. 300.43(a)]

The question is not whether teachers will address the transition needs of students with disabilities but how they will address these needs. There are two approaches for incorporating instruction, services, and community experiences into a student's program—one focus is through a pedagogical component and the other one is through a legislative component. For the pedagogical component, school personnel involved in program development for students with disabilities need to consider how successful progression through secondary school and the transition into postschool activities can occur. Students' programs should address each of the areas noted in the above IDEA 2004 regulations, including instruction, community experiences, employment, and daily living skills, if appropriate. In each of these areas the focus should be on the student's abilities, current level of competency, and classes or settings that will be appropriate for the student's goal-based instruction. During transition planning, team members need to consider the level of severity of the student's disability and the degree of inclusive participation in the school program.

Greene (2009) provides an example of how to expand the concept of transition planning in inclusive settings. This model has four pathways for transition planning for students with different levels of ability and future plans. The first two pathways are for students who are included in the general education classes for all or most of their middle and secondary years and plan to transition into some form of postsecondary education (college or university, community college, or vocational school), live independently in the community, and work full time at competitive employment. The educational program for these students provides training that will lead to a successful completion of their transition goals. Teachers who have these students in their classes need to address their transition goals in their classes. Pathways three and four are for students who are included in some of the general education classes during their middle and secondary school years. However, these students do not plan to transition into postsecondary education, but plan to live semi-independently in the community and work full time in competitive employment. They will need supports as adults to successfully manage these goals. Teachers who have these students in their classes will need to collaborate with students, their families, counselors, and special education teachers to ensure their transition goals are addressed (Greene, 2009).

IDEA 2004 requires schools to develop an individualized transition plan (ITP) as part of the IEP process, when the student reaches the age of 16. According to Murdick, Gartin, and Crabtree (2007), the ITP addresses "the needs of the student as he or she 'transitions' into the community from the school setting" (p. 99). This additional section must address the needed transition services through the development of a specific transition plan for each secondary student with a disability. This plan must be based on an age-appropriate transition assessment.

The ITP must include the following IDEA 2004 regulations:

1. Appropriate measurable postsecondary goals based upon age appropriate transition assessments related to training, education, employment, and, where appropriate, independent living skills; and
2. The transition services (including courses of study) needed to assist the child in reaching those goals. [34 C.F.R. 300.320(b)]

The ITP should be a description of services and supports that must be included in students' academic programs to assist in their future goals "to live independently, establish social lives, become lifelong learners, and sustain employment" (Bassett & Kochlar-Bryant, 2006, p. 2). Moreover, this program must be based on age-appropriate assessments that focus on issues related to transition.

TRANSITION ASSESSMENT FOR PLANNING

A transition assessment is "an ongoing process of collecting information on the student's strengths, needs, preferences, and interests as they relate to the demands of current and future living, learning, and working environment" (Sitlington, 2007, p. 1). This assessment of the student's transition needs is essential for the development of a viable transition plan and provides the basis for an outcomes-oriented plan. In essence, "the transition team chooses assessments that provide technically sound data to promote the student's movement toward his or her postsecondary goals" (Flexer & Luft, 2008, p. 106).

Transition assessments should begin informally during the elementary school and continue with increasing formality into secondary school. Transition assessments should be comprehensive, addressing all of the student's areas of need including vocational, career, personal, social, and living (Carter, Trainor, Sun, & Owens, 2009). According to Sitlington (2007), the purposes of transition assessments are (1) to determine the student's level of career development, (2) to identify the student's needs, strengths, interests, and preferences as they relate to postsecondary goals, (3) to identify a focus of study to attain these goals, (4) to identify the self-determination skills needed to reach the identified goals, (5) to identify any specific accommodations, supports, or assistive devices the student may need, and (6) to complete the IDEA 2004–required Summary of Performance (SOP) document that must be completed when the student exits secondary school.

The individual student's program and needs dictate the choice of assessment methods. Teachers can use either formal (typically standardized methods) or informal assessment methods. According to Walker, Kortering, and Fowler (2007), formal transition assessment methods include adaptive behavior and daily living skills assessments, general and specific aptitude tests, interest inventories, intelligence tests, achievement tests, temperament inventories or instruments, career maturity or employability tests, self-determination assessments, and transition planning inventories. Formal assessment measures are most often completed by the student's career-vocational teacher, special education teacher, or the general education teachers.

In addition to formal assessments, classroom teachers may use informal assessment methods such as interviews and questionnaires, direct observation of student performance, curriculum-based assessments, and/or environmental analysis when assisting students in determining their future goals (Walker et al., 2007). An example of an often-used transition assessment-planning instrument is The Outcome/Skill Checklist for Transition Planning (Roessler, 1998). This assessment tool is aligned with the Life-Centered Career Education (LCCE) Curriculum (Brolin, 2004), a comprehensive curriculum guide for teachers who want to incorporate career education into their programs. According to Schloss et al. (2007), the LCCE "focuses on the total life plan of an individual, facilitating growth and development in all life roles and settings" (p. 284). Table 4.3 provides web resources for transition assessment tools.

Another frequently used model of transition assessment is Person-Centered Transition and Assessment Planning. The term "person-centered" is a general term describing an array of approaches to transition that empower self-determination in youth with disabilities and their families by helping them identify their future goals and supporting their more active involvement in the transition process ("Ten Tips to Prepare Your Child for Success," 2005). This active involvement by the individual with a disability serves to assist in the development of self-determination and self-advocacy skills as the student transitions into postsecondary life.

Person-centered assessment focuses on the identification of high-quality, meaningful outcomes and is considered to be a means to foster dignity and respect for the person with a disability. According to Rusch (2008), it "is a continuous process of information gathering and decision making" (p. 183). The person with the disability and his or her family members direct the process. In the assessment component of this process the individual's needs, values, and interests are identified. Next the student and the other members of the group identify the

TABLE 4.3 ● Transition Assessment and Planning Tools

Title/Author/Date	Informational Websites
Outcomes-Based Planning Steere, Wood, Pancsofar, & Butterworth (1990)	https://fp.auburn.edu/rse/trans_media/08_ Publications/06_Transition_in%20Action/ chap11.htm
Personal Futures Planning Mount & Zwernick (1988)	http://www.pbis.org/pbis_newsletter/ volume_2/issue1.aspx
McGill Action Plan Vandercook, York, & Forest (1989)	http://www.circleofinclusion.org/english/pim/ seven/maps.html
Essential Life Planning Smull & Harrison (1992)	http://www.allenshea.com/brochure.pdf http://learningcommunity.us/documents/ FPTGuide.11-03.pdf
Choosing Options and Accommodations *for Children (COACH)* Giangreco, Cloninger, & Iverson (1993)	http://www.uvm.edu/~mgiangre/ed.html http://www.uconnucedd.org/pdfs/ Inclusion%20Notebook/TIN_Fall04.pdf
Group Action Planning Turnbull & Turnbull (1997)	https://fp.auburn.edu/rse/trans_media/ 08_Publications/02_Conf_Proceedings/ Proceedings4/12a_TURNBULL.pdf www.ttac.odu.edu/Articles/person.html

appropriate personal, community, and family supports needed to meet the student's needs. Person-centered assessment and planning has an individual focus, not a system focus. When using this assessment instrument, the team is encouraged to use a planning process that is based on the individual's future dreams. In addition it involves the family as well as the individual in the development process and emphasizes supports that foster self-determination skills and commitments by all those who are involved (Rusch, 2008). Rusch also stated that person-centered assessment is essentially "focused on opportunity enhancement" (2008, p. 63). That is, it takes an individual's strengths, which create opportunities, and provides supports to enhance those strengths.

A useful example of how to use the person-centered philosophy in assessment for transition plan development is described in the "Adult Lifestyles Planning Cycle" (Garcia & Menchetti, 2003). A number of other person-centered planning programs are considered forms of person-centered assessment and planning, as well. Each of these programs focuses on encouraging students to express their vision for the future—that is, where they see themselves when it comes to education, employment, and life in the community. In addition, person-centered assessment and planning includes a section where the team identifies supports needed by students to achieve their vision. In this process, all people involved are viewed as supports whose role is to facilitate the achievement of their personal visions.

THE TRANSITION PLANNING TEAM

Career vocational and transition services for students with disabilities have evolved over the years in response to educational and legislative changes (Mellard, 2005). In the past, special educators were primarily responsible for initiating the transition planning process. However, IDEA 2004 requires members of the student's IEP team to be involved in the preparation of the ITP. Regardless of who takes the leadership role, transition services should be planned by a team of individuals that includes, but is not limited to, the student, school personnel knowledgeable about the student's abilities and skills, and personnel from the community and adult service agencies. The parents should also attend. Once students with disabilities reach the age of majority, which is 18 years in most states, they represent themselves and their parents can attend only if their student wishes.

In an ideal situation, a variety of individuals who have an involvement in the student's present or future should be attending the transition plan meeting. The specific group of individuals involved should be related to the likely futures of the student. For example, a student who needs assisted employment and living supports would likely have a different ITP team than one who planned on attending a postsecondary educational program. Individuals who should be on the majority of teams include the student, parents or guardians, special education teacher, general classroom teachers, and a representative from the administration. Table 4.4 describes the roles of these individuals, plus the roles of others who might be added to the team, depending on the student's likely future in the community.

The most important individual on the team that develops an individual transition plan is the student. Since the meeting is addressing the student's future, then the student should provide information on his or her wishes and dreams concerning the future. To assure the student's active involvement, Hendricks and Wehman (2009) suggest that students should act as the team leader. This serves to encourage their involvement in the process and also helps them develop self-determination skills. Parents or guardians are also critical team members. Parents typically know their children better than anyone else, including school personnel. Rather than having known the student for a few years, parents have known the student for a lifetime. Not

TABLE 4.4 ● Roles of Individuals Involved in Transition Plan Development

Team Member	Roles
Student	Serves as self-advocate In charge of meeting when possible Expresses dreams and preferences Serves as chief decision maker at age of majority
Parent(s)	Provide parental views of dreams and preferences Allows student to serve as decision maker when age of majority is reached Assures guarantee of rights until rights transfer
Special education teacher	Provides assessment(s) of potential Provides description of strengths and weaknesses
Content teachers	Provides assessment(s) of potential Provides description of strengths and weaknesses
Administrative representative	Ensures rights of student and parents Ensures district's fiscal responsibilities can be met
Vocational teacher	Provides assessment(s) of potential related to vocational skills Provides description of strengths and weaknesses related to vocational skills
School counselor	Provides assessment(s) related to postsecondary education and training opportunities Provides description of strengths and weaknesses related to postsecondary education and training opportunities Provides guidance on postsecondary education and training
Rehabilitation counselor	Provides information on employment opportunities Provides information on postsecondary financial supports
Therapists	Provides assessment(s) related to postsecondary therapy opportunities Provides description of strengths and weaknesses related to postsecondary therapy needs
Community living specialists	Provides information on community living supports

only do they know their student better than school personnel, but also parents (or guardians) have an important interest in where and what their child does upon graduation or release from school. While school personnel complete their responsibility when students leave school, parents (guardians) remain in the student's life. They can speak of the student's goals and infuse their view of the present and the future in the discussion.

Special education teachers who are, or have been, working with the student are also essential to the process. They can provide essential information concerning the student's past achievements, potential future issues, and information concerning the next step in the transition process. They will also assist in designing students' academic programs and helping them establish their educational goals. The school district's special education supervisor represents the interests of the district. While this individual does not have to attend ITP meetings, someone should be designated to represent the district. The person representing the administration ensures students' needs are met and represents the district in matters of policy and financial commitments. Vocational or other content area teachers might attend to determine how the student will interact with the general education curriculum. Content area teachers provide information on required standardized curricula and examinations that students may need to complete their transition plan and secondary school. Vocational instructors provide an assessment of the students' skills in relationship to others seeking the same competitive position. In addition, vocational instructors provide important information concerning the next steps to competitive employment.

As students near the age of majority, defined as 18 in most states, personnel from community and adult service agencies might also attend transition meetings. For students wishing to continue their education, an adult education specialist might attend; for students more likely to enter employment, a vocational rehabilitation counselor might need to attend. For students who will likely move into a new living environment, but who need supports, an assisted living coordinator, a support services coordinator, or a case worker might need to attend. When planning the transition for students who may need ongoing therapy or medical supports, professionals such as occupational therapists, physical therapists, speech therapists, or nurses might be needed to provide current information on the student's needs and to recommend future treatments or therapies. In addition, students who use assistive technology might need someone on their planning committee who can give advice for these supports and individuals who need to have financial support of Medicaid might need a Medicaid specialist on their team. The exact nature of the student's ITP planning team should be determined on a case-by-case basis, depending on the student's needs and likely postschool futures. Table 4.5 summarizes some of the transition services commonly offered by various community agencies. School personnel need to consider, on an individual basis, which of these agencies should be involved in the process.

TABLE 4.5 ● Common Community Agencies and the Transition Services They May Offer

Agency/Program* (Purpose and Funding Source)	Examples of Employment Services	Examples of Postsecondary Education Services	Examples of Adult and Independent Living Services
Vocational Rehabilitation Agency assists people with cognitive, sensory, physical, or emotional disabilities to attain employment and increased independence. Funded by federal and state money, VR agencies typically operate regional and local offices. VR services typically last for a limited period of time and are based on an individual's rehabilitation plan. If needed, an individual with disabilities can request services at a later time, and a new rehabilitation plan will be developed.	• Vocational guidance and counseling • Medical, psychological, vocational, and other types of assessments to determine vocational potential • Job development, placement, and follow-up services • Rehabilitation, technological services and adaptive devices, tools, equipment, and supplies	• Apprenticeship programs, usually in conjunction with Department of Labor • Vocational training • College training toward a vocational goal as part of an eligible student's financial aid package	• Housing or transportation supports needed to maintain employment • Interpreter services • Orientation and mobility services

(continued)

TABLE 4.5 ● *(continued)*

Agency/Program* (Purpose and Funding Source)	Examples of Employment Services	Examples of Postsecondary Education Services	Examples of Adult and Independent Living Services
Mental Health and Mental Retardation Agencies provide a comprehensive system of services responsive to the needs of individuals with mental illness or mental retardation. Federal, state, and local funding are used to operate regional offices; local funding is often the primary source. Services are provided on a sliding payment scale.	• Supported and sheltered employment • Competitive employment support for those who need minimal assistance		• Case management services to access and obtain local services • Therapeutic recreation, including day activities, clubs, and programs • Respite care • Residential services (group homes and supervised apartments)
Independent Living Centers help people with disabilities to achieve and maintain self-sufficient lives within the community. Operated locally, ILCs serve a particular region. ILCs may charge for classes, but advocacy services are typically available at no cost.	• Information and referral services • Connecting students with mentors with disabilities	• Advocacy training • Connecting students with mentors with disabilities	• Advocacy training • Auxiliary social services (e.g., maintaining a list of personal care attendants) • Peer counseling services • Housing assistance • Training in skills of independent living (attendant management, housing, transportation, career development) • Information and referral services • Connecting with mentors
Social Security Administration operates the federally funded program that provides benefits for people of any age who are unable to do substantial work and have a severe mental or physical disability. Several programs are offered for people with disabilities, including Social Security Disability Insurance (SSDI), Supplemental Security Income (SSI), Plans to Achieve Self-Support (PASS), Medicaid, and Medicare.	Work incentive programs which may include: • Cash benefits while working (e.g., student-earned income) • Medicare or Medicaid while working • Help with any extra work expenses the individual has as a result of the disability • Assistance to start a new line of work	• Financial incentives for further education and training	• Medical benefits • Can use income as basis for purchase or rental of housing

*Name of agencies or programs may differ slightly from state to state.

Source: From *Transition planning: A Team Effort* (pp. 4-5), by S. H. de Fur, 1999. Washington, DC: NICHCY.

THE TRANSITION PLAN

As noted, IDEA requires that schools include transition planning as part of students' IEPs when they reach their 16th birthday. Other than saying that it must include appropriate, measurable postsecondary goals, based on age-appropriate assessments in areas of training, education, employment, and independent living skills, and provide the necessary services to enable a student to achieve those goals, IDEA does not elaborate on the design or composition of the plan. While not mandated by federal law, most school districts incorporate ITPs in the IEP process for students reaching their 16th birthday. By using the annual IEP development and review process schools are able to address all of the goals and objectives of students, including academic, social, and others that apply for the school year plus those related to transition.

Basset and Kochlar-Bryant (2006) emphasized that the ITP should describe the services that schools will provide to facilitate their social, academic, and vocational success as adults. Therefore, transition plans should not be focused on an academic year, similar to the IEP, but on services that will be provided to help students in the future. One way of describing this concept is future-based programming. ITP teams are building programs that focus on the needs of students after they exit school.

While there are minimal federal guidelines related to transition plans, there are several essential elements of a good plan. These include (Smith, Polloway, Patton, & Dowdy, 2012):

- Students and family members must be actively involved in the process.
- Students' strengths, interests, and preferences must be taken into consideration.
- Goals and activities must be results-oriented.
- Goals and activities must focus on helping students move successfully from school environments to postschool environments.
- All of the variables associated with adult life should be considered.

Smith et al. (2012, p. 498) describe a transition plan for a student named Jim, who had primary difficulties with academic skills, behavioral control, and lack of self-advocacy. Jim is very concerned about passing the state exit in reading and language, and wants desperately to obtain his driver's license. Table 4.6 shows the transition components of Jim's IEP.

Age of Majority

By middle and secondary school, students are important members of their planning process and should be actively involved in the development of their transition plans. This student-focused planning is essential when one considers an additional component of IDEA 2004. This is the requirement that transfers the primary decision-maker role from parents to students upon reaching the age of majority, which is defined as 18 years in most states. According to IDEA 2004 regulations:

> Beginning not later than one year before the child reaches the age of majority under State law, the IEP must include a statement that the child has been informed of the child's rights under Part B of the Act, if any, that will transfer to the child on reaching the age of majority. . . . [34 C.F.R. 300.320(c)]

The transfer of rights from parents to students can result in controversy for parents, students, and those teachers involved in the program.

The IDEA also requires schools to notify students of their upcoming age of majority, and the subsequent transfer of rights, 1 year prior to the student achieving this age. After reaching the age of majority, students must indicate in writing that these rights have been explained, and

TABLE 4.6 ● Jim's IEP: Transition Components

Unique educational needs, characteristics, and measured present levels of academic achievement and functional performance (PLOPs).	Special education, related services and supplemental aids and services (based on peer-reviewed research to the extent practicable); assistive technology and modifications or personnel support.	Measurable annual goals and short-term objectives (progress markers),[1] including academic and functional goals to enable students to be involved in and make progress in the general curriculum and to meet other needs resulting from the disability.
(Including how the disability affects student's ability to participate and progress in the general curriculum.)	(Including anticipated starting date, frequency, duration, and location for each.)	(Including progress measurement method for each goal.)

Instruction

Self-advocacy PLOP: Jim is unaware of his legal rights under Section 504 and ADA, and he is unable to request appropriate accommodations he would need in given situations, such as a large lecture class. He becomes embarrassed and anxious when discussing his disability and its affects on his school performance, and he becomes angry or tries to change the subject.

Community

Driver's license PLOP: Jim has been driving for a year on a learner's permit and is concerned that he cannot pass the written test required for his license, although he is confident of all his driving and related skills except map reading.

Employment and other

Not needed at this time. Jim intends to enroll in the computer network support program at Leland Community College (LCC) and is on track for a regular diploma. He is a tech lab assistant this year and is doing very well.

1. Small group instruction from special ed teacher in relevant rights, procedures, and remedies under Section 504, ADA, and IDEA
   - Role playing in describing needed accommodations to employers, professors, and other adult life figures of authority.
   - Services to begin Tuesday, Sept.15; two thirty-minute sessions weekly until goals are met.
   - (L&R) Protection and Advocacy will assist teacher and provide materials at no cost. (Verified by phone—M. Adams)
   - LCC Office of Disability Services will meet with Jim to set up an accommodation plan. (Verified by phone—S. Holvey)

2. Within two weeks from the date of this IEP, the driver training instructor will inform Jim about accommodations available in the state, if any, for licensing people with reading disabilities. Then she and Jim will develop a plan to follow through and that plan will be added to this IEP no later than Oct. 10.
   - (L&R) DMV will assist instructor and will provide information on test accommodations. (Verified by phone—J. Hill)
   - Instruction in map reading and route highlighting.

Goal 1: Given a twenty-five-item objective test over basic rights and procedures under Section 504 and ADA, Jim will pass with a score of 75 percent or better.

Goal 2: In hypothetical role-play scenarios of disability-based discrimination, Jim will calmly and accurately explain to an employer, professor, or other representative of the postschool world his rights and remedies under Section 504 and ADA.

Goal 3: Given a real-world meeting with the Director of Disability Services at LCC, Jim will describe the effect of his disability in a school situation and will explain what accommodations help him to meet expectations.

Goal 4: Jim will become a competent driver in Jefferson state and will take the licensing exam on March 15. By March 1, given a practice exam administered under real-world conditions, Jim will score at least 70 percent.

Goal 5: Given a city map, Jim will accurately highlight six common routes he routinely follows and four routes he will use next year, when he is attending LCC, e.g., from his home to the mall, from his home to LCC, etc.

---

[1]For students who take an alternative assessment and are assessed against other than grade level standards, the IEP **must** include short-term objectives (progress markers). For other students, the IEP **may** include short-term objectives. The IEP **must** for all students clearly articulate how the student's progress will be measured; and that progress must be reported to parents at designated intervals.
Source: From *Better IEPs: How to Develop Legally Correct and Educationally Useful Programs* (p. 145), by B. D. Bateman and M. A. Linden, 2006, Verona, WI: Attainment.

then they have the right to make decisions about their IEP, placement, and other issues around the provision of special education (Smith et al., 2012).

The transfer of rights often results in parental concern if they are not being included in the special education process when they continue to be the primary support for their child. In addition, some students may not be willing to participate or be able to clarify plans for their future, nor be able to identify skills needed or personal responsibilities as a result of a lack of self-advocacy skills and experiences (Mellard, 2005). For students determined to be incapable of participating at this level and protecting their rights, courts may grant guardianship of the student to parents or other guardians (Smith et al., 2012).

The inclusion of students in person-centered planning activities as well as the provision of training in self-advocacy early on in the school program can help in avoiding such situations. As Mellard (2005) states, "[T]he educational environment and ITP—and IEP-related meetings— provide some of the best training opportunities for students to develop their self-advocacy skills and gain a broader understanding of career and lifestyle issues they are confronting" (p. 3). Therefore, the requirements to include students in their IEP/ITP development, the practice of providing students opportunities to take a leadership role in their IEP/ITP development, and the mandate to transfer rights from parents to students upon reaching the age of majority actually provide opportunities for students to be more self-determined and to develop self-advocacy skills, which they will need as young adults after exiting high school.

SUMMARY

For all students, the transition from high school to adult life is a prospect that can be both exciting and frightening. For students with disabilities, it may be even more so as they may encounter barriers to successful postschool employment and/or education as well as with successful independent living in the community. For teachers who are planning to help students on this journey, it will be your responsibility to assist the students in successfully completing the course of study as it relates to your class. For teachers who have students with disabilities in their class, the process will require you to form linkages with other educational personnel as well as with professionals in other human service agencies, including employment and training, adult services, and rehabilitation. As Bassett and Kochlar-Bryant (2006) say, these students will "need additional support and preparation to make the journey" (p. 1). Thus, all teachers and other school professionals who will be working with students in middle and secondary school will need to be aware of their needs as they plan for, and successfully complete, their journey into the world of adult life.

ACTIVITIES

1. When teachers assist students in determining future vocations and careers, the teacher must know the mental and physical demands of that work. Therefore, it is essential that teachers explore unfamiliar vocational territory. Upon leaving high school, many former students need to locate entry-level work. Identify one entry-level job that is done outdoors and explain the duties and demands of that work. Next identify an entry-level job that is performed indoors and do the same.

2. Select a company in your town. Observe the workers and record the tasks that they perform. Then list the job titles of all the workers within this company.

REFERENCES

Bassett, D. S., & Kochlar-Bryant, C. A. (2006). Strategies for aligning standards-based education and transition. *Focus on Exceptional Children, 39*(2), 1–19.

Bassett, D. S., & Lehmann, J. (2002). *Student-focused conferencing and planning.* Austin, TX: Pro-Ed.

Bos, C. S., & Vaughn, S. (2006). *Strategies for teaching students with learning and behavior problems* (6th ed.) Boston: Allyn & Bacon/Pearson.

Brolin, D. E. (2004). *Life-centered career education.* Reston, VA: Council for Exceptional Children.

Carter, E. W., Trainor, A. A., Sun, Y., & Owens, L. (2009). Assessing the transition-related strengths and needs of adolescents with high-incidence disabilities. *Exceptional Children, 76*(1), 74–94.

Cronin, M. E., Patton, J. R., & Wood, S. J. (2005). *Life skills instruction: A practical guide for integrating real-life content into the curriculum* (2nd ed.). Austin, TX: Pro-Ed.

Deshler, D. D., & Schumaker, J. B. (2006). *Teaching adolescents with disabilities: Accessing the general education curriculum.* Thousand Oaks, CA: Corwin Press.

Duplass, J. A. (2006). *Middle and high school teaching: Methods, standards, and best practices.* Boston: Houghton Mifflin.

Flexer, R. W., Baer, R. M., Luft, P., & Simmons, T. J. (2008). *Transition planning for secondary students with disabilities* (3rd ed.). Upper Saddle River, NJ: Merrill/Pearson.

Flexer, R. W., & Luft, P. (2008). Transition assessment. In R. W. Flexer, R. M. Baer, P. Luft, & T. J. Simmons, *Transition planning for secondary students with disabilities* (3rd ed., pp. 103–133). Upper Saddle River, NJ: Merrill/Pearson.

Garcia, L. A., & Menchetti, B. M. (2003). The adult lifestyles planning cycle: A continual process in planning personally satisfying adult lifestyles. In D. L. Ryndak & S. Alper (Eds.), *Curriculum and instruction for students with significant disabilities in inclusive settings* (2nd ed., pp. 277–306). Boston: Allyn & Bacon.

Giangreco, M. F., Cloninger, C. J., & Iverson, V. (1993). *Choosing options and accommodations for children (COACH): A planning guide for inclusive education.* Baltimore: Paul H. Brookes.

Greene, G. (2009). Transition pathways. In C. Kochlar-Bryant & G. Greene, *Pathways to successful transition for youth with disabilities: A developmental approach* (2nd ed., pp. 264–293). Upper Saddle River, NJ: Merrill/Pearson.

Hendricks, D. R., & Wehman, P. (2009). Transition from school to adulthood for youth with autism spectrum disorder. *Focus on Autism and Other Development Disabilities, 24*(2), 77–88.

Individuals with Disabilities Education Improvement Act of 2004. 20 U.S.C. §1400 et seq.

Individuals with Disabilities Education Improvement Act of 2004. 34 C.F.R. §300 et seq.

Mellard, D. (2005). Strategies for transition to postsecondary educational settings. *Focus on Exceptional Children, 37*(9), 1–19.

Mount, B., & Zwernik, K. (1988) *It's never too early, it's never too late: An overview of personal futures planning.* St. Paul, MN: Governor's Planning Council on Developmental Disabilities.

Murdick, N. L., Gartin, B. C., & Crabtree, T. (2007). *Special education law* (2nd ed.). Upper Saddle River, NJ: Merrill/Pearson.

Neece, C. L., Kraemer, B. R., & Blacher, J. (2009). Transition satisfaction and family well being among parents of young adults with severe intellectual disabilities. *Intellectual and Developmental Disabilities, 47*(1), 31–43.

Roessler, R. (1998). Making the transition: An outcome/skill checklist for transition planning. *LCCE Insider,* 3–6.

Rosenberg, M. S., O'Shea, L. J., & O'Shea, D. J. (2006). *Student teacher to master teacher: A practical guide for educating students with special needs* (4th ed.). Upper Saddle River, NJ: Merrill/Pearson.

Rusch, F. R. (2008). *Beyond high school: Preparing adolescents for tomorrow's challenges* (2nd ed.). Upper Saddle River, NJ: Merrill/Pearson.

Schloss, P. J., Schloss, M. A., & Schloss, C. N. (2007). *Instructional methods for secondary students with learning and behavior problems* (4th ed.). Boston: Allyn & Bacon/Pearson.

Sitlington, P. L. (2007). Overview of transition assessment. In P. L. Sitlington, D. A. Neubert, W. H. Begun, R. C. Lombard, & P. J. Leconte, *Assess for success: A practitioner's handbook on transition assessment* (2nd ed.). Thousand Oaks, CA: Corwin/Sage.

Smith, T. E. C., Gartin, B. C., Murdick, N. L., & Hilton, A. (2006). *Families and children with special needs: Professional and family partnerships.* Upper Saddle River, NJ: Pearson.

Smith, T. E. C., Polloway, E. A., Patton, J. R., & Dowdy, C. A. (2012). *Teaching students with special needs in inclusive settings* (6th ed.). Upper Saddle River, NJ: Pearson.

Smull, M., & Harrison, S. B. (1992). *Supporting people with severe reputations in the community.* Alexandria, VA: National Association of State Mental Retardation Program Directors.

Steere, D. E., Wood, R., Pancsofar, E., & Butterworth, J. (1990). Outcome-based school-to-work transition planning with severe disabilities. *Career Development for Exceptional Individuals, 13,* 57–69.

Ten tips to prepare your child for success in adulthood. (2005). *Exceptional Parent, 42.*

Turnbull, A. P., & Turnbull, H. R. (1997). *Families, professionals, and exceptionality: A special partnership.* Upper Saddle River, NJ: Merrill/Pearson.

Vandercook, T., York, J., & Forest, M. (1989). The McGill action planning system (MAPS): A strategy for building vision. *Journal of the Association for the Severely Handicapped, 14,* 205–215.

Walker, A. R., Kortering, L. J., & Fowler, C. H. (2007). *Age-appropriate transition assessment guide.* Charlotte, NC: National Secondary Transition Technical Assistance Center (NSTTAC).

School/Family Collaboration in a Middle/Secondary Inclusive Classroom

Study Questions

1. School/family partnerships are of great importance to special education teachers, but why would such partnerships be important to middle and secondary teachers?

2. What would be a broad definition of family and a narrow definition of family? As a teacher, what is the implication of your definition of family?

3. What is the impact on a family of having a child with a disability? How can you as a teacher apply this information in working with parents?

4. What are areas of diversity you may encounter as a teacher? What is the teacher's responsibility to dealing with diversity in the classroom? What is the teacher's responsibility to the classroom and its students if the family's beliefs run counter to the teacher's beliefs?

INTRODUCTION

Prior to the passage of IDEA, many parents of students with disabilities were minimally involved in the educational programs of their children. This may have been because of their being passive, or more than likely was the result of school personnel simply taking the lead and not involving family members. IDEA requires that school personnel engage cooperatively with parents in the education of children with disabilities. As a result, the parental role changed from passive recipient of educational services to active participant with rights guaranteed by legislation. Under IDEA, parental participation is required in the identification and eligibility process as well as in placement decisions and annual program planning. In other words, parents must have the opportunity to be involved in every step of the special education process. Once students with disabilities reach the age of 16, the involvement of parents extends to students, who become involved members of the transition planning team focusing on preparing students for postsecondary, adult life. To protect the rights of students with disabilities and their families, the law includes a required system of due process and procedural safeguards. Schools are no longer allowed to make educational decisions about students with disabilities without parental involvement.

Unfortunately, regardless of their legal rights to be involved, many parents continue to participate passively in the educational process of their children (Turnbull, Turnbull, Erwin, & Soodak, 2010). This lack of involvement could be the result of parents not understanding their rights, not believing that their involvement is really necessary, or being intimidated by school personnel who seem to have a great deal more knowledge about special education than they do. Regardless of why, school personnel must take proactive steps to increase parental involvement. School personnel should make the commitment to encourage school/family partnerships through shared responsibilities, shared decision making, and parity for all participants. To meet this goal, family empowerment and family-centered services must be the foundation of school–family partnerships (Taylor, Smiley, & Richards, 2009).

COLLABORATION

Collaboration is a framework for two or more individuals to work together as equal partners to make decisions that will lead to positive changes (Welch, 2000). In an educational setting the goal of collaboration is to improve services for students through the efforts of families and schools working together as equal partners who share resources, decisions, and responsibilities.

Because IDEA stresses the importance of involving students with disabilities and their families in the educational process, school–family collaboration is an important component of

TABLE 5.1 ● Web Resources on Collaboration

Collaboration	Web Resources
Family–school collaboration and problem solving	http://www.udel.edu/cds/pbs/downloads/PBSFSCnonotes.ppt
National Coalition for Parent Involvement in Education	http://www.ncpie.org/DevelopingPartnerships/
National Dropout Prevention Center/Network: Family Engagement	http://www.dropoutprevention.org
Teacher–parent collaboration: printables, articles, and resources	http://www.teachervision.fen.com

providing appropriate educational services to students with disabilities. During the special education process, including referral, assessment, and IEP meetings, collaboration occurs formally. Less formal collaborative efforts occur when families work with schools to ensure culturally sensitive services, expand trust between the school and its constituency, and develop a sense of community and shared responsibilities. The role of family members as collaborators differs greatly from their former role of recipients of services. The new role of families as collaborators requires families to become full and equal partners with educators and school systems. Teachers are full participants in both informal and formal collaboration that occurs with students with disabilities, their families, and school colleagues. For many secondary level teachers this is a new role, one that requires the recognition and understanding of the various concepts of family and their implications for the education of students with disabilities. Table 5.1 provides a list of web resources related to collaboration.

Impact of Family Involvement

Family involvement in the education of their children can have a significant, positive impact on student achievement in terms of attendance, more positive attitudes, better grades, increased motivation, and higher test scores (Izzo, Weissberg, Kasprow, & Fendrich, 1999; Kellough & Kellough, 2008). In 2001, Catsambis found that students in middle and secondary schools who had parents with high parental academic expectations and high levels of encouragement exhibited high academic achievement regardless of race, socioeconomic status, or parental level of education. Several other studies have found that greater involvement by parents fosters positive attitudes toward school, improves homework habits, reduces absenteeism and dropping out, and enhances academic achievement (Sui-Cho & Willms, 1996). Sui-Cho and Willms (1996) found that parental involvement demonstrated by discussing school activities and helping students plan their programs had the strongest relationship to academic achievement. The story of Sophia provides a real-life example of family involvement.

Standards and Family Involvement

Because of the strong research base supporting family involvement in educational programs, professional standards for the teaching profession include school, family, and community relations as an area in which teachers must demonstrate proficiency. According to a 2001 report published by the Harvard Family Research Project (Caspe, 2001, p. 3), standards have been:

> . . . issued by professional or certifying organizations that expect teachers to:
>
> • Work with and through parents and families to support children's learning and development. [National Board for Professional Teaching Standards (NBPTS)]

SIDE BAR

5.1 The Story of Sophia

Sophia is 12 years old and in the sixth grade. She receives special education services because of her learning disabilities in the area of reading. Her family came to the United States from Guatemala before she was born. Spanish is spoken as the primary language in the home. She is the youngest of six children and one of three children born in the United States. She has never been outside of the United States, but other members of her extended family have moved to the United States and lived with her family as they made the transition. Her family works in the building trades. Her oldest brother works closely with their father in securing and negotiating contracts for the family. In many ways, her brother has become the spokesperson for the family.

Sophia's teacher, Ms. Jordan, was concerned that as Sophia transitioned to upper secondary grades she might encounter more academic challenges because of her learning difficulties. During study times, Sophia is highly distractible. In the past, it was thought that Sophia might have ADHD, but the diagnosis was never confined. Therefore, Ms. Jordan wanted to improve the effectiveness of Sophia's study time by developing her self-monitoring skills. She wanted to develop a self-monitoring plan for Sophia to use both at school and at home.

Ms. Jordan sent a note to the family written in both English and Spanish asking for a conference. She asked if the parents and Sophia could come together, and suggested that any other family members would also be welcome. She also offered to meet at the school, their home, or another suggested locale. Ms. Jordan said that she would meet with them at any time or day convenient for them, noting that the school building was open from 7:30 A.M. until 7:30 P.M.

Sophia was pleased to be asked to attend the meeting that was focused on helping her become a more effective student. She agreed to carry the note to the parents and to return with her parents' response. The next day Sophia had the parents' answer. The parents asked for a meeting at the school after 4:00 and also asked that the older brother be included because of his English skills.

The day before the meeting, the teacher asked Sophia if there were any courtesies that might make the family welcome. Sophia taught Ms. Jordan to say "Hello" and "Thank you for coming," so that she could greet the family in Spanish. Sophia and the teacher decided to have some bottled water, sodas, and cookies available to offer the family although Sophia did not think that they would eat or drink. Ms. Jordan and Sophia selected some of Sophia's best work to show her parents to assure her parents that she was doing well in school. Ms. Jordan did not want the parents to think that Sophia was "in trouble with the teacher" for fear that she would be punished for doing poorly in school.

The family, Sophia, and Ms. Jordan met in the school conference room since it had a table and comfortable chairs. Sophia acted as hostess and offered the refreshments. She also showed her work products and Ms. Jordan pointed to the exemplary work that Sophia was producing. Ms. Jordan then mentioned that Sophia would soon change schools and that there would also be a change in the way homework would be given. Ms. Jordan said that she wanted Sophia to be able to "study more efficiently." The brother Thomas asked if Sophia was a problem in the classroom. Ms. Jordan said that Sophia was a pleasure in the classroom and Sophia beamed. Ms. Jordan reiterated that Sophia was a good sixth-grade student but when she went to seventh grade, there was more homework. So, she wanted to teach Sophia how to do her homework more effectively, meaning quickly and correctly.

Ms. Jordan asked where Sophia did her homework. Thomas said that she did her homework at the kitchen table. Ms. Jordan showed the family a kitchen timer and asked if they had one and they said that they did. She asked if Sophia could use it to time her homework and the family agreed. Ms. Jordan gave the family a copy of a checklist that she and Sophia had developed. It was written in English and Spanish and contained two questions: (1) Did you work the entire time without stopping? and (2) How much work did you complete? Sophia was to set the timer at 5 minutes. When the timer went off, she was to answer the questions and then walk around the kitchen stretching. At the end of the homework session, a family member signed the paper. The next day she was to return it to Ms. Jordan, and they would discuss Sophia's progress. During study times at school, Ms. Jordan would use the same timer and as Sophia improved in her concentration, the time would be lengthened to the goal of 15 minutes without a break. Ms. Jordan asked if this plan was agreeable to the family. The family agreed to allow Sophia to participate. As the meeting closed, Ms. Jordan thanked the family members and shook hands. She hugged Sophia and thanked the family for allowing Sophia to be her student.

- Know the importance of establishing and maintaining a positive collaborative relationship with families to promote academic, social, and emotional growth of children. [National Council for Accreditation of Teacher Education (NCATE)]
- Propagate communication between home and school that is regular, two-way, and meaningful. [National Parent Teacher Association (PTA)]
- Foster relationships with school colleagues, parents, and agencies in the larger community to support student's learning and well-being. [Interstate New Teacher Assessment and Support Consortium (INTASC)]
- Communicate about mathematics goals to help families and other caregivers. [National Council of Teachers of Mathematics (NCTM)]
- Maintain an open, friendly, and cooperative relationship with each child's family, encourage their involvement in the program, and support the child's relationship with his or her family.

Legal Mandate for Family Involvement

Not only does research support family involvement in education, but several federal laws actually mandate such involvement. Legislation, including Section 504 of the Vocational Rehabilitation Act, the Individuals with Disabilities Education Act (IDEA), and the No Child Left Behind Act (NCLB) (formerly the Elementary and Secondary Education Act, or ESEA) all include sections addressing the need for parental involvement (Murdick, Gartin, & Crabtree, 2007). These laws stress the importance of involving the students and families in the education process and actually mandate certain steps in the process.

For public schools providing special education services to students with disabilities, the most important legislation mandating specific actions is the IDEA. Prior to the passage of IDEA in 1975, many schools avoided trying to get parental involvement in the education of their children. IDEA requires schools to take certain steps to ensure parental involvement in the process. The basis for parental involvement is the due process rights afforded parents and students under IDEA. These include the right to receive notice before the school takes certain actions with their children; the right to consent before the school takes certain actions with their children, and the right to a due process hearing if the family and school disagree on the educational program for a particular child. Table 5.2 describes each of these parental rights.

TABLE 5.2 ● Parental Rights Under IDEA

Right to Notice—Parents have a right to be notified by the school before taking any actions regarding referral, evaluation, placement, or programming.

Receive a Copy of Child's Records—Parents have a right to examine and get a copy of their child's records at any time. School cannot withhold any records on a child when parents request a copy.

Right to Consent—Parents have a right to consent regarding the initial testing of the child and whether or not the child is placed in special education. Schools cannot conduct an initial evaluation or place the child in any special education program without parental permission.

Right to an Independent Evaluation—Parents have a right to secure an independent evaluation of their child if they do not agree with the school's evaluation. School personnel must consider the results of an independent evaluation when making decisions about the child. Parents may have to pay for the independent evaluation.

Right to Mediation—If the school and parent do not agree on the child's educational program, parents can voluntarily enter into mediation. Parents continue to have a right to require a due process hearing.

Right to a Due Process Hearing—Parents have a right to request an impartial, due process hearing if there is a disagreement on the child's educational program. A hearing officer, a non-biased third party, listens to the schools' and parents' issues and makes a mandatory ruling on the case.

THE FAMILY

There are many different views and definitions of family. Traditionally, a family was described as a group of individuals living together in a single dwelling (Smith, Gartin, Murdick, & Hilton, 2006). This was primarily composed of a father, mother, and children. Sometimes this also included an extended family in which one or more grandparents live in the home. For the purposes of the U.S. government, the term *family* is defined as a group of two or more people related by birth, marriage, or adoption who reside together (U.S. Census Bureau Population Survey, 2004). Researchers have used different definitions of family. For example, Poston et al. (2003) defined *family* as two or more individuals who regard themselves as a family and who carry out the functions that families typically perform.

With family defined in so many different ways, it is important for teachers and school personnel to consider families using a broad definition; using a narrow definition could possibly omit persons who could have a major impact on the child. Regardless of how family is defined, school personnel must not lose sight of the fact that a child's family is a critical factor in a child's life, meaning that their involvement in school activities is critically important to the child's educational program. Any preconceived ideas about what a family should look like must be discarded by educators to enable them to accept any child's family, regardless of its configuration (Smith, Polloway, Patton, & Dowdy, 2012). When working with families that are not considered a traditional family unit, educators must be aware of possible personal biases and avoid actions based on this bias. To do otherwise would be unethical and could have a negative impact on students (Smith et al., 2006).

Characteristics of Families

While educators must view each family as a unique entity, there are some common characteristics found in most families, such as a set of norms or rules that influence the behaviors of each member of the family unit. These family norms result from religious, cultural, and ethnic beliefs which provide the framework for family behaviors and result in the uniqueness of each family (McCubbin, Thompson, Thompson, McCubbin, & Kaston, 1993). Without a doubt, families in the 21st century differ significantly from families 30 and 40 years ago. Some of the differences found in families today include:

- Many families are single-parent families, usually headed by a mother.
- Single-parent families headed by mothers often are low-income families.
- Different family structures, such as gay or lesbian couples, are more prevalent.
- Many families do not speak English as their primary language.
- Many families have two working parents.
- Cultural diversity among families is much greater.

Family members are involved in the educational programs of their children within the context of their culture, beliefs, and current situation. The U.S. Census Bureau (2004) projected that more than 50% of the population of the United States will be comprised of minorities by the year 2042, and that by 2023, more than half of all children in U.S. public schools will be from minority groups. With the cultural diversity of this country increasing dramatically (Johnson & Lichter, 2010), school personnel must be more cognizant than ever of different cultural beliefs and how they may impact children in schools. For example, some parents may espouse religious beliefs that do not support the involvement of medical personnel when their child is ill. This view may be very difficult for school personnel to accept because of concerns for the child. In these situations, discussions should be held to determine actions that are allowed by the school should the child become ill during school hours. In some cultures family members defer or acquiesce to teachers' expertise instead of expressing their own ideas. While this is considered a form of respect for teachers, it could result in family members not being active participants in the educational process. When working with parents with this belief, full family involvement may be difficult to obtain. One way to assist schools in this situation is to contact a liaison within the family's community, such as another parent from the same cultural group who is actively involved in their child's educational program for assistance.

In some instances, the family's culture may impact future planning for students with disabilities and the school's ability to implement transition plans. For example, in some cultures, students with disabilities, especially female students, are not expected to live independently after high school. Therefore, their families may not see the need for vocational training, independent living skills development, or self-determination supports because they assume the child will be cared for by members of her extended family. Regardless of the configuration of the student's family or the family's cultural beliefs, school personnel must recognize and accept the fact that family members generally want what is best for their child.

A first step in accepting children and families from different cultures is for educators to develop an understanding of how they view different cultures. Some questions that educators can ask themselves to ascertain their beliefs include (Cartledge & Kourea, 2008, p. 355):

1. What is the racial or gender breakdown of the students that I typically send from my class for disciplinary actions?
2. How often do I send the same students for disciplinary actions?
3. What messages am I communicating to the students who are the recipients of these actions?
4. What messages am I communicating to their classmates?
5. Is the behavior of my students getting better? How do I know? If it is not getting better, why not?
6. Do I dispense disciplinary referrals fairly on the basis of race and gender?
7. Are disciplinary actions therapeutic or simply punitive?
8. Do I distinguish culturally specific behaviors from behavioral inadequacies?
9. If students have substantial behavioral differences, have I taught them the skills that they need to know?
10. Am I punishing students for my lack of skill in effective behavior management?
11. Do I punish students because of my lack of skill in effective instruction?

By answering these questions, educators can determine their feelings about students from different cultural groups.

Family Life Cycle

The family life cycle refers to the developmental changes in the family unit that occur over time to accommodate the changes in the needs of family members. Turnbull and Turnbull (2001) developed a framework for understanding the changes that occur in most families. As the family moves from one stage to the next, the basic structure of the family—including its functioning, relationships, and interactions—changes. The most stressful time for a family is the time when there is a transition from one stage to the next, such as the movement of their children from primary school (ages 5–12) to adolescence (ages 12–21) to adulthood (ages 21+). For families who have children with disabilities, transition times may be particularly challenging.

Adolescence presents unique concerns and challenges for parents of all children. Some of these issues include their emerging sexuality, possible rejection and isolation from their peer groups, physical and emotional changes of puberty, and development of vocational goals and possibly securing postsecondary educational opportunities. To assist families to successfully navigate issues during transition, school personnel can provide support by incorporating curricular content where appropriate, directly related to life cycle family issues.

Tips for Communicating with Families

There is no way that schools can maximally impact the educational opportunities with children without parental involvement; and there is no way that schools can maximize parental involvement without good communication. When school personnel work with families, it is important to communicate with all of the significant members of the family. This could include parents, grandparents, aunts, uncles, or siblings since any of these may be critical decision makers within their family. There are numerous things school personnel can do to enhance communication with families. Some recommendations include: (1) Be an active listener with parents; (2) always be respectful of parents, especially when parents are upset; (3) discuss specific educational and behavior expectations and goals of the child; (4) make positive comments about the child; (5) establish regular communication with family members and communicate frequently; (6) begin meetings with welcoming, introducing individuals present, and reviewing any previous meetings that may have been held; and (7) do not assume parents know and understand how to assist their child (Brandes, 2005).

IMPACT OF A CHILD WITH DISABILITIES ON THE FAMILY

The identification of a child as having a disability affects the entire family and produces a variety of responses from each family member. These could include grief, loss, denial, guilt, bargaining, anger, depression, acceptance, stress (Quintero & McIntyre, 2010; Smith et al., 2006). By the time students with disabilities enter middle or secondary school, most family members have had ample time to deal with some of these reactions. However, each family member's perceptions and feelings are unique since each family member views the impact of the disability from a different stance. Indeed, families and family members differ greatly in the interpretation of the disability; for example, one family member may view deafness as a tragedy while another family member may view it as a crisis, another as an unfortunate circumstance, and another as a unique characteristic of the child. Therefore, educators in secondary schools must be prepared for a variety of different reactions from family members of students with disabilities.

Kubler-Ross (1969) described the impact on parents when they learn that their child has a disability as a five-step grieving process: (1) denial, (2) bargaining, (3) anger, (4) depression, and (5) acceptance. There are several assumptions with the Kubler-Ross model, including:

- Parents go through all steps.
- Parents move from step to step in sequential order.
- Movement is an orderly process.
- Failure to progress at a reasonable rate or remaining at a step indicates a problem in the parent's life or lack of acceptance or resolution of an issue or feeling.
- Unresolved feelings are abnormal, are destructive to family, and need resolution.

The Kubler-Ross model was acceptable for many years, but more recently, researchers have begun to question some of the assumptions underlying the model. For example, Smith, Jaffe-Gill, and Segal (2009) noted that Kubler-Ross never intended for these stages to be a rigid framework that applies to everyone who mourns. The most likely conclusion regarding family reactions to having a child with a disability is that such reactions are unique for each family and family member. School personnel need to realize that the presence of a child with a disability presents many challenges for families, so they must be prepared to collaborate with families to ensure an appropriate education for the student.

Parents and Stress

All parents experience stress during the parenting process. However, families that include a child with a disability have increased stress (Turnbull, Turnbull, & Wehmeyer, 2010). Families of children with disabilities show higher percentages of lower family incomes and more single-parent households, two factors that can add to stress (Hodapp & Krasner, 1994). Other sources of stress related to children with disabilities include:

- Financial burden
- Additional behavior issues
- Problems with siblings
- Frustration with educational systems
- Lack of understanding about the full impact of the disability
- Concern for the future of the child
- Individual family factors, such as marital solidarity, financial resources, religious heritage, and availability of external supports
- Age of diagnosis
- Severity of disability
- Type of disability

School personnel need to be aware of sources of stress and how they may impact on family members in their reaction to a child's disability as well as their involvement in the child's educational program.

Siblings and Stress

The siblings of the youth with disabilities also have issues and challenges that result from the disability. It is likely that between 15% and 20% of students have a sibling with a disability (Smith et al., 2012). Siblings have the same feelings of loss and grief as do the parents and other family members. Additionally, siblings may be dealing with the stigma and embarrassment of having a brother or sister with a disability. Siblings face some specific issues related to the presence of a disability in the family. For one thing, siblings often become a caregiver and supervisor for their brother or sister with a disability (Quintero & McIntyre, 2010). This could result in their having less time than their peers for schoolwork, and more importantly, social opportunities. Often, adolescents with a disability may overidentify with their siblings, refusing to allow personal space and personal time for the siblings to spend with their friends. While not all siblings have problems, many do have issues. Hutton and Caron (2005) found that (1) 38% were resentful or jealous of their siblings; (2) 12% were fearful of their sibling; (3) 12% felt sadness because of their sibling, and (4) 6% felt awkward because of their sibling. Only 12% of the siblings in the study accepted their disabled sibling like they would have accepted another sibling. Often, siblings report feelings of guilt and confusion and, unlike adults, lack the maturity and experience to deal with such issues. To reassure siblings, Smith et al. (2006) recommended that parents and other adults consider implementing the following actions:

- Provide siblings with information concerning the disability.
- Include siblings in family and school meetings.
- Inform them of the changes and stresses currently on the family.
- Work for equity with regard to the family duties and responsibilities.
- Prevent the siblings from becoming a second parent in areas of sibling care and discipline.

It is critical that educators remember the needs of siblings, include them in activities, and encourage teen attendance in support groups. Educators can provide information for the sibling to learn more about disability, its causes, and its impact. Educators can also provide the sibling with a safe environment to talk about personal concerns and feelings. Schools can become a safe haven for the sibling to vent without fear of judgments or rejection. You can provide the sibling with support through the use of books and examples that explore the issues siblings may have and are not comfortable discussing. The top children's books that portray in a positive manner children with disabilities have been identified by Prater and Dyches (2008). Table 5.3 provides a list of these books for students in grades 5–12.

Extended Family and Stress

Extended family members, especially grandparents, can be a source of love and acceptance to family members and to the youth with disabilities. There are numerous things they can do to facilitate acceptance of the child with a disability and help the other members of the family deal with their child and sibling. Extended family members can support the child's parents by taking children for an afternoon, an overnight, or a brief vacation, thereby providing a renewal time for the parents. The extended family can influence the child's development by allowing the youth the opportunity to practice age-appropriate life skills in multiple settings. By providing a safe haven for the youth with disabilities, the extended family can buffer the student from the daily demands of being an adolescent.

Extended family can also be a source of stress. When grandparents and other extended family members show a lack of understanding of the disability, have inappropriate expectations for the child with the disability, or continue to blame one or both parents for the child's disability, then the potential support becomes a major liability. Therefore, it is important for teachers to recognize the potential impact extended family members may have in a student's life. If they are an integral part of the family then you may ask the parents if they would like to include them in school activities and meetings; if they are not supportive you need to realize the added stress factor upon the family.

Professionals and Family Stress

While professionals provide services and supports to individuals with disabilities and their family, they can also be a source of stress (Bennet, Lee, & Lueke, 1998; Parette & Petch-Hogan, 2000). For example, school personnel who exhibit negative attitudes concerning the involvement of parents in school environments are a stressor for those parents seeking such involvement (Bennett et al., 1998; Howart, 1998). For some families who do not seek or want the help of professionals, any assistance provided may increase parental stress (Meyer & Bailey, 1993). Stress also increases when professionals demonstrate a lack of knowledge, respect, and/or appreciation for the family's preferences, values, or culture (Smith, 1993). Depending on the type of disability, the family may not see a need for the professional to be involved and therefore may view your attempts to help as inappropriate and stressful.

TABLE 5.3 ● Books Portraying Positive Images of Children with Disabilities

Title, Author (Illustrator or photographer, if any), Publisher, and Year	Disability	Awards	Type of Book	Grade Level
Al Capone Does My Shirts, Gennifer Choldenko, Putnam, 2004	Autism	Newbery Honor	Chapter	5+
The Bus People, Rachel Anderson, Holt, 1989	Various disabilities		Chapter	5+
The Curious Incident of the Dog in the Night-Time, Mark Haddon, Random House, 2003	Autism	Dolly Gray	Chapter	9+
Freak the Mighty, Rodman Philbrick, Scholastic, 1993	Learning disabilities; orthopedic and other health impairments		Chapter	6+
Kissing Doorknobs, Terry Spencer Hesser, Delacorte, 1998	Emotional/behavioral disorders		Chapter	7+
Life Magic, Melrose Cooper, Holt, 1996	Other health impairment; learning disabilities		Chapter	4+
Lois Lowry Trilogy, *The Giver* (2000), *Gathering Blue* (2002), and *Messenger*, Delacorte Books for Young Readers, 2005	Various disabilities	Newbery Medal for *The Giver*	Chapter	6+
Rules, Cynthia Lord, Scholastic, 2006	Autism; orthopedic impairment; communication disorders	Newbery Honor	Chapter	4+
So B It, Sarah Weeks, HarperCollins, 2004	Intellectual disabilities	Dolly Gray	Chapter	6+
Tru Confessions, Janet Tashjian, Holt, 1997	Intellectual disabilities	Dolly Gray	Chapter	4+
The View from Saturday, E. L. Konigsburg, Aladdin, 1996	Orthopedic impairment	Newbery Medal	Chapter	4+
The Westing Game, Ellen Raskin, Penguin, 1978	Orthopedic impairment	Newbery Medal	Chapter	4+
Yours Turly, Shirley, Ann M. Martin, Holiday House, 1988	Learning disabilities		Chapter	4+
I Am an Artichoke, Lucy Frank, Laurel Leaf, 1993	Emotional/behavioral disorders		Chapter	7+
My Louisiana Sky, Kimberly Willis Holt, Random House, 1998	Intellectual disabilities		Chapter	6+
Risk 'n Roses, Jan Slepian, Philomel, 1990	Intellectual disabilities		Chapter	5+
A Single Shard, Linda Sue Park, Random House, 2001	Orthopedic impairments	Newbery	Chapter	5+
Welcome Home, Jellybean, Marlene Fanta Shyer, Scribner's Sons, 1978	Intellectual disabilities		Chapter	5+
Wish on a Unicorn, Karen Hesse, Holt, 1991	Intellectual disabilities		Chapter	4+

Source: From "Books That Portray Characters with Disabilities," by M. A. Prater and T. T. Dyches, 2008, *Teaching Exceptional Children, 40*, pp. 34–35. Used with permission.

When parents visit the school to meet with the educational team, they may react to questions and statements from a frightened, anxious, or concerned state. School personnel must recognize the possibility that parental responses to suggestions may trigger an emotional reaction as opposed to a rational response. The best course of action for school personnel is to listen to what parents say as well as what they don't say. School personnel should try to identify the emotional state that suggestions elicit from parents, knowing that this may not be a reaction to what is being said but to what they are hearing. It is therefore imperative that teachers and other school professionals become aware of and sensitive to the feelings of family members concerning interactions with professionals (Paul, Porter, & Falk, 1993). Establishing a trusting relationship may be the most important thing teachers can do when working with families of children with disabilities.

FAMILIES FROM DIVERSE BACKGROUNDS

The "melting pot" theory, predicting that American society would become more homogeneous over the years has not happened. In fact, the American society has become more heterogeneous; it is now more diverse than ever and the trend continues. By the year 2020, half of the students in the United States will come from diverse, nonwhite backgrounds (Gollnick & Chinn, 2009). A diverse background is not limited to ethnicity, primary language, and geographic origin, but includes differences in age, gender, language and communication style, religious beliefs, socioeconomic status, sexual preference, and ability (Gollnick & Chinn, 2009).

Diversity in Family Structure

Today's families may not fit the traditional (and somewhat artificial) concept of one working dad, one stay-at-home mom, and two children. Following is an adapted list of differing family structures and the potential challenges that each might encounter (Ray, 2005):

1. *Single-parent families* may experience stress and isolation and are likely to live in poverty. However, children may have a closer relationship with their parent, may be more independent, and may have a healthier self-image.
2. *Blended families* (where parents each have children from other relationships) may have to deal with sibling rivalry as well as resolving issues of bonding and child rearing (including discipline). However, the standard of living for the family may improve with marriage as well as feelings of improved security and happiness as the two parents have more time to meet the social and parenting needs of the children.

   However, if the student with disabilities lives in two separate households during the year, school-related problems can occur. Following is a list of school-related issues encountered by parents of children living in two separate households during the school year (adapted from Smith et al., 2006):
   - Variable amounts of time available for homework and school problems
   - Pressures competing for family resources (financial and time)
   - Additional parent conferences
3. *Multigenerational families* may have different values in the two households concerning school behavior and performance. Multigenerational families (including grandparents or other relatives) may face legal issues if adoption has not occurred, economic issues, and energy/vitality challenges. Difficulties can also occur if there are different parenting styles and expectations among those with responsibility for the child's parenting. However, special bonds often develop among the child, the grandparents, and other extended

family members in the household. The extended family can provide additional persons who can nurture and parent the children. According to Demo and Cox (2000), when family members share in the care of children, it creates a strong network of support and social relationships.

4. *Foster families* may result in stress for all family members as well as concerns of not knowing what might occur next in the child's life. Since this family is temporary by definition, creating a strong family bond is difficult. However, in cases of abuse or neglect, a foster family may be a safe refuge for the child. Foster parents have received training and have access to supports to assist the child who needs physical or psychological help.

5. *Gay/lesbian families* often face discrimination and societal abuse as well as legal issues that might exclude one of the parents from access. In 2006, Pawelski et al. reported that nearly 10 million students have gay or lesbian parents. A common concern of these parents is that they feel isolated from the children's schools (Bos, van Balen, van den Bloom, & Sandfort, 2004). For example, there is a lack of nontraditional families in the standard curriculum, and they report high levels of bullying of their children (Mercier & Harold, 2003; Ray & Gregory, 2001). Additionally, some teachers may have issues with this lifestyle preference and feel uncomfortable with these parents. Teachers may even avoid communicating with the parents or asking them to become involved in classroom or school activities. However, research covering 20 years or more has found that a parent's sexual orientation does not affect a child's gender identity, self-concept, behavior, intelligence, or personality characteristics (American Academy of Pediatrics, 2003; Demo & Cox, 2000; Perrin, 2002; Sailor, 2004).

Tips for Working with Families of Diverse Family Structures

It is important for middle and secondary teachers to take an active role in increasing family involvement and in welcoming members of families into their classrooms. Friend and Cook (2007, p. 5) presented some general tips to assist you in working with diverse family structures:

- Be sure to know the correct last names of every parent, regardless of the family structure.
- Avoid language that implies that "family" refers only to traditional family structure.
- For recently formed families, offer information on their children's strengths and abilities.
- Avoid making requests that may place parents in an uncomfortable position related to time or money. Some families cannot afford to contribute materials for classrooms, and some parents cannot come to conferences during typical school hours or on a specific day; therefore, teachers need to offer options and alternatives when making requests of family members.
- Remember that projects and activities that presume students are part of a traditional family may not be appropriate—for example, alternatives to creating a family tree may be in order.
- In some cases—for example, when grandparents are raising children—you may need to explain school procedures.
- Perhaps, most important, all educators should reflect on their own beliefs about nontraditional families and set aside any assumptions they may have about them. Being positive with students and families and being alert to, and stopping, the teasing of students from these families are important responsibilities that you may have.

Bower (2008) provided a set of tips for working with families of same-sex partners. However, the tips are relevant to all types of diversity based on family structure. Following are suggestions from lesbian mothers for educators:

- Be inclusive in curriculum.
- Be respectful of all families.

- Provide a physically and emotionally safe environment for children from diverse families. (Note: Be aware of bully prevention.)
- Ask parents about family structures rather than assuming. (Note: Send home a flyer about home situations including "Who is your family?" and "Who lives with your child?")
- Rethink permission slips and provide several blank signature lines.
- Create time and space for discussion of differing family structures. (Note: Develop a family mosaic representing important people in the students' lives and read books containing nontraditional families.)
- Be sensitive about holidays (e.g., Mother's Day, Father's Day) and allow students who wish to complete two projects or encourage them to make a project for all the person(s) important to them (i.e., grandmother, grandfather, aunt, uncle, two mothers, or two fathers).
- Embrace differences rather than minimize them.
- Talk about diversity in a nonjudgmental manner.
- Make learning about the students and their families a priority.
- Develop strong antibullying and teasing policies, both schoolwide and class-specific.
- Create a classroom where differences are accepted.

Although as a secondary level teacher, you may not have significant amounts of interaction with some parents, you will be meeting with family members during open house hours, parent–teacher meetings, IEP meetings, and so forth. You will need to assess your own biases and language as well as class curriculum to ensure that it is friendly to all types of families.

Diversity in Culture and Language

The cultural heritage of a family affects the family's reaction to disability. The etiology of the disability in American educational culture relates to medical causality, and treatments based on scientific or research findings. In other cultures, the cause is fate, spiritual or religious visitation, punishment, retribution, or reprisal. The different cultural meanings and view of disability can result in conflict, or tension, between the family of the student with disabilities and the school personnel. Therefore, you need to be aware of the potential for conflict and of the family's beliefs concerning disability, its causation, and impact on the child's future.

For example, the word *handicapped* may have an alternative meaning to persons of differing cultures (the term means "crazy" to some). Many Native American cultures do not have a word for "disability" (Robinson-Zanartu, 1996), which results in the youth with disabilities being integrated into the community and given tasks based on the individual's skills and abilities (Stewart, 1977). Often the demands of a culturally different life are defined as what is required for functioning in the student's home environment and the expectations of what will be needed in the child's future environment (Harry, 1995). As a result, you should be aware of the family's culture and what that means so that you can adjust services and educational goals to reflect the needs of the student within the family's cultural context.

Researchers have frequently found that culturally diverse families are often passively involved in educational planning (Harry, 1992). The cultural heritage of some family members may ascribe the responsibility for education to school personnel because of their respect for schools and teachers. Possibly, some family members are accustomed to, and accepting of, the school making decisions concerning the education of students. Others may believe that the school holds them responsible for the student's failure or disability. Then, others may believe that the school does not want, or need, their involvement (Smith et al., 2006; Taylor et al., 2009). Some parents may feel intimidated by school personnel. They may lack trust for professionals who have insufficient knowledge of the student's culture or do not exhibit a desire to increase communication and cultural awareness as part of the educational process (Harry, 2002). Teachers should be aware that although collaboration is necessary in order to provide optimal educational experiences for students with disabilities, schools do have the ultimate authority to make educational decisions. This unspoken inequality may impact on the comfort that families may have when working with school personnel. If school personnel and families are to build a collaborative relationship that is based on trust, respect, and mutual understanding, it is important for teachers to seek information on the culture and language of the families of students. In order for teachers to have successful collaborative partnerships with families, they must listen well and focus on the feelings and attitudes as well as the words of the family. Remember that today parent participation in educational decision making is a right secured by law, and school personnel must be proactive in encouraging parents to participate in the process.

Tips for Working with Families of Cultural and Language Differences

When there is a mismatch between teacher and student backgrounds, school personnel may need advice and support in order to effectively meet the needs of students and their families (Delpit, 1995). There are several actions teachers can take to address this mismatch. These include:

- Learning about yourself and your cultural identification
- Reflecting on your personal culture and experiences and determining how they are different from the cultures and experiences of your students
- Identifying different cultural groups represented in the classroom
- Working with someone from the same cultural group for guidance and knowledge
- Learning some common words that could be used in greetings for students who speak a different language
- Minimizing the use of written materials for students who speak a different language
- Sending written communications in the student's native language
- Using interpreters if necessary to improve oral communication
- Being an excellent listener

Developing a Culturally Sensitive Classroom

To develop a culturally sensitive classroom, teachers need to explore how students view some culturally bound concepts. Vaughn, Bos, and Schumm (1997) suggest the following general areas with questions that teachers and school personnel can use when finding out more about students and their cultures. Teachers can ask students these questions or just observe students and infer the answers to the questions. Asking students directly is a better approach, because the inferential approach could be impacted by the teacher's bias.

- *Time:* How do students perceive time? How is timeliness regarded in their cultures?
- *Space:* What personal distance do students use in interactions with other students and with adults? How does the culture determine the space allotted to boys and girls?
- *Dress and foods:* How does dress differ by age, gender, and social class? What clothing and accessories are considered acceptable? What foods are typical?
- *Rituals and ceremonies:* What rituals do students use to show respect? What celebrations do students observe, and for what reasons? How and where do parents expect to be greeted when visiting the class?
- *Work:* What types of work are students expected to perform, and at what age, in the home and community? To what extent are students expected to work together?

- *Leisure:* What are the purposes for play? What typical activities are done for enjoyment in the home and community?
- *Gender roles:* What tasks are performed by boys? By girls? What expectations do parents and students hold for boys' and girls' achievements, and how does this differ by subject areas?
- *Status:* What resources (e.g., study area and materials, study assistance from parents and siblings) are available at home and in the community? What power do parents have to obtain information about the school and to influence educational choices?
- *Goals:* What kinds of work are considered prestigious or desirable? What role does education play in achieving occupational goals? What education level does the family and student desire for the student?
- *Education:* What methods for teaching and learning are used in the home (e.g., modeling and imitation, didactic stories and proverbs, direct verbal instruction)?
- *Communication:* What roles do verbal and nonverbal languages play in learning and teaching? What roles do conventions such as silence, questions, rhetorical questions, and discourse style play in communication? What types of literature (e.g., newspapers, books) are used in the home and in what language(s) are they written? How is writing used in the home (e.g., letters, lists, notes) and in what language(s)?
- *Interaction:* What roles do cooperation and competition play in learning? How are children expected to interact with teachers? (Vaughn et al., 1997, p. 278)

In addition, teachers should evaluate their classroom and the school environment, to determine the cultural sensitivity of the school. The following are suggestions to help school personnel provide an educational environment that is sensitive to students' and families' cultures and languages:

- Provide information to families in their primary language using their preferred method (notes, telephone calls, face-to-face meetings, or tape recording).
- Include all family members who are important to the student.
- Use a respectful form of address such as Mr., Mrs., Ms., or Dr. Be sure to err on the side of formality, especially if speaking to older family members.
- Attend social events and community functions held in the community.
- Locate and use a cultural guide(s) who can help you in understanding the cultural aspects of nonverbal communication, appropriate manners, gender roles, medical practices, child-rearing practices, rites of passage, and specific beliefs and folkways that might influence your relationship with the family.
- Develop a survival vocabulary of key words and phrases in the family's language.
- Conduct meetings in family-friendly settings such as community centers, houses of worship, a library, or a site suggested by the family or cultural guide.
- Allow the needs of the family to dictate the time and place of meetings whenever possible. Be sensitive to issues such as work and childcare conflicts, transportation issues, and cultural and religious restrictions related to gender, location, and meeting times.

SCHOOL AND FAMILY COLLABORATION

The most recent reauthorization of IDEA (2004) continues to mandate parental involvement in the education of their children. Parents have specific rights, previously cited, that give them an equal voice in decisions about the education of their children. Often, parents are eager to become involved with the education of their young children. Unfortunately, the involvement level of many parents decreases as students get older. This is extremely unfortunate regarding students with disabilities. During their adolescent years critical decisions are made that will facilitate their transition from school to postschool environments. Parents need to be involved in these decisions. After all, they are not only partners but the senior partner in the collaborative efforts for their children (Cavkaytar & Pollard, 2009).

The fact that parents have a right to be involved in the education of their children can also be viewed as a burden. Parents are asked more today than ever before to expand their roles in the educational process (Turnbull et al., 2010). With parental involvement being critical, and many parents not wanting to participate at the level that is required, schools must develop strategies to increase parental involvement at all levels. School personnel cannot step back and acknowledge that parents choose not to participate; school personnel must do everything they can to secure such involvement.

Parents may be uninvolved for a variety of reasons. School personnel should determine why they are uninvolved and implement strategies to increase their involvement. Some parents may simply feel that their ideas and suggestions have gone unheard over the years. While many may have eagerly attended assessment and IEP meetings when their child was younger, they may have become somewhat cynical that school personnel did not listen to their ideas. Still others may have determined that school personnel likely know what is best for their child and have basically turned decision making over to them.

Parent and school collaborative efforts fail for several different reasons. Summers et al. (2005) noted that these include professionals feeling unprepared and unsupported by their school districts to work with parents; problems with communication; and disagreeing about what may be best for the child. Regardless of why parents may be uninvolved with secondary students with disabilities, schools must encourage and reinforce involvement. Decisions will be made during middle school and high school that will likely impact the student's future; parents need to be involved in these decisions.

Encouraging Parental Participation

One of the most important things school personnel can do to encourage parents and school partnerships is to listen to family members. If parents believe that school personnel are actually listening to them it will go a long way in establishing trust and encouraging families to work with the school. When parents think the school is inviting them to participate but really do not care what they have to say, then the likelihood that they will continue to be involved will diminish quickly. Active listening is a method of listening which also assures the speaker that you understand the message sent. Active listening allows you to convey both verbally and non-verbally that you are attending to the message and that the input is valuable. There are several formats for active listening, but the simplest is the four-step process of (1) *paraphrase* (restate) the speaker's message, (2) *encourage* the speaker to keep talking, (3) *reflect* feelings conveyed in the speaker's message, and (4) *probe* to secure additional information or clarification of the information.

A more advanced model for active listening involves 10 steps. These steps focus on acknowledging what is spoken, giving verbal and nonverbal feedback, summarizing what is said, and giving additional feedback. Table 5.4 describes all 10 steps in this active listening model. School personnel must be active listeners to facilitate communication and parental involvement. Many parents and other family members feel like school personnel do not listen to them, even though they are in the same meeting and provide some superficial acknowledgment of what is said. Active listening shows parents that school personnel are really listening and considering their input, which is invaluable for building a trusting relationship.

TABLE 5.4 ● Steps in Active Listening

1. *Acknowledge* the information and demonstrate you are listening with verbal and nonverbal cues. For example, the listener can look at the speaker and nod.
2. *Restate* the speaker's message and allow time for the speaker to correct misunderstood information or feelings. The listener can use "You feel as if . . ." statements.
3. *Reflect* the speaker's body language and spoken language to indicate both understanding and affirming of similar understandings. The listener uses nonverbal reflection such as smiles, frowns, and body position such as leaning forward toward the speaker.
4. *Interpret* by being empathetic, encouraging the person to talk, and asking for clarification when more information is needed. This is not a reflection or restatement, but often poses a question, "Do you mean . . . ?" or ask for more information, such as "Did you mean that . . . ?"
5. *Summarize* the relevant information and check for accuracy with the speaker. Do not judge or provide suggestions at this point. The listener might use "I understood you to say that . . ."
6. *Probe* or ask a clarifying question or two. These questions will assure the speaker that you are seeking understanding, which will support your credibility with the speaker.
7. *Give feedback* that will affirm their insights and ideas, but do not offer criticism. If you add to the statement "this is good, *because . . .*" the listener will demonstrate greater sincerity instead of programmed agreement.
8. *Support* statements will validate the speaker's information, ideas, or concerns. The listener might say, "What you did was a rational response to the situation?" or "I can see why you say that."
9. *Check perceptions* is an essential step if the listener is interpreting correctly the information and impressions gleaned from the speaker. The listener must summarize or sum up what the speaker has been saying.
10. *Be quiet.* By being quiet, you show that you are listening to the speaker and not talking too much. Also being quiet allows time for thinking to occur. However, use this only after you have established an accepting environment where support is evident, so that the quiet is supportive and not an interrogation technique.

TABLE 5.5 ● Ways to Increase Parental Participation in the IEP Process

- Establish trust with parents
- Empower parents
- Focus on improving communication skills
- Use a wide variety of communication options
- Be sensitive to cultural and language differences
- Show a caring attitude about the student
- Ensure parents understand the nature of an inclusive educational program
- Support parents in home interventions
- Provide reinforcement to parental efforts

Source: Information from Smith, T. E. C., Polloway, E. A., Patton, J. R., & Dowdy, C. A. (2012). *Teaching students with special needs in inclusive settings* (6th ed.) Upper Saddle River, NJ: Merrill/Pearson.

In addition to really listening to parents and taking into consideration their input, school personnel can increase parental involvement in educational decision making for their student in middle and secondary schools in several other ways. Table 5.5 describes additional ways to encourage family–school collaboration.

Establish Trust with Parents.   One of the most important things school personnel can do to enhance school–family collaboration is to establish trust. Many parents are untrusting of schools for a variety of reasons. These could include their own negative experiences in school; possible negative experiences of other children in the family; or feelings that the school does not really care what they think about their child's education. Establishing trust can be a time-consuming effort; however, if schools are truly interested in strengthening their collaborative relationship with parents they should address this issue.

Empower Parents. Many parents feel unempowered when dealing with teachers and other school officials. After all, parents may not have the formal education that school personnel have, and they also may not understand the educational jargon often used by teachers and others. Parents need to feel that they are equal partners, and in reality the senior partners, in the collaborative relationship. This means school personnel need to encourage parents not only to provide input into discussions but to actively participate and even take the lead in decision making.

Focus on Improving Communication Skills. As noted previously, communication is key in establishing and maintaining collaborative relationships between parents and school personnel. Teachers should never assume that parents know what is going on with their child. Over communication is better than under communication. Take advantage of formal means of communication, such as letters and information sheets, as well as informal means such as phone calls, e-mails, and face-to-face conversations.

Use a Wide Variety of Communication Options. As noted above, schools should not rely on formal communication alone. Many parents may actually prefer more informal means of communicating. Home visits are powerful in providing communication opportunities as well as building trust.

Be Sensitive to Cultural and Language Differences. With the increasing diversity of our society, many families are from different cultural groups than teachers. School personnel must be sensitive to the culture and language of the family and not assume that individuals from different cultural groups share the same social values as they do. Being sensitive to different cultural and language characteristics can encourage trust between parents and school personnel.

Show a caring attitude about the student. Parents want to know that school personnel care about their child. School personnel need to be positive about the student and the student's future. Showing a caring attitude and pointing out the positive attributes of the student help establish a trusting relationship.

Ensure Parents Understand the Nature of an Inclusive Educational Program. School personnel often assume that parents understand educational practices. Discussing issues that parents are unaware of can make parents feel unempowered. Therefore, when discussing educational issues with parents and other family members, school personnel must explain in understandable lay terms the proposed educational programs. The word *inclusion* may even be misunderstood. At all times, teachers and others must not talk down to parents. Explaining educational practices to them in terms they will understand, without talking down to them, will greatly assist in strengthening the relationship between parents and school personnel.

Support Parents in Home Interventions. Schools only have a few hours each day to provide interventions for a child who is having difficulties. Parents, on the other hand, have many more opportunities. Schools should work with parents to provide them with support and encouragement to implement home interventions. The chances of a child benefiting from educational interventions are increased if family members reinforce activities that are occurring in the school.

Provide Reinforcement to Parental Efforts. Parents need to know they are doing a good job. Working with students with disabilities can be frustrating for teachers, but it can also be very frustrating for parents. School personnel need to positively reinforce parents for any level of participation, including attending meetings, actively participating in meetings, and implementing home interventions.

SUMMARY

The practice of school–family collaboration provides a method for you and the families of your students to pursue the common goal of excellence in education. Unfortunately, educators often have poorly developed skills in working as partners with families. To improve your skills, consider using the following suggestions. You should expand your definition of family to include more than that of mother, father, and child/children to that of a more inclusive family concept. You will need to discover the norms and rules that govern each family in your classroom. When possible, you should determine the impact the child's disability has on the individual family members as well as on the extended family unit. It is also essential that you recognize the role stress plays in the life of the family and you should identify the stressors that are within your control and that of the school. With your cultural guide, you should discuss cultural differences that may otherwise hinder the collaboration process as well as identify ways to mitigate these barriers. Finally, you should use the information gained to design a culturally sensitive classroom that provides your students with a safe and accepting learning environment.

In summary, as you are planning your classroom, you will need to consider whether you believe that a secondary teacher can and should collaborate with the families of *all* students in the classroom. It is important you remember that although all families should be included in notes, websites, and so forth, so that they can be aware of what is currently happening in your classroom, not all families will need or want extensive involvement with the teacher or the school. Your responsibility is to provide ways in which parents and other family members can collaborate with you at their level of need so that their child can have a successful educational experience as he or she transitions through secondary school and into postsecondary life.

ACTIVITIES

1. You are to conduct a face-to-face interview with an adult who has a disability *or* the parent of a secondary student with a disability, using the questions provided. You will need to write the interview in question and answer (Q & A) format. When conducting the interview use statements such as "Tell me more" or "What else can you think of," to ensure the most complete answers possible. You will then summarize the information and write your reflections of the experience.

Section One: Introduction

Write an opening paragraph telling about the person interviewed. Information should include: age, year in school or grade completed in school, ages and number of siblings and other pertinent family dynamics. You should disclose your relationship to the person (friend, brother, cousin, etc.) if any. You may choose to use first names or initials to protect identities.

Section Two: Q & A for the Adult with a Disability

Would you please describe your disability?
When did you first discover that you had this disability?
How has this disability affected your quality of life?

Have you had problems with accessibility due to your disability? Please explain where and when you have had problems.
What has been the most challenging part of having this disability?
What are some of the most valuable experiences you've had?
What have been your experiences with school personnel?
What have they done that has been most helpful?
What have they done that has been least helpful or maybe even harmful?
What would you want me to do/not do in terms of my interactions with you?
I am just learning about students with disabilities and how to work effectively with them in a classroom. What other information would you like me to know about working with people with special needs?

Section Two: Q & A for the Parent of a Student with a Disability

Would you please describe your child's disability?
How did you learn that your child had a disability?

Do you think you were given adequate information about your child's special needs at the time you were informed of his or her disability?

What information would have been most valuable in helping you adjust to having a child with special needs?

How does your child's disability affect other people in your family and your family life in general?

What has been the most challenging part of having a child with a disability?

What special strengths or abilities do you see in your child?

What have been your experiences with school personnel? What have they done that has been most helpful?

What type of services does your child receive in the school setting?

Has your child made social/academic progress in school? Please explain.

I am just learning about students with disabilities and how to work effectively with them in a classroom. What information would you like me to know about interacting with parents of special needs children?

Section Three: Reflection

Write a summary of what you have learned from the interview, specifically identifying any new information. Tell how you as a teacher will use this information in your future career.

2. Occasionally, there is a book (fiction or nonfiction) that demonstrates the impact disability has on family. Tracey Koretsky wrote such a novel, titled *Ropeless*. This book is available online at http://www .readropeless.com/buy.html. The author is also available to chat with readers and provide a unique view of her book.

REFERENCES

American Academy of Pediatrics (AAP). (2003). Family pediatrics: Report of the task force on the family. *Pediatrics, 111*, 1541–1571.

Bennett, T., Lee, H., & Lueke, B. (1998). Expectations and concerns: What mothers and fathers say about inclusion. *Education and Training in Mental Retardation and Developmental Disabilities, 33*, 108–122.

Bos, H. M. W., van Balen, F., van den Bloom, C., & Sandfort, T. G. (2004). Minority stress, experience of parenthood, and child adjustment in lesbian families. *Journal of Reproductive and Infant Psychology, 22*(4), 291–304.

Bower, L. A. (2008). Standing up for diversity: Lesbian mothers' suggestions for teachers. *Kappa Delta Pi Record, 44*, 181–183.

Brandes, J. A. (2005). Partners with parents. *Intervention in School and Clinic, 41*(1), 52–54.

Cartledge, G., & Kourea, L. (2008). Culturally responsive classrooms for culturally diverse students with and at-risk for disabilities. *Exceptional Children, 74*(3), 351–371.

Caspe, M. (2001). *Family-school-community partnerships: A compilation of professional standards of practice.* Cambridge, MA: Harvard Graduate School of Education, Harvard Family Research Project.

Catsambis, S. (2001). Expanding knowledge of parental involvement in children's secondary education: Connection with high school seniors' academic success. *Social Psychology of Education, 5*(2), 291–304.

Cavkaytar, A., & Pollard, E. (2009). Effectiveness of parent and therapist collaboration program (PTCP) for teaching self-care and domestic skills to individuals with autism. *Education and Training in Developmental Disabilities, 44*(3), 381–395.

Delpit, L. (1995). *Other people's children: Cultural conflict in the classroom.* New York: New Press.

Demo, D. H., & Cox, M. J. (2000). Families with young children: A review of research in the 1990s. *Journal of Marriage and the Family, 62*, 876–895.

Friend, M., & Cook, L. (2007). *Interactions: Collaboration skills for school professionals* (5th ed.). Boston: Pearson.

Gollnick, D., & Chinn, P. (2009). *Multicultural education in a pluralistic society* (8th ed.). Upper Saddle River, NJ: Merrill/Pearson.

Harry, B. (1992). *Cultural diversity, families, and the special education system.* New York: Teachers College Press.

Harry, B. (1995). African American families. In B. Ford, F. Obiakor, & J. Patton (Eds.), *Effective education of African American exceptional learners* (pp. 211–233). Austin, TX: Pro-Ed.

Harry, B. (2002). Trends and issues in serving culturally diverse families of children with disabilities. *Journal of Special Education, 36*(3), 131–138, 147.

Hodapp, R. M., & Krasner, D. V. (1994). Families of children with disabilities: Findings from a national sample of eighth-grade students. *Exceptionality, 5*(2), 71–81.

Howart, A. (1998). Empowering family members to work as partners with professionals. In A. Hilton & R. Ringlaben (Eds.), *Best and promising practices in developmental disabilities*. Austin, TX: Pro-Ed.

Hutton, A. M., & Caron, S. L. (2005). Experiences of families with children with autism in rural New England. *Focus on Autism and Other Developmental Disabilities, 20,* 180–189.

Individual with Disabilities Education Improvement Act of 2004, P.L. 108–446.

Izzo, C. V., Weissberg, R. P., Kasprow, W. J., & Fendrich, M. (1999). A longitudinal assessment of teacher perceptions of parent involvement in children's education and school performance. *American Journal of Community Psychology, 27,* 817–839.

Johnson, K. M., & Lichter, D. T. (2010). Growing diversity among America's children and youth: Spatial and temporal dimensions. *Population and Development Review, 36*(1), 151–176.

Kellough, R. D., & Kellough, N. G. (2008). *Teaching young adolescents: Methods and resources for middle grades teaching*. Upper Saddle River, NJ: Merrill/Pearson Education.

Kubler-Ross, E. (1969). *On death and dying*. New York: Macmillan.

McCubbin, H. I., Thompson, E. A., Thompson, A. I., McCubbin, M. A., & Kaston, A. J. (1993). Culture, ethnicity, and the family: Critical factors in childhood chronic illness and disability. *Pediatrics, 91,* 1063–1070.

Mercier, L. R., & Harold, R. D. (2003). At the interface: Lesbian-parent families and their children's schools. *Children and Schools, 25*(1), 35–47.

Meyer, E. C., & Bailey, D. B. (1993). Family-centered care in early intervention: Community and hospital settings. In J. L. Paul & R. J. Simeonsson (Eds.), *Children with special needs: Family, culture, and society* (2nd ed.). Fort Worth, TX: Harcourt Brace Jovanovich.

Murdick, N. L., Gartin, B. C., & Crabtree, T. (2007). *Special education law* (2nd ed.). Upper Saddle River, NJ: Merrill/Pearson.

Parette, H. P., & Petch-Hogan, B. (2000). Facilitating culturally/linguistically diverse family involvement. *Teaching Exceptional Children, 33,* 4–10.

Paul, J. L., Porter, P. B., & Falk, G. D. (1993). Families of children with disabling conditions. In J. L. Paul & R. J. Simeonsson (Eds.), *Children with special needs: Family, culture, and society* (2nd ed.). Fort Worth, TX: Harcourt Brace Jovanovich.

Pawelski, J. G., Perrin, E. C., Foy, J. M., Allen, C. E., Crawford, J. E., Del Monte, M., Kaufman, M.,

Klein, J. D., Smith, K., Springer, S., Tanner, J. L., & Vickers, D. L. (2006). The effects of marriage, civil union, and domestic partnership laws on the health and well-being of children. *Pediatrics, 118,* 349–364.

Perrin, E. C. (2002). Technical report: Coparent or second-parent adoption by same-sex parent. *Pediatrics, 109,* 341–344.

Poston, D., Turnbull, A., Park, J., Mannan, H., Marquis, J., & Wang, M. (2003). Family quality of life: A qualitative inquiry. *Mental Retardation, 41*(5), 313–328.

Prater, M. A., & Dyches, T. T. (2008). *Teaching about disabilities through children's literature*. Westport, CT: Libraries Unlimited.

Quintero, N., & McIntyre, L. L. (2010). Sibling adjustment and maternal well-being: An examination of families with and without a child with an autism spectrum disorder. *Focus on Autism and Other Developmental Disabilities, 25*(1), 37–46.

Ray, J. A. (2005). Family-friendly teachers: Tips for working with diverse families. *Kappa Delta Pi Record, 41*(2), 72–76.

Ray, J. A., & Gregory, R. (2001, Winter). School experiences of the children of lesbian and gay parents. *Family Matters, 59,* 28–34.

Robinson-Zanartu, C. (1996). Serving Native American children and families: Considering cultural variables. *Language, Speech, and Hearing Services in Schools, 27,* 373–384.

Sailor, D. H. (2004). *Supporting children in their home, school, and community*. Boston: Pearson/Allyn & Bacon.

Smith, C. (1993). Cultural sensitivity in working with children and families. In J. L. Paul & R. J. Simeonsson (Eds.), *Children with special needs: Family, culture, and society* (2nd ed., pp. 113–121). Fort Worth, TX: Harcourt Brace Jovanovich.

Smith, M., Jaffe-Gill, E., & Segal, J. (2009). Coping with grieving and loss: Support for grieving and bereavement. Retrieved from: http://www.helpguide.org/mental/grief_loss.htm

Smith, T. E. C., Gartin, B. C., Murdick, N. L., & Hilton, A. (2006). *Families and children with special needs*. Upper Saddle River, NJ: Pearson.

Smith, T. E. C., Polloway, E. A., Patton, J. R., & Dowdy, C. A.(2012). *Teaching students with special needs in inclusive settings* (6th ed.). Upper Saddle River, NJ: Merrill/Pearson.

Stewart, J. (1977). Unique problems of handicapped Native Americans. In *The White House Conference on Handicapped Individuals* (Vol. 1, pp. 438–444). Washington, DC: U.S. Government Printing Office.

Sui-Cho, E. H., & Willms, J. D. (1996). Effects of parental involvement on eighth-grade achievement. *Sociology of Education, 69,* 126–141.

Summers, J. A., Hoffman, L., Marquis, J., Turnbull, A., Poston, D., & Nelson, L. L. (2005). Measuring the quality of family-professional partnerships in special education services. *Exceptional Children, 72*(1), 65–81.

Taylor, R. L., Smiley, L. R., & Richards, S. B. (2009). *Exceptional students: Preparing for the 21st century.* Boston: McGraw-Hill Higher Education.

Turnbull, A., Turnbull, H., Erwin, E., & Soodak, L. (2010). *Families, professionals, and exceptionality: Positive outcome through partnerships and trust* (5th ed.). Upper Saddle River, NJ: Merrill/Pearson.

Turnbull, A., Turnbull, H., & Wehmeyer, M. L. (2010). *Exceptional lives: Special education in today's schools* (6th ed.). Upper Saddle River, NJ: Merrill.

Turnbull, A. P., & Turnbull, H. R. (2001). *Families, professionals, and exceptionalities: Collaborating for empowerment* (4th ed.). Upper Saddle River, NJ: Merrill/Prentice Hall.

U.S. Census Bureau. (2004). *Statistical Abstract of the United States: 2004.* Washington, DC: Author.

Vaughn, S., Bos, C. S., & Schumm, J. S. (1997). *Teaching mainstreamed, diverse, and at-risk students.* Boston: Allyn & Bacon.

Welch, M. (2000). Collaboration as a tool for inclusion. In S. E. Wade (Ed.), *Inclusive education: A casebook and readings for prospective and practicing teachers* (pp. 71–96). Mahwah, NJ: Erlbaum.

6

Classroom Management and Adolescents with Disabilities

Study Questions

1. Define classroom management and explain how it can impact student learning.

2. Give examples of research-based organizational structures that support learning in the following areas: classroom space, seating arrangements, classroom climate, and classroom rules and procedures.

3. Explain how the planning and conducting of instruction can impact classroom management.

4. Give examples of research-based principles impacting the planning and implementation of extra space instruction in the following areas: academic learning time, available instructional time, selection of instructional grouping, and selection of instructional strategies.

INTRODUCTION

Managing classrooms to facilitate effective learning is a challenge for all educators. Frequently, problems with classroom management skills are the primary reason many teachers give for leaving the field of teaching. Unlike elementary classrooms, where teachers typically work with the same group of 20 to 30 students for the entire school day, at the secondary level teachers usually teach different students for each period of the day, meaning that they may have more than 100 different students on a daily basis. Although classroom management is a challenge for all teachers, the large number of students taught in secondary classrooms and the wide range of students' skills further complicate effective classroom management. Secondary teachers have a primary role of teaching specific content, such as history, biology, or English. Without good classroom management skills it may be very difficult for teachers to focus on teaching this content and for students to learn the content. Classroom management supports a positive classroom environment where teachers can be more effective teachers and students can learn more efficiently.

Classroom management is a general term that incorporates a number of different components; it is not simply disciplining students. Classroom management includes the physical organization of the classroom, appropriate and specific rules and procedures, instructional plans, and methods for addressing both positive and negative student behaviors. In effectively managed classrooms, teachers not only understand the different classroom conditions and student behaviors important for creating positive learning environments, but they also focus on creating these conditions (Emmer, Evertson, & Worsham, 2006).

COMPONENTS OF CLASSROOM MANAGEMENT

Classroom management includes multiple components. In order for teachers to effectively implement an effective classroom management program they must address each of these different components. Figure 6.1 depicts numerous components included in a comprehensive classroom model.

Organization of Classroom Space

According to some researchers, the organization of the space where learning occurs is where teachers should begin to develop an effective classroom management program (Lang, 2001; Sommer, 1977; Taylor-Green, Brown, Nelson, & Longton, 1997). Early research indicated that

```
Organization of Classroom Space
        Furniture Arrangement
        Lighting
        Color Scheme and Decorations
        Equipment
        Equipment Storage
Seating Arrangement
        Desk Arrangement
        Access to Content
Classroom Climate
Classroom Norms
        Classroom Rules
        Classroom Procedures
Planning and Conducting Instruction
        Content
        Learning and Instructional Time
        Instructional Strategies
```

FIGURE 6.1 ● Components of Classroom Management

student behaviors are more appropriate when the physical arrangement of the classroom supports instructional expectations (Evans & Lowell, 1979; Weinstein, 1977; Weinstein, 1979). The organization of the physical environment includes the furniture arrangement, lighting, color scheme and decorations, equipment and its storage, and cleanliness. Classrooms should be organized with the overall goal of creating a space where learning can be maximized. Before other facets of classroom organization, such as procedures and instructional methods can be developed, decisions concerning the organization of the physical space must be made (Bonus & Riordan, 1998).

Seating Arrangement

The seating arrangement and workspaces for students are important components of classroom organization, as well. In determining these aspects of classroom organization, the age and grade of students, content to be learned, and learning activities should all be considered. For example, a word-processing classroom might have tables that are bolted to the floor and facing the teacher in order to reduce the possibility of damaging the equipment. A political science classroom, on the other hand, might have desks or tables that can be moved to promote discussion. Teachers who use cooperative learning activities want to ensure that the classroom arrangement facilitates this instructional approach.

The most common desk arrangement in middle and secondary schools consists of rows, either vertical or horizontal, facing the teacher. This arrangement is often called traditional seating or theater seating (Duplass, 2006). Other types of seating arrangements include round table seating (desks in a circle around the perimeter of the room but facing a central focus), group seating (desks in groups of four or five), half-circle seating (desks facing a central point but in one or two curved rows) and paired seating, also known as desk tops together (pairs of desks facing each other).

The arrangement of desks and workspaces can have a significant impact on student behavior, learning, and social interactions. For example, it has been determined that students who are in a classroom using the traditional seating arrangement learn and participate more when they are seated in the "action zone," which is the front or middle rows (McCrosky & McVetta,

1978; Wulf, 1977). Researchers have also found that teachers tend to communicate and react more favorably to students within those areas, without even realizing it (Daly & Suite, 1981; Ridling, 1994). Teachers should therefore evaluate the type of activities they use as well as the amount of student–student and student–teacher interactions that are desired for particular classrooms. In other words, desks and other workstations should be arranged to support the type of instructional activities that are planned for the class, such as lecture, cooperative learning groups, independent work seating, or center seating.

The arrangement of student seating not only impacts instruction but also influences student empowerment. Student empowerment is involved in seating arrangements when students determine where they sit. The question teachers often ask is whether student seat assignments should be by student choice or by teacher assignment. The majority of research in this area was completed during the 1970s and 1980s, and found that students who self-selected their own seating were more relaxed and participatory than those whose seating was assigned by teachers (Dykman & Reis, 1979; Totusek & Staton-Spicer, 1982).

While students' age and grade are important factors in decisions about classroom arrangement, so too are the content areas and planned activities. There are several additional issues that should be taken into consideration when determining classroom arrangements. These include the following:

1. Independent work areas should be located away from the high-traffic and congested areas in the room (Emmer, Evertson, & Worsham, 2003).
2. Furniture and equipment should be placed so that there is easy access to all areas of the room (Emmer et al., 2003; Shores, Gunter, & Jack, 1993).
3. Teachers should have a clear view of all students (Shores et al., 1993).
4. Teachers should have access to all students (Shores et al., 1993).
5. Students should have a clear view of the teacher, boards, materials, projector screens, or any items used during instruction (Horne-Martin, 2002; Weinstein, 2007).

Classroom Climate

The classroom "climate" is the fusion of the physical organization with the social organization of the classroom. The social organization of classrooms, which includes the classroom ambiance, has been considered an important facet of organization for learning since the Maslow and Minz (1956) study of people's interactions in different types of spaces. That particular study indicated that individuals feel better and work better when they are in an environment that is clean, comfortable, and attractive. Educators need to take this into consideration when designing classroom space, considering the "feel" as well as the "look" of the classroom environment, because both factors impact student behavior (Borich, 2004).

Classroom Norms

In addition to the physical organization and classroom climate, it is important for teachers to identify the classroom norms that will be used in making decisions on how the class works together to learn. These classroom norms, or principles, go beyond the behavioral issues and establish a set of explicit beliefs that are translated into behaviors, attitudes, and rewards (Anderson, 1981; Lenz & Deshler, 2004). In his 1970 seminal research examining the differences in orderly and disorderly classrooms, Kounin found that teachers in orderly classrooms communicated their expectations of classroom behavior to their students better than teachers in classrooms where student behavior was not as good. Established expectations of behavior within the classroom are known as rules and procedures (Emmer et al., 2006;

Evertson & Emmer, 1982). *Rules* are written to clarify teacher and school expectations of behavior. *Procedures*, also known as routines, are used to indicate expectations for a specific activity as opposed to the general classroom behavioral expectations indicated in a set of rules. Procedures allow classrooms to run efficiently, thereby saving time that can be used for instructional activities. Good teachers establish, teach, and reinforce both rules and procedures (Babkie, 2006; Brophy & Good, 1986; Evertson, 1985).

Developing Classroom Rules and Procedures

Classroom rules are defined as the "general expectations or standards for classroom conduct" (Good & Brophy, 2008, p. 77) and are often called "class policies" or "class guidelines" (Emmer et al., 2006). Research has indicated that for classroom rules to be useful in communicating expectations and be followed by students, they should be written in a positive format. Additionally, they should be stated in a clear, straightforward manner (Bicard, 2000; Boonstrum, 1991; Emmer et al., 2006; Good & Brophy, 2008).

In many classrooms, teachers formalize their expectations for appropriate behavior and subsequent learning success by establishing a set of rules with accompanying *procedures*. Procedures are routines students follow when completing various classroom activities. Rules, when accompanied with procedures, make it clear to students exactly what behaviors are expected. Expectations are critical in good classroom management; the better the students' understanding of expectations, the more likely the classroom will be an orderly learning environment.

Involving students in the development of classroom rules and procedures gives students ownership of the expected behaviors as well as responsibility for following the rules and procedures (Salend & Sylvestre, 2005). Involving students in rule preparation should begin early in the year with a discussion of the purpose for rules and their relationship to successful learning. After classroom rules and procedures are established, they must be explicitly taught to all students. Steps in the development and implementation of rules and procedures are included in Table 6.1.

TABLE 6.1 ● Steps to Teach Rules and Procedures

Define terms clearly	Do not use ambiguous rules and procedures. Describe the terms used in rules and procedures and ask questions to ensure that all students understand.
Provide examples	Give examples of appropriately following rules and procedures. Use positive examples of how rules and procedures are followed correctly rather than examples of how rules and procedures are not followed.
Discuss rationale for rules and procedures	Explain the rationale for the rules and procedures. Students are likely to follow rules and procedures if they understand the reasons for them.
Discuss consequences	Explain the consequences when rules and procedures are not followed.
Teach routines	Discuss routines that must be followed, especially for specific activities such as labs and other classes where traditional instruction does not occur. Example, when using cooperative learning groups, what are the rules and procedures that should be followed?

PLANNING AND CONDUCTING INSTRUCTION

In addition to identifying and delineating rules and procedures, it is essential that teachers specifically plan the instructional content that will be presented and implement instruction to meet the needs of students in the class. Although this topic may not seem related to classroom management, the teachers' classroom management skills impact their efficient use of instructional time and therefore successful learning by students (Duplass, 2006). If teachers do not have a sound instructional plan, having rules and procedures in place may be unimportant. Inappropriate student behaviors, not to mention a lack of learning, often occur when students are not instructionally challenged. If the instruction is at an inappropriate level for students or if it is presented in a way that is not motivating, efficient learning will not occur and inappropriate behaviors are likely (Kerr & Nelson, 2006).

Planning for instruction includes several steps. First, teachers must decide on the content to be covered and the amount of time for the instruction. With student diversity becoming greater, classes may include students with a wide range of academic skills. Therefore, teachers must select the content to be taught taking into consideration this variability. Due to benchmark tests and state standards, content is frequently set by educational agencies. If the content is prescribed, teachers need to focus more on the delivery of the content to keep students engaged.

Learning and Instructional Time

Following determination of the content, teachers need to determine how much time they will have to teach a particular topic. The amount of instructional time is an important variable because it directly impacts student learning (Carroll, 1963). In addition to the allocation of instructional time, the amount of time in which students are actively engaged in the learning process is important. Student's active time on task has been called "engaged time" or "academic learning time (ALT)," and refers to the amount of time students are successfully involved with the content (Smith, 2000; Weinstein, 2007). The actual amount of time is impacted by a variety of factors, including:

- Actual time allocated to the class
- Motivation of students
- Efficiency of instruction
- Social interactions of students
- Inappropriate behaviors

During the school day, the amount of time middle and high school teachers have with students in a particular class is limited. Although elementary school teachers allot specific amounts of time as content specific, these time allotments are not as rigidly defined as those in middle and secondary schools where the day is typically divided into 50-minute periods. In an effort to address this issue of time constraint, some secondary schools have allotted time differently using block schedules of 80- or 90-minute segments or instituting alternating-day schedules to allow more time for teachers to instruct their students (Fleming, Olenn, Schoenstein, & Eineder, 1997). Unfortunately, an analysis of results from research studies indicated mixed results on the impact of block scheduling on learning for students (Mattox, Hancock, & Queen, 2005; Nichols, 2005; Zepeda & Mayers, 2006). These results simply show that extending the amount of time available for instruction does not ensure that active learning time will increase. The key is teachers' incorporating active learning into in-depth planning of the instructional milieu.

TABLE 6.2 ● Summary of Instructional Strategies

SMALL GROUP INSTRUCTION

Small group instruction usually means five or fewer students learning together (Kellough & Kellough, 2008). Research indicates that such small group instruction can result in high levels of academic success for students (Smith, 2000; Walters, 2000). In some cases, small group learning, using "breakout sessions," may be used in an informal manner to complement whole class instruction.

COOPERATIVE LEARNING

Cooperative learning is "a successful teaching strategy in which small teams, each with students of different levels of ability, use a variety of learning activities to improve their understanding of a subject" (*Cooperative Learning*, n.d.). There are four research-based principles of cooperative learning (Johnson & Johnson, 1999; Slavin, 1995). These include:
- *Heterogeneous*—groups represent various ability levels.
- *Group accountability*—the group is responsible for achieving the goal.
- *Positive interdependence*—cooperative learning must be planned so that each individual must work with the others for the goal to be achieved.
- *Individual accountability*—each team member must be held individually accountable for his or her own actions in progressing toward the assigned activity goal.

DIFFERENTIATED INSTRUCTION

Differentiated instruction is described as a philosophy that takes into consideration students' strengths, interests, skills, and readiness in instructional planning and delivery. Five elements of differentiated instruction include: content, process, products, affect, and learning environment.

After planning for instruction, the actual delivery of instruction is an important element in classroom management. There are numerous instructional techniques teachers can use to increase student engagement and learning. These include:

- Small group instruction
- Cooperative learning
- Differentiated instruction

Table 6.2 summarizes these instructional strategies. The specific strategies used are unimportant. The critical factor for teachers is to utilize a variety of techniques to increase student engagement and learning.

MAINTAINING APPROPRIATE BEHAVIORS

While rules and procedures, physical organization of the classroom, instructional content, and how students are grouped for instruction are all critical elements in classroom management, the most critical component is the ability of teachers to establish and maintain appropriate behaviors. In order to maintain effective learning environments, teachers must incorporate proactive, positive practices for maintaining appropriate behaviors. In addition, teachers need to recognize that preventing inappropriate behaviors by emphasizing positive behavioral interventions is more effective for managing student behaviors than reacting to inappropriate behaviors (Algozzine & Kay, 2002).

Positive Behavioral Supports

One method that focuses on positive interventions is *positive behavioral supports* (PBS). This preventive approach is supported in the 2004 reauthorization of the Individuals with Disabilities Education Improvement Act. IDEA requires schools to consider the use of positive behavioral supports in programs for students with disabilities. The use of PBS is an "application of a behaviorally based systems approach to enhancing the capacity of schools, families, and communities to design effective environments that improve the fit or link between research-validated practices and the environments in which teaching and learning occur" (U.S. Department of Education [USDOE], 2000, p. III-8). Specifically, positive behavioral supports use proactive methods including positive reinforcement, prompts, and cues to elicit appropriate behavior in specific situations (Stormont, Lewis, & Beckner, 2005).

Although PBS was originally developed for use with students with severe behavior problems, it has been found to be successful in teaching appropriate behavior responses to students with milder behavioral issues (Marquis et al., 2000). According to Henley (2006, p. 213):

> Proactive behavioral supports are derived from an analysis of student behaviors and the classroom dynamics that influence these behaviors. When teachers analyze events that trigger problem behaviors, they can adjust classroom variables to promote constructive behavior. . . . Rather than addressing deficits in student behavior, proactive behavioral supports promote the idea of looking for strengths. Building on individual capacity is the surest path to achieving positive change.

Schoolwide Positive Behavioral Supports

As a result of teachers successfully using positive behavioral supports in inclusive classrooms with students who have behavioral problems, some schools have begun to expand the model schoolwide. Using positive behavioral supports in an entire school is called *schoolwide positive behavioral supports* (SWPBS), and is described as "a systematic and effective approach for improving student behavior broadly across school environments" (Freeman et al., 2006, p. 4). It is a systems level approach that can be used by school personnel to implement practices that meet the needs of all students in the school, not just those with disabilities (Turnbull et al., 2002). SWPBS is based on several core themes, including (Freeman et al., 2006):

A. The social culture of the whole school should provide a foundation for student success.
B. Prevention of behavioral problems should be emphasized instead of reaction to behavioral incidents.
C. The teaching of appropriate social and behavioral skills is essential.
D. All staff should be involved in active data collection.
E. Behavior support practices should be developed and implemented using a three-tiered continuum of supports.

In addition, SWPBS incorporates an array of specific procedures for school personnel to use, including (1) an emphasis on systems change that supports the use of effective educational practices by all teachers and other personnel who are involved (Freeman et al., 2006); (2) a continuum of supports to match educational interventions with student needs (Carr et al., 2002); (3) a team-based strategy development and implementation; (4) schoolwide language concerning educational practice and interventions; and (5) a common vision for addressing the academic, behavioral, and social needs of all the children (Horner, Sugai, Todd, & Lewis-Palmer, 2005; Liaupsin, Jolivette, & Scott, 2004).

Empowering Students

Many researchers and educators believe that disruptive and inappropriate student behaviors, especially at the middle and secondary school levels, are actually attempts by students to acquire some control over their own lives (Curwin & Mendler, 1988). Early research by Kounin (1970) indicated that good classroom managers actually involved students in the management of their own behaviors before inappropriate behaviors could occur, a form of student empowerment. Empowering students gives them some control over their lives and the learning process itself (Larrivee, 2005) and can motivate students to both learn and accept responsibility for their own actions (Jolivette, Wehby, Canale, & Massey, 2001). Student involvement can take the form of participation in classroom rule development, identification of rewards for completion of work and the exhibition of appropriate behaviors, and identification of consequences for noncompletion of work and the exhibition of inappropriate behaviors (Emmer et al., 2006). Student empowerment can also take the forms of self-instruction, self-reinforcement, time management (see Chapter 9), and self-determination (see Chapter 13).

SIDE BAR

6.1 The Story of Sophia

Sophia, a 12-year-old who is in the sixth grade, has learning disabilities in the area of reading and written communication. Her family came to the United States from Guatemala before she was born. Spanish is spoken as the primary language in her home. She is the youngest of six children and one of the three children born in the United States. Sophia's teacher, Ms. Jordan, was concerned that as Sophia transitioned to the upper secondary grades she might encounter more academic difficulties because of her disabilities. During study times, Sophia is highly distractible. In the past, it was thought that Sophia might have ADHD, but the diagnosis was never confirmed. Therefore, Ms. Jordan wanted to improve the effectiveness of Sophia's study time by developing her self-monitoring skills. She wanted to develop a self-monitoring plan that Sophia could use both at school and at home.

THE ORIGINAL BIP. The goal of the behavioral intervention plan was for Sophia to learn how to do her homework more effectively—that is, quickly and correctly. Sophia was to use a kitchen timer to time how long she spends on her homework. Ms. Jordan gave the family a copy of a checklist that she and Sophia had developed together. It was written in both English and Spanish and contained only two questions: (1) Did you work the entire time without stopping? and (2) How much work did you complete? Sophia was to set the timer at 5 minutes. When the timer sounded, she was to answer the questions and then walk once around the kitchen stretching. She was to continue this procedure until

her homework was completed. At the end of the homework session, a family member signed the paper. The next day Sophia was to return the signed form to Ms. Jordan, and they would discuss Sophia's progress. During study times at school, Ms. Jordan would use the same timer and as Sophia improved in her concentration, the time would be lengthened to the goal of 15 minutes without a break.

RESULTS OF THE INTERVENTION. Sophia's family members were committed to Sophia's success in school. Sophia worked nightly at the kitchen table, used the timer, and within the first week extended the time to 15 minutes without a break. Sophia was completing all of her assigned homework nightly. At school she followed the same procedure, but encountered more difficulty with work completion. Within the first week she was working for an uninterrupted 15 minutes, but percentage of work completion remained below 50%. The graphs below indicate the improvement in completion but it remained at an unacceptable level. Three weeks passed with progress, but the classroom teacher was concerned that the rate of progress was slow.

THE NEXT STEP. During the last 3 weeks, Ms. Jordan has sent notes to the family on Sophia's progress. Now Ms. Jordan sent a note to the family stating that Sophia was improving, but perhaps more could be done to help her complete the schoolwork. The teacher arranged for a second meeting with the family, but also asked the special education teacher, Mrs. Ramos, to attend. The family

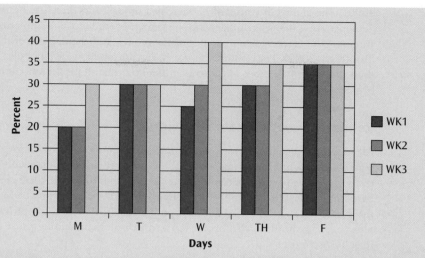

agreed to come, as did Sophia and Mrs. Ramos. The teacher hoped that Mrs. Ramos could provide some suggestions concerning how to improve Sophia's skills, particularly in reading since Sophia had a diagnosed learning disability in reading and written communication.

THE SECOND MEETING. At the second meeting in the school conference room, Sophia acted as hostess, offering refreshments to the family, Mrs. Ramos, and Ms. Jordan. Ms. Jordan reviewed the plan and told the group of the progress that Sophia had made. Ms. Jordan stressed the fact that Sophia had improved her focus so much that the group should consider that objective met. When working at home Sophia was completing all her work so Ms. Jordan wanted to know how Sophia was able to do that every night. Sophia said that she sat at the table until the work was complete. She also said that if she had trouble reading or understanding what she was reading, one of her siblings would explain it to her. Her mother and father nodded in agreement. Her father said, "All the children help one another. It is the way our family does its work." Ms. Jordan had charts showing Sophia's progress for the last 3 weeks for her at-school completion rate.

Ms. Jordan said that the bar graph showed that Sophia had improved in her work completion rate, but she wanted

to know what things interfered with Sophia completing her assignments. Sophia said that she didn't have enough time. She said that she read slower than her classmates and that the books were sometimes hard to understand. Mrs. Ramos asked about the reading level of the books and assignments. She suggested that Sophia be given a prepared study guide to help her know what was important about the assignments and to focus the class assignments on the important concepts being taught. This change might help to reduce the time necessary for Sophia to complete her class work. Sophia's parents were concerned that the teachers were letting Sophia "get by with something." However, both teachers reassured them that Sophia would be expected to learn the same content as the other students. The change would mean that Sophia would have materials based on her reading level. Then, her brother John said that reading was important and that Sophia needed to learn to read better. The teachers agreed, although Sophia looked concerned. Ms. Jordan asked if the teachers could have 3 weeks to try the new plan of modifying the reading materials. During this time, Mrs. Ramos would give Sophia some reading tests and see where Sophia needed extra reading help. The family agreed to meet again in 4 weeks.

Modeling Appropriate Behaviors

Once classroom rules have been designed, teachers and students should model the appropriate behaviors, attitudes, values, and social responses. Modeling appropriate behaviors is a form of behavioral demonstration or imitation to prompt the exhibition of the requisite appropriate behavior (Henley, 2006). Modeling may be demonstrated by teachers, other students, someone outside the classroom, or by video self-modeling (Alberto & Troutman,

2009). The choice of who will be seen as a model, and therefore be the most effective for demonstrating the behavior, depends on the age of students, the similarity of the model to the students, the perceived competence of the model, and the prestige of the model (Alberto & Troutman, 2009). For example, if your behavior model were a popular student in the class, then that person is more likely to be influential than a model who is not socially accepted by peers.

Reinforcing Appropriate Behaviors

All students act and behave appropriately some time each day. Unfortunately, although research has shown that appropriate behaviors are likely to be repeated and increased when positively recognized by teachers and other significant individuals (Beaman & Wheldall, 2000; Zirpoli, 2005), teachers and others often ignore these behaviors because the behaviors are the preferred, expected behaviors (Zirpoli, 2005). In order for appropriate behaviors to be repeated, they must be reinforced. Ignored behaviors, including those that are appropriate, may be discontinued.

Positive reinforcement is the provision of a rewarding consequence (a reinforcer) following the target behavior. Positive reinforcement increases the likelihood that the behavior it follows will be repeated (Alberto & Troutman, 2009). As a result, one way to increase desired behaviors is to follow that behavior with a positive reinforcer. *Reinforcers*, the consequences for behaviors, fall into two classes: primary reinforcers and secondary reinforcers.

Primary reinforcers are directly reinforcing to most individuals. Primary reinforcers do not represent the reinforcement—they are the reinforcement. Examples of primary reinforcers include edibles, such as candy or popcorn, and sensory items, such as listening to music on headphones or using sensory brushes (Maag, 2004). Primary reinforcers are frequently used with young children or individuals who are just learning a particular behavior or skill. Individuals with cognitive impairments also respond well to primary reinforcers.

Secondary reinforcers are also known as conditioned reinforcers. They do not provide any direct reinforcement, but are associated with items that are reinforcing. Secondary reinforcers are of four types: tangible items (badges, posters, stickers), privileges or activities (class responsibilities, activity or homework exceptions), generalized items (tokens, grades, points, extra credits), and social opportunities (social time, seating arrangements, teacher or friend proximity, expressions of support) (Alberto & Troutman, 2009). Table 6.3 lists examples of primary and secondary reinforcers.

According to Alberto and Troutman (2009), three things must occur in order for teachers to successfully use positive reinforcement. *First*, the reinforcer selected must be considered desirable by the students. If the reinforcer is not desirable it will not have the desired effect of increasing the behavior. Reinforcement occurs naturally in nature as well as in educational settings, but whether the reinforcement is considered to be positive or aversive depends on the individual.

The *second* factor that must be present is the manner in which the reinforcer is presented, specifically the timing of the reinforcing item or event following the desired behavior. For a relationship to become established between the behavior and the reinforcer, the reinforcer must be presented immediately after the behavior's occurrence. This *immediacy requirement* is one of the most difficult for teachers to meet. Busy classrooms and other distractions often result in teachers forgetting or delaying the reinforcement and thereby diminishing its impact.

The *third* factor that must be present is that of contingency. In other words, the receipt of the reinforcement is based upon (that is, contingent on) the desired behavior. This *contingency* relationship is based on the *Premack principle* that "makes students' preferred behavior

TABLE 6.3 ● Examples of Primary and Secondary Reinforcers

PRIMARY REINFORCERS	SECONDARY REINFORCERS
Food	Social Stimuli
Liquids	Opportunity to Engage in Preferred Activities such as:
Sleep	Make a special project
Shelter	View a video
Sex	Work with art supplies
Sensory Reinforcers such as:	Tangible Reinforcers such as:
Music	Awards
Colored lights	Posters of Rock or Sport Stars
Sweet smells	Video Games
Sharp or sweet tastes	Privileges such as:
Soft or furry textures	Homework reduction
Swings or rockers	Access to computers
	Access to music
	Access to library
	Access to gym
	Free time
	Excused from test

Source: Adapted from P. A. Alberto and A. C. Troutman, 2009, *Applied Behavior Analysis for Teachers* (8th ed.). Upper Saddle River, NJ: Merrill/Pearson.

dependent on the occurrence of a less preferred behavior in order to increase the preferred behavior" (Larrivee, 2005, p. 187). An example of the Premack principle is: "When your assignments are completed, you can use the class computer." This contingency requirement establishes a relationship between the behavior and the reinforcer.

DECREASING INAPPROPRIATE BEHAVIORS

Although preventive methods are the best approach to classroom management, there are times when inappropriate behaviors occur and teachers have to focus their efforts on decreasing behaviors. There are times when teachers have to respond to student behavior that may be aggressive, abusive, or disruptive to learning and teaching (Larrivee, 2005). In order for teachers to deal effectively with these behaviors, they must be prepared to use long-term strategies, not simply short-term interventions sometimes known as "cease and desist" methods. When identifying effective practices to decrease inappropriate behaviors, Weinstein (2007, p. 314) proposes five principles to guide the teacher's choice:

1. Disciplinary strategies must be consistent with the goal of creating a safe, caring classroom environment.
2. Keep the instructional program going with a minimum of disruption.
3. Whether or not a particular action constitutes misbehavior depends on the context in which it occurs.
4. Match the severity of the disciplinary strategy with the misbehavior you are trying to eliminate.
5. Be "culturally responsive," because differences in norms, values, and styles of communication can have a direct effect on student behavior.

Responding to Minor Inattention and Misbehavior

Due to the nature of adolescence, many of the misbehaviors that occur in middle and secondary classrooms can be classified as minor inattention or minor misbehaviors. When dealing with these types of problems, the goal for teachers is to eliminate the behaviors quickly so that there are limited distractions for the rest of the class (Good & Brophy, 2008). Teachers should therefore choose methods that will be effective and redirected before the behavior escalates. To be successful at this level of behavior management, teachers must practice classroom monitoring consistently—that is, they should display "withitness," or the ability to teach and monitor the room at the same time (Duplass, 2006; Kounin, 1970).

Changing the classroom environment is one of the simplest things teachers can do to change behaviors. Changing the classroom environment can decrease chronic behavior problems, prevent behavior problems for students who are at risk, and allow children with minimal or no problem behavior to access learning without interruption (Guardino & Fullerton, 2010, p. 9). Guardino and Fullerton (2010) describe three steps to change classroom environments: observing the classroom to determine which behaviors need to be changed; modifying the environment based on the observations; and following up by evaluating the impact of the changes. Figure 6.2 provides a description of each of these steps.

Cues and *redirection* are two methods that can be used for refocusing students on appropriate learning tasks. These methods "do not give undue attention to the misbehavior and they do not interfere with the flow of instructional activity" (Emmer et al., 2006, p. 173). They allow for minimal actions from teachers that do not impede instruction. *Redirection* can occur through the use of nonverbal communication. Specific actions might include (Emmer et al., 2006; Good & Brophy, 2008; Weinstein, 2007):

- Eye contact (the "teacher look")
- Gestures (hand signals signifying stop)
- Physical proximity (walking or standing near the student or students)
- Verbal communication such as name dropping (saying the student's name or using the student's name in the instruction)
- Response requests (calling on the student to respond to a lesson item)

It may be suggested that a physical tap or touch on the shoulder or head of the student is an appropriate method for redirecting behaviors. However, this is not considered an appropriate action in middle and secondary schools. When using any form of redirection, teachers should not ask questions about the behavior or use any form of threat. The purpose should simply be to get students back on task (Good & Brophy, 2008).

In some instances, misbehaviors may occur only briefly or be fairly unobtrusive. In such cases, teachers may create more disruptions when they take certain actions than when they simply ignore the behavior. When choosing to ignore in these situations, teachers need to monitor the classroom closely and judge whether the behavior is becoming more intense or occurring more frequently (Weinstein, 2007).

Extinction is different from the ignoring just described. It is "the discontinuation or withholding of the reinforcer of a behavior that has previously been reinforcing the behavior" (Walker, Shea, & Bauer, 2007, p. 179). This is a useful method but its success is dependent on the teacher's ability to identify the reinforcer–behavior relationship and to consistently remove that reinforcer from the situation for a sufficient period of time. For example, if students are reinforced when they get out of their seat by the teacher telling them to sit down (which brings attention to the student), ignoring the students, which results in their not getting the attention, could result in the extinction of the inappropriate behavior. When using this method, of course, teachers must ensure that withholding the reinforcer does not result in the behavior

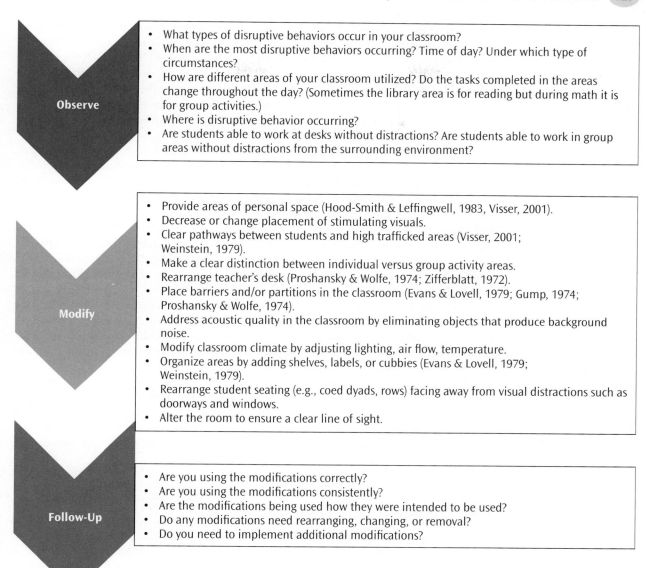

Observe
- What types of disruptive behaviors occur in your classroom?
- When are the most disruptive behaviors occurring? Time of day? Under which type of circumstances?
- How are different areas of your classroom utilized? Do the tasks completed in the areas change throughout the day? (Sometimes the library area is for reading but during math it is for group activities.)
- Where is disruptive behavior occurring?
- Are students able to work at desks without distractions? Are students able to work in group areas without distractions from the surrounding environment?

Modify
- Provide areas of personal space (Hood-Smith & Leffingwell, 1983, Visser, 2001).
- Decrease or change placement of stimulating visuals.
- Clear pathways between students and high trafficked areas (Visser, 2001; Weinstein, 1979).
- Make a clear distinction between individual versus group activity areas.
- Rearrange teacher's desk (Proshansky & Wolfe, 1974; Zifferblatt, 1972).
- Place barriers and/or partitions in the classroom (Evans & Lovell, 1979; Gump, 1974; Proshansky & Wolfe, 1974).
- Address acoustic quality in the classroom by eliminating objects that produce background noise.
- Modify classroom climate by adjusting lighting, air flow, temperature.
- Organize areas by adding shelves, labels, or cubbies (Evans & Lovell, 1979; Weinstein, 1979).
- Rearrange student seating (e.g., coed dyads, rows) facing away from visual distractions such as doorways and windows.
- Alter the room to ensure a clear line of sight.

Follow-Up
- Are you using the modifications correctly?
- Are you using the modifications consistently?
- Are the modifications being used how they were intended to be used?
- Do any modifications need rearranging, changing, or removal?
- Do you need to implement additional modifications?

FIGURE 6.2 ● Steps to Changing Classroom Environment

Source: From "Changing Behaviors by Changing the Classroom Environment," by C. A. Guardino and E. Fullerton, 2010, *Teaching Exceptional Children, 42,* 8–13.

escalating to the point where instruction cannot occur. In middle level or secondary classrooms, control over reinforcement (particularly those from attention-seeking behaviors) is difficult if not impossible (Alberto & Troutman, 2009; Chance, 1998).

When minor misbehaviors continue or escalate to a more serious level, teachers must take actions to limit the behaviors. One way is to implement consequences for such behaviors. *Consequences of rule violations* are often identified at the time class rules and procedures are designed. In some instances, violations of schoolwide rules and specific consequences are stated in the school policy. When possible, consequences should be natural, or logical consequences of the behavior (Weinstein, 2007). *Natural consequences* are "based on the natural flow of events, taking place without teacher intervention" (Larrivee, 2005, p. 201). An example of a natural consequence would be students not getting to go on a field trip because they arrive at school late. *Logical consequences*, on the other hand, only occur as a result of teacher interventions, although they should be related to the behavior (Weinstein, 2007). Teachers should never use consequences that are arbitrary and not clearly related to the behavior.

One set of consequential methods is known as the *differential reinforcement strategies*, or as positive reductive strategies (Walker et al., 2007). This set of methods is "the process of reinforcing an appropriate behavior in the presence of one stimulus and, simultaneously, not reinforcing an inappropriate behavior in the presence of another stimulus" (p. 176). The use of differential reinforcements is easy to begin and maintain by teachers, aides, therapists, and others associated with the student (Gongola & Daddario, 2010). There are four main types of differential reinforcement procedures: differential reinforcement of other behaviors (DRO), differential reinforcement of alternative behaviors (DRA), differential reinforcement of incompatible behaviors (DRI), and differential reinforcement of lower rates of behavior (DRL). Table 6.4 summarizes each of these procedures.

When using the DRO procedure, the teacher determines that the student's behavior must be eliminated for specified amounts of time. As a result, the student is reinforced when not exhibiting a certain behavior during that specified time period. Other appropriate behaviors continue to be reinforced and if the behavior does occur, it is ignored unless it is dangerous to the student or others in the classroom or too disruptive.

The DRI method is used for behaviors that can only be decreased if replaced by other behaviors. In the DRI procedure, a behavior is identified which cannot occur concurrently with the inappropriate behavior. This "replacement" behavior is then reinforced and the targeted inappropriate behavior is ignored. For example, a student cannot be in his or her seat and out of his or her seat at the same time. So the student is reinforced when the appropriate behavior

TABLE 6.4 ● Differential Reinforcement Procedures

Term	Definitions
DRI	*Incompatible behavior:* Reinforcement is provided for the occurrence of a behavior that is physically incompatible with the behavior to be reduced (e.g., reinforcing a student for keeping their hands folded in their lap rather than touching other students).
DRA	*Alternative behavior:* Reinforcement is provided for the occurrence of a target behavior that is an alternative to the behavior being reduced (e.g., reinforcing a student for squeezing a squish ball rather than picking at their head).
DRO	*Other behavior:* Reinforcement occurs for engaging in any response other than the target behavior for a set interval of time (e.g., reinforcing a student for any other behavior other than head picking).
DRL	*Low rates of behavior:* Reinforcement occurs for low rates of a target behavior. For DRL to be appropriate, the target behavior must be relatively acceptable, although if occurring frequently or at high levels of intensity, the behavior would be constituted as disruptive (e.g., reinforcing a student for participating only 3 times per class period rather than 12 times per class period).

Source: From "A Practitioner's Guide to Implementing a Differential Reinforcement of Other Behaviors Procedure," by L. C. Gongola and R. Daddario, 2010, *Teaching Exceptional Children, 42,* 14–20.

(in the seat during independent work time) occurs; out of seat behavior is ignored unless it is disruptive to classroom learning.

If the behavior is inappropriate only because of the frequency of its occurrence, then the DRL procedure would be appropriate. In the DRL procedure, students are reinforced for lowering the number of times a behavior occurs. This form of differential reinforcement is often used in conjunction with student self-management and self-reinforcement. For example, when using this method, the teacher and student would discuss the inappropriate behavior, identify the number of times the behavior occurs during the class period, choose a target number of times the behavior will occur, choose an appropriate reinforcement for reaching the target number, and then allow the student to monitor the behavior. The teacher will monitor the behavior periodically and provide reinforcement to the student on a predesignated schedule (Alberto & Troutman, 2009; Maag, 2004).

Many middle and secondary teachers voice concerns about difficulties in implementing various classroom management procedures in today's diverse classrooms. Oftentimes, they find it difficult to implement such procedures effectively. To address this concern, and simply because it's good practice, many educators advocate involving the student in his or her own behavior management (Weinstein, 2007). Student *self-management procedures*, also known as cognitive-behavioral interventions, include self-monitoring or self-recording of the frequency of behavior occurrence, self-evaluation of the intensity and frequency of the behavior, and self-reinforcement for the exhibition of appropriate behaviors or the omission of inappropriate behaviors (Larrivee, 2005; Zirpoli, 2005). The use of self-management procedures supports the philosophy that middle and secondary level students should be learning to regulate their own behaviors and accept responsibility for them. It is definitely a form of self-determination.

Shogren, Wehmeyer, Palmer, Soukup, Little, et al. (2008) have identified eight components of self-management and self-determination:

1. choice making
2. decision making
3. problem solving
4. goal setting and attainment
5. self-observation, evaluation, and reinforcement
6. self-instruction
7. self-advocacy and leadership
8. self-awareness.

Of these, self-determination skills, self-observation, evaluation, and reinforcement are critical for managing one's own behaviors. Students who are self-observant know whether or not they are abiding by classroom rules and procedures. Through their self-evaluation and reinforcement, they are able to successfully manage their own behaviors.

Self-determination, including skills related to self-management, can be taught. Several researchers have studied the efficacy of teaching these skills and have determined that students can actually learn the skills to self-manage (Price, Wolensky, & Mulligan, 2002). Eisenman (2007) suggests that students have opportunities to make choices in the classroom. Through positive reinforcement of good choices, students can learn how to monitor and manage their own behaviors.

Sebag (2010, p. 24) proposes a self-advocacy behavior management (SABM) model that includes five steps:

Step 1   Weekly grade (WG) report: Student and teacher complete daily conduct forms that address major areas of concern.

Step 2   Student–teacher conference: Student identifies/names conduct struggle by reviewing and reflecting on conduct forms during student–teacher conferences.

TABLE 6.5 ● Self-Advocacy Behavior Management—Five-Step Process

Step	The Student Should	The Teacher Should	Helpful Hints
1: The Weekly Grade (WG) Report	Always have WG form visible and accessible.	Monitor WG form and mark WG domains throughout the lesson.	Oral and written feedback on WG should be immediate and specific.
2: Student–Teacher Conference	Student and teacher hold one-on-one conference to review WG. See Step 3 below. Step 3 takes place during the conference.	Student and teacher hold one-on-one conference to review WG. See Step 3 below. Step 3 takes place during the conference.	Make the conference a unique and welcoming experience for all students.
3: Develop Goal & Strategy	(a) Review WG and reflect. (b) Identify and name conduct struggle(s). (c) Devise goal and strategy.	Guide and coach the student through (a), (b), and (c) of Step 3. Articulate these only when student is unable to. The teacher should articulate any consequence.	Student should lead this process to the greatest extent possible. The teacher guides and scaffolds. The teacher might use follow-up questions in order to cognitively guide the student to articulate (a), (b), and (c) of Step 3.
4: Follow-up Conference	(a) Reflect on goal and strategy from previous WG conference. (b) Repeat (a), (b), and (c) of Step 3 for current WG.	Same as Step 3.	Same as Step 3.
5: Adjustment(s) to Goal & Strategy	Adjust goal and/or strategy if original goal and/or strategy are not producing results.	To the greatest extent possible, guide and coach the student through the process. Articulate these only when student is unable to.	Student should lead this process to the greatest extent possible and the teacher guides and scaffolds. Use follow-up questions in order to cognitively guide the student to articulate this.

Source: From "Behavior Management Through Self-Advocacy," by R. Sebag, 2010, *Teaching Exceptional Children, 42,* 22–29.

Step 3 Develop goal and strategy: Student devises a strategy to address the struggle.
Step 4 Follow-up conference: Student reflects on the effectiveness of the strategy.
Step 5 Adjustment(s) to goal and strategy: Student makes necessary adjustment(s) to goals and/or strategy for further progress.

Table 6.5 is a quick reference guide to Sebag's five-step process.

BEHAVIOR INTERVENTION PLANNING

Teachers and parents need to be proactive in preventing inappropriate behaviors from occurring, or dealing with them appropriately when they occur. In these instances a behavior intervention plan should be developed. IDEA 2004 mandates that schools develop such a plan for students with disabilities whose behaviors interfere with their learning or the learning of others; who put peers at risk with their behavior problems; and whose behavior results in severe disciplinary actions (Smith, Polloway, Patton, & Dowdy, 2008).

Determining Underlying Causes

A first step in behavior intervention planning is to develop an understanding of the cause of the behavior. A functional behavior analysis is a good way to determine what factors are related to the behavioral problems. A functional behavior analysis is a systematic procedure that describes "why a behavior occurs by analyzing the behavior and generating hypotheses about its purpose or intended function. Ultimately, these hypotheses should assist school personnel in identifying interventions that change the student's undesirable behavior" (Fad, Patton, & Polloway, 2006, p. viii). When developing the hypotheses, what occurs before the behavior and after the behavior are used to determine the function of the behavior. Examples of functions include escaping or avoiding something unpleasant, frustration, or attention seeking. School personnel typically use a form when conducting a functional behavior assessment (see Figure 6.3).

Once a behavior analysis is complete, a behavior intervention plan can be developed. Assumptions underlying the development of behavior intervention plans include (Smith, Polloway, Patton, & Dowdy, 2004, p. 107):

- Behavior problems are best addressed when the causes (i.e., functions) of the behaviors are known.
- Interventions that are based on positive intervention strategies are more effective than punitive ones.
- Dealing with difficult behaviors demands a team approach.

Behavioral intervention plans typically include (1) specific behavioral goals, (2) proposed interventions, (3) responsible staff, (4) and evaluation methods, criteria, and schedule. Figure 6.4 provides an example of a behavior intervention plan.

PUNISHMENT

Punishment is the least successful method of reducing inappropriate behaviors. Unfortunately, many teachers think of punishment as their primary means for managing classroom behaviors. Punishment can be defined as applying something unpleasant afterward as a behavioral consequence. Punishment in classrooms is typically one of three different forms—reprimands, time-out, and response cost. Reprimands are when the teacher presents something unpleasant after a behavior. In secondary schools this is frequently a verbal reprimand, when students are told what they have done wrong. Time-out is when students are denied access to reinforcement. Having students leave a group would be a form of time-out, as well as requiring them to sit in a particular place in the classroom, alone from their peers. Finally, response cost means that students lose something that is valuable to them. This could include free time, a privilege such as going to the lunch room early, or not having to turn in homework over the weekend. When using response cost, consider the following suggestions (Smith et al., 2008, p. 432):

- Explain clearly to students how the system works and how much one will be fined for a given offense.
- Make sure all penalties are presented in a nonpersonal manner.
- Confirm that privileges that are lost are indeed reinforcing to students.
- Make sure that all privileges are not lost quickly, resulting in a situation in which a student may have little or no incentive to behave appropriately.
- Tie in this procedure with positive reinforcement at all times.

Behavior # 3   Physical aggression fighting

Precipitating Conditions (Setting, time, or other situations typically occurring *before* the behavior)	Specific Behavior (*Exactly* what the student does or does not do)	Consequences (Events that typically *follow* the behavior)	Function of the Behavior (*Hypothesized purpose[s]* the behavior serves)
☒ unstructured time in hallways/on the bus	Casey pushes, hits, trips other students, often students who are smaller; Casey's aggression occurs more often when no adults are watching her (on bus; in halls).	☒ teacher attention	☐ escape/avoidance
☐ academic instruction in		☒ peer attention	☐ gaining attention
		☒ verbal warning/reprimand	☒ expression of anger
☐ when given a directive to		☐ loss of privilege (what kind?)	☐ frustration
			☒ vengeance
☒ when close to smaller students		☐ time out (where/how long?)	☐ seeking of power/control
			☒ intimidation
☐ when provoked by		☒ detention (how long?) after school	☐ sensory stimulation
			☐ relief of fear/anxiety
☐ when unable to		☐ removal from class	☐ other _____
			_____
☒ other when unsupervised		☒ in-school suspension (how long?) 3 days	_____
			_____
☐ none observed		☐ other _____	_____

Specific Assessment Techniques Used to Analyze This Behavior

☒ Observation   ☐ Student Interview   ☒ Administrative Interview   ☒ Parent Interview

☒ Behavior Checklist/Rating Scale   ☐ Video/Audio Taping   ☒ Teacher Interview   ☐ Other _____

Relating Information/Considerations

Academic: Low grades-homework not turned in

Family: Casey's behavior has disrupted family life. Mother reports she is afraid of Casey.

Social/Peer: Few friends   **Other:** _____

FIGURE 6.3 ● Example of a Functional Behavior Assessment

Source: From T. E. C. Smith, E. A. Polloway, J. R. Patton, and C. A. Dowdy, 2004, *Teaching Students with Special Needs in Inclusive Settings* (4th ed., p. 214). Used with permission.

Evaluation

Progress Codes:
/ = ongoing
X = mastered
D = discontinued

Specific Goal(s)	Proposed Intervention(s)	Person(s) Responsible	Methods	Criterion	Schedule Date	Code
1. Casey will increase respectful language in class, including saying "yes, sir" or "yes, ma'am" when requested to do something.	1. Contract for • positive comments • saying "yes, ma'am" or "yes, sir" • refrain from verbal threats	1. Student Teachers Counselor	– Contract forms – Discipline referrals	1. Respectful language 90% of time	9/1/99 10/15/99 12/1/99 1/15/00 3/1/00 4/15/00 6/1/00	
2. Casey will decrease verbal threats and teasing.	2. Delay release from classroom to hallway by 5 minutes	2. Teachers		2. Contract • positive comments: 5 per day • "yes" responses: 80% of time • verbal threats: fewer than 8 per 6 weeks		
3. Casey will decrease aggressive incidents toward peers (fighting, hitting, tripping).	3. Continuum of responses to aggression: • Parent–Asst. Principal conference and suspension to AEP for 3 days • Go to antiaggression classes • Notify probation officer	3. Parents Assistant Principal Counselor		3. Aggression: No incidents in next 6 weeks		

These goals were developed with consideration of the following information:

☐ Parent concerns regarding special circumstances: _____

☐ Teacher/administrator concerns regarding special circumstances: _____

☑ Outside agency/professional concerns regarding special circumstances:
Probation officer requires notification.
_____
_____
_____

FIGURE 6.4 ● Sample Behavioral Intervention Plan

Source: From *Behavioral Intervention Planning: Completing a Functional Behavioral Assessment and Developing a Behavioral Intervention Plan, Revised Ed.* (p. 40), by K. M. Fad, J. R. Patton, and E. A. Polloway, 2000, Austin, TX: PRO-ED. Copyright 2000 by PRO-ED, Inc. Reprinted with permission.

SUMMARY

Classroom management is a critical element in today's schools because of its relationship to effective learning. Indeed, without a well-managed classroom, students cannot learn to their maximum ability levels. Often a lack of classroom management skills is a primary reason teachers leave the profession. There are numerous components of classroom management. These include organization of classroom space, classroom climate, classroom rules, and classroom procedures.

The planning and conducting of instruction is a very important component in classroom management. Indeed, the content that is taught, the level of student ability, and the instructional methods used are related to how students learn. It is very difficult for students to follow rules and procedures when they are frustrated with the level of content that is being taught.

Teachers have to maintain appropriate behaviors and diminish inappropriate behaviors. It is always easier to have a proactive, preventive classroom management system than a reactive system that addresses manifested behavior problems. One preventive model is the use of positive behavioral supports, which uses modeling appropriate behaviors, positive reinforcement, prompts, and cues to elicit appropriate behaviors. Some schools implement a schoolwide positive behavior support system. Research has shown this to be an effective method of classroom management because all students understand expectations in every school setting.

There are times when inappropriate behaviors occur and teachers have to decrease those behaviors in order to promote a positive learning environment. Methods of doing this include changing the classroom environment, providing cues and redirection, using extinction, and reinforcing differential behaviors. For some students, behavior intervention planning is necessary, which requires a systematic approach to behavioral analysis and behavioral planning.

ACTIVITIES

1. Observe the procedures for opening class in a middle or secondary classroom. These might include, but are not limited to, turning in homework, picking up graded assignments, and locating materials missed when absent from class. Record your observations. Next observe the ending of class including, but not limited to, picking up and storing materials used in class, future assignments and homework, and gathering personal possessions. Record your observations. Write a reflection comparing your observation to the recommendations in the chapter. Then, develop opening and closing procedures for your future classroom.

2. Observe a 10-minute instructional segment in a middle or secondary general education classroom and in a resource room. Keep a chart of the number of times the teacher provides a comment meant to be reinforcing and the number of times the teacher provides a comment meant to be a punishment or consequence for noncompletion of work or inappropriate behaviors. Compare the two charts and write a reflection on your observation applying the research-based information in the chapter.

3. Often school policies impact the teacher's use of rewards and penalties. Ask school personnel if such policies (either formal or informal) exist within the school. Write a brief paper reporting the policies and comparing these with the research-based procedures presented in this chapter.

REFERENCES

Alberto, P. A., & Troutman, A. C. (2009). *Applied behavior analysis for teachers* (8th ed.). Upper Saddle River, NJ: Merrill/Pearson.

Algozzine, B., & Kay, P. (Eds.). (2002). *Preventing problem behaviors.* Thousand Oaks, CA: Corwin.

Anderson, L. (1981). Instruction and time-on-task: A review. *Journal of Curriculum Studies, 13,* 289–303.

Babkie, A. M. (2006). 20 ways to be proactive in managing classroom behavior. *Intervention in School and Clinic, 41*(6), 184–187.

Battistich, V., Solomon, D., & Delucchi, K. (1993). Interaction processes and student outcomes in cooperative learning groups. *Elementary School Journal, 94,* 19–32.

Beaman, R., & Wheldall, K. (2000). Teachers' use of approval and disapproval in the classroom. *Educational Psychology, 20*(4), 431–447.

Bicard, D. F. (2000). Using classroom rules to construct behavior. *Middle School Journal, 31*(5), 37–45.

Bonus, M., & Riordan, L. (1998). *Increasing student on-task behavior through the use of specific seating arrangements.* (ERIC Document Reproduction Service No. ED422129).

Boonstrum, R. (1991). The nature and function of classroom rules. *Curriculum Inquiry, 21,* 193–21.

Borich, G. D. (2004). *Effective teaching methods* (5th ed.). Upper Saddle River, NJ: Pearson Merrill Prentice Hall.

Brooks, D. M. (1985). The teacher's communicative competence: The first day of school. *Theory Into Practice, 24*(1), 63–70.

Brophy, J., & Good, T. (1986). Teacher behavior and achievement. In M. C. Wittrock (Ed.), *Handbook of research on teaching* (pp. 328–376). Upper Saddle River, NJ: Prentice Hall.

Caldwell, J., Huitt, W., & Graeber, A. (1982). Time spent in learning: Implications for research. *Elementary School Journal, 82*(5), 471–480.

Carr, E. G., Dunlap, G., Horner, R. H., Koegel, R. L., Turnbull, A. P., Sailor, W., Anderson, J., Albin, R. W., Koegel, L. K., & Fox, L. (2002). Positive behavior support: Evolution of an applied science. *Journal of Positive Behavior Interventions, 4,* 4–16.

Carroll, J. (1963). A model of school learning. *Teachers College Record, 64,* 723–735.

Chance, P. (1998). *First course in applied behavior analysis.* Long Grove, IL: Waveland.

Chiu, M. M. (2004). Adapting teacher interventions to student needs during cooperative learning: How to improve student problem solving and time on-task. *American Educational Research Journal, 41*(2), 365–399.

Coalition for Evidence-Based Policy. (2003). *Identifying and implementing educational practices supported by rigorous evidence: A user friendly guide.* Washington, DC: U.S. Department of Education, Institute for Education Sciences.

Cohen, E. G. (1994). Restructuring the classroom: Conditions for productive small groups. *Review of Educational Research, 64,* 1–36.

Coloroso, B. (2002). *Kids are worth it! Giving your child the gift of inner discipline.* New York: Avon Books/Harper Collins.

Cooperative learning. (n.d.). Retrieved July 24, 2008, from *http://edtech.kennesaw.edu/intech/cooperativelearning.htm*

Curwin, R. L., & Mendler, A. N. (1988). *Discipline with dignity.* Alexandria, VA: Association for Supervision and Curriculum Development.

Daly, J. A., & Suite, A. (1981). Classroom seating choice: Teacher perceptions of students. *Journal of Experimental Education, 50*(2), 64–69.

Duplass, J. (2006). *Middle and high school teaching: Methods, standards, and best practices.* Boston: Houghton Mifflin.

Dykman, B. M., & Reis, H. T. (1979). Personality correlates of classroom seating position. *Journal of Educational Psychology, 71*(3), 346–354.

Eisenman, L. T. (2007). Self-determination interventions: Building a foundation for school completion. *Remedial and Special Education, 28*(1), 2–8.

Emmer, E. T., Evertson, C. M., & Worsham, M. E. (2003). *Classroom management for secondary teachers.* Boston: Allyn & Bacon.

Emmer, E. T., Evertson, C. M., & Worsham, M. E. (2006). *Classroom management for middle and secondary high school teachers* (7th ed.). Boston: Allyn & Bacon.

Evans, G., & Lovell, B. (1979). Design modification in an open-plan school. *Journal of Educational Psychology, 7*(1), 41–49.

Evans, W., Tokarczyk, J., Rice, S., & McCray, A. (2002). Block scheduling: An evaluation of outcomes and impact. *The Clearing House, 75*(6), 319–323.

Evertson, C. M. (1980). *Differences in instructional activities in high- and low-achieving junior high classes.* Paper presented at the annual meeting of the American Education Research Association, Boston. (ERIC Document Reproduction Service No. ED19554).

Evertson, C. M. (1985). Training teachers in classroom management: An experimental study in secondary school classrooms. *Journal of Educational Research, 79,* 51–55.

Evertson, C. M. (1994). Classroom rules and routines. *International encyclopedia of education* (2nd ed.). Oxford: Pergamon.

Evertson, C. M., & Emmer, E. T. (1982). Effective management at the beginning of the school year in junior high classes. *Journal of Educational Psychology, 74*(4), 485–498.

Fad, K., Patton, J. R., & Polloway, E. A. (2006). *Behavioral intervention planning: A comprehensive guide for completing a functional behavioral assessment and developing a behavioral intervention plan* (3rd ed.). Austin, TX: Pro-Ed.

Fisher, C. W., Berliner, D. C., Filby, N. N., Marliave, R., Cahen, L. S., & Dishaw, M. M. (1980). Teaching behaviors, academic learning time, and student achievement: An overview. In C. Denham & A. Lieberman (Eds.), *Time to learn* (pp. 7–32). Washington, DC: U. S. Department of Education.

Fleming, D. S., Olenn, V., Schoenstein, R., & Eineder, D. (1997). *Moving to the block: Getting ready to teach in extended periods of learning time.* (An NEA Professional Library Publication). Washington, DC: National Education Association.

Frederick W. (1977). The use of classroom time in high schools above and below the median reading score. *Urban Education, 11,* 459–464.

Freeman, R., Eber, L., Anderson, C., Irvin, L., Horner, R., Bounds, M., & Dunlap, G. (2006). Building inclusive school cultures using school-wide PBS: Designing effective individual support systems for students with significant disabilities. *Research & Practice for Persons with Severe Disabilities, 31*(1), 4–17.

Gabriel, A. E. (1999). Brain-based learning: The scent of the trail. *Clearing House, 72,* 288–290.

Gettinger, M., & Seibert, J. K. (1995). Best practices for increasing academic learning time. In A. Thomas & J. Grimes (Eds.), *Best practice in school psychology-III* (pp. 943–954). Washington, DC: National Association for School Psychologists.

Gongola, L. C., & Daddario, R. (2010). A practitioner's guide to implementing a differential reinforcement of other behaviors procedure. *Teaching Exceptional Children, 42,* 14–20.

Good, T., & Brophy, J., (2008). *Looking in classrooms* (10th ed.) Boston: Allyn & Bacon.

Goodlad, J. L. (1984). *A place called school.* New York: McGraw-Hill.

Guardino, C. A., & Fullerton, E. (2010). Changing behaviors by changing the classroom environment. *Teaching Exceptional Children, 42,* 8–13.

Gump, P. V. (1974). Operating environments in schools of open and traditional design. *School Review, 82,* 575–593.

Henley, M. (2006). *Classroom management: A proactive approach.* Upper Saddle River, NJ: Merrill/Pearson.

Hood-Smith, N. E., & Leffingwell, R. J. (1983). The impact of physical space alternation on disruptive classroom behavior: A case study. *Education, 104,* 224–231.

Horne-Martin, S. (2002). Environment-behavior studies in the classroom. *Journal of Design and Technology Education, 9,* 2.

Horner, R. H., Sugai, G., Todd, A. W., & Lewis-Palmer, T. (2005). Schoolwide positive behavior support. In L. M. Bambara & L. Kern (Eds.), *Individualized supports for students with problem behaviors* (pp. 359–390). New York: Guilford Press.

Jacobs, G. M., Power, M. A., & Inn, L. (2002). *The teacher's sourcebook for cooperative learning: Practical techniques, basic principles, and frequently asked questions.* Thousand Oaks, CA: Corwin Press.

Johnson, D. W., & Johnson, R. T. (1999). *Learning together and alone: Cooperative, competitive, and individualistic learning* (5th ed.). Boston: Allyn & Bacon.

Johnson, D. W., Johnson, H., Stanne, M., & Garibaldi, A. (1990). Impact of group processing on achievement in cooperative groups. *Journal of Social Psychology, 130,* 507–516.

Johnson, D. W., Johnson, R. T., Holubec, E. J., & Roy, P. (1984). *Circles of learning: Cooperation in the classroom.* Alexandria, VA: Association for Supervision and Curriculum Development.

Jolivette, K., Wehby, J. H., Canale, J., & Massey, G. N. (2001). Effects of choice-making opportunities on the behavior of students with emotional and behavioral disorders. *Behavioral Disorder, 26,* 131–145.

Karweit, N. (1989). Time and learning: A review. In R. E. Slavin (Ed.), *School and classroom organization.* Hillsdale, NJ: Lawrence Erlbaum.

Kauffman, J. M., Mostert, M. M., Trent, S. C., & Hallahan, D. P. (2002). *Managing classroom behavior: A reflective case-based approach* (3rd ed.). Boston: Allyn & Bacon.

Kazdin, A. E. (1977). *The token economy: A review and evaluation.* New York: Plenum Press.

Kellough, R. D., & Kellough, N. G. (2008). *Teaching young adolescents: Methods and resources for middle grades teaching* (5th ed.). Upper Saddle River, NJ: Merrill/Pearson.

Kerr, M. M., & Nelson C. M. (2006). *Strategies for addressing behavioral problems in the classroom* (5th ed.). Upper Saddle River, NJ: Merrill/Pearson.

Kounin, J. S. (1970). *Discipline and group management in classrooms.* New York: Holt, Rinehart and Winston.

Kutash, K., & Duchnowski, A. J. (2006). Creating environments that work for all youth: Increasing the use of evidence-based strategies by special education teachers. *National Center on Secondary Education and Transition Research to Practice Brief: Improving Secondary Education and Transition Services through Research, 5*(1), 1–6.

Lang, D. E. (2001). Teacher interactions within the physical environment: How teachers alter their space ad/or routines because of classroom character. (ERIC Document Reproduction Service No. ED472265).

Larrivee, B. (2005). *Authentic classroom management: Creating a learning community and building reflective practice.* Boston: Allyn & Bacon/Pearson.

Leinhardt, G., Weidman, C., & Hammond, K. M. (1987). Introduction and integration of classroom routines by expert teachers. *Curriculum Inquiry, 17*(2), 135–176.

Lenz, B. K., & Deshler, D. D. (2004). *Teaching content to all: Evidence-base inclusive practices in middle and secondary schools.* Boston: Allyn & Bacon/Pearson.

Leonard, L. J. (2001). *Erosion in instructional time: Teacher concerns.* (ERIC Document Reproduction Service No. ED460119).

Liaupsin, C. J., Jolivette, K., & Scott, T. M. (2004). School-wide systems of support: Maximizing student success in schools. In R. B. Rutherford, M. M. Quinn, & R. Sathur (Eds.), *Handbook of research in emotional and behavioral disorders* (pp. 487–501). New York: Guilford Press.

Lotan, R. (2006). Managing groupwork in the heterogeneous classroom. In C. M. Evertson & C. S. Weinstein (Eds.), *Handbook of classroom management: Research, practice, and contemporary issues.* Mahwah, NJ: Lawrence Erlbaum.

Maag, J. W. (2004). *Behavior management: From theoretical implications to practical applications* (2nd ed.). Belmont, CA: Thompson/Wadsworth.

Malone, B. G., & Tietjens, C. L. (2000). Re-examination of classroom rules: The need for clarity and specified behavior. *Special Services in the Schools, 16,* 159–170.

Marks, H. M. (2000). Student engagement in instructional activity: Patterns in the elementary, middle, and high school years. *American Educational Research Journal, 37*(1), 153–184.

Marquis, J. G., Horner, R. H., Carr, E. G., Turnbull, A. P., Thompson, M., Behrens, G. A., Magito-McLaughlin, D., McAtee, M. L., Smith, C. E., Anderson-Ryan, K., & Doolabh, A. (2000). Meta analysis of positive behavior supports. In R. M. Gersten, E. P. Schiller, & S. Vaughn (Eds.), *Contemporary special education research: A syntheses of the knowledge base on critical instructional issues* (pp. 137–178). Mahwah, NJ: Lawrence Erlbaum.

Martella, R. C., Nelson, J. R., & Marchard-Martella, N. E. (2003). *Managing disruptive behavior in the schools.* Boston: Allyn & Bacon.

Maslow, A. H., & Minz, N. L. (1956). Effect of esthetic surroundings: Initial effects of three esthetic conditions upon perceiving "energy" and "well-being" in faces. *Journal of Psychology, 41,* 247–254.

Mattox, K., Hancock, D. R., & Queen, J. A. (2005). The effect of block scheduling on middle school students' mathematics achievement. *NASSP Bulletin, 89,* 3–13.

McCrosky, J. C., & McVetta, R. W. (1978). Classroom seating arrangement: Instructional communication theory versus student preferences. *Communication Education, 27,* 101–102.

McGarity Jr., J. R., & Butts, D. P. (1984). The relationship among teacher classroom management behavior, student engagement and student achievement of middle and high schools science students of varying aptitude. *Journal of Research in Science Teaching, 21*(1), 55–61.

Murdick, N., & Petch-Hogan, B. (1996). Inclusive classroom management: Using preintervention strategies. *Intervention in School and Clinic, 31,* 172–176.

Nastasi, B. K., & Clements, D. H. (1991). Research on cooperative learning: Implications for practice. *School Psychology Review, 20,* 110–131.

National Commission on Excellence in Education. (1983). *A nation at risk: The imperative for educational reform.* Washington, DC: Government Printing Office.

National Education Commission on Time and Learning. (1994). *Prisoner of time.* Washington, DC: Government Printing Office.

Nelson, J., Lott, L., & Glenn, H. S. (2000). *Positive discipline in the classroom: Developing mutual respect, cooperation, and responsibility in your classroom.* Roseville, CA: Prima.

Nichols, J. D. (2005). Block-scheduled high schools: Impact on achievement in English and language arts. *The Journal of Educational Research, 98*(5), 299–309.

Odom, S. L., Brantlinger, E., Gersten, R., Horner, R. H., Thompson, B., & Harris, K. R. (2005). Research in special education: Scientific methods and evidence-based practices. *Exceptional Children, 71,* 1–22.

Price, L. A., Wolensky, D., & Mulligan, R. (2002). Self-determination in action in the classroom. *Remedial and Special Education, 32*(2), 109–115.

Proshansky, E., & Wolfe, M. (1974). The physical setting and open education. *School Review, 82,* 557–574.

Reid, R. (1996). Research in self-monitoring: The present, the prospects, the pitfalls. *Journal of Learning Disabilities, 29,* 317–331.

Rhode, G., Jenson, W. R., & Reavis, H. K. (1993). *The tough kid book.* Longmont, CO: Sopris West.

Ridling, Z. (1994). *The effects of three seating arrangements on teachers' use of selective interactive verbal behaviors.* (ERIC Document Reproduction Service No. ED369757).

Ross, J. A. (1995). Effects of feedback on student behavior in cooperative learning groups in a grade 7 math class. *The Elementary School Journal, 96*(2), 125–143.

Salend, S., & Sylvestre, S. (2005). Understanding and addressing oppositional and defiant classroom behaviors. *Teaching Exceptional Children, 37*(6), 32–39.

Schniedewind, N., & Davidson, E. (2000). Differentiating cooperative learning. *Educational Leadership, 58*(1), 24–27.

Scott, T. M., Nelson, C. M., & Liaupsin, C. J. (2001). Effective instruction: The forgotten component in preventing school violence. *Education and Treatment of Children, 24,* 309–322.

Sebag, R. (2010). Behavior management through self-advocacy. *Teaching Exceptional Children, 42,* 22–29.

Shapiro, E. S., DuPaul, G. J., & Bradley-King, K. L. (1998). Self-management as a strategy to improve the classroom behavior of adolescents with ADHD. *Journal of Learning Disabilities, 31*(6), 545–555.

Shernoff, D. J., Csikszentmihalyi, M., Schneider, B., & Shernoff, E. S. (2003). Student engagement in high school classrooms from the perspective of flow theory. *School Psychology Quarterly, 18*(2), 158–176.

Shogren, K. A., Wehmeyer, M. L., Palmer, S. G., Soukup, J. H., Little, T. D., Garner, N., & Lawrence, M. (2008). Understanding the construct of self-determination. *Assessment for Effective Intervention, 33*(2), 94–107.

Shores, R. E., Gunter, P. L., & Jack, S. (1993). Classroom management strategies: Are they setting events for coercion? *Behavioral Disorders, 18,* 92–102.

Slavin, R. E. (1985). An introduction to cooperative learning research. In R. Slavin, S. Sharan, S. Kagan, R. Hertz-Lazarowitz, C. Webb, & R. Schmuch (Eds.), *Learning to cooperate, cooperating to learn* (pp. 5–15). New York: Plenum Press.

Slavin, R. E. (1990). Achievement effects of ability grouping in secondary schools: A best-evidence synthesis. *Review of Educational Research, 60*(3), 471–499.

Slavin, R. E. (1995). *Cooperative learning: Theory, research and practice* (2nd ed.). Boston: Allyn & Bacon.

Slavin, R. E. (1996). Cooperative learning in middle and secondary schools. *Clearing House, 69,* 200–204.

Smith, B. (2000). Quantity matters: Annual instructional time in an urban school system. *Educational Administration Quarterly, 36*(5), 652–682.

Smith, D. J., Young, K. R., West, R. P., Morgan, D. P., & Rhode, G. (1988). Reducing the disruptive behavior of junior high school students: A classroom self-management procedure. *Behavioral Disorders, 18,* 231–239.

Smith, K. A. (2000). Going deeper: Formal small-group learning in large classes. *New Directions for Teaching and Learning, 81,* 25–46.

Smith, T. E. C., Polloway, E. A., Patton, J. R., & Dowdy, C. A. (2004). *Teaching students with special needs in inclusive settings* (4th ed.). Boston: Allyn & Bacon.

Smith, T. E. C., Polloway, E. A., Patton, J. R., & Dowdy, C. A. (2008). *Teaching students with special needs in inclusive settings* (5th ed.). Boston: Allyn & Bacon.

Sommer, R. (1977). Classroom layout. *Theory into Practice, 16*(3), 174–175.

Stormont, M., Lewis, T. J., & Beckner, R. (2005). Positive behavior support: Applying key features in pre-school settings. *TEACHING Exceptional Children, 37,* 42–48.

Tankersley, M. (1995). A group-oriented contingency management program. *Preventing Behavior Analysis, 10,* 349–367.

Taylor-Green, S., Brown, D., Nelson, L., & Longton, J. (1997). School-wide behavioral support: Starting the year off right. *Journal of Behavioral Education, 7*(1), 99–112.

Thorson, S. A. (2003). *Listening to students: Reflections on secondary classroom management.* Boston: Allyn & Bacon.

Tiberius, R. G. (1999). *Small group teaching: A troubleshooting guide.* London: Kagan Press.

Totusek, P. F., & Staton-Spicer, A. Q. (1982). Classroom seating preference as a function of student personality. *Journal of Experimental Psychology, 50*(3), 159–163.

Tudge, J. R. H. (1992). Processes and consequences of peer collaboration: A Vygotskian analysis. *Child Development, 63,* 1364–1379.

Turnbull, A., Edmonson, H., Griggs, P., Wickham, D., Sailor, W., Freeman, R., Guess, D., Lassen, S., McCart, A., Park, J., Riffel, L., Turnbull, R., & Warren, J. (2002). A blueprint for schoolwide positive behavior support: Implementation of three components. *Exceptional Children, 68*(3), 377–402.

U.S. Department of Education. (2000). *Twenty-second annual report to Congress on the implementation of the Individuals with Disabilities Education Act.* Washington, DC: Author.

Visser, J. (2001). Aspects of physical provision for pupils with emotional and behavioural difficulties. *Support for Learning, 16*(2), 64–68.

Vygotsky, L. (1962). *Thought and language.* Cambridge, MA: MIT Press.

Vygotsky, L. (1978). *Mind in society: The development of higher psychological processes.* (Edited by M. Cole, V. John-Steiner, S. Scribner, & S. Souberman). Cambridge, MA: Harvard University Press.

Walker, H. M., Ramsey, E., & Gresham, F. M. (2004). *Antisocial behavior in schools: Evidence-based practices* (2nd ed.). Belmont, CA: Wadsworth.

Walker, J. E., & Shea, T. M. (1999). *Behavior management: A practical approach for educators.* Upper Saddle River, NJ: Merrill/Pearson.

Walker, J. E., Shea, T. M., & Bauer, A. M. (2007). *Behavior management: A practical approach for educators* (9th ed.). Upper Saddle River, NJ: Merrill/Pearson.

Walters, L. S. (2000). Putting cooperative learning to the test. *Harvard Education Letter, 16*(3), 1–6.

Webb, N. M. (1985). Student interaction and learning in small groups: A research summary. In R. Slavin, S. Sharan, S. Kagan, R. Hertz-Lazarowitz, C. Webb, & R. Schmuck (Eds.), *Learning to cooperate, cooperating to learn* (pp. 147–172). New York: Plenum Press.

Weinstein, C. S. (1977). Modifying student behavior in an open classroom through change in the physical design. *American Educational Research Journal, 14*, 249–262.

Weinstein, C. S. (2007). *Middle and secondary classroom management: Lessons from research and practice* (3rd ed.). Boston: McGraw-Hill.

Weinstein, R. (1979). *Student perceptions of differential teacher treatment.* Washington, DC: Department of Health, Education, and Welfare, Bureau of Education of the Handicapped.

Workman, E. A. (1998). *Teaching behavioral self-control to students* (2nd ed.). Austin, TX: Pro-Ed.

Wulf, K. M. (1977). Relationship of assigned classroom seating area to achievement variables. *Educational Research Quarterly, 2*(20), 56–62.

Zepeda, S. D., & Mayers, R. S. (2006). An analysis of research on block scheduling. *Review of Educational Research, 76*(1), 137–170.

Zifferblatt, S. M. (1972). Architecture and human behavior: Toward increasing understanding of a functional relationship. *Educational Technology, 12*, 54–57.

Zirpoli, T. J. (2005). *Behavior management: Applications for teachers* (4th ed.). Upper Saddle River, NJ: Merrill/Pearson.

CHAPTER

7

Coteaching

Study Questions

1. Define *coteaching* and explain its five essential elements.

2. Friend and Cook (2010) list six coteaching models. Define each and list advantages and disadvantages. Tell how each can be used in the middle and secondary school classrooms.

3. While coteaching specifically involves two or more teachers providing instruction within the same space to the same students, its success is dependent on the actions of others within the school environment. Explain the roles of these persons and how they may impact coteaching.

4. What are some effective actions to take when wishing to implement coteaching?

INTRODUCTION

Unlike public school teachers 50 years ago who taught in classrooms that were fairly homogeneous, as a result of the increased diversity ethically, socioeconomically, and educationally, today's teachers must be competent to teach students who represent a wide range of characteristics. The inclusion of students with disabilities in general education classes has added to the diversity in public school classrooms and resulted in a significant need for collaboration among general classroom teachers, special education teachers, related services personnel, and parents. In today's middle and secondary schools, diversity is a fact. Students with limited English language skills, students who are culturally different, students with special gifts and talents, and students with disabilities are simply a part of the student population. As middle and secondary school teachers struggle to teach these diverse learners, collaboration becomes an essential element of professional interaction. Through collaborative interactions with colleagues, teachers can receive professional support as they provide appropriate educational opportunities to the diverse learners in the classroom. The collaborative style of interaction is in contrast to the traditional school structure of teacher isolation and one teacher for one class. Today's teachers are encouraged to share specialized knowledge, responsibility for students, and accountability for student learning—in other words, to work together.

Collaboration is not a process but a way of thinking, planning, sharing, and working together. It is when two or more individuals work together to accomplish a common purpose. With regard to teachers, it means two or more teachers working together to effectively meet the needs of students. There is simply no way one teacher can meet the needs of today's heterogeneous group of students without assistance. The growing diversity found in public schools has, in effect, played a key role in the expansion of collaboration among school professionals (Mastropieri, Scruggs, Graetz, Noland, Gardizi, et al., 2005).

COOPERATIVE TEACHING MODEL

One teaching strategy firmly grounded in collaboration is *coteaching*, an educational model where general and special education teachers are simultaneously present in the same classroom and share instructional duties (Sileo & van Garderen, 2010). Friend and Cook (2010) noted that coteaching "occurs when two or more professionals jointly deliver substantive instruction to a diverse, blended group of students in a single, physical space" (p. 113). Team teaching, a form of cooperative teaching, has existed for many years, usually in the form of two general education teachers joining their two classes together for instruction. As a result of the inclusion movement of adding students with disabilities to the general classroom population, team teaching evolved into a model where general education teachers and special education teachers created instructional teams to effectively address the learning needs presented by special education students as well as other students with learning difficulties. In this model, each teacher has an important contribution to make to the instructional process; instructional planning, presentation, assessment, and decision making are shared. Coteaching, therefore, is when the content expertise of the general classroom teacher is combined with the information access expertise of special education teachers to create a unique partnership for addressing the needs of students with disabilities (Villa, Thousand, & Nevin, 2008). The result is the best of both worlds—biology teachers, history teachers, and foreign language teachers who know their subject content, teamed with special education teachers who have expertise in making the content accessible to students who have learning problems.

Hourcade and Bauwens (2003) propose five elements whose presence defines coteaching today. The first element is that of *cooperative presence*. In other words, both teachers are physically present in the classroom together. The second element is *cooperative planning*, where the teachers meet regularly to design and prepare lessons together. The third element is *cooperative presenting*, where both teachers are present and actively involved in presenting class instruction. The fourth element, *cooperative processing*, occurs when both teachers are responsible for monitoring and evaluating the results of instruction. The fifth element is *cooperative problem solving*, where both teachers work together to solve classroom issues. In other words, you as the teacher who plans to coteach will work with another teacher, usually a special education teacher, and cooperatively plan, implement, and monitor all facets of your educational program.

Benefits of Coteaching

There are numerous benefits to the coteaching model. Probably the most important is that a coteaching classroom provides the opportunity for students with disabilities to access the general education curriculum, a requirement of IDEA, while receiving support from a special education teacher. It also assists general classroom teachers in meeting the unique needs of students with disabilities and other students who are experiencing learning difficulties. Content specialists often do not have the knowledge or experience to meet the needs of students with unique learning needs. Similarly, special education teachers typically do not have an in-depth knowledge of the content in secondary classes. A coteaching arrangement provides the opportunity for two teachers to bring different types of expertise to the classroom, making it more likely that the needs of all students will be met (Magiera, Smith, Zigmond, & Gebauer, 2005). In addition to the benefit of maximizing the expertise of two teachers, other benefits of coteaching include:

- Better opportunities to monitor students for learning
- Better opportunities to monitor students for behavior
- Improved academic achievement for students with disabilities (Walsh & Jones, 2004)
- Better access to the general curriculum for students with disabilities (Walsh & Jones, 2004)

Coteaching definitely has its benefits. One teacher, sharing her thoughts on coteaching, stated the following (Salend, Gordon, & Lopez-Vona, 2002, p. 196):

> We get along very well. We are both flexible and have developed similar expectations for students and similar classroom management styles. We feed off each other's comments and teaching styles. We switch which groups we work with so that we both get to perform a variety of roles with all our students. We work together, develop together, and bounce things off each other. Working as a team makes you feel good.

The coteaching model is beneficial to students and teachers. With school populations becoming more diverse, including students with wide and varying levels of academic preparedness, schools must find a way to meet the needs of all students; cooperative teaching can provide such an opportunity.

Research Base for Coteaching

Reviews of the research on various aspects of coteaching, although anecdotal and limited, have indicated that teachers consider the coteaching organizational structure to have a positive effect on student achievement (Keefe, Moore, & Duff, 2004; Murawski & Swanson, 2001; Scruggs,

Mastropieri, & McDuffie, 2007; Weiss, 2004). Dieker and Murawski (2003) examined findings on coteaching at the secondary level. Their findings, generally positive, emphasized the importance of coteacher training, shared planning time, and mastery of the content being taught by both teachers (general and special education).

There have also been some negative findings related to coteaching. These include the fact that schools tend to have larger class sizes in coteaching classrooms (Dieker & Murawski, 2003); the lack of teacher training in the use of coteaching in the classroom (Keefe et al., 2004); inadequate planning time provided for the coteachers; and lack of administrative support for this organizational plan (Scruggs et al., 2007).

While there are pros and cons to the cooperative teaching model, research indicates that the model is a promising strategy for meeting the needs of the growing diverse population in secondary classrooms. However, teachers involved in coteaching have reported the following barriers to its successful implementation: (1) a lack of training and preparation for teachers wishing to participate in coteaching, (2) a lack of shared planning time for the participating teachers, and (3) a lack of administrative support for this organizational model. Two additional barriers are language and vision. When a general educator and a special educator decide to use coteaching, they need to develop a common language for discussing, planning, and successful delivery of instruction. This can be difficult because both groups bring their own language into the partnership (Friend & Cook, 2010). Second, coteachers must discuss their philosophies of education, how children learn, and how they teach. Developing a common language and identifying common beliefs will assist in developing a classroom philosophy which will then become their basis for instructional delivery and classroom management (Friend & Cook, 2010).

Before Beginning a Coteaching Model

In an effort to meet the needs of students, many schools have implemented a cooperative teaching model. Wanting to implement such a model simply because it is successful does not mean that schools can move to this model quickly. A coteaching model should not be implemented without a great deal of planning. Magiera and colleagues (2005) suggested schools take the following steps prior to implementing a coteaching model:

1. Attend coteaching workshops as a team. Teachers who will be working as a coteaching team should attend workshops on coteaching, as a team, prior to implementing the model. At this time both teachers can discuss their visions of what the coteaching classroom should look like, so they are working cooperatively prior to its beginning.
2. Request common planning time. Planning time for coteaching teams is a critical component. Without ample time to plan, coteaching will not be successful. During their planning time, teachers should discuss needs of specific students, determine how content will be delivered, and determine what roles each team member will fill. School leaders should ensure a common planning time for coteachers prior to implementing the model.
3. Put both teachers' names on the board, handouts, notes to families, and exams. In other words, make it clear to everyone, including students, other teachers, and parents, that the classroom belongs to both individuals. Coteachers must feel an equal ownership of the classroom and time with the students.
4. Become familiar with content standards. General classroom teachers likely have an understanding of the content standards they must address. For coteachers to be effective, both teachers need to have a thorough understanding of the standards so their efforts will target the achievement of those standards.

All parties involved in collaborative educational efforts, including general and special education teachers who are coteaching a classroom, must use shared decision making (Frattura & Capper, 2007). If a coteaching arrangement is going to be successful, both teachers must feel ownership in the classroom, among students, and with educational programs.

Selection of Coteachers

One of the most important aspects in implementing a coteaching program is the selection of teachers to be coteachers. Coteachers must be able to communicate well, get along with each other, share common beliefs, and desire to work as a team. Some teachers, regardless of the benefits of the model, will simply refuse to be involved. Other teachers may want to be involved in a coteaching arrangement but may not be suitable for such an arrangement. As a result, administrators must select teachers for coteaching who they think will be active team members who understand their role in the model (Salend, 2008). Although there is no one type of teacher who would make an ideal coteacher, certain common characteristics are typical among successful coteachers. These include (Walther-Thomas, Korinek, McLaughlin, & Williams, 2000):

- Professional competence
- Personal confidence
- Respect of colleagues
- Professional enthusiasm
- Respect for colleagues' skills and contributions
- Good communication and problem-solving skills
- Personal interest in professional growth
- Flexibility and openness to new ideas
- Effective organizational skills
- Previous experience teaming with others
- Willingness to invest extra time in the process as needed
- Commitment to planning weekly with partner
- Voluntary participation in coteaching

Role of General Educators

General classroom teachers and special education teachers must fill some specific roles in order to create an effective coteaching model. Unfortunately, in the past, very few middle and secondary general educators and special educators have been prepared for collaborative roles within the classroom. Traditional programs focused on preparing teachers to teach alone in a classroom without collaborating with other educators. General classroom teachers were prepared to teach a subject in a classroom, without assistance, and special education teachers were prepared to teach students with disabilities, also without assistance from others teachers. With the need to collaborate growing concurrently with the increasing diversity of schools, preparation programs are changing. Middle and secondary teachers are now developing collaborative strategies and sharing students as part of the secondary school experience. Special education teachers are being prepared to be collaborative partners with other educators to delivery appropriate instruction. While characterized as focusing primarily on content and not on individual student needs, the role of secondary teachers is changing partly because of the No Child Left Behind Act of 2001, which requires all general educators to make the curriculum accessible to all students, including those with special needs. This law has resulted in all educators assuming responsibility for all students, a very positive step that supports the inclusion of students with disabilities in general education classrooms.

With the spread of inclusive classrooms, secondary teachers are being asked to provide instruction to many students who were previously taught in special education classrooms. This has resulted in the need for general classroom teachers to reach out to special education teachers for support. With inclusion being the legal and professional mandate, the best model for providing this support is some form of collaboration. Cooperative teaching is a model that provides support to general classroom teachers while providing the opportunity for students with disabilities to receive their instruction in general classrooms with their nondisabled peers.

Role of Special Educators

Now that students receive special education and specialized services in general education classrooms, coteaching offers new opportunities for both educators to share and learn (Hourcade, 2008). As noted, the traditional role of special educators is to provide instructional interventions to students with disabilities in special education settings. Most were not prepared to work with general classroom teachers in a cooperative teaching model. The role of the special educator in coteaching can vary according to his or her competency in the subject content. However, in any coteaching situation the special education teacher should be involved in all aspects of the academic program, including planning instruction, implementing instruction, assessing fairly and giving grades, monitoring classroom activities, and assisting in classroom management.

Special education teachers have specialized knowledge concerning disabilities, how disabilities may impact cognition, and instructional strategies that might lessen that impact (Murray, 2004). As a result, they bring a wealth of knowledge to the cooperative team that can be used to make content accessible for all students. Rice, Drame, Owens, and Frattura (2007) reported that general education teachers appreciated "special educators' ability to be proactive in introducing new ideas regarding curriculum, instruction, inter-disciplinary connections, assistive technology, and strategies to address the needs of individual learners" (p. 13). Through the use of coteaching, students receive the benefits of exposure to general education curriculum and expectations while receiving supports to enable them to meet classroom expectations.

Regardless of specific roles, coteachers must be compatible. When coteachers work well together, students benefit. Likewise, when they do not work well together, students may suffer. Research has shown that academic content knowledge, high stakes testing, and coteacher compatibility are all directly related to coteaching success (Mastropieri et al., 2005).

Strengthening Coteaching Relationships

Coteaching has been shown to be a successful model for schools to address the needs of diverse students, including those with disabilities. However, simply implementing a coteaching model does not guarantee success: Some coteaching efforts are successful; some coteaching efforts fail. The following factors are related to successful coteaching (Mastropieri et al., 2005):

- An outstanding working relationship
- Strengths as motivators
- Time for coplanning

TABLE 7.1 ● Areas Related to Successful Coteaching

Outstanding Working Relationship—Good working relationships are critical.
Strengths as Motivators—Good coteachers are strong motivators for their students.
Time Allocated for Coplanning—probably the most important area of successful coteaching.
Appropriate Curriculum—Get students involved in the curriculum and learning process.
Effective Instructional Skills—Effective instructional approaches have to be used.
Disability-Specific Teaching Adaptations—Specific adaptations/accommodations must be
    implemented.
Expertise in the Content Area—Both teachers need to have knowledge of the content area.

Source: From "Case Studies in Co-Teaching in the Content Areas: Successes, Failures, and Challenges," by
M. A. Mastropieri, T. E. Scruggs, J. Graetz, J. Norland, W. Gardizi, and K. McDuffie, 2005, *Intervention
in School and Clinic, 40*, 260–270.

- Solid curriculum
- Effective instructional skills
- Exceptional disability-specific teaching adaptations
- Expertise in the content area

Table 7.1 describes each of these areas. Even though they have all been identified as being related to successful coteaching programs, the relationship between the two teachers and time for planning are commonly listed as the most critical components.

When coteaching works well it provides an excellent means of providing educational opportunities for students with disabilities and their nondisabled peers. School personnel should therefore implement strategies or actions to strengthen the coteaching relationship, including planning and instruction, assessment, enhancing the partnership, extending the team's reach, and maintaining perspective (Stivers, 2008). Table 7.2 describes actions within each of these areas that can strengthen coteaching models.

Several strategies can enhance the likelihood of coteaching being successful. These include professionalism, the ability to articulate and model instruction to meet student needs, the ability to accurately assess student progress, the ability to analyze teaching and teaching styles, the ability to work with a wide range of students, and knowledge of course content (Rice et al., 2007). Dukes and Lamar-Dukes (2009) suggest 10 important subsystems that are important when designing cooperative teaching programs. These include basic issues such as classroom workspace and communication, as well as teachers' belief systems and vision for their classrooms. Table 7.3 describes each of the 10 subsystems.

Regardless of efforts to plan and implement coteaching models effectively, there are times when teachers involved in these efforts develop conflicts. When this occurs it is likely that the most damage to the relationship will be the impact on students. As a result, there must be a mechanism in place to deal with such teacher–teacher conflicts. Conflict resolution should be part of professional development programs. "In cooperation with school administrators, the educational support team can plan and develop effective processes to manage a wide range of possible conflicts among teachers (e.g., differences in classroom management techniques)" (Dukes & Lamar-Dukes, 2009, p. 21). If teacher–teacher conflicts continue they can quickly reverse the positive impact that cooperative classrooms may have had.

TABLE 7.2 ● Twenty Ways to Strengthen Coteaching Relationships

PLANNING AND INSTRUCTION

1. Set aside large blocks of time for planning. Coteachers need several hours each month for uninterrupted planning for new units and differentiated lessons.
2. Adapt planning tools to suit your needs. There are several planning tools available that can greatly assist coteachers.
3. Lobby for instructional materials that support coteaching. Teachers must request new materials that are needed to successfully implement a coteaching model.
4. Try new models of coteaching. If one particular coteaching approach is not effective, teachers should try different models that may result in success.
5. Use your time strategically. Take advantage of having two teachers in the classroom and maximize the use of the time that is available for planning and instruction.
6. Reexamine the layout of your classroom to be sure it continues to be well-suited to your evolving coteaching practices. Classroom furniture and desk arrangments may need to change to fit different coteaching practices.

ASSESSMENT

7. Give and get feedback, twice as fast. Coteachers should use brief assessments and informal measures to determine the effectiveness of their instruction.
8. Clarify your understanding of each other's grading expectations. Ensure that both teachers understand and accept each other's grading expectations to maintain a smooth grading process.
9. Experiment with ways to share responsibility for grading. Try different ways to grade students to take advantage of having two teachers who share the grading process.

ENHANCING YOUR PARTNERSHIP

10. Recognize the little things that can mean a lot. Having both teachers' names on the board, report cards, and other communications helps both teachers feel like equal partners.
11. Pay attention to parity. Both coteachers must be considerate of each other's need for parity and implement practices that emphasize this parity.
12. Acknowledge problems early and honestly. Problems that result in coteaching arrangements must be addressed quickly before attitudes and feelings become involved.
13. Address conflicts in a manner that is comfortable for both of you. Coteachers need to deal with conflicts in a way that is comfortable to both parties.
14. Learn to let it go. Teachers who are committed to coteaching partnerships must learn to not dwell on issues that are unimportant and remain focused on making the coteaching classroom successful for all students.

EXTENDING YOUR REACH

15. Attend a professional development workshop together. Attending professional meetings together provides an opportunity for both coteachers to develop a similar understanding of issues related to their coteaching assignments. It also aids in feelings of parity.
16. Model collaborative skills. Coteachers need to model collaboration for students who can then use the same skills for cooperative learning and other collaborative events.
17. Volunteer to serve as mentors to new coteaching pairs. After experiencing a coteaching arrangement, teachers should mentor new coteaching pairs to enhance the likelihood of their success.

MAINTAINING PERSPECTIVE

18. Create a mission statement. Coteachers need to have a common mission or vision for their classroom; taking the time to create a mission statement will facilitate success of the coteaching effort.
19. Honor your sense of humor. Coteachers need to express humor in their day-to-day activities because it helps build cooperative teams.
20. Remember: Coteaching is not a marriage. Coteachers need to understand that they do not have to be best friends; they merely need to have a good working relationship that builds learning opportunities for students.

Source: From "Strengthen Your Co-Teaching Relationship," by J. Stivers, 2008, *Intervention in School and Clinic, 44*, 121–125.

TABLE 7.3 ● Ten Subsystems Important in Designing Cooperative Teaching Programs

Belief and Vision—Believing and having the vision that all students can benefit from inclusive programs.

Time—Collaboration and coteaching requires time for planning and implementing programs.

Classroom (Work) Space—All teachers need to feel like they have ample workspace.

Documentation—Documenting services provided to students is a good way to determine effectiveness of the program.

Conflict Resolution—Schools need to have a conflict resolution process because conflicts occasionally arise between team members.

Initial and Ongoing Professional Development—Coteachers and other professionals involved in collaboration need professional development that allows them to work together to solve problems related to such collaboration.

Fluid and Open Lines of Communication—Communication must be stressed among all team members, and all team members must feel comfortable with their communication opportunities.

Standards and Practice—Teachers have to adhere to effective instructional practices.

Data Collection and Review—Collecting and analyzing data/information is the best way to determine what practices are effective.

Program Evaluation—All programs need to be evaluated, including collaborative educational programs, to ensure they are modified as needed to improve outcomes.

Source: From "Inclusion by Design: Engineering Inclusive Practices in Secondary Schools," by C. Dukes and P. Lamar-Dukes, 2009, *Teaching Exceptional Children, 41,* 16–23.

COTEACHING MODELS

Coteaching is not a single approach; there are numerous ways to implement this strategy. The coteaching model selected for use in middle and secondary classrooms will depend on the teachers involved, the content being taught, and the focus of the lessons. Ultimately, the most important consideration should be the needs of the learners, the demands of the curriculum, and the impact of the instructional delivery in supporting student learning. Effective middle and secondary level teachers should become comfortable and skilled in the use of all six frequently used models: (1) teaming; (2) one teaching, one observing; (3) one teaching, one assisting; (4) station teaching; (5) parallel teaching; and (6) alternative teaching (Friend & Cook, 2010). Table 7.4 describes each of these models, and Figure 7.1 visually depicts each model. In addition, other coteaching models may have special education teachers splitting time between two classes or serving as a resource to different classrooms, depending on a particular need.

Teaming

When teachers speak of coteaching, teaming is the strategy that most often comes to mind. Teaming occurs "when two or more people plan, teach, assess, and assume responsibility for all the students in a classroom" (Thousand, Villa, & Nevin, 2006, p. 244). In this model, teachers typically alternate the instructional lead. Teaming is also the strategy that requires the greatest level of mutual trust and commitment between teachers and as a result often brings the greatest personal rewards to the coteachers. When interviewed about this model's usage, coteachers often report that teaming results in a synergy that enhances their students' participation and revitalizes them as teachers (Friend & Cook, 2010).

TABLE 7.4 ● Coteaching Models

WHOLE CLASS MODELS	
Teaming	Both teachers are actively engaged in teaching the whole class. Teachers alternate the instructional lead.
One Teaching, One Observing	One teacher teaches the lesson; other teacher observes students' responses and takes data.
One Teaching, One Assisting	One teacher teaches the lesson; other teacher records attendance or completes other clerical duties.
	One teacher teaches the lesson; other teacher leaves the classroom teaching students outside of class or runs class-related errands.
	One teacher teaches the lesson; other teacher prepares the homework or materials for a later lesson.
DIVIDED CLASS MODELS	
Station Teaching	Class is divided into at least two teacher-supported stations; additional stations may be used as independent station or supervised by the coteachers or other personnel. Each station covers different content, but all students will rotate through all stations.
Parallel Teaching	Class is divided into two equal-sized heterogeneous groups; each teacher instructs the small group on the same lesson.
Alternative Teaching	One teacher teaches a small group of less than half the class on a topic; other teacher instructs the larger group on another topic.

Source: Adapted from "Co-Teaching Revisited: Redrawing the Blueprint," by A. Kloo and N. Zigmond, 2008, *Preventing School Failure, 52*(2), 12–20.

One challenge coteachers may encounter when using teaming is the meshing of teaching styles, pacing, instructional format preferences, and use of humor. While teachers may have differences in each of these components, they still must complement each other (Friend & Cook, 2010). A second challenge is that both teachers need to be comfortable and competent taking the roles of leader and supporter at different times (Thousand et al., 2006). The third challenge is coteaching may be difficult for a novice teacher. Even with veteran teachers, they should not feel obligated to undertake teaming unless they feel comfortable with the concept and the strategies to be used (Friend & Cook, 2010). Finally, coteachers who decide to use teaming need to check with each other frequently to determine if each is comfortable and satisfied with the model. Coteachers should begin the teaming experience with an open discussion of individual needs and should periodically allow time for discussing classroom issues during the coteaching relationship.

One Teaching, One Observing

In the "one teaching, one observing" model, one coteacher is assigned to observe behavioral, social, and academic functioning of the students in the classroom while the other coteacher conducts the instruction to the entire class. The observing teacher systematically collects data on individual students, a small group of students, or the entire class. One potential challenge

(a) One Teaching/One Helping

(b) Parallel Teaching

(c) Station Teaching

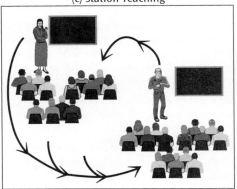

(d) Alternative Teaching

(e) Team Teaching

FIGURE 7.1 ● Coteaching Models

Source: From S. J. Salend, 2008, *Creating Inclusive Classrooms: Effective and Reflective Practices* (6th ed., p. 161). Upper Saddle River, NJ: Merrill/Pearson. Used with permission.

when using the one teaching, one observing model is it could result in the overuse of a specific role by one of the coteachers. For example, when one coteacher is consistently assigned as observer, that teacher might be viewed as a teacher's aide, not an equal teacher in the class-room. Likewise, the other coteacher might be viewed as the "real" teacher in the class. Thus, a perception of unequal parity, or inequality, in the roles of the teachers may occur. Both teachers need to guard against this possibility by changing roles periodically (Friend & Cook, 2010).

Prior to undertaking a one teaching, one observing class session, coteachers should determine who will observe (person or group), what will be observed, why the observation is needed, and what method will be used in the observation. For example, if there is a student who is off task regularly, the observing teacher may focus on this student to determine the number of times the student (1) refuses to do the work or (2) distracts other students from working. The observing teacher could use a frequency chart and tally the occurrences of each behavior. This information can be used in making critical instructional decisions (Friend & Cook, 2010).

One Teaching, One Assisting

In the "one teaching, one assisting" model, one coteacher teaches and the other coteacher supports the instructional process. The coteacher who is teaching is primarily responsible for preparing the lesson, leading instruction, and managing the classroom. The assisting coteacher's responsibility is to walk around the classroom assisting students who need redirection or providing support to those students with questions or concerns. The advantage of this strategy is that it takes relatively little joint planning and provides a role to a teacher who may be weak in the content being taught. It is also a strategy that needs little joint planning, meaning that can be used in situations when joint planning time is limited (Friend & Cook, 2010).

Challenges that might be present with the one teaching, one assisting model include the potential for the assisting coteacher to lose parity through overuse of this strategy, resulting in undermining the credibility of the assisting coteacher in the classroom. A second challenge is the distraction created by a teacher moving throughout the classroom while the other teacher is presenting the lesson. This movement can become a visual distraction for some students or even for the presenting coteacher. It can also become an auditory distraction if the assisting coteacher whispers or speaks to students while the lesson is occurring. Perhaps a greater challenge presented by this model is the need to determine if a student is simply seeking attention from the teacher or from peers. Another problem is that the presence of an assisting coteacher could inadvertently encourage students to be dependent learners. Thus, this model may reinforce the behaviors related to learned helplessness that appear in some students, especially those with disabilities. A third challenge is that in playing a supportive role with individual students, the coteacher may inadvertently begin to block the student–student interactions present in the general education classroom. If a teacher is seen to hover around an individual student, it could lead to stigmatization of the student and an interruption of the normal class interactions that would be beneficial to the student (Friend & Cook, 2007; Thousand et al., 2006). Therefore, although the one teaching, one assisting model is a strategy that can be used easily in most classrooms, it should be used sparingly because of the challenges associated with its use.

Station Teaching

Station teaching is a coteaching approach where both coteachers provide instruction to the class by dividing the content so that each coteacher has specific content to plan and teach. The material to be taught is provided in specific areas of the room called "stations." In station teaching, students move from one station to another according to a schedule while the teachers introduce and supervise the completion of activities related to the specific content they have introduced. This strategy requires both teachers to be responsible for planning and delivering the curricular content. The coteachers deliver different components of the lesson content, but do so at the same time, maintain the same pace so that they begin and end at the same time, have parity or equality in the classroom, and hold equal status as teachers (Friend & Cook, 2010; Kloo & Zigmond, 2008; Thousand et al., 2006). In some classrooms more than two stations may be used in combination with independent work assignments. The independent work assignments can be completed with a peer tutor, visiting expert, paraprofessional, student teacher, or another adult who might be assigned to the classroom. Station teaching has the advantage of student learning opportunities through multiple teaching styles and lower student–teacher ratios. For students with exceptional learning needs this model supports the concept of differentiated instruction and, therefore, promotes easier inclusion into the class.

One challenge when using station teaching is the potential for increased noise and movement within the classroom, which can increase distractions and create the potential for disruptive behaviors. Strategies to counter these challenges include preferential seating for students with distractibility issues; study carrels; sound-muffling headphones for those doing independent work; and altered classroom arrangements to help separate the teachers and the groups of students (Friend & Cook, 2010).

A second challenge is the increase in transition times. Transition time is often a time of increased noise and misbehavior and can be a time-consuming process. To speed the process and reduce noise and misbehaviors, coteachers might move instead of the students. A second strategy is to teach students how to move quietly and efficiently, while keeping their hands and materials in check. After providing instruction, coteachers will need to actively reinforce students' appropriate transition behaviors (Friend & Cook, 2010). One more challenge when using this model is to avoid the development of a class within a class. Coteachers need to ensure that all of the students are taught by both coteachers, to avoid routinely grouping the same students together with the same coteacher. Ensuring heterogeneity in the groups and rotating supervision can easily address this challenge (Thousand et al., 2006).

Parallel Teaching

Parallel teaching occurs when two teachers divide the class evenly and each delivers instruction to a heterogeneous group of students. Decisions teachers make on the composition of student groups should be based on the philosophy that diversity should be maintained within the larger class group. In this model, teachers jointly plan the instruction and then each delivers the instruction to his or her assigned group using identical instructional strategies and materials. The benefit is that all students receive essentially the same instruction, but in a smaller group with one of the coteachers. Unlike in station teaching, coteachers using the parallel method do not exchange groups during the class period, although to reduce the possibility of a class within a class occurring, the groups may be changed daily, weekly, or when the instructional lesson changes (Friend & Cook, 2010).

According to Thousand and colleagues (2006), parallel teaching has at least eight variations: (1) splitting the class where the class is evenly divided between the two teachers; (2) using station teaching, as discussed previously; (3) rotating groups where coteachers rotate among two or more groups of students while each teaches the same topic to a different group of students; (4) rotating groups where each teacher teaches a different component of the lesson and the teachers rotate between groups instead of having students rotate between teachers; (5) monitoring student groups when cooperative learning is used; (6) monitoring experiment or lab activities by both teachers for a given number of student lab groups; (7) providing a student learning style focus with each coteacher utilizing materials based on either visual, kinesthetic, or auditory learning styles; and (8) providing supplementary instruction where one coteacher instructs a concept or skill and the other coteacher helps students apply it or generalize it to relevant environments. Several of these variations are also described by Friend and Cook (2010) with different titles.

An advantage of parallel teaching is that it results in lower teacher–student ratios. Its use is highly appropriate for drill-and-practice activities, test reviews, projects needing close teacher supervision, and activities where student discussion is essential (i.e., preparing for debates or point/counterpoint presentations). Another advantage of the smaller class size is increased participation by all students, including those who might be reluctant to enter into discussions in large groups.

Similar to station teaching, there may be increased noise and activity levels when using parallel teaching. Coteachers can use similar strategies to deal with these distractions that were suggested in the previous section. Having groups separate to opposite corners of the room may also help in reducing excessive noise. Other challenges of this approach could include difficulties in pacing and the need for both teachers to be knowledgeable and competent in all content being taught. To address this challenge, coteachers need to discuss the content to develop a common understanding and ensure that both groups receive similar information. Content outlines, study guides, or content maps may help both teachers with pacing. In addition, coteachers may simply watch and listen to each other and adjust the instructional pace accordingly (Friend & Cook, 2010; Thousand et al., 2006).

Alternative Teaching

Alternative teaching is a coteaching strategy in which a small group of students is selected and provided instruction that is different from the instruction provided to the larger group of students in the class. This strategy is often used to provide preteaching to students with special learning needs or intensive instruction for those encountering learning difficulties. It can also be used as an enrichment strategy for students already competent in the content. This strategy is also effective for students who have missed information previously presented.

The challenge when using alternative teaching is the risk of stigmatization for students in the selected group. To reduce this possibility, all students in the class could be rotated through the small group during a reasonable time period (week, month, grading period, etc.). A variation to the model provides an opportunity for students to volunteer for the group for an in-depth discussion, questions, or reviews. This variation has an inherent risk of attracting students who are seeking attention. To prevent this from happening, teachers can communicate with students prior to asking for volunteers to encourage particular students to participate. It is critical that both teachers routinely provide instruction in the small group to avoid the possibility that either is labeled as the teacher for students who are having academic difficulties. Records should also be kept on which students are attending the small group to ensure that all students are rotated to that group periodically. Composition of the groups should be fluid and vary according to student needs.

ROLE OF SCHOOL PERSONNEL IN COTEACHING

Most research on coteaching has emphasized the roles of the teachers who are participating in the classroom. However, coteaching can be implemented using other professionals, such as paraprofessionals, counselors, administrators, therapists, or even parents and volunteers. While these nonteaching partners can be extremely useful in implementing a coteaching model, school personnel must always recognize their limitations because of minimal training in pedagogy, classroom management, and other important areas related to teaching.

Role of Paraprofessionals

Paraprofessionals function as important members of the instructional team because their role is to provide assistance and supports for students, often focusing on students with special needs who are included in general education classrooms. Paraprofessionals are therefore available to provide support for teachers in delivering instruction and support for students with learning and behavior problems. Since they are typically in classrooms most of each day, they are able to observe the students in a variety of activities. Their insight could be useful in understanding students' academic problems, behavioral challenges, abilities, and social issues. Often paraprofessionals become invisible to students and may therefore be in a position to observe behaviors that are often hidden from teachers. The challenge for paraprofessionals is to ensure that they do not become a stigmatizing factor for students they assist. Because they are an important member of a child's instructional team in a cotaught classroom, their attendance in developing intervention plans is important. If they are unable to attend these meetings, teachers should make an effort to solicit their input and ideas at different times.

Teacher–paraprofessional teams are not always as effective as they could be. This may be due to teachers finding themselves in supervisory roles with paraprofessionals and without having the necessary skills to establish and maintain a positive, working relationship. Since paraprofessionals represent a very important resource for collaborative teams, it is imperative that teachers develop a better understanding of how to work with them to assist students who are having learning problems. Devlin (2008) has identified 20 ways to create effective teacher–paraprofessional teams. These include discussing work style preferences, practicing effective listening, and using a collaborative problem-solving process. Table 7.5 describes these 20 steps.

Role of Administration

The support of school administrators in implementing and maintaining a successful coteaching program is critical. In fact, without their support it is extremely difficult to maintain a viable coteaching program. There are numerous areas where administrative support is important. These include (1) assisting in scheduling; (2) assigning students to your classrooms; (3) ensuring an appropriate number of students in the cotaught classroom; (4) creating planning time opportunities for coteachers; (5) considering the time requirements for coteachers when assigning extra duties; and (6) providing opportunities for coteachers to attend professional development together. One of the more important requirements for successful coteaching is planning. School administrators need to provide coteachers with opportunities for planning time. If they have to find their own planning time outside the regular school day it is unlikely coteachers will want to continue the model. A supportive administration may be able to configure teaching assignments to allow the coteachers the same planning period, or at least provide occasional opportunities for joint planning. Administrators can also influence school districts on policy matters that might facilitate coteaching efforts. For example, the size of a cotaught class might remain the same as a typically taught class instead of increased numbers since there are two teachers in the class, or the cotaught class might have the same distribution of special education students or others with exceptional learning needs as the typical general education classes. Administrators also decide when teachers are asked to substitute in another class during their planning period and can assist coteachers by helping them avoid loss of planning time.

Role of Other Professionals

In addition to teachers, paraprofessionals, and administrators, there are other professionals in schools who could be valuable resources on coteaching teams. These include school counselors, physical and occupational therapists, behavioral intervention specialists, speech-language pathologists, school nurses, and vocational rehabilitation specialists. Each of these professionals could play an important role in coteaching arrangements, particularly around a particular topic. For example, a rehabilitation counselor could assist a general classroom teacher in classes

TABLE 7.5 ● Ways to Create Effective Teacher–Paraprofessional Teams

- Discover your paraprofessional's interests and skills. This indicates your interest in the paraprofessional and your desire to be a team.
- Communicate that you are a team. Ensure that your communications, oral and written, indicate that the paraprofessional is part of the team.
- Talk about work style preferences. Have a discussion with the paraprofessional about work style preferences, such as punctuality, classroom management styles, and other issues that occur on a daily basis in the classroom.
- Develop a personal job description that includes ethical guidelines. Create a list of job duties and expectations for the paraprofessional; include ethical guidelines such as confidentiality to ensure the paraprofessional understands roles played by team members.
- Convey your role as instructional leader. Discuss your own roles with the paraprofessionals to ensure that they understand your specific roles; emphasize the legal responsibility.
- Be proactive regarding classroom and behavior management. Make sure that the paraprofessional understands the classroom and behavior management plans and how they will be implemented.
- Discuss the issue of confidentiality. Stress the importance of confidentiality to the paraprofessional, emphasizing the legal requirements that must be upheld.
- Set clear priorities for student learning, and communicate these to your paraprofessional. Make sure your paraprofessional understands what, how, and why something is taught.
- Give frequent constructive feedback. Make sure you provide feedback to the paraprofessional to positively reinforce appropriate actions and suggest improvements in other areas.
- Be aware of how you communicate. Do not "talk down" to your paraprofessional and always be respectful of his or her role in the instructional process.
- Delegate decision making to your paraprofessional. Allow the paraprofessional to make some decisions in the classroom to reinforce his or her role as a team member.
- Practice effective listening. Make sure you listen to your paraprofessional by truly paying attention to what he or she has to say.
- Establish formal planning times. Just as coteachers need planning time, so too do teachers and their paraprofessionals. Formal planning times ensure that the planning will occur.
- Hold brainstorming sessions. Include paraprofessionals in brainstorming sessions about specific students or situations. Often paraprofessionals have ideas that teachers may not consider.
- Include your paraprofessional. Invite paraprofessionals to IEP meetings and other formal meetings where their opinions and observations can be helpful.
- Provide training beyond what is expected by the school system. Many paraprofessionals can be used more effectively with more training. Don't underestimate their abilities.
- Use a collaborative problem-solving process. Include paraprofessionals in problem-solving sessions and encourage their active participation.
- Integrate your paraprofessional into the entire classroom setting. Rotate responsibilities in the classroom, when possible, to engage the paraprofessional in most of the activities instructional process.
- Be open. Establish an honest, open relationship with your paraprofessional and encourage him or her to share opinions and ideas as well.
- Incorporate laughter into each day. Have fun. Most people enjoy their jobs if they have some fun, and people who enjoy their jobs are likely to be more productive workers.

Source: Adapted from "Create Effective Teacher–Paraprofessional Teams," by P. Devlin, 2008, *Intervention in School and Clinic, 44,* 41–44.

focusing on vocational opportunities and a school counselor could assist in classes focusing on self-determination, social skills, and mental health. When considering the use of a coteaching model, teachers need to examine the roles of all professionals who will be involved in the implementation of this method.

STRATEGIES USED IN IMPLEMENTING COTEACHING

When preparing to coteach, teachers interested in the model should first visit with the school principal about the idea. School administrators can enable the project, provide resources including planning time, modify teaching and student schedules, and answer questions when they arise (Murawski & Dieker, 2004; Murray, 2004). Principals can be a strong advocate for coteaching as an organizational model. In addition, when they support coteaching they become advocates for coteachers attempting to implement the model. As with any new initiative in the school, there will be differing degrees of awareness, proficiency, and acceptance of coteaching. As a result, teachers interested in implementing a coteaching model should provide literature for the principal and other teachers explaining the model. Providing principals with this information will give them the necessary tools to advocate for the program. This administrative advocacy will greatly assist in developing an understanding and acceptance of coteaching by other teachers and parents (Murawski & Dieker, 2004; Murray, 2004).

Following consultation with and approval from the school administration, teachers interested in implementing a coteaching model must begin planning for its implementation. A first step may be getting to know each other better. Since coteaching requires teachers to work closely together in the same classroom, they need to be very familiar with each other. There are several books available that describe activities designed for teachers who are getting ready to coteach, including *Collaboration: A Success Strategy for Special Educators* (Cramer, 1998) and *Cooperative Teaching: Rebuilding and Sharing the Schoolhouse* (Hourcade & Bauwens, 2003). These two books can provide encouragement for prospective coteachers. In planning a coteaching classroom, the new coteachers must have opportunities to plan and discuss their classroom, and do the following (Friend & Cook, 2010; Gately & Gately, 2001; Johnston, Tulbert, Sabastian, Devries, & Gompert, 2000; Murray, 2004; Vaughn, Schumm, & Arguelles, 1997):

- Share their core beliefs concerning teaching
- Share their dreams for the classroom
- Share their vision of how the classroom will function
- Determine roles and responsibilities for each other
- Establish classroom expectations
- Discuss parity issues
- Discuss ownership of students
- Determine space usage
- Determine classroom rules and procedures
- Determine grading responsibilities and expectations
- Determine behavioral expectations and consequences
- Discuss how regular feedback to each other will take place

After planning for the coteaching opportunity, the one thing that remains is to prepare students for the change in how they will be taught. This means that when students arrive in class on the first day they will need an introduction to the new organizational method. Families of students should be notified before the beginning of the school year that there will be two teachers in the classroom and how the classroom will function. For families who have not been notified, an information meeting may be helpful after the school year has begun. Regardless of when parents and students are provided information about the classroom, they should meet with both coteachers, who need to be consistent in their interpretation of the classroom model. Students and their parents should be provided information regarding how the classroom will function, including how instruction will be delivered, how students will be evaluated, and how discipline will be maintained. Additionally, the overall rationale behind the coteaching model, including its strengths and weaknesses, should be discussed.

Research on coteaching has revealed that teachers assume a wide variety of leading and supporting roles in coteaching arrangements, ranging from quiet support to functioning in a true teacher partnership (Morocco & Aguilar, 2002; Weiss & Lloyd, 2003). It should be realized that all coteachers have an important role in planning, implementing, and supporting instruction. Both teachers have active roles in teaching content while integrating specialized instruction into the class. In summary, collaboration through coteaching is a rapidly growing phenomenon in the schools. Those teachers who have used the coteaching model have described it as an effective means of meeting legislative and regulatory mandates. In addition, they have stated that coteaching provided a positive experience for both teachers.

EVALUATING COOPERATIVE TEACHING

Cooperative teaching can be an extremely successful model for working with students in middle and secondary schools, including those with disabilities and other learning problems. However, at times, cooperative teaching programs are unsuccessful. In one such instance, a teacher wrote the following (Salend et al., 2002, p. 196):

> I don't think I'd like to work in this type of program again. She felt like a visitor in my classroom, and we never connected personally. We struggled because of differences in roles, teaching and communication styles, and philosophy. The students also were confused. They felt that I was the teacher and she was my aide. I felt like she was always watching me and judging me. We didn't know how to do it and received little support from our principal.

Obviously this teacher did not have a good coteaching experience. While research supports the model, it is not always implemented successfully and often teachers who think they want to participate in the model find out later that they cannot give up the autonomy they have in their traditional classroom.

Once a cooperative teaching program is established, school personnel should conduct an ongoing evaluation to ensure the program's success. The last thing schools need is to implement a program that will not be successful and continue with that program in the future. Evaluating cooperative teaching programs can provide information to administrators to help them make decisions about continuing a particular program or making changes to the program that will hopefully lead to success.

Evaluating cooperative teaching programs requires the collection of information. This can be accomplished in several ways, including employee interviews and surveys, best practices checklists, and observations. Observing cooperative teaching classrooms can be an effective way to determine how the model is working. The following questions can be the focus of such an observation (Salend et al., 2002, p. 198):

- What roles do teachers perform? Are these roles meaningful?
- How often and for how long are teachers interacting with each other?
- Who is initiating and ending these interactions?
- What is the nature of these interactions (e.g., cooperative, reciprocal, supportive, complementary, individualistic)?
- Which students are the recipients of these interactions?
- What are the outcomes of these interactions for teachers and their students?
- What factors appear to promote and limit these interactions?

Directions: Please indicate your feeling about the following statements using this scale:

Strongly Disagree	Disagree	Neutral	Agree	Strongly Agree
(1)	(2)	(3)	(4)	(5)

1. I like working in a cooperative teaching team. 　　　　　　　　　1 2 3 4 5
2. Students benefit from being taught by a cooperative teaching team. 　1 2 3 4 5
3. I feel like this is our classroom. 　　　　　　　　　　　　　　　1 2 3 4 5
4. Students with disabilities receive fewer specialized services as a result of cooperative teaching. 　1 2 3 4 5
5. My students' families are satisfied with our cooperative teaching arrangement. 　1 2 3 4 5
6. Other professionals are supportive of our cooperative teaching arrangement. 　1 2 3 4 5
7. Our cooperative teaching team has sufficient time to communicate effectively. 　1 2 3 4 5
8. Our cooperative teaching team shares responsibility for all instructional and noninstructional activities. 　1 2 3 4 5
9. Our cooperative teaching team blends the teaching styles, philosophies, talents, and expertise of both teachers. 　1 2 3 4 5
10. Working in a cooperative teaching team has encouraged me to try new instructional strategies. 　1 2 3 4 5
11. Our school district provides the necessary support from others, resources, and training to implement cooperative teaching effectively. 　1 2 3 4 5
12. I enjoy teaching more because I work in a cooperative teaching team. 　1 2 3 4 5
13. I like having another adult in the classroom. 　　　　　　　　　　1 2 3 4 5
14. It is easy to communicate with my cooperative teaching partner. 　1 2 3 4 5
15. I perform a subordinate role in our cooperative teaching team. 　　1 2 3 4 5
16. I have benefited professionally and personally from working as a cooperative teaching team. 　1 2 3 4 5
17. My workload has increased as a result of working in a cooperative teaching team. 　1 2 3 4 5
18. I am satisfied with the schoolwide and districtwide policies regarding cooperative teaching teams. 　1 2 3 4 5
19. I would like to continue to work in a cooperative teaching team. 　1 2 3 4 5

FIGURE 7.2 ● Sample Survey of Teachers

Source: From S. J. Salend, 2011, *Creating Inclusive Classrooms: Effective and Reflective Practices* (7th ed., p. 152). Upper Saddle River, NJ: Merrill/Pearson. Used with permission.

Salend (2008) provides a sample survey that can be used with coteachers that will also provide information for the evaluation. Figure 7.2 describes this survey. After collecting information, an analysis should be made by administrators and teachers involved in the cooperative teaching classroom to determine any areas that need to be changed that will improve the program.

SUMMARY

Collaboration related to education can be defined as two or more teachers working together to accomplish a common purpose. Coteaching is a strategy that is grounded in collaboration. In this model, two teachers, typically a special education teacher and general classroom teacher, work together in the same classroom in a variety of different arrangements to deliver instruction to the same group of students. Coteaching and other collaborative teaching models are more important today than ever because of the growing diversity of students in public schools. This diversity includes students with

disabilities who are mostly educated with their nondisabled peers for most of each school day.

There are numerous benefits to coteaching for both teachers and students. Students without disabilities even benefit from the model. Schools interested in implementing a coteaching model should plan in advance rather than simply starting a coteaching program. Teachers need to develop a thorough understanding of each other's vision, philosophy, classroom management style, grading practices, and preferred instructional strategies prior to implementing the model. Coteachers must have ample planning time, both before the model is implemented and during its use, in order to effectively meet the needs of students in the classroom.

There are several variations of the coteaching model. These variations are dependent on specific roles played by each coteacher and should be used depending on the nature of students in the classroom and preferences of the coteachers. Finally, coteaching can involve more than teachers. Teachers can develop coteaching arrangements with paraprofessionals, therapists, counselors, and even parents. Regardless of the makeup of the coteaching team, the model can be extremely successful and beneficial to a diverse student population.

ACTIVITIES

1. With one of your classmates select a type of coteaching and design a lesson using the selected model. Present it to the class.

2. For a greater challenge, design a training program on coteaching. Demonstrate each of the models of coteaching by using that model in that section of the training.

3. Observe a classroom where teachers are using coteaching as an instructional strategy. Write a summary of the teaching that occurred. After the instruction is concluded, ask the teachers how they decided who was the presenter and who was the supporter. Ask how much planning time they used in preparation for the class. Ask the teachers to briefly describe how accommodations are made for students with disabilities in the areas of curriculum, instruction, and evaluation. Ask who does the grading and who does the discipline. Ask about their ideas on working with parents and the roles that they have or share when parents request a meeting with the teacher. Write a report on the answers to the questions. Then summarize your reaction to the cotaught classroom.

REFERENCES

Cramer, S. F. (1998). *Collaboration: A success strategy for special educators.* Boston: Allyn & Bacon.

Devlin, P. (2008). Create effective teacher–paraprofessional teams. *Intervention in School and Clinic, 44,* 41–44.

Dieker, L. A., & Murawski, W. W. (2003). Co-teaching at the secondary level: Unique trends, current trend, and suggestions for success. *The High School Journal, 86*(4), 1–13.

Dukes, C., & Lamar-Dukes, P. (2009). Inclusion by design: Engineering inclusive practices in secondary schools. *Teaching Exceptional Children, 41,* 16–23.

Frattura, E., & Capper, C. A. (2007). New teacher teams to support integrated comprehensive services. *Teaching Exceptional Children, 39*(4), 16–21.

Friend, M., & Cook, L. (2010). *Interactions: Collaboration skills for school professionals* (6th ed.). Upper Saddle River, NJ: Pearson Education.

Gately, S. F., & Gately Jr., F. J. (2001). Understanding co-teaching components. *Teaching Exceptional Children, 33*(4), 40–47.

Hourcade, J. J. (2008). Collaboration in the schools: Enhancing success for students with developmental disabilities. In H. P. Parette & George R. Peterson-Kaplan (Eds.), *Research-based practices in developmental disabilities* (2nd ed., pp. 589–609). Austin, TX: Pro-Ed.

Hourcade, J. J., & Bauwens, J. (2003). *Cooperative teaching: Rebuilding and sharing the schoolhouse* (2nd ed.). Austin, TX: Pro-Ed.

Johnston, S. S., Tulbert, B. L., Sebastian, J. P., Devries, K., & Gompert, A. (2000). Vocabulary development: A collaborative effort for teaching content vocabulary. *Intervention in School and Clinic, 35*(5), 311–315.

Keefe, E. B., Moore, V., & Duff, F. (2004). The four "knows" of collaborative teaching. *TEACHING Exceptional Children, 36*(5), 36–42.

Kloo, A., & Zigmond, N. (2008). Co-teaching revisited: Redrawing the blueprint. *Preventing School Failure, 52*(2), 12–20.

Magiera, K., Smith, C., Zigmond, N., & Gebauer, K. (2005). Benefits of co-teaching in secondary mathematics classes. *Teaching Exceptional Children, 37*(3), 20–24.

Mastropieri, M. A., Scruggs, T. E., Graetz, J., Noland, J., Gardizi, W., & Mcduffie, K. (2005). Case studies in co-teaching in the content areas: Successes, failures, and challenges. *Intervention in School and Clinic, 40,* 260-279.

Morocco, C. C., & Aguilar, C. M. (2002). Coteaching for content understanding: A schoolwide model. *Journal of Educational and Psychological Consultation, 13,* 315-347.

Murawski, W. W., & Swanson, H. L. (2001). A meta-analysis of co-teaching research: Where are the data? *Remedial and Special Education, 22,* 258–267.

Murawski, W. W., & Dieker, L. A. (2004). Tips and strategies for co-teaching at the secondary level. *Teaching Exceptional Children, 36*(5), 52–58.

Murray, C. (2004). Clarifying collaborative roles in urban high schools: General educators' perspectives. *Teaching Exceptional Children, 36*(5), 44–51.

Rice, N., Drame, E., Owens, L., & Frattura, E. M. (2007). Co-instructing at the secondary level: Strategies for success. *Teaching Exceptional Children, 39*(6), 12–18.

Salend, S. J. (2008). *Creating inclusive classrooms: Effective and reflective practices* (6th ed.). Upper Saddle River, NJ: Merrill/Pearson.

Salend, S. J. (2011). *Creating inclusive classrooms: Effective and reflective practices* (7th ed.). Upper Saddle River, NJ: Merrill/Pearson.

Salend, S. J., Gordon, J., & Lopez-Vona, K. (2002). Evaluating cooperative teaching teams. *Intervention in School and Clinic, 37,* 195–200.

Scruggs, T. E., Mastropieri, M. A., & McDuffie, K. A. (2007). Co-teaching in inclusive classrooms: A metasynthesis of qualitative research. *Exceptional Children, 73,* 392–416.

Sileo, J., & van Garderen, D. (2010). Creating optimal opportunities to learn mathematics: Blending co-teaching structures with research-based practices. *Teaching Exceptional Children, 42*(3), 14–21.

Stivers, J. (2008). Strengthen your co-teaching relationship. *Intervention in School and Clinic, 44,* 121–125.

Thousand, J. S., Villa, R. A., & Nevin, A. I. (2006). The many faces of collaborative planning and teaching. *Theory into Practice, 45*(3), 239–248.

Vaughn, S., Schumm, J. K., & Arguelles, M. E. (1997). The ABCDE's of co-teaching. *Teaching Exceptional Children, 30*(2), 4–10.

Villa, R., Thousand, J., & Nevin, A. (2008). *A guide to co-teaching: Practical tips for facilitating student learning* (2nd ed.). Thousand Oaks, CA: Corwin.

Walsh, J. M., & Jones, B. (2004). New models of cooperative teaching. *Teaching Exceptional Children, 36,* 14–18.

Walther-Thomas, C., Korinek, L., McLaughlin, V. L., & Williams, B. (2000). *Collaboration skills for school professionals* (4th ed.). White Plains, NJ: Longman.

Weiss, M. P. (2004). Co-teaching as a science in the schoolhouse: More questions than answers. *Journal of Learning Disabilities, 37,* 218–223.

Weiss, M. P., & Lloyd, J. (2003). Conditions for co-teaching: Lessons from a case study. *Teacher Education and Special Education, 26*(1), 27–41.

8

Differentiated Instruction

Study Questions

1. Define *differentiated instruction* and explain its usefulness in meeting the needs of a diverse classroom.

2. Explain the six principles that are the basis of differentiated instruction.

3. Explain and give examples of the five elements that teachers most often address when planning instruction.

4. Explain *backward design* and list questions teachers may ask when implementing this method of planning.

5. Why is differentiated instruction useful in middle and secondary classrooms?

INTRODUCTION

Today, most middle and secondary general education classrooms include students with special learning needs, among them students with cultural and language differences, exceptional talents, mild to moderate disabilities, as well as typical middle and secondary level students. This diversity of students is the result of state and federal law and regulations as well as current educational philosophy; teachers must be prepared to educate all children in general education settings. With the diversity of classrooms growing annually, there is no way teachers can effectively teach a classroom of students the same material using the same methods for the entire class. One teaching method or style for all children simply does not work; today's diverse students learn differently, are at different levels, and differ from one another in significant ways.

In addition to the change in the mix of students in the classrooms, the curriculum in today's schools is strongly influenced by state and national content and performance standards. Indeed, the No Child Left Behind Act of 2001 (NCLB) is often cited as a driving force in the standards-based reform movement (Van Garderen & Whittaker, 2006; Nolet & McLaughlin, 2000; Stodden, Galloway, & Stodden, 2003; Tomlinson, 2000). The challenging question in schools then becomes: How can teachers address these standards and at the same time meet the needs of all students in today's diverse classroom? The answer most often provided is that teachers must understand and use evidence-based practices in the selection of curricular and instructional strategies for the classroom. They must differentiate content area instruction (Anderson, Yilmaz, & Wasburn-Moses, 2004; Schloss, Schloss, & Schloss, 2007).

Curriculum refers to the broader view of education or schooling as "the courses offered, the overall experience provided a child by the school, the program included in a particular subject field, or in some cases, the sum total of experiences afforded school age children regardless of school sponsorship" (Meyen, 1981, pp. 20–21). Curriculum also refers to "what is taught in the school and consists of learning outcomes that society considers essential for success" (Mercer & Mercer, 2001, p. 170). *Instruction* is the process or method of presenting the curriculum. In other words, the curriculum is "a program, a plan, content, and learning experiences" whereas the instruction is "methods, the teaching act, implementation, and presentation" (Oliva, 2001, p. 8). Therefore, for teachers to be informed and effective, they must understand what constitutes the curriculum in their school, how to design evidence-based instruction, and be able to identify effective instructional strategies that will assist their students in the acquisition of instructional goals related to the curriculum.

Orlich, Harder, Callahan, and Gibson (2001) identified four important findings related to instructional planning. This information supports the belief that teachers' individual skills in completing planning activities will have a significant impact on the effectiveness of which instructional planning models are used in specific content area classrooms.

EVIDENCE-BASED PRACTICES ON CONTENT AREA STRATEGIES

Content area instruction is when teachers provide instruction to students in areas such as social studies, science, foreign language, math, and literature (Bryant, Smith, & Bryant, 2008). In the majority of middle and secondary level classrooms this instruction is teacher-directed and emphasizes the specific content or subject matter. One of the major problems experienced by students in middle and high school content classes is difficulty in reading (Bryant et al., 2000; Unrau, 2008). This is a significant issue because three of the major content areas (language arts/English, science, and social studies) focus heavily on the use of content area text-books as the major method for knowledge acquisition. This is especially true for students with learning and behavioral difficulties or language differences, for whom there are some specific problems that may directly impact classroom instruction. For instance, students reduce their opportunity for classroom success if they "lack the strategies and skills that enable their typically achieving peers to benefit fully from textbook-based instruction" (Bryant et al., 2008, p. 538). This lack of prerequisite reading skills or the level of language skills becomes an important issue when teachers utilize cooperative groups and activity learning with students who may not have skills to be fully involved in the group learning process (Bryant et al., 2008; Bryant, Ugel, Thompson, & Hamff, 1999).

Social studies and language arts/English subjects are often taught as back-to-back, or blocked, courses. This integration of content has been seen as a means to apply literary concepts to history/social studies instruction and thus to allow the students to "conduct inquiry and develop reasoning skills while fostering knowledge acquisition and concept attainment" (Unrau, 2008, p. 375). In the science content area, science-focused activities and discovery learning are often used as a means of learning content. But the issue of reading, as well as deficiencies in organizational and planning skills, may impede student learning in these content areas. Mathematics is often not included when teachers think of problems that students may have in reading, but the use of symbols both in the form of reading words and in numbers is an integral part of teaching in this content area. Thus, for students with special learning needs, the lack of higher level language development and usage, organizational and planning problems, and reading issues may be significant barriers to success in the classroom. Because of the diversity present in the middle or secondary classroom, teachers must address the individual characteristics and needs of students in order to enhance the chances of their learning success.

After considering the student issues noted above, it is apparent that you must be competent in identifying evidence-based methods for use in your classroom so that student success can be achieved. The first step in utilizing evidence-based strategies is to address the needs of students in your inclusive middle or secondary classroom. According to Unrau (2008), there are a number of research-based strategies that can be used by teachers in all content areas because they "transfer productively to each and every discipline without jeopardizing the core knowledge and skills of the discipline" (p. 364). Table 8.1 provides examples of evidence-based practices for use in the secondary classroom.

Secondly, you should be prepared to, and skilled in, when and how to adapt your classroom structure, lesson organization, and teaching presentation. Research indicates that teachers who are willing to adapt their teaching to meet individual student needs often find that the adaptation assists other students in the classroom as well (Schumm et al., 1995). According to Haager and Klingner (2005), teachers can be successful in the use of adaptations if they not only have accepting attitudes about students and the students' ability to learn, but are also confident in their own ability to teach. Schumaker and Lenz (1999) have developed a six-step guide that is useful for teachers who are planning to develop adaptations in the classroom. The steps in this process are as follows:

1. Create a plan for making adaptations.
2. Identify and evaluate the demands on the student.
3. Determine the purpose or aim of the adaptations.
4. Determine the type of adaptation needed.
5. Inform the students and parents about the adaptation.
6. Implement, evaluate, and adjust the adaptations. (as cited in Haager & Klingner, 2005, pp. 339–342)

An instructional model that has been suggested as one that provides teachers with a guide for using evidence-based methods is called the differentiation of instruction model. According

TABLE 8.1 ● Examples of Evidence-Based Practices for Secondary Classroom

Use multiple motivational methods	Alexander, 2003; Brewster & Pager, 2000; Eichinger, 1997; Good & Brophy, 2003; Moje & Dillon, 2006
Use informal assessments throughout the lessons	Kibby, 1995; Solomon & Morocco, 1999
Incorporate activities to develop content-specific vocabulary	Beck, McKeown, & Kucan, 2002; Nagy & Scott, 2000; National Reading Panel, 2000; Tan & Nicholson, 1997
Introduce comprehension strategies such as graphic organizers and knowledge representations	Caverly, Mandeville, & Nicholson, 1995; Hyerle, 1996; Lieberman & Langer, 1995
Use writing (whether through the use of pencil or computer) as a means to encourage learning	Andrews, 1997; Richards & Gipe, 1995; Yager, 2004
Teach critical reading skills to use with both print and nonprint materials	Bean, Chappell, & Gillan, 2004; Beck, McKeown, Hamilton, & Kucan, 1997; Brozo, 2006; Tanner & Casados, 1998
Introduce and train in the use of collaborative learning strategies	Allen, 2000; Manzo, Manzo, & Thomas, 2005; Slavin, 1995

to Tomlinson (2000), "differentiation is simply attending to the learning needs of a particular student or group of students, rather than the more typical pattern of teaching the class as though all individuals in it were basically alike" (p. 149). Following is a description of this model, also known as differentiated instruction.

DIFFERENTIATED INSTRUCTION

D *ifferentiated instruction* is defined as "the planning of curriculum and instruction using strategies that address student strengths, interests, skills, and readiness in flexible learning environments" (Gartin, Murdick, Imbeau, & Perner, 2002, pp. 1–8). In other words, it is not a teaching plan, nor an instructional strategy, but a philosophy that guides your thoughts about, and actions with, children in the classroom (Tomlinson, 2000). In fact, when teachers discuss the planning and implementation of instruction based on the philosophy of differentiation within the instructional arena, they address the five elements that can easily be modified within the curriculum. These five elements are content, process, products, affect, and learning environment. Structuring of the learning environment is discussed more thoroughly in Chapter 6, and only briefly in this section as part of the discussion of all five elements and their interaction when differentiated instruction.

The idea of differentiation of instruction evolved from the work of several education theorists (Armstrong, 2000, 2003; King-Sears, 1997; Tomlinson, 1999a). As a result, this concept addresses the educational conditions concerning accommodation and adaptation required by the Individuals with Disabilities Education Improvement Act of 2004 (IDEA). Differentiation of instruction is based on three premises: (1) that students bring different strengths, interests, backgrounds, and learning needs to the classroom; (2) that students learn at different rates and in different ways using different modalities; and (3) that students apply knowledge and skills differently, especially when the knowledge and skills are more complex.

In conjunction with these three premises and to assist teachers in developing a repertoire of skills, Tomlinson and Eidson (2003) listed six principles that teachers considering the differentiation of instruction model should understand.

The first principle is, "Good curriculum comes first." Thus, the teacher's task is to ensure that the curriculum is interesting, important, and cogent. Methods to enhance this aspect of the curriculum should be identified and used in all content area classes.

The second principle is, "All tasks should be respectful of each learner." Using this principle, teachers develop tasks that are interesting and their expectations should be for students to think and respond at a high cognitive level.

The third principle is, "When in doubt, teach up!" In other words, plan lessons that stretch students, rather than protect them during the process of learning. Identify and provide varying supports to enhance the chances of success for all students in the classroom.

The fourth principle is, "Use flexible grouping." Flexible grouping is based on specific learning needs, preferences, strengths, or interests of the students. The teaching plan must include times for both small and large group instruction. In other words, students are to be grouped and regrouped as appropriate for learning activities. Group membership should be varied so that all students work together at some time throughout the day or week. These interactions can provide opportunities for respectful interactions as well as opportunities for positive exchanges among students.

The fifth principle is, "Assess students in many ways at many times." Thus, do not limit assessments to only two: a preassessment and a final assessment. Consider assessment as part of the process of teaching; provide assessments in many forms and use them to maximize opportunities to learn about students.

The final principle is, "A portion of the student grade should reflect the student's growth." All students should receive acknowledgment and rewards for doing their best. This principle, of course, depends on the teacher addressing the needs of the students and preparing lessons that support student learning. This differentiation of instruction can occur on several levels according to the complexity of the classroom material and the characteristics of the students in the specific class. In general, students should be challenged to reach higher level goals and all work required of students should be important and interesting.

When students in a classroom present extreme variance in their learning abilities, some form of individualized instruction is essential. Unfortunately, research shows that teachers use a limited number of methods—only ones they feel competent and comfortable using (King-Sears & Cummings, 1996). Therefore, it is critical that teachers expand their teaching repertoire to include instructional strategies and teaching methods based on the needs of students, not on personal preference (McDiarmid, Ball, & Anderson, 1998). Lenz and Deshler (2004) state, "The art and craft of skillful teaching involves not only knowing what techniques to use, but when to use them, how to use them, and how to monitor when the techniques are working for the students" (p. 230).

Although some schools use the terms *accommodation* and *adaptation* interchangeably, this discussion does not. Accommodation is a change to the input, or output, of instruction. In other words, it is related to the instructional outcome *without* changing the content or the conceptual level (Lenz & Deshler, 2004; Taylor, Smiley, & Richards, 2009). There is no change to the curriculum or the assessment, but a change to the method used to demonstrate the acquisition of the skill or knowledge. A common practice seen in many classrooms is the teacher allowing students with dexterity difficulties to submit assignments by using a computer instead of a pencil or pen. Accommodations can include the use of supplemental materials and texts at different reading levels, audiotapes and videotapes, highlighted written materials, and note-taking organizers, to name just a few.

Adaptation, on the other hand, is a change made to the *conceptual level* of the instruction, but keeps the curricular content the same (Lenz & Deshler, 2004; Taylor et al., 2009). An example of a teacher practice is "tiered" instruction (Tomlinson & Eidson, 2003; Tomlinson & Kiernan, 1997). In tiered instruction, the teacher presents the class with information concerning the procedures to use in completing the class activity, but divides the students into groups so that the students can practice the process using activities of varying degrees of complexity. A second method of providing for adaptation includes providing supports for students with special learning needs (e.g., those with an IEP, or ESL students) that modify the level of difficulty based on the individual needs of the student. A common practice seen in many classrooms is the teacher allowing students with memory or language difficulties to match terms to definition when other students are asked to write the term from memory when a definition is given or where 20 words are to be defined and only 10 are required for the student with special learning needs.

Research during the 1980s and 1990s focused on the issues presented by this diversity of student needs and the effectiveness of the methods used by teachers to meet them (Brantlinger, 1993; Cohen & Lotan, 1995; Evans, 1985; Evertson, Sanford, & Emmer, 1981; Mevarich & Kramarski, 1997; Newmann, 1992; Rothenberg, McDermott, & Martin, 1998). From this research four evidence-based practices for differentiating instruction were identified: (1) matching of assignments to student ability levels; (2) providing students with multiple levels of reading materials, including textbooks and supplementary materials; (3) preparing assignments on different ability levels; and (4) planning instruction that will accommodate the needs of individual students (Good & Brophy, 2000; Janney & Snell, 2000). The Association for Supervision and Curriculum Development (ASCD) has been a strong proponent of differentiated instruction and has sought to encourage teachers to use these research-based teaching practices. In fact, Good and Brophy (2000) found that teachers are more effective if they incorporate these research findings when planning instruction.

KEY CONCEPTS IN USING DIFFERENTIATION OF INSTRUCTION

Using the differentiation of instruction model involves a *backward design* for planning. This design requires teachers at the beginning of the instructional planning process to pose a series of questions to focus the planning process on the end goal and on the steps leading up to that goal. For example, a teacher may ask, "What enduring understandings do I want my students to develop? How will my students demonstrate their understanding when the unit is completed? How will I ensure that students have the skills and understand the concepts required in the summative evaluation?" (GREECE Central School District, 2008). Table 8.2 provides a list of web resources related to differentiation of instruction.

The answers to these questions are used as the basis for designing instruction in the differentiated model. These responses indicate what is worth knowing in the content area curriculum at this time. After identifying what is worth knowing, then examine the essential five elements (content, process, product, affect, and learning environment) of differentiated instruction as part of the planning process. A brief description of the five elements follows.

Content

In planning instruction using differentiation of instruction, the *content* of the curriculum should be considered first. Content includes *what* you plan to teach (the curriculum and the

TABLE 8.2 ● Differentiation of Instruction Web Resources

The Access Center

www.k8accesscenter.org/training_resources/mathdifferentiation.asp

CAST: Universal Design for Learning (Differentiated Instruction)

www.cast.org/publications/ncac/ncac_diffinstruc.html

Delving into Differentiation in Middle School: How to Implement Differentiation

www.mamleonline.org/resources/differentiation/implement.htm

Enhance Learning with Technology: Strategies for Differentiating

http://members.shaw.ca/priscillatheroux/differentiatingstrategies.html

Internet4Classrooms: Differentiated Instruction

www.internet4classrooms.com/di.htm

NWREL: Increasing Student Engagement and Motivation

www.nwrel.org/request/oct00/textonly.html

Resource Guide for the Standards and Rubric for School Improvement: Differentiated Instruction

www.schoolsmovingup.net/cs/az/view/az_in/18

materials) and *how* you will give students access to the materials and the ideas—that is, the approaches you will use to assist students in learning the what (i.e., the curriculum). Thus the initial step in the differentiated instruction model is a review of the content to be studied, including the required information, or enduring understandings, that students should have acquired when the end of the lesson has been reached (GREECE Central School District, 2008). Examples of the types of questions that might be asked include: What is essential that *all* students learn of this curricular content? What is essential that *most,* but not all, students learn of this curricular content? What is essential that *some* students learn of this curricular content? The answers to these questions will assist the teacher in selecting a framework for presenting the curricular content material. (For more information, explore the planning pyramid by Schumm, Vaughn, and Leavell [1994] and the planning pyramid for inquiry and understanding by Unrau [2008]). Teachers should use multiple means of presenting content; for example, include visual access through graphs, timelines, and pictures and auditory access through audiotapes, videotapes, and music as well as the traditional printed content written providing multiple reading levels for easier access. Figure 8.1 provides additional examples. In some instances, teachers may not have the freedom to change the curriculum significantly as the content may be prescribed by a required curriculum guide developed by the local school district or the state department of education. In that case, teachers may utilize the other two components (process and product) to achieve the requisite individualization.

Process

Once the content has been addressed, teachers develop questions that assist in the process of deciding how best to differentiate the manner in which the instruction will be presented. According to the Council for Exceptional Children (CEC, 2005), *process* is defined as the method that you, the teacher, select or design in order to present the content, and the method by which

Concept-based teaching
Curriculum compacting
Learning contracts
Mini-lessons
Orbital studies
Varied supports

- Audio/video recorders
- Note-taking organizers
- Highlighted print materials
- Digest of key ideas or key vocabulary

Varied text and resource materials

- Visual access through graphic organizers, charts, pictures, graphs, multilevel reading materials, supplemental reading materials, wall or shelf displays, websites
- Auditory access through tapes, music, and videos
- Kinesthetic access through manipulatives, science materials, and tools

FIGURE 8.1 ● Examples: Differentiation of Content

the students are to respond to the content. It is the *how* of acquiring the knowledge, understanding, and skills that were identified as the learning objective for the content area. In other words, these are the instructional activities that will help students learn the curriculum and come to understand the information presented in the classroom. Figure 8.2 provides additional examples.

Again, the questioning technique is helpful to identify the most appropriate method for introducing the content while at the same time meeting the diverse needs of students. Examples of questions include: What is the purpose of the lesson? What are the specific individualized needs and strengths of the students? How do the students learn best? What methods would best guide them in understanding the essential ideas or concepts of the content? What methods would be most effective in assisting the students to relate the new information to previous information they have learned? The answers to these questions will help teachers identify the most appropriate process, or teaching method, to use with students with diverse learning needs. Examples of process methods that might be used in differentiating instruction include tiered

Cubing
Learning logs
Graphic organizers
Literature circles
Community problem solving
Learning centers
Compacting
Journals
Jigsaw
Role playing
Model making
Labs
Interest centers
Choice boards
Tiered assignments

FIGURE 8.2 ● Examples: Differentiation of Process

lessons (Tomlinson, 1999b), entry points (Gardner, 1993), learning centers, cubing strategy, and tic-tac-toe menus (Billmeyer & Barton, 1998).

Product

In differentiation of instruction, the demonstration of students' mastery of the knowledge or skills you have identified and, therefore, the effectiveness of the process is through the product (CEC, 2005). *Products* are those things that show what the student has learned and can be used as the assessment items through which students demonstrate the acquisition of knowledge, understanding, and skills being taught. It is important to offer students multiple ways of demonstrating what they know and can do with the content. No instructional design is complete without a means of demonstrating that the instructional goal has been attained. Possible means for students to demonstrate their knowledge and skill acquisition include writing a paper, play, or imaginary interview; painting a picture; and constructing a timeline with date-related illustrations. Figure 8.3 provides additional examples.

After the questions concerning the content and the process have been answered, then identify *product* questions, that is, questions whose answers indicate each student's "understanding performance" (Perkins, 1991). In differentiation of instruction, questions to ask when selecting the products of the lesson being designed include: What should students have learned at the end of the lesson or unit? What should students understand? What application of the knowledge should students be able to do? How will successful completion of the lesson be recognized? To answer these questions, teachers might use concrete products such as "essays, videos, dramatizations, and experiments" (Gartin et al., 2002, pp. 6–52). Teachers might also select from products that fit into Renzulli's seven product categories—artistic, performance, spoken, visual, model/construction, leadership, and written products (Renzulli, Leppien, & Hays, 2000). Or use abstract products such as cognitive structures and affective structures that verify that student learning has occurred (Gartin et al., 2002). In the differentiation of instruction model, the product also includes various assessment options that teachers can use and/or modify to meet students' diverse needs. For example, you might use assessment procedures other than the typical paper and pencil tests, such as authentic assessment, portfolio assessment, student work presentations, or scoring guides and rubrics. You select the assessment procedure according to the answers that result from the product questions.

Based on Bloom's taxonomy
Based on Gardner's theory of multiple intelligences
Design webpage or wiki
Design a game
Conduct a debate
Choreograph a dance
Write a newspaper article
Develop a rap, rhythm, song, or chant
Be a mentor
Write and/or produce a play
Write and/or record music
Present a mock trial
Develop an advertising campaign
Create charts or diagrams to explain an idea or concept
Design and/or create costumes
Compile and annotate a set of Internet resources
Create a photo essay

FIGURE 8.3 ● Examples: Differentiation of Products

Affect

Affect is how students link their thoughts and feelings in the classroom. It encompasses students' feelings and emotions about themselves, their work, and the classroom as a whole (Tomlinson, 2003). All students need to feel that they are important to the group as a whole and they need to be accepted and valued for who they are. Students learn better if they feel safe and secure, both physically and emotionally (Bryk & Schneider, 2003; Good, Grumley, & Roy, 2003; Marzano & Marzano, 2003; Schaps, 2003).

Teachers will need to plan so that each student is challenged academically and feels the demand of high expectations (Tomlinson & Eidson, 2003). For example, what excites one student in the classroom may discourage another. In the classroom, a successful teacher addresses both student affect and cognition. When addressing affect, the teacher must plan to establish an environment in which all learners are valued and accepted. Additionally, teachers must react to situations in a manner that exhibits their valuing and acceptance of all learners in the classroom. Tomlinson and Eidson (2003) developed the list of actions for the teacher to consider when establishing a supportive classroom environment. Two important actions discussed by Tomlinson and Edison (2003) are respect and self-reflection. Teachers must assist students in learning to respect themselves and their peers and, thus, demonstrate an acceptance of the commonalities and differences within the classroom. In addition, teachers need to support students as they learn how to be reflective about problems in their relationships and develop a feeling of competency in their ability to effectively solve problems.

Learning Environment

The goal of a classroom using differentiated instruction is to construct a flexible learning environment where important work is happening. The *learning environment* is the way the classroom feels and functions. A flexible learning environment is the cornerstone of a differentiated classroom. Teachers will need to consider their space, the amount of time available for instruction, the materials on hand, and their rules and procedures. The question for teachers to address is, "How can I arrange the classroom to allow students of differing readiness levels, learning styles, and interests to learn and grow?" Teachers should design their learning environment to encourage flexibility in the methods used to engage students. While lecture is often used for this purpose, other methods include videos, role playing, peer tutoring, cooperative learning, and instructional games. These should be included to better meet the needs of all students. Table 8.3 provides additional questions for teachers to consider when planning the classroom learning environment.

TABLE 8.3 ● Questions to Consider When Planning the Learning Environment

- How can the furniture be arranged so that students can rearrange it into work groups or into quiet personal spaces?
- When classroom furniture cannot be rearranged or moved is there a way for the students to organize the space to allow for work groups or for personal quiet retreats?
- Where can books, materials, and artifacts be stored so that they are available, but not distracting?
- What amount or type of movement in the room is acceptable? Who can move about? How often? How is movement defined and how can it be accomplished quietly, efficiently, and without disturbing others?
- What signals can the teacher use and what signals can the student use?
- How can we teach the students to use the books, supplies, materials, products, and classroom furniture appropriately?
- What consequences have been instituted for use when or if materials are used inappropriately? How does the student signal that the materials are inadequate or missing?

It is essential for you to construct a learning environment that allows students to use the space, furniture, and materials as they need. An important question to ask is, "How can I plan the space that will allow students a safe place to learn and grow?" The learning environment must address the safety needs of students and provide support for the students to take learning risks. Class rules and procedures help set the tone of the classroom. As Tomlinson (2003) states, "In differentiated classrooms, teachers continually assess student readiness, interest, learning profile, and affect. Teachers then use what they learn to modify content, process, product, and the learning environment to ensure maximum learning for each member of the class" (p. 6).

IMPLEMENTING DIFFERENTIATION OF INSTRUCTION IN MIDDLE AND SECONDARY CLASSROOMS

When planning to teach using differentiation of instruction, the teacher's goal is to have students be successful learners. The teacher accomplishes this goal by providing students with curriculum and instruction that (1) meets the needs of all learners, (2) is respectful of their diversity, and (3) supports their learning by addressing both needs and strengths. To assist teachers in designing a classroom based on the differentiation of instruction model, they are encouraged to answer the following set of planning questions: What do I need to know about my students? What content will I teach? How will I teach this content? How will I accommodate differing learning needs? How will I assess student learning? How will I differentiate instruction in the specific content areas? Each of these questions will be addressed next.

What Do I Need to Know About the Students?

When planning to teach using differentiation of instruction, teachers will first seek to discover students' qualities that may impact their learning. To discover these qualities teachers will review the academic histories of the students, their interests, how they learn best (perhaps using Gardner's theory of multiple intelligences or asking their family members), and by learning what individual students already know and what they might want to know. Many teachers develop learning profiles for their students so that the information is organized and readily available for use in planning instruction.

What Content Will I Teach?

Today's teachers are required to meet national, state, and school district academic standards. The use of differentiation of instruction allows them to use these standards to direct the curriculum and focus on instructional objectives. However, national, state, and school district academic standards do not dictate how teachers can plan to meet these standards. The teacher's role, therefore, remains one of instructional designer. Using differentiation of instruction also requires teachers to design relevant instruction focusing on essential learning based on individual student characteristics. Differentiation of instruction requires teachers to prepare a plan to modify and adjust the curriculum to better match these characteristics and needs.

Teachers follow a series of steps in order to prepare lessons to meet both students' needs and the required standards for that grade and/or content area. The first step in this process is to identify the concepts or ideas that are most important for the students to know and understand. In other words, the teacher should look for the "big idea." When students understand the big idea, then they not only learn the facts, but they also apply the facts critically.

Second, teachers begin to formulate essential questions. The essential questions help determine if the planned learning activities reflect what is important for students to know, understand, and perform. Having made this determination, teachers will be better able to focus instructional planning.

The final step is for teachers to design the specific unit of instruction. To begin designing the unit, they first write the unit questions. Unit questions layer specific content and facts onto the previously identified essential questions. In this process, teachers consider the big question and the little questions. The little questions are part of the big question and address specific content and skills. Teachers work to ensure that these little questions (say, four questions or less) are as interesting as possible, because these are the questions that students will be exploring. With the framework of essential questions and unit questions developed, teachers then design the learning activities to address students' unique characteristics. Therefore, teachers first choose the unit theme, then the essential questions that need to be answered, the unit question, the curriculum standards, the content or topics, the skills, and finally possible assessment products.

How Will I Teach This Content?

Once the information has been gathered and the essential knowledge and skills identified, teachers are ready to design challenging activities. Heacox (2002) describes challenging activities as those that are rigorous, relevant, and complex. Each student in the classroom needs to feel challenged by assignments that require the use of higher level thinking skills. Like many other teachers when they are designing what will be taught, you may want to use Bloom's *Taxonomy of Educational Objectives* (1984). Bloom's six levels of thinking are knowledge, comprehension, application, analysis, evaluation, and synthesis. Using Bloom's taxonomy helps teachers to categorize activities by the level of challenge and complexity. This organizational format makes it easier to adapt and modify activities in order to develop a wider range that better matches the characteristics and needs of the diverse learners in the classroom.

A second option when designing or adapting learning activities is to use Gardner's (1993) theory of multiple intelligences. Each student has varying strengths in both thinking and learning, and by planning the instruction to address these strengths, students will learn more easily. The greater the variety of activities offered to students, the greater the chance of them successfully meeting the instructional objectives.

How Will I Accommodate Differing Learning Needs?

When a teacher offers a lockstep curriculum with lecture as the main learning strategy, then classroom management is relatively easy. When a teacher offers greater variety and challenge in the curriculum, however, the management of the classroom can become a greater challenge. The question becomes one of how to accommodate the differing learning needs of students and still maintain management of the classroom. During instruction if students are brought together to focus on a common task, then teachers will have less difficulty in providing assistance and supervision. Therefore, an essential characteristic of classrooms using differentiation of instruction is the use of flexible grouping. *Flexible grouping* allows students with similar learning goals, needs, or preferences to work together. Depending on the task, teachers may select, or may allow students to select, the group membership. The concept of flexible grouping demands that group membership will change according to the task and/or the needs of the students. See Figure 8.4 for examples of grouping.

> Flexible grouping
> Small group instruction
> Cooperative learning
> Interest groups
> Group investigations
> Independent studies

FIGURE 8.4 ● Examples of Grouping

While flexible grouping is one method of responding to the needs of students, cooperative grouping is another. *Cooperative groups* are determined by either the teacher or the students, with the members of the group working on the same task over a period of time. The purpose of cooperative grouping is to develop interpersonal and team-oriented skills. When you choose to use this grouping strategy, the focus is on development of collaborative skills as well as academic learning.

Another type of grouping you might use is *short-term instructional grouping*. The purpose of this form of instructional grouping is to allow teachers to match students with similar instructional needs. Teachers may allow a group of students who have conquered the learning task to work on a special project or an accelerated learning task. In the same way, teachers may pull together those students needing additional instruction, support, and guidance to accomplish the learning objective. Often this type of group is used when mass absences (e.g., due to sickness or extracurricular activities) have occurred and you need to reintroduce the instruction on materials students have missed.

How Will I Assess Student Learning?

In the differentiation of instruction process, three types of assessments are used: preassessments and pretests, formative assessments, and summative assessments. Teachers often use preassessments to determine the students' current knowledge or skill. The preassessment is particularly important when using differentiation of instruction because instruction is based on what students already know and what they need to learn. Students who show proficiency in a particular area can move to other content area objectives, thus extending or enriching their learning.

Formative assessments occur during the learning process. These assessments are used to alter the activity based on whether learning is progressing as desired. Formative assessments have been the focus of much research (Bangert-Downs, Kulik, & Kulik, 1991; Bangert-Downs, Kulik, Kulik, & Morgan, 1991; Black & William, 1998; Crooks, 1988; Fuchs & Fuchs, 1986; Hattie, 1992; Kluger & DeNisi, 1996; Marzano, 2006; Natriello, 1987). The combined research has resulted in four important findings: Formative assessment should (1) be formative in nature, (2) be frequent, (3) be related to student progress in meeting the instructional objectives, and (4) assist students in improving their performance.

Also important is the *summative,* or *final, assessment*, which occurs at the end of a unit of learning. Traditionally, the final grade is a deep-rooted fixture in the American education system. It is a shorthand way of communicating how students are doing. When teachers decide to use a summative assessment, they will need to decide for what skill this assessment will be used. In other words, they should develop the assessment to determine what the students will be able to do with the content material that has been covered. The decision hinges on what skills the teacher wants the assessment to indicate that the students can do. In other words, to show successful learning, do the students need to be able to explain, interpret, apply, place in perspective, demonstrate empathy, or grow in self-knowledge (Wiggins & McTighe, 2005)?

It is important for students to understand criteria for the teacher appraisal of the results of the summative evaluation. The criteria for appraisal should be written on the language level of the students and should be clear, specific, and concise. The chosen criteria should be based on high expectations, not just on what is passable work, and should be written in a positive form. In addition, teachers must describe the minimum acceptable criteria, while not limiting students' work. Heacox (2002) writes, "Grades = Rigor" (p. 120). Differences in grades should not be based on the amount of work, but on the level of challenge in the work. Thus, the prepared criteria should clearly demonstrate the belief that all students can think and learn at more complex levels of thinking.

Assessing student achievement can be exciting for both the teacher and the students. The evaluation process should never be demeaning or insulting. The assessment should allow students the opportunity to show what they have learned while the teacher cheers them on to academic excellence.

How Will I Differentiate Instruction in the Specific Content Areas?

Although each of the four major content areas (language arts/English, science, social studies/history, and mathematics) have very different learning goals and teaching strategies, they also have classroom and student characteristics that are similar. As a result, there are evidence-based strategies that incorporate the differentiation of instruction philosophy that can be used across all four content areas. Three groups of these strategies will be briefly discussed—concept-based/unit teaching, text and resource material (orbital studies) variation, and support system variations.

Concept-based teaching is the practice of emphasizing the key concepts and principles within a lesson or unit of information. According to Tomlinson (2001), "concepts are the building blocks of meaning" (p. 74). Students with special learning needs often have difficulty in content area classrooms as a result of the emphasis on learning factual information. As the amount of specific information builds, they often forget previous essential information. Without a basic understanding of the reason the material is being taught—that is, what the purpose of learning this content is—students often fail to attend for the amount of time required for true memory to occur.

One example when concept-based teaching is often used is in unit teaching. Unrau (2008, p. 386) described a curriculum triangle to incorporate content differentiation into the middle and secondary unit planning process in the following manner:

> Differentiated instruction is based on a reality: Not all students can or will learn all the content presented to them, nor will they all learn it in the same way. Trilevel curriculum enables teachers to graphically see the essential content they expect *all* their students to master, the content they expect *some* of their students to gain, and the content they expect only a *few* of their students to learn.

A second evidence-based differentiation of instruction strategy is *text and resource material variation*. As discussed previously, one of the major barriers to successful learning is student inability to access information from content area textbooks and written materials. The use of materials in multiple forms and on multiple levels can lessen this problem. Teachers who prepare a classroom resource library have on hand materials at varying levels that use different methods of information presentation (e.g., audio, video, print). A useful method that correlates with text and resource materials variation is called *orbitals,* or *orbital studies* (Stevenson, 1992; Tomlinson, 2001). Orbital studies are student-selected investigations that revolve or orbit around some facet of the specified content of the unit. This method allows students to focus on essential content and do so at their own level of ability.

Support system variation is the third evidence-based method for use in differentiating content instruction. Examples of support system variations include note-taking organizers and/or graphic organizers, critical information highlighting, key idea digests that are sometimes included in teacher-developed survival packets, and learning partners (also called study buddies, reading partners, or peer scribes) (Janney & Snell, 2000; Tomlinson, 2001, 2003). (See Haager & Klingner [2005] for an expanded discussion of various adaptations for differentiating content instruction.) These variations to the accepted method for presenting content area material or for student completion of independent content area readings and activities allow for student differences without compromising the integrity of the curriculum.

SIDE BAR

8.1   Lachesa in Science Class

Mr. Watson teaches math and science at Stonewall High School. Lachesa is a student in his math/science class. Mr. Watson is planning a unit on cell theory and knows that he will need to address Lachesa's special learning needs. He knows that her reading and math levels are in the lower quartile. Also, she has cerebral palsy with lower limb spasticity and uses a wheelchair. She has some involvement with her upper extremities and has difficulty with handwriting.

Mr. Watson first identified what he wanted all students to learn, what most of the students should learn, and what some of the students should learn. He believed that all of the students should know the three parts of cell theory and be able to label correctly the two types of cells (prokaryotic and eukaryotic). Most students will be able to describe the function of each component of these cells and be able to compare and contrast animal and plant cells. Some students will be able to distinguish between an organism and a community of cells.

He then determined that the microscope might be difficult for Lachesa to use, especially if it were placed on a tall counter. He decided to address this potential difficulty by having the class work as partners. He also set a workstation on one of the lower desks to accommodate both a chair and a wheelchair. This workstation also had a laptop with the worksheets in digital format. Using the digital format, Lachesa could type the required information instead of trying to handwrite the answers in the small lines provided.

Mr. Watson also provided several ways to access the materials. First, he simplified the text. Second, he provided study guides and self-scoring practice sheets. He also allowed students to use a computer-based self-study program containing a variety of practice exercises.

To process the information, he put the pairs of students together to form six groups of four (two sets of pairs). Each student was assigned two vocabulary words to teach the other group members. Mr. Watson assigned the group membership and ensured that the group members varied in abilities and skill levels so that the members could help each other learn the meaning of the words through demonstration, explanation, or research. Later Mr. Watson planned to use whole class instruction to demonstrate the use of the microscope and the assigned activities at each station. Students are required to complete the assignment sheets either by hand or using the computer.

To meet Lachesa's learning needs, Mr. Watson modified the learning environment, used both flexible grouping and whole class instruction, modified content, and modified process. Therefore, he acted on four of the five elements of differentiated instruction. In the diverse classrooms of today, these modifications also help those with poor reading skills, English language learners, and those who are gifted. Teachers who design differentiated classrooms find that environments designed using differentiated instruction enable all students to work at their personal best.

SUMMARY

This chapter has presented an overview of differentiation of instruction and provided examples of evidence-based strategies for differentiating instruction available for use by middle and secondary teachers. For successful learning to occur in today's classrooms, it is important for teachers to develop a repertoire of knowledge and skills to better meet the diverse needs of students. Teachers often employ their own principles and incorporate their own individual methods and modifications that are often identified with differentiated instruction. As a result of this, they may expect differentiated instruction to be simple to implement, but in fact the opposite is true. Because of the perceived simplicity of the differentiated planning model, some teachers may be misled into thinking that instructional design will be both simple to develop and simple to implement. Adequately meeting the needs of *all* learners in middle and secondary education classrooms has been and often continues to be a problem under traditional circumstances (Baker & Zigmond, 1990; Schumm et al., 1994). The challenges are simply more acute in an era of high stakes testing and elevated standards. Today teachers must identify and use research-based practices in planning and educating middle level and secondary students in content area classrooms. The use of differentiated instruction methodology has been shown to assist teachers in meeting this goal.

ACTIVITIES

1. Interview a middle school or secondary teacher who teaches in your content area. Ask what are the most frequent accommodations requested for students with disabilities. Then ask what are the most frequent modifications used in the classroom to differentiate instruction for those students who have difficulty learning the course content. Group these into content, process, product, affect, and learning environment.

2. Do a web search for examples of differentiated instruction within your content area.

3. Design a training program on differentiated instruction. Provide examples of each of the following: content, process, product, affect, and learning environment

REFERENCES

Alexander, R. (2003). *The path to competence: A lifespan developmental perspective on reading.* Paper commissioned by the National Reading Conference. Retrieved July 23, 2008, from http://www.nrconline.org

Allen, J. (2000). *Yellow brick roads: Shared and guided paths to independent reading 4–12.* Portland, ME: Stenhouse.

Anderson, S., Yilmaz, O., & Wasburn-Moses, L. (2004). Middle and high school students with learning disabilities: Practical academic interventions for general education teachers—A review of the literature. *American Secondary Education, 32*(2), 19–38.

Andrews, S. E. (1997). Writing to learn in content area reading class. *Journal of Adolescent & Adult Literacy, 41*(2), 141.

Armstrong, T. (2000). *Multiple intelligences in the classroom* (2nd ed.). Alexandria, VA: ASCD.

Armstrong, T. (2003). *The multiple intelligences of reading and writing: Making words come alive.* Alexandria, VA: ASCD.

Baker, J. M., & Zigmond, N. (1990). Are regular classes equipped to accommodate students with learning disabilities? *Exceptional Children, 56,* 515–526.

Bangert-Downs, R. L., Kulik, C. C., Kulik, J. A., & Morgan, M. T. (1991). The instructional effect of feedback on test-like events. *Review of Educational Research, 61*(2), 213–238.

Bangert-Downs, R. L., Kulik, J. A., & Kulik, C. C. (1991). Effects of classroom testing. *Journal of Educational Research, 85*(2), 89–99.

Bean, J. C., Chappell, V. A., & Gillan, A. M. (2004). *Reading rhetorically* (brief edition). New York: Pearson/Longman.

Beck, I. L., McKeown, M. G., Hamilton, P. L., & Kucan, L. (1997). *Questioning the author: An approach for enhancing student engagement with text.* Newark, DE: International Reading Association.

Beck, I. L., McKeown, M. G., & Kucan, L. (2002). *Bringing words to life: Robust vocabulary instruction.* New York: Guilford.

Billmeyer, R., & Barton, M. L. (1998). *Teaching reading in the content areas. If not me, then who?* (2nd ed.). Aurora, CO: Mid-continent Regional Educational Laboratory (MCREL).

Black, P., & William, D. (1998). Assessment and classroom learning. *Assessment in Education, 5*(1), 7–75.

Bloom, B. S. (1984). *Taxonomy of educational objectives: Book 1 cognitive domain.* New York: Longman.

Brantlinger, E. (1993). *The politics of social class in secondary school: Views of affluent and impoverished youth.* New York: Teachers College Press.

Brewster, C., & Pager, J. (2000). *Increasing student engagement and motivation: From time-on-task to homework.* Retrieved July 23, 2008, from http://www.nwrel.org/request/oct00/textonly.htm

Brozo, W. G. (2006). WebQuests: Supporting inquiry with primary sources. *Thinking Classrooms, 7*(1), 47–48.

Bruner, J. S. (1960). *The process of education.* Cambridge, MA: Harvard University Press.

Bryant, D. P., Smith, D. D., & Bryant, B. R. (2008). *Teaching students with special needs in inclusive classrooms.* Boston: Pearson/Allyn & Bacon.

Bryant, D. P., Ugel, N., Thompson, S., & Hamff, A. (1999). Strategies to promote content area reading instruction. *Intervention in School & Clinic, 34*(5), 293–302.

Bryant, D. P., Vaughn, S., Linan-Thompson, S., Ugel, N., Hamff, A., & Hougen, M. (2000). Reading outcomes for students with and without reading disabilities in general education middle-school content area classes. *Learning Disability Quarterly, 23*, 238–252.

Bryk, A., & Schneider, B. (2003). Trust in schools: A core source for school reform. *Educational Leadership, 60*(5), 40–44.

Caverly, D., Mandeville, T., & Nicholson, S. A. (1995). PLAN: A study-reading strategy for informational text. *Journal of Adolescent & Adult Literacy, 39*(3), 190–199.

Cohen, E., & Lotan, R. (1995). Producing equal-status interaction in the heterogeneous classroom. *American Education Research Journal, 32*, 99–120.

Council for Exceptional Children (CEC). (2005). *Universal design for learning: A guide for teachers and education professionals.* Arlington, VA: CEC and Merrill/Pearson Education.

Crooks, T. J. (1988). The impact of classroom evaluation practices on students. *Review of Educational Research, 58*(4), 438–481.

Eichinger, J. (1997). Successful students' perception of secondary school science. *School Science and Mathematics, 97*(3), 122–131.

Evans, J. (1985). *Teaching in transition: The challenge of mixed ability grouping.* Philadelphia: Open University Press.

Evertson, C., Sanford, J., & Emmer, E. (1981). Effects of class heterogeneity in junior high school. *American Education Research Journal, 18*, 219–232.

Fuchs, L. S., & Fuchs, D. (1986). Effects of systematic formative evaluation: A meta analysis. *Exceptional Children, 53*, 199–208.

Gardner, H. (1993). *Multiple intelligences: The theory in practice.* New York: Basic Books.

Gartin, B. C., Murdick, N. L., Imbeau, M., & Perner, D. E. (2002). *How to use differentiated instruction with students with developmental disabilities in the general education classroom.* Arlington, VA: Division on Developmental Disabilities, CEC.

Good, E. P., Grumley, J., & Roy, S. (2003). *A connected school.* Chapel Hill, NC: New View Publications.

Good, T. L., & Brophy, J. E. (2000). *Looking in classrooms* (8th ed.). New York: Longman.

Good, T. L., & Brophy, J. E. (2003). *Looking in classrooms* (9th ed.). New York: McGraw-Hill.

GREECE Central School District. (2008). *Backward design: Beginning with the end in mind to design multi-genre thematic units.* Retrieved June 20, 2008, from www.greece.k12.ny.us/instruction/ELA/6-12/Backward-Design/Overview.htm

Haager, D., & Klingner, J. K. (2005). *Differentiating instruction in inclusive classrooms: The special educator's guide* (pp. 331–389). Boston: Pearson/Allyn & Bacon.

Hattie, J. A. (1992). Measuring the effects of schooling. *Australian Journal of Education, 36*(1), 5–13.

Heacox, D. (2002). *Differentiating instruction in the regular classroom: How to reach and teach all learners, grades 3–12.* Minneapolis, MN: Free Spirit.

Hyerle, D. (1996). *Visual tools for constructing knowledge.* Alexandria, VA: ASCD.

Individuals with Disabilities Education Improvement Act, 20 U.S.C. 1400 *et seq.* (2004).

Janney, R. E., & Snell, M. E. (2000). *Teachers' guide to inclusive practices: Modifying schoolwork.* Baltimore: Brookes.

Kibby, M. W. (1995). *Practical steps for informing literacy instruction: A diagnostic decision-making model.* Newark, DE: International Reading Association.

King-Sears, M. E. (1997). Best academic practices for inclusive classrooms. *Focus on Exceptional Children, 29*(7), 1–22.

King-Sears, M. E., & Cummings, C. S. (1996). Inclusive practices of classroom teachers. *Remedial and Special Education, 17*, 217–225.

Kluger, A. N., & DeNisi, A. (1996). The effects of feedback interventions on performance: A historical review, a meta-analysis and a preliminary intervention theory. *Psychological Bulletin, 119*, 254–284.

Lenz, B. K., & Deschler, D. D. (2004). *Teaching content to all: Evidence-based inclusive practices in middle and secondary schools.* Upper Saddle River, NJ: Pearson.

Lieberman, M., & Langer, E. (1995) Mindfulness and the process of learning. In P. Antonacci (Ed.), *Learning and context.* Cresskill, NJ: Hampton Press.

Manzo, A., Manzo, U., & Thomas, M. M. (2005). *Content area literacy: Strategic teaching for strategic learning* (4th ed.). Hoboken, NJ: John Wiley.

Marshall, J. D., Sears, J. T., & Schubert, W. H. (2000). *Turning points in curriculum: A contemporary American memoir.* Upper Saddle River, NJ: Merrill/Pearson.

Marzano, R. J. (2006). *Classroom assessment and grading that work.* Alexandria, VA: ASCD.

Marzano, R. J., & Marzano, J. (2003). The key to classroom management. *Educational Leadership, 61*(1), 6–13.

McDiarmid, G. W., Ball, D. L., & Anderson, C. W. (1998). Why staying one chapter ahead doesn't really work: Subject specific pedagogy. In M. C. Reynolds (Ed.), *Knowledge base for the beginning teacher* (pp. 193–206). Elmsford, NY: Pergamon.

Mercer, C. D., & Mercer, A. R. (2001). *Teaching students with learning problems* (6th ed.). Upper Saddle River, NJ: Merrill/Pearson.

Mevarich, Z., & Kramarski, B. (1997). IMPROVE: A multidimensional method for teaching mathematics in heterogeneous classrooms. *American Education Research Journal, 34*, 365–394.

Meyen, E. (1981). *Developing instructional units for the regular and special education teachers* (3rd ed.). Dubuque, IA: Brown.

Moje, B. M., & Dillon, D. R. (2006). Adolescent identities as demanded by science classroom discourse communities. In D. E. Alvermann, K. Hinchman, D. W. Moore, S. Phelps, & D. R. Waff (Eds.), *Reconceptualizing the literacies of adolescents' lives* (2nd ed., pp. 85–106). Mahwah, NJ: Erlbaum.

Nagy, W. E., & Scott, J. A. (2000). Vocabulary processes. In M. L. Kamil, P. B. Mosenthal, P. D. Pearson, & R. Barr (Eds.), *Handbook of reading research* (Vol. III, pp. 269–284). Mahwah, NJ: Erlbaum.

National Reading Panel. (2000). *Report of the national reading panel: Teaching children to read.* Bethesda, MD: National Institute of Child Health and Human Development.

Natriello, G. (1987). The impact of evaluation processes on students. *Educational Psychologist, 22*(2), 155–175.

Newmann, F. (Ed.). (1992). *Student engagement and achievement in American secondary schools.* New York: Teachers College Press.

No Child Left Behind Act of 2001, 20 U.S.C. 6301 *et seq.* (2002).

Nolet, V., & McLaughlin, M. J. (2000). *Accessing the general curriculum: Including students with disabilities in standards-based reform.* Thousand Oaks, CA: Corwin.

Oliva, P. F. (2001). *Developing the curriculum* (5th ed.). New York: Longman.

Orlich, D. C., Harder, R. J., Callahan, R. C., & Gibson, H. W. (2001). *Teaching strategies: A guide to better instruction* (6th ed.). Boston: Houghton Mifflin.

Perkins, D. N. (1991). Educating for insight. *Educational Leadership, 49*(2), 4–8.

Renzulli, J. S., Leppien, J. H., & Hays, T. S. (2000). *The multiple menu model: A practical guide for developing differentiated curriculum.* Mansfield Center, CT: Creative Learning Press.

Richards, J., & Gipe, J. (1995). What's the structure? A game to help middle school students recognize common writing patterns. *Journal of Reading, 38*(8), 667–669.

Rothenberg, J., McDermott, P., & Martin, G. (1998). Changes in pedagogy: A qualitative result of teaching heterogeneous classes. *Teaching and Teacher Education, 14*, 633–642.

Schaps, E. (2003). Creating a school community. *Educational Leadership, 60*(6), 31–33.

Schloss, P. J., Schloss, M. A., & Schloss, C. N. (2007). *Instructional methods for secondary students with learning and behavior problems* (4th ed.). Boston: Pearson/Allyn & Bacon.

Schumaker, J. B., & Lenz, B. K. (1999). *Adapting language arts, social studies, and science materials for the inclusive classroom.* Reston, VA: The Council for Exceptional Children.

Schumm, J. S., Vaughn, S., & Leavell, A. G. (1994). Planning pyramid: A framework for planning for diverse students' needs during content instruction. *Reading Teacher, 47*, 608–615.

Schumm, J. S., Vaughn, S., Haager, D., McDowell, J., Rothlein, L., & Saumell, L. (1995). General education teacher planning: What can students with learning disabilities expect? *Exceptional Children, 61*, 350–352.

Slavin, R. E. (1995). *Cooperative learning* (2nd ed.). Boston, MA: Allyn and Bacon.

Solomon, M. Z., & Morocco, C. S. (1999). The diagnostic teacher. In M. Z. Solomon (Ed.), *The diagnostic teacher: Constructing new approaches to professional development* (pp. 231–246). New York: Teachers College Press.

Stevenson, C. (1992). *Teaching ten to fourteen year olds.* New York: Longman.

Stodden, R. A., Galloway, L. M., & Stodden, N. J. (2003). Secondary school curricula issues: Impact on postsecondary students with disabilities. *Exceptional Children, 70,* 9–25.

Tan, A., & Nicholson, T. (1997). Flashcards revisited: Training poor readers to read words faster improves their comprehension of text. *Journal of Educational Psychology, 89,* 276–288.

Tanner, M. L., & Casados, L. (1998). Promoting and studying discussions in math classes. *Journal of Adolescent and Adult Literacy, 41*(5), 342–350.

Taylor, R. L., Smiley, L. R., & Richards, S. B. (2009). *Exceptional students: Preparing teachers for the 21st century.* Boston: McGraw-Hill.

Tomlinson, C. A. (1999a). *The differentiated classroom: Responding to the needs of all learners.* Alexandria, VA: ASCD.

Tomlinson, C. A. (1999b). Mapping a route toward differentiated instruction. *Educational Leadership, 57*(1), 12–16.

Tomlinson, C. A. (2000). Reconcilable differences: Standards-based teaching and differentiation. *Educational Leadership, 58*(1), 6–11.

Tomlinson, C. A. (2001). *How to differentiate instruction in mixed-ability classrooms* (2nd ed.). Upper Saddle River, NJ: Pearson Merrill/Pearson.

Tomlinson, C. A. (2003). *Fulfilling the promise of the differentiated classroom: Strategies and tools for responsive teaching.* Alexandria, VA: ASCD.

Tomlinson, C. A., & Eidson, C. (2003). *Differentiation in practice: A research guide for differentiating curriculum, grades 5–9.* Alexandria, VA: ASCD.

Tomlinson, C. A., & Kiernan, L. J. (1997). *Differentiating instruction.* Alexandria, VA: ASCD.

Unrau, N. (2008). *Content area reading and writing: Fostering literacies in middle and high school cultures* (2nd ed.). Upper Saddle River, NJ: Merrill/Pearson.

Van Garderen, D., & Whittaker, C. (2006). Planning differentiated multicultural instruction for secondary inclusive classrooms. *TEACHING Exceptional Children, 38*(3), 12–20.

Wiggins, G., & McTighe, J. (2005). *Understanding by design* (expanded 2nd ed.). Alexandria, VA: ASCD.

Yager, R. E. (2004). Science is not written, but it can be written about. In E. W. Saul (Ed.), *Crossing borders in literacy and science instruction* (pp. 95–107). Newark, DE: International Reading Association.

9 Strategies Instruction

Study Questions

1. What are instructional strategies?

2. How can instructional strategies be used to assist middle and high school students in content classes?

3. What are the three main areas of instructional strategies?

4. What is the strategies instructional model and how can it be used?

5. What are some examples of strategies for acquiring, storing, and disseminating information?

INTRODUCTION

Students with disabilities are receiving more and more of their education in general education classrooms, taught by general classroom teachers. With the No Child Left Behind Act of 2001 and the Individuals with Disabilities Education Act (IDEA) requiring that students with disabilities (1) meet the same standards as students without disabilities, (2) have access to the general education curriculum, and (3) be served with nondisabled peers to the maximum extent appropriate, the growing challenge for educators is to provide educational opportunities that will lead to success for these students.

While there is a sound philosophical and legal basis for this reality, many of these students will struggle without significant supports. As the curricular demands increase in secondary schools, many students with disabilities will not be successful, not because they lack the necessary cognitive abilities, but because they do not have the skills and strategies necessary to deal with information presented in science, math, and other content classes (Deshler, 2005). Lack of skills in reading, organization, memory, attention, and test-taking may result in academic difficulties for students with disabilities.

Many students with disabilities are capable of achieving academic success in general education classrooms. However, they often experience roadblocks to this success. In order to help students overcome these roadblocks, teachers need to help enhance their learning skills, memory, and motivation. Strategy instruction "offers promise for helping students with mild disabilities to set goals, devise or select effective ways to approach a task, and monitor their own performance" (Meese, 2001, p. 56). Through strategies instruction, teachers focus on helping students with disabilities become independent, active decision makers in their own lives.

Students use learning strategies as a way to learn effectively, efficiently, and independently (Swanson & Deshler, 2003). They are "tools that students use to access and interact successfully with subject content. Various strategies help students read, write, think, demonstrate competence, interact socially, and build community" (Land, 2009, p. 5). Often, if students do not have good learning strategies they are passive learners and are unsuccessful in academic tasks. A learning strategies–based model helps students become more aware of different skills that will improve their learning. It shifts the role of the teacher from teaching information to helping students learn how to learn (Mercer & Pullen, 2009).

With the ability to use strategies, many students with disabilities can become independent learners. While this may not be critical for students in elementary schools, where teachers traditionally provide more hands-on instruction, as students move to secondary and postsecondary educational settings, and eventual employment, it becomes critical. This is due to the increased academic demands of secondary and postsecondary educational settings and increased demands for individual learning in employment settings. While colleges and universities must comply with Section 504 and the ADA, these laws do not require services to the extent of IDEA, meaning that it is up to secondary schools to help students develop skills that can facilitate their success during and after middle and high school.

Tutoring and other direct instructional approaches can be effective in facilitating academic success; however, a better approach is to provide students with tools they can use to become successful independent learners. Teaching students how to use strategies that will make them independent learners is a better approach than providing them with direct supports that can result in their being service-dependent. Teaching learning strategies is similar to the old adage that teaching a person to fish is better than simply giving him fish. Once students become proficient in better ways to learn on their own they are much more likely to be successful, independent learners than if they are simply provided direct instructional supports. Strategies instruction can help prepare them for this opportunity.

There are several assumptions underlying a strategies instructional model (SIM) approach. Some of these include (Horowitz, 2009, p. 1):

- Most adolescents (even older students who are low achievers) can learn to function successfully and independently in mainstream settings.
- The role of the SIM-trained teacher is to teach low-achieving adolescents strategies that will enable them to become independent learners.
- The role of the classroom content teacher is to encourage "strategic behavior" and to deliver subject matter information in ways that students can understand and recall.
- Adolescents should have a major voice in deciding what strategies they are learning, how fast they need to master them, and how much (and what kinds of) support they need, to make these strategies their own.

While there are hundreds of strategies, no single learning strategy is the answer for problems experienced by all students; teachers must guide students to find strategies that work best for each one of them (Center for Research on Learning, 2009).

TEACHING STUDENTS HOW TO USE STRATEGIES

Although studies have found that strategies can have a positive impact on student learning, unless students know how to use them effectively they are of limited benefit. Students regularly use strategies in their learning, storing, and retrieving of information and knowledge. Many students learn these strategies on their own, without any formal instruction; however, some students with disabilities who need to use these strategies do not learn how to use them without direct instruction. Teachers, therefore, must be proactive in teaching students how to use learning strategies.

The goal of teaching learning strategies is for students to become capable of independently using the strategy in various settings and situations (Swanson & Deshler, 2003). To achieve this goal, strategies must be taught and students must have opportunities to use them in classrooms. This requires collaboration between special education teachers, who would likely teach these skills and strategies, and general education content teachers who should encourage and reinforce students to use them (Deshler, 2005). In one study, Bulgren et al. (2006) found that while general educators believe that part of their role in secondary classrooms is to teach strategies along with content, they are not in favor of others coming into their classrooms to teach strategies to students. This means that in some classrooms, the general classroom teachers will teach the strategies as well as the content. Whether the special education teacher or general education teacher teaches strategies is unimportant. The important thing is that strategies are taught and students are encouraged and given opportunities to use them.

Effectively using learning strategies is similar to using other skills; unless students have multiple opportunities to use strategies that have been taught, they will not use them effectively. Swanson and Deshler (2003, p. 131) suggested several stages that need to be completed if students are to learn to use learning strategies independently. These include:

1. Verbal practice designed to help students understand and talk about the intent of each step of the strategy and to learn each strategy step to a mastery level so that it can be automatically applied to respond to a curricular demand
2. Controlled practice and feedback, designed to give students practice using the strategy in controlled materials (i.e., ones written at the students' instructional level) so that they focus on applying the strategy to materials that are not overly difficult

3. Advance practice and feedback, designed to give students practice using the strategy on materials that approximate actual grade level difficulty materials
4. Generalization designed to give students practice applying the strategy to a broad array of new materials and circumstances

Schumaker et al. (2006) described a course used to teach students how to improve their literacy levels by using strategies. This course consists of teaching several strategies, using a specific sequence for each strategy. First, the strategy is described, then modeled by the teacher. Following verbal practice, students practice with a partner or independently. After practicing the strategy, integration and generalization occur. The entire teaching sequence is reinforced with guided practice. The teaching model can be described as (1) watch me—modeling; (2) let's do it together—guided practice; and (3) you do it—practice doing it yourself.

THE STRATEGIES INSTRUCTIONAL MODEL

Deshler and Schumaker (1988) introduced the strategies instructional model (SIM) as a comprehensive model for using learning strategies. SIM is an instructional system that focuses on helping students with diverse learning needs achieve success in general education classrooms by providing appropriate materials as well as methods and strategies. The SIM includes:

- Curricular materials that can be modified to meet the unique learning needs of students
- Routines for teachers to facilitate the success of students with learning problems
- Strategies that students can use

The strategies instructional model includes teacher- and student-focused interventions. In other words, the SIM impacts the way teachers teach as well as the way students learn. The teacher-focused interventions include ways that teachers present information that, in turn, facilitates learning for students with diverse learning needs. Four conditions exist when using this model (Lenz & Deshler, 2004, p. 355):

1. Both group and individual needs are valued and met.
2. The integrity of the content is maintained.
3. Critical features of the content are selected and transformed in a way that promotes learning for all students.
4. Instruction is carried out in a partnership with students.

This model requires teachers to think about what they want to teach, and organize and present information in such a way that students with diverse learning needs can actually learn the content.

STUDENT-FOCUSED INTERVENTIONS— LEARNING STRATEGIES

Using the strategies instructional model, or a similar model aimed at arming students with learning skills, requires teachers to facilitate the use of a variety of student-focused interventions, or learning strategies. While there are numerous strategies that can benefit students, they can generally be organized into three groups: (1) strategies that help students acquire information; (2) strategies that help students store and keep the information; and (3) strategies that help students show what they have learned (Schumaker & Deshler, 2003).

Teachers need to evaluate students to determine the most useful strategies. While there are no assessments specifically designed to determine which strategies would be helpful to students, teachers need to use informal assessments, such as observations, to make such a determination. One way to use informal assessment is to develop a checklist with items related to specific strategies, to determine which ones students use and which ones would likely be beneficial in a student's academic success. The response to intervention (RTI) model could also be used to determine specific strategies (Hardcastle & Justice, 2006). Teachers could teach students to use certain strategies and determine if their use made a difference in the student's academic performance. If the strategy was determined to be useful, then the teacher could provide opportunities for the student to use that particular strategy. On the other hand, if the strategy proved not useful, then the teacher could move on to another possible strategy. The remainder of the chapter describes some strategies that fall under the three areas listed previously. These are only examples of strategies that are available; literally, hundreds of strategies could be included.

STRATEGIES TO ACQUIRE INFORMATION

Strategies that help students acquire information include those that deal with reading and listening, skills that account for a major amount of learning in middle and secondary grades where modeling and hands-on instruction decreases. Once students reach upper elementary grades, the demands for acquiring information through reading grow significantly each year. Unfortunately, as the grade level increases, the demand to acquire information through reading complex materials grows. As a result, many students who have significant deficits in literacy find it extremely difficult to do well in school past early elementary years. Students with reading deficits must be taught how to use strategies that will enable them to be more successful in acquiring information through reading.

Similarly, as students progress through school their need to acquire information through listening becomes increasingly important. As students reach upper elementary grades and middle school, their need to take notes and acquire information through listening increases. Even though an instructional trend is for more active involvement in the learning process, many teachers continue to teach using a didactic model where students learn primarily through listening. In classrooms where teachers use a more cooperative, active learning model, students still must have good listening and note-taking skills to take maximum advantage of cooperative learning and other group activities. For students who have difficulty acquiring information through listening, success may be impacted. Therefore, teaching students strategies that will help them acquire information through listening is important. The following describes various strategies that are helpful for students in their acquisition of knowledge.

Strategies for Reading

Reading is a critical skill for all students, but especially as students progress through middle and secondary grades. Without the ability to acquire information from reading textbooks or other materials, students will unlikely be successful.

The use of strategies has been shown to be effective for students with reading difficulties. While many students develop their own strategies for dealing with content materials, other students, including many students with disabilities, must be taught how to use specific strategies. They also must be given opportunities to practice those strategies and then be encouraged and reinforced for generalizing strategies to different situations.

Deficits in reading often impede success of students with disabilities in middle and secondary content classes. Students unable to read and comprehend materials associated with a class, whether it is from a textbook, handout, or other sources, are at a distinct disadvantage; and this disadvantage increases with each grade level. Therefore, for this group of students, teachers must facilitate the use of strategies to circumvent reading deficits.

In order for students to successfully acquire information from reading materials they must be fluent readers. "Fluency means that students can read text with accuracy, expression, speed, and with comprehension" (Faber, 2006, p. 24). In order to be fluent students must have good decoding and vocabulary skills, as well as a large repertoire of sight words. Fluent readers are able to focus on the meaning of the reading materials, which results in comprehension—the ultimate goal of reading. There are several strategies that can assist students in developing fluency and comprehension.

Decoding Strategies.   Many students with disabilities have major problems with decoding. Decoding can be described as skills necessary for students to read words that are unknown. Archer, Gleason, and Vachon (2003) noted that difficulties with decoding may be the major obstacle for students with poor reading skills in secondary schools. If students spend inordinate amounts of time decoding words, they do not have an opportunity to focus on the content for comprehension—the major purpose of reading. If they are unable to decode the reading material, they are unlikely to learn the information presented. Lebzelter and Nowacek (1999) described several strategies to assist secondary students with decoding skills.

Word Identification Strategy.   The word identification strategy was developed by Lenz and Hughes (1990). The strategy helps students who have reading problems to decode unfamiliar words. This seven-step strategy, called DISSECT, requires students to take advantage of context clues, breaking words into known components. The seven DISSECT steps are as follows (Ellis, Deshler, Lenz, Shumaker, & Clark, 1991):

Discover the context. The student skips unknown words and after reading the sentence, tries to guess the word based on its context.

Isolate the prefix. The student identifies any prefix and draws a box around it.

Separate the suffix. The student, similar to the previous step, identifies any suffix.

Say the stem. The student says the stem word that is left after the prefix and suffix have been deleted.

Examine the word. The student uses the rule of twos and threes to divide the stem word into a pronounceable word.

Teachers need a systematic method for teaching any strategy. Lenz and Hughes (1990) recommended an additional seven-step process to teach students how to use DISSECT. These steps could be used to teach any strategy that focuses on reading.

Step 1   Students are assessed using a 400-word, timed reading test to determine reading ability and grade level. Following the assessment, results are shared with students who must agree, in writing, to learn the strategy.

Step 2   The teacher explains the steps in the strategy and sets dates to achieve strategy goals.

Step 3   Teachers use a think-aloud strategy as they move through each step of the strategy; students then model this think aloud.

Step 4   Students describe, in their own words, how the strategy works. They can only move on to step 5 when they reach 100% on a "rapid-rate oral practice" and 80% on recognizing a list of prefixes and suffixes.

Step 5   Students record reading a passage at their reading level and move to step 6 only when their reading accuracy reaches 99%.

Step 6   Students repeat step 5 but with increasingly difficult reading materials.

step 7   Students are assessed with grade level reading materials, and after making six or fewer errors, make a written commitment to generalize the reading strategy for other school assignments.

WIST. Another decoding strategy described by Lebzelter and Nowacek (1999) is the word identification strategy training, or WIST. This program includes four specific strategies that were used successfully by Lovett et al. (1994) in a study of preadolescent students with dyslexia. The program includes different strategies, and allows students to use a specific strategy for different situations. The strategies include (1) word identification by analogy; (2) vowel variations; (3) SPY, or seek the part you know; and (4) peeling off. Having four strategies in the program gives students the opportunity to use the one that is most appropriate for a specific word. For example, if the student cannot determine an analogy for an unknown word, another strategy can be used. The four-strategy program gives students options that are very important when trying to decode unknown words. Table 9.1 describes each of these strategies in more detail.

Vocabulary Building Strategies. Vocabulary is directly linked to comprehension and fluency. As students read a passage, either they have to stop and determine the meaning of words they do not know, or they simply continue with their reading without a real understanding of what they have read. In either case, fluency and comprehension will be negatively impacted. Therefore, improving students' vocabulary will help with their fluency and comprehension. Following are several strategies teachers can use to help students improve their vocabulary skills.

Learning Walls. Learning walls can assist students in developing vocabulary associated with particular lessons. While some middle and secondary teachers may think learning walls are more appropriate at the elementary level, when used properly they can provide assistance for older learners. Teachers begin the learning wall by identifying important words, formulas, concepts, or other information that students must know before they can be successful in class. Charts that include this information are posted in prominent places around the room. These

---

TABLE 9.1 ● Word Identification Strategy Training (WIST)

WORD IDENTIFICATION BY ANALOGY

Uses the analogy or compare/contrast approach
Students compare unfamiliar words with known words using rhyming and patterns
Students learn a list of words using whole word approach
Example: Students use known words *kick* and *her* to decode *bicker*

VOWEL VARIATIONS

Students learn vowels have multiple pronunciations
Students are taught different vowel pronunciations in the order they occur
Example: Students try to decode *find* using a short *i*; after determining that is incorrect, they try the long *i*

SEEK THE PART YOU KNOW (SPY)

Students look for small, known words in other words
Example: In *abundance*, students may know *bun* and *dan* which would help decode the word

PEELING OFF

Students peel off prefixes and suffixes and use another strategy to decode
Example: To decode *unpacking*, students would peel off *un* and *ing* and decode *pack* using the vowel variation strategy

---

Source: From "Reading Strategies for Secondary Students with Mild Disabilities," by S. Lebzelter and E. J. Nowacek, 1999, *Intervention in School and Clinic, 34,* 212–219.

charts can be enhanced with color and graphics, but the key element is the information presented (Faber, 2006).

Once the learning wall has been posted, teachers need to help students learn to use the information. Two games teachers can use are Guess the Word and Wordo. In Guess the Word, the teacher provides clues to students who must identify which word or concept on the learning wall matches. In Wordo, students use a sheet with empty squares, similar to a bingo card, and write words from the learning wall in each square. The teacher calls out different words and the first student to cover all of the words in a line wins the game (Faber, 2006). These are examples of ways a learning wall can be used; teachers only need to use their creativity to develop different ways of using the strategy.

Sorts.   Sorts is another way of improving students' vocabulary. Using this approach, teachers provide students with a list of words and ask them to sort the words using different groupings. An open sort would be when students sort the list of words any way they want, while a closed sort would be when the teacher provides categories for the sorts. After students have sorted their words they should present them to the class and explain their rationale for the sort.

Morphemic Analysis.   Morphemic analysis is a method students use to understand the meaning of a word using word parts. Students break a word into syllables, pulling off prefixes and suffixes until they identify a root word. Frequently identifying the root word and understanding the meaning of prefixes and suffixes will allow students to understand the meaning of the word.

Weekly Vocabulary List.   Still another way of increasing students' vocabularies is with weekly vocabulary lists. Similar to spelling lists in elementary grades, vocabulary lists focus on specific words that students can learn weekly. These words should be associated with the content that is being presented. For example, a chapter or unit on physical science would include words vastly different from one on a literature course where students have to read *Moby Dick*. When using vocabulary lists, teachers should focus on a few specific words, and provide lots of practice time during the week to use the words in context.

Strategies for Comprehension

Once students read fluently they can focus their attention on comprehension. For many students with reading difficulties, comprehension is the primary area of weakness. Unfortunately, comprehension is the key to acquiring information from reading materials. If students are unable to comprehend what they read they likely will be unable to achieve success in content subject areas.

Comprehension strategies are "sets of steps that good readers use to make sense of what they are reading" (Faber, 2006, p. 25). Good readers typically use comprehension strategies without even thinking about them. However, for many students with reading difficulties, these strategies must be taught (Faber, 2006). As with other strategies, when teaching comprehension strategies, teachers should model the strategy, use the strategy together, and then give students opportunities to practice using the strategies independently. Following are examples of strategies to help students improve their comprehension skills.

Embedded Story Strategy.   One study investigated the effects of using embedded learning strategy instruction on the literacy skills of secondary school students. In this study, one group of students, including seven students with learning disabilities, was provided embedded story-structure instruction, while another group, which also included seven students with learning disabilities, was provided comprehensive skill instruction. The embedded story-structure instruction consisted of three components: a self-questioning strategy, a story-structure analysis, and a summary writing strategy.

Figure 9.1 depicts a graphic organizer for the embedded story-structure instruction. Here, students learned to use reporter's questions (*who, what, how, when, where, which,* and *why*) when reading a story. Results of the study revealed that students using the embedded story-structure strategy had significantly higher posttest scores than students receiving the comprehensive strategy instruction. This was true not only for students with disabilities, but also for students without disabilities, whose scores also improved significantly compared to their non-disabled peers receiving the comprehensive strategy instruction (Faggella-Luby, Schumaker, & Deshler, 2007).

Name_____ Title_____ Date_____

Who are the main characters?

	Characters	Clues/Description
• Protagonist	_____	_____
• Antagonist	_____	_____
• Other	_____	_____
	_____	_____

• *What is the control conflict?*

Person vs. Person
Person vs. Nature
Person vs. Ideal
Person vs. Self

• *How does the central conflict begin?* (Initiating Event)

• *When does the story take place?* (Time)

• *Where does the story take place?* (Place and Background Info)

• *Which decision or event is the climax (or turning point)?* (Climax)

• *How does the central conflict end/resolve?* (Resolution)

• *Why does the author tell us the story in this way?* (Theme)

Story Structure Picture:

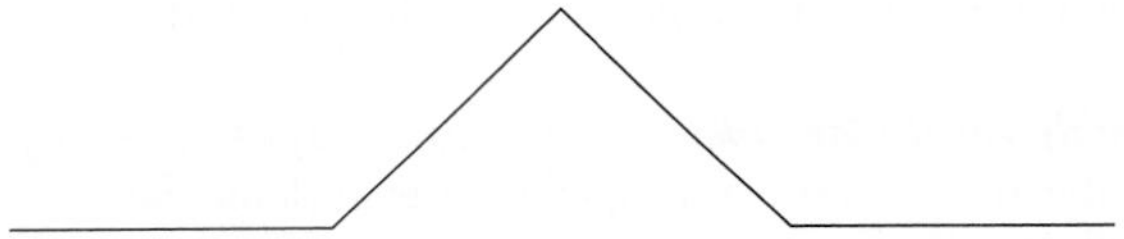

Summary:
_____
_____
_____
_____
_____
_____
_____
_____
_____
_____
_____

FIGURE 9.1 ● Graphic Organizer for Embedded Story-Structure Instruction

Source: "Embedded Learning Strategy Instruction: Story-Structure Pedagogy in Heterogeneous Secondary Literature Classes," by M. Faggella-Luby, J. S. Schumaker, & D. D. Deshler, Spring 2007, *Learning Disability Quarterly, 30*, pages 131–144. Copyright 2007 by the Council for Learning Disabilities. Reprinted with permission.

SQ3R Reading Method.   The SQ3R strategy has been used by teachers and students for many years. This method simply provides steps for students to follow when reading for comprehension. It emphasizes the importance of becoming familiar with the overall reading material prior to beginning reading, and developing questions that can be answered during reading. The components of the SQ3R strategy are (1) *survey* the reading material; (2) develop *questions* while surveying; (3) *read* the material looking for answers to your questions; (4) *recite* or orally ask questions about what has been read; and (5) *review* the reading material over the next several days. Table 9.2 expands these steps.

Paraphrasing and Summarizing.   Good readers typically paraphrase and summarize what they have read. Unfortunately, many students who are not good readers will simply read the material without performing these tasks. These students need to be taught how to paraphrase and summarize, using the following steps:

- Read a passage.
- Ask yourself what the passage is about.
- Ask yourself what is happening.
- Make up a summary of what happened.

TABLE 9.2 ● SQ3R Reading Strategy

Survey the chapter	Title of chapter, headings, subheadings Captions under pictures, charts, graphs, maps Review questions or study guides Read introductory and concluding paragraphs Read summary
Question surveying	Make questions out of title, headings, subheadings Read any questions at end of chapter or end of sections Ask what was said about the chapter when assigned Ask what you already know about the topic
When starting to **Read**	Look for answers to questions Answer questions at beginning and end of chapters Read captions again Note bolded or other highlighted words Study pictures, graphs, charts, etc. Read slower for difficulty sections Read parts that are unclear again Read one section at a time
Recite after reading a section	Ask yourself questions about what you have read or summarize what you have read Take notes in your own words Use as many senses in reciting as you can; the more senses the better
Review	Review daily by writing questions for notes or highlighted materials Page through text or notes to review content Orally recite and write answers to questions Use flash cards for difficult questions Use mnemonic devices for material that needs to be memorized

Source: From Study Guides and Strategies. www.studygs.net/texred2.htm

When teaching students how to use paraphrasing and summarizing, the teacher and students might read a passage together and perform the steps orally. After modeling the practice, the teacher could ask students to read the passage and then guide them to ask questions and develop a summary. Finally, the teacher would have students read a passage independently and apply the steps.

RAP.   A strategy similar to paraphrasing and summarizing is called RAP. The basic premise is for students to *read* a passage, *ask* questions about the passage, and then *put* the ideas or information into their own words.

Story Map.   Many students can benefit greatly from visual representations of what they have read. A story map can assist students to visualize how information fits together, thereby improving their comprehension. When using a story map, students can work independently or in groups. After reading a passage, they map out the major facts, activities, and characters from the content. By placing this information in circles, they can then connect the circles to reflect different relationships among the different map points.

Reciprocal Teaching.   The reciprocal teaching strategy requires students to read part of an assignment, and based on that reading predict what will occur in a following section. The method involves four steps—summarize, clarify, question, and predict. After reading a section, students summarize what they have read. If there are questions they can go back to clarify parts of the passage. Then they ask themselves what was important in the passage. Finally, they predict what will happen in the subsequent section, and then follow a similar routine after reading that part.

Reciprocal teaching can be used independently, but it can also be an effective group or paired-reading process. The key to this strategy, as well as other comprehension strategies, is to get students to focus on the content. Developing questions related to materials prior to reading the materials is an excellent way of helping students focus.

Strategies for Acquiring Information from Textbooks

Many different strategies have been developed to assist students in reading and comprehending textbooks. Since a great many middle and secondary classes remain textbook-based, students' ability to read and comprehend information from textbooks is critical for their academic success (Hallahan, Lloyd, Kauffman, Weiss, & Martinez, 2005). Students are generally required to read textbook assignments as part of their learning requirements. Students unable to acquire meaningful information from these materials will likely have significant difficulty in content classes. Many learners devise their own strategies for acquiring information from textbooks. However, for many students with disabilities, some of these strategies may need to be taught.

Gore (2004) described three ways of enhancing the use of textbook instruction. The first is preteaching vocabulary. Reading comprehension is predicated on students' knowledge of vocabulary. While some students learn new vocabulary words as they move through the content, many students need explicit vocabulary instruction prior to attempting a reading assignment. Therefore, teachers should identify words in a reading assignment that may not be within the students' vocabulary and provide vocabulary instruction prior to the reading assignment.

Teaching text structure is a second suggestion by Gore (2004). Teaching students how the text is structured, such as the importance of headings, bold or italicized words, numbers or letters to summarize points, and margin notes can provide clues for students looking for important information in a passage. Looking for words that signify importance, such as *furthermore*, *consequently*, and *in conclusion*, can also signal an important part of a passage (Salend, 2008).

Highlighting textbooks is the third suggestion provided by Gore (2004). Highlighting the text is an excellent means for helping students gain information from textbooks. While many students highlight their own textbooks, this is a strategy that can be completed for students. While highlighting the text may take time initially, teachers can ensure that the highlighted textbooks are given to students with reading difficulties during future years. Also, other students can follow a highlighted text to highlight other textbooks. Using highlighted textbooks is a useful strategy for the following reasons (Gore, 2004, p. 105):

- Assures discrimination between critical and not so critical information
- Focuses attention on the most important information
- Eliminates frustration when discrimination is assisted
- Increases motivation when frustration is eliminated

The following describes additional strategies to assist students with textbook reading.

SCROL.   Grant (1993) devised a strategy to help students use textbooks and other instructional materials, called SCROL. When using this strategy, students learn how to use text headings during their reading to assist in their understanding of the content. The SCROL strategy uses the following steps:

Survey. Students read headings and subheadings and ask themselves what they know about the topics and what will be presented.

Connect. Students determine how the headings are related and provide key words that show these connections.

Read. Students read the material and develop an outline of the major ideas.

Outline. During this step, students actually write down the headings and major ideas.

Lookback. Students review the headings and subheadings and check the validity of their outline.

The KWL Reading Method.   The KWL reading method can help students understand their text reading, and it is designed to be used by groups or by an entire class. The method works well with the discussion component when used by a group; however, it can be used independently as well. The KWL method uses the following steps:

Know. Students think about the topic and list what they already know. This helps students focus on the reading content prior to the reading, and helps students identify keywords, terms, and phrases. Students write down this information in a table they have created, under the column "What We Know."

Will or *want.* Next, students devise a series of questions regarding what they want to know about the topic. Students develop questions based on the information they gather after previewing the table of contents, headings, pictures, charts, figures, tables, and other components in the reading material. These questions go into the table, under the column "Will."

Learned. At this stage, students answer the questions they listed in the previous step. This can be accomplished during or after the reading and discussions. Students list their answers and check what they have learned with what they wanted to learn (Faber, 2006).

Strategies for Note-Taking

In addition to acquiring information through reading, students in middle and high schools acquire a significant amount of information through listening. This requires students to take notes for future study. Note-taking in middle and secondary content classes becomes more important as students matriculate through the grades. This includes taking notes during lectures and class discussions and taking notes while reading material. Most students learn to take notes independently; however, for many students with disabilities, note-taking strategies need to be taught. It is very difficult for students to be successful in secondary and postsecondary educational settings without the ability to take efficient notes.

Note-Taking from Oral Presentations.   Students in secondary schools must be able to take notes because of the teaching model used by many secondary teachers. While more secondary teachers are using cooperative learning and other active learning strategies in their classrooms, there are still many teachers who lecture at least part of the time, resulting in the need for students to be able to take coherent notes that are useful for learning. Even in situations where students are learning from each other, efficient note-taking can be extremely beneficial. On the surface, note-taking might be considered a simple process, but in actuality it is complex. Taking useful notes is much more than simply writing down information that has been presented. Effective note-taking requires students to do the following (Gore, 2004, p. 79):

1. Sustain their attention
2. Comprehend what the teaching is saying
3. Discriminate between critical and irrelevant information
4. Paraphrase the information into a note format
5. Organize it in a coherent way
6. Record it readably and quickly

Unfortunately, many students with disabilities have difficulties with one or more of these skills, which results in their being at a significant disadvantage when trying to acquire information from oral materials. It is important for students to learn to take effective notes. There are several strategies that can assist students; however, while learning how to use these strategies, teachers could provide notes to students so they will not miss content while learning how to take notes.

Strichart and Mangrum (2010) described three stages of note-taking: (1) getting ready to take notes, (2) taking notes, and (3) taking actions after note-taking. Before students can effectively take notes, they must be ready; they must have their paper, writing utensils, and any note-taking guides ready when the teacher begins the lesson. It is also helpful for students to review previous materials related to the lesson. This helps them prepare for the content that will be presented. Finally, if there has been a reading assignment prior to the lesson, having read this material will also prepare students for the content that will be presented by the teacher. In addition to being ready for taking notes, there are several strategies that can be helpful when students are actually taking notes. The following describes some of these strategies.

Guided Notes.   Guided notes use a "skeleton outline" that students follow as a guide to take notes. The detail level of the guide should depend on the needs of students. Some students, for example, may need only a guide that includes major headings while others may need a guide with major headings and several levels of subheadings. Regardless of the level, students fill in their guide as the teacher presents information. Guided notes can assist students in the following ways (Gore, 2004, p. 83):

- Increase attention because the students are actively engaged
- Increase perception because three modalities are involved
- Increase discrimination between essential and nonessential information because the teacher has guided the note-taking process
- Decrease confusion because the student is guided through the note-taking process with three modalities involved
- Increase memory if used with the daily review

Simply providing the template for guided notes is not a guarantee that students will use it effectively. Teachers can take several steps to help students successfully use guided notes. Prior to the class, teachers can provide cues to help students focus on particular content, ask questions, and lead discussions about the upcoming lesson. After the class, teachers can go over notes with individual students or in small groups; lead a class review; and have students exchange notes to check for content and accuracy (Study Guides and Strategies, 2009). Albeit simple, these steps can be critical in the successful use of guided notes by students.

Strategic Note-Taking.   Familiarity with a subject makes taking notes easier than when taking notes over unknown material. Therefore, students need to utilize any information that they may know about a topic. Strategic note-taking provides students with a note-taking strategy that incorporates previously learned information. Students actually begin the process by recording what they already know about the topic prior to the lesson. Figure 9.2 provides a sample strategic note-taking form.

There are numerous strategies to help students actually take notes, but after the note-taking session, there are other actions that students should take to assist them in the learning process. This includes comparing notes with other students to verify the content; seeking clarification from the teacher or reference materials about information not understood; and rewriting notes to avoid future misunderstanding of abbreviations or gaps in notes (Strichart & Mangrum, 2010).

Record/Reduce/Recite/Reflect/Review.   An important component of note-taking is what occurs after the notes have been taken. In other words, a student may take great notes, but if there are no actions after the notes have been taken, the student may still have difficulty remembering the information or effectively using the notes at a later date. When using this strategy, students use a notebook and develop a format prior to the note-taking opportunity. There are several steps involved in this process, most of which take place after the initial note-taking. When using this process, students take the following steps (Study Guides, 2009):

- Record notes on one section.
- After class, reduce the notes using keywords, phrases, or questions.
- Then recite, or talk aloud from memory, what has been learned from the lesson.
- Think over what has been learned and connect it to previously known facts.
- Then review notes prior to the next class or next test.

Note-Taking from Textbooks.   In addition to taking notes during class, either from teachers or other students, taking notes from textbooks or other written materials is also important for students. It is much more efficient to study notes from a text than going back over the entire text again. Good ways to facilitate taking notes while reading a text include (1) writing down questions as content is read; (2) listing vocabulary that is new to the reader; and (3) when permissible, emphasizing parts of the material by highlighting parts either through the use of a highlighter or underlining (Salend, 2008). The following describes one strategy to assist students in taking notes from written materials.

Power Notes.   Gore (2004) described the use of power notes for helping students organize notes from a textbook. Using this strategy, students, often working in pairs, identify the title of the chapter (power 1), bold subheadings within the chapter (power 2), and pull information from subheadings (power 3). This process helps students organize information and may even serve as a motivator for students who view the activity as a puzzle. This particular note-taking strategy alerts students about the nature of the content and gets them ready to focus on particular topics. Any process that helps students focus can greatly aid in their note-taking.

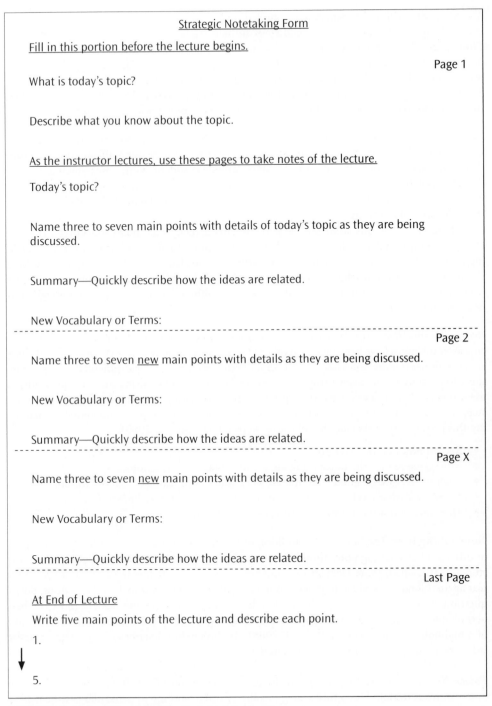

FIGURE 9.2 ● An Abbreviated Strategic Notetaking Form

Source: Reprinted with permission from J. R. Boyle & M. Weishaar (2001). "The Affects of Strategic Notetaking on the Recall and Comprehension of Lecture Information for High School Students with Learning Disabilities." *Learning Disabilities Research & Practice, 16*, p. 136. Copyright © 2001 John Wiley & Sons.

Organizational Tools

Poor organizational skills are common among students with a variety of disabilities (Smith, Polloway, Patton, & Dowdy, 2008). Without the ability to organize reading, taking notes, writing papers, and studying efforts, students will have significant difficulties being successful in general education classrooms. Many students simply need help in organizing their notes and learning efforts. Because many students with mild disabilities who are included in general education classrooms have problems with organizing and retaining information, oral and graphic organizers can be invaluable for their academic success. These are simply tools that can be used either before a lesson (called advance organizers) or after a lesson (called post organizers) to help students determine and understand the important information in the lesson (Salend, 2008).

Advance organizers are used before a lesson to help orient students to the information that will be presented, whereas post organizers come after a lesson and help students review and remember what has been presented. Advance and post organizers can take several forms, and can be oral or graphic; both help students acquire and/or remember information.

Oral Organizers.   A student's oral organizers can be either advance or post organizers. Advance oral organizers provide students an oral "heads up" about information that is about to be presented. For example, teachers can provide this comment prior to giving lecture notes:

> "Class, in the next 45 minutes we are going to talk about the primary reasons why the United States entered World War II. First, we will talk about changes in the German and Japanese governments and some of the issues they faced that resulted in some of their actions. After this topic we will talk about the initial expansions of these countries and some of the reactions from other countries. Finally, we'll talk about immediate actions that resulted in the United States declaring war on Germany and Japan."

By giving an oral outline of what the lecture will include, the teacher has helped students organize their notes and has alerted them to the organization of the lesson.

Post oral organizers provide students with a summary of the lesson and help students validate their notes and understand the most important parts of the lesson. For example, after the above described lecture, the teacher could say:

> So, the primary steps leading to the American involvement in World War II included (1) the rise to power of Adolf Hitler and the need for raw materials in Japan; (2) German and Japanese expansion in western Europe and China; and (3) the Japanese attack on Pearl Harbor."

This sort of post oral organizer helps students summarize and validate the facts that they have learned.

Other examples of oral organizers include:

- Making simple statements such as "listen up" before stating a fact
- Making simple statements such as "this is an important point" before stating a fact
- Saying at the end of a lesson, "I want you to remember these things we just talked about . . ."
- Saying at the end of a lesson, "Now let's summarize the key points, which were . . ."

Graphic Organizers.   Another type of organizer, which can be either advance or post, is a graphic organizer. Graphic organizers can be described as an organizational tool that teachers can use to help students organize information for maximum learning (Baxendell, 2003). There are numerous types of graphic organizers. Baxendell (2003) described four commonly used types: cause-and-effect diagrams, sequence charts, main-idea-and-detail

TABLE 9.3 ● Types of Graphic Organizers

CAUSE-AND-EFFECT DIAGRAMS

- Cut across all subject areas
- Used in reading stories to demonstrate results of character's actions
- Used in writing instruction to help organize student compositions
- Used in social studies to show events leading to major issues in history
- Diagrams are developed to show cause-and-effect relationships

SEQUENCE CHARTS

- Used to show chain of events
- Used in reading to summarize key elements of the passage/story
- Used in social studies to show timelines
- Used in science to show steps in a scientific experiment
- Order of events must be visually clear

MAIN-IDEA-AND-DETAIL CHARTS

- Helps students determine main idea and details of a reading assignment
- Used in all subject areas
- Students compose five sentence paragraphs

COMPARE-CONTRAST DIAGRAMS

- Venn diagram is an example
- Displays similarities and differences between two or more ideas

Source: From "Consistent, Coherent, Creative: The 3 C's of Graphic Organizers," by B. W. Baxendell, 2003, *Teaching Exceptional Children, 35*, 46–53.

charts, and compare-and-contrast diagrams. Each of these graphic organizers works best with particular information. Table 9.3 summarizes these types of advance organizers and their appropriate use.

Salend (2008) uses different terms to describe graphic organizers. A directional graphic organizer can be used to help students understand the process, procedures, sequence, and timelines of events. For example, students could learn the events leading up to the Civil War by using this type of graphic organizer. A second type described by Salend (2008) is a comparative graphic organizer. This type of organizer helps students understand the similarities and differences between two or more concepts. Figure 9.3 shows a comparative graphic organizer.

STRATEGIES FOR STORING AND RETRIEVING INFORMATION

The second component of learning strategies deals with storing and retrieving information. If students cannot store and retrieve what they have learned, then the initial learning becomes significantly less important. Just as there are strategies that can assist students in acquiring information, there are also a variety of strategies that can help students store and retrieve the information.

Mnemonic Strategies

Many students use mnemonic strategies to help store and retrieve information. Mnemonic strategies include verbal or visual clues that will help students remember and retrieve information.

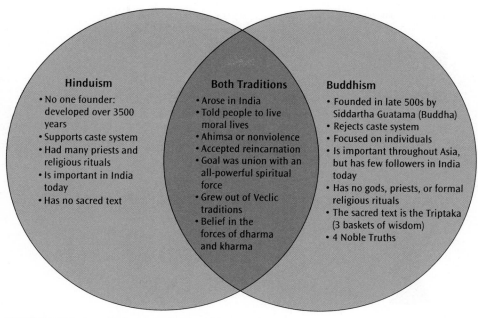

Hinduism
- No one founder: developed over 3500 years
- Supports caste system
- Had many priests and religious rituals
- Is important in India today
- Has no sacred text

Both Traditions
- Arose in India
- Told people to live moral lives
- Ahimsa or nonviolence
- Accepted reincarnation
- Goal was union with an all-powerful spiritual force
- Grew out of Veclic traditions
- Belief in the forces of dharma and kharma

Buddhism
- Founded in late 500s by Siddartha Guatama (Buddha)
- Rejects caste system
- Focused on individuals
- Is important throughout Asia, but has few followers in India today
- Has no gods, priests, or formal religious rituals
- The sacred text is the Triptaka (3 baskets of wisdom)
- 4 Noble Truths

FIGURE 9.3 ● Sample Comparative Graphic Organizers

Source: S. J. Salend (2008). Creating inclusive classrooms: Effective and reflective practices (6th ed.), p. 479. Used with permission.

Meese (2001) noted three different mnemonic strategies: the keyword method, reconstructive elaborations, and the pegword method.

Keyword Method. In the keyword method, students find words that sound like target words, make up a story using the words, and visualize a picture that demonstrates the story. This method is effective for the following reasons (Gore, 2004, p. 183):

- Memory is enhanced when material is presented auditorily and visually and because the information requires students to elaborate on material that is made concrete and meaningful.
- Motivation is elevated by the playful nature of the strategies.
- Attention is increased when motivation is elevated.

Often the keyword is one that sounds like the word used in the image. For example, if a student is trying to remember the word *crane,* he might have a mental image of a bird in the rain.

Reconstructive Method. The reconstructive mnemonic method is more aptly used with more abstract information. Meese (2001) used an example of a picture of Uncle Sam looking over Europe and saying, "This is not my war," as a way of remembering the position of the United States prior to the beginning of World War II. Using the reconstructive method, students can visualize just about anything that could be related to the fact or facts being remembered. Another example would be visualizing two planes and two tall buildings to help remember the events of September 11, 2001.

Pegword Method. The pegword method can be used when students are trying to remember a particular order of words. Rhyming words are frequently used as the pegwords to help students

California 1 Collie on a Bun

Texas 2 Shoe Taxi Wearing Shoes

New York 3 Tree New Fork in Tree

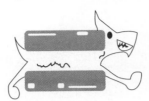

Florida 4 Snore Flowers Snoring

Pennsylvania 5 Hive Bees Bring Pens Back to the Hive.

FIGURE 9.4 ● Pegword Mnemonics to Teach the Five Most Populous States

Source: M. C. Gore (2004). Successful inclusion strategies for secondary and middle school teachers: Keys to helping struggling learners access the curriculum. p. 185. Used with permission.

remember the sequence of letters. Pegword mnemonics is effective for the following reasons (Gore, 2004, p. 184):

- Memory is enhanced when information is elaborated, given concreteness, and is meaningful, as well as when information is encoded in multiple modalities.
- Motivation is elevated by the playful nature of the strategies.
- Attention is increased when motivation is elevated.

Figure 9.4 shows the use of pegword mnemonics to teach the five largest U.S. states.

First Letter Mnemonics.   Another mnemonic strategy that can be used effectively is called the *first letter mnemonics* (Sabornie & deBetencourt, 2004). This strategy can be used when students need to learn a large amount of material. Using this strategy, students will do the following (Lenz & Deshler, 2004):

- Identify lists of information that need to be learned.
- Select an appropriate title or label for each set of information.

- Select a mnemonic device for each set of information.
- Create study cards with the information.
- Use cards to rehearse and learn the information.

Research has shown that using this form of mnemonic strategy can be extremely helpful in learning large amounts of information (Lenz & Deshler, 2004).

An example of a first letter mnemonic strategy would be for a student wanting to learn the last 10 presidents of the United States, in order. The presidents are Eisenhower, Kennedy, Johnson, Nixon, Ford, Carter, Bush, Clinton, Bush, and Obama. A first letter mnemonic strategy might be the following phrase: "**E**very **k**ind **j**ake **n**eeds **f**ond, **c**aring, **b**eautiful, **c**harismatic, **b**rainy, **o**ldtimers." By students remembering a silly jingle, they might be able to remember the last 10 presidents.

In addition to mnemonic strategies, there are other strategies that can help students remember what they have learned. Carter, Prater, and Dyches (2009) suggest the following ideas:

Use pictures and encourage visualization. Use pictures in class to help students remember information. These pictures can be posted on walls, shown on overhead projectors or elmos, or drawn on a chalkboard. Students could even draw their own pictures.

Encourage students to verbalize, or to talk about what they are learning. Give students opportunities to talk about what they are learning. Active, involved learning is much more efficient than passive learning. Encourage and reinforce students for using their own words to describe what they are learning.

Incorporate concrete learning experiences in instruction. Being able to relate information to concrete learning experiences makes learning easier. For example, showing students a Skinner box in class when talking about Skinner's experiments with pigeons and operant conditioning could facilitate learning and memory about this topic.

Incorporate recall enhancement routines in lessons. Use mnemonic devices while teaching. Develop the support and show how it can be used during the lesson.

Promote the use of external memory. Encourage students to use supports to help them learn and remember information. These supports can be as simple as paper and pencil to take notes, or as complex as laptop computers.

STRATEGIES FOR EXPRESSING LEARNED MATERIALS

In the end, students must be able to show what they have learned in our ever-increasing system of accountability. Being able to perform on tests and other outcome measures is more important today than ever before. Some students can learn and store information but have great difficulty expressing what they have learned on tests, homework, oral reports, and written assignments. For this group of students, strategies can facilitate their expressing of what they have learned.

Writing Strategies

Writing assignments can be extremely difficult for many students, including those with disabilities. Similar to reading and taking effective notes, the need to effectively express oneself in writing becomes more important as students progress through the grades. While some students have the ability to express themselves well in essays and research papers, others need instruction. One way to approach a writing assignment is to break it into several specific steps. These include (Study Guides, 2009):

- Develop your topic.
- Identify your audience.
- Research your topic.
- Organize and prewrite the paper.
- Develop an initial draft and write a completed paper.
- Revise the paper.
- Proofread for final version.

The learning strategies curriculum (Deshler & Schumaker, 1988) includes five writing strategies on sentence writing, paragraph writing, error monitoring, inspecting, and theme writing. Teachers have opportunities to select the strategy that best fits the needs of their students, eventually teaching students to select the strategy that would be the most appropriate. Table 9.4 describes these strategies. Studies on each of these strategies have shown that students with learning disabilities, and other students, can learn and implement strategies to improve writing effectively (Schumaker & Deshler, 2003).

Hallahan and colleagues (2005) included several of the strategies found in the learning strategies curriculum, with slight modifications. The following strategies can assist students with writing skills (Hallahan et al., 2005, p. 439):

- *Sentence writing:* Students learn how to recognize and write simple, compound, complex, and compound-complex sentences.
- *Paragraph writing:* Students learn how to outline ideas, select a point of view, select appropriate tense, and sequence ideas in an effort to compose organized, complete paragraphs.
- *Error monitoring:* Students learn how to find and correct errors in their writing.
- *Theme writing:* Students learn how to write a five-paragraph theme.

Teachers can use guided feedback to help students improve their writing skills. When using such a strategy, teachers may want to have a writing checklist available to assist students in understanding the writing process. Figure 9.5 shows an example of such a writing checklist.

Test-Taking Strategies

Students with disabilities are currently held accountable for their outcomes similar to those without disabilities. As a result, their performance on tests is extremely important. Test-taking strategies can help students with disabilities exhibit improved outcomes. In fact, all students can benefit from test-taking strategies. For students with disabilities, it is often imperative that specific strategies are taught to facilitate their success. Test scores do not always accurately reflect what a student actually knows. If the purpose of assessment is to determine students' knowledge, then teaching them how to take tests that accurately reflect their knowledge level is important. Carter and colleagues (2009) provide the following general examples of how teachers can improve student test performance:

- Inform students regarding what, when, and how they will be tested.
- Provide students with reminder notes several days before the test will be administered.
- Remind students to come prepared physically for the assessment.
- Provide a healthy, positive, and confident atmosphere.
- Provide practice tests using the format of the actual test with items that closely align with the questions students will encounter.
- Teach relaxation and adrenalin-reducing techniques.

TABLE 9.4 ● Writing Strategies

SENTENCE WRITING STRATEGY
- Students write four types of sentences
- Sentences are simple, compound, complex, and compound-complex
- Students write four simple sentences
- Once simple sentences are mastered, students learn how to write 10 variations related to compound, complex, and compound-complex
- After learning to write all 14 sentences, students have a myriad of sentence types

PARAGRAPH WRITING STRATEGY
- Student learns how to list ideas related to a topic
- Plan point of view and verb tense
- Plan sequence of ideas to be expressed
- Write various sentences to pull paragraph together

ERROR MONITORING STRATEGY
- Used to help students find and correct writing errors
- Draft of written product is written on every other line
- Student checks for organizational errors
- Student checks for capitalization, punctuation, spelling, and appearance
- Errors are noted with strike-outs or circles with correction written in space above
- Students recopy corrected version

INSPECTING STRATEGY
- Students check and correct errors using computerized spellchecker
- Students find incorrect words and select correct version from spellchecker
- Students sound out words and try other options if unsure of correct spelling
- Strategy includes computerized set of lessons teachers can download

THEME WRITING STRATEGY
- Helps students write well-organized themes
- Students think about what they know about a topic and do research on areas where they need additional information
- Students use a theme writing diagram to organize information
- Structure includes introductory paragraph, three or more detail paragraphs, and concluding paragraph
- Paragraphs are connected with transitions
- Students then edit for errors

Source: From "Can Students with LD Become Competent Writers?" by J. B. Schumaker and D. D. Deshler, 2003, *Learning Disability Quarterly, 26,* 129–141.

- Provide external reinforcement for effort.
- Teach students to attribute success/failure to personal effort and not to forces outside their control.
- Teach students general test-taking strategies that can apply to many different tests.
- Teach students strategies that are specific to the type of question being asked.
- Teach students strategies specific to high stakes testing.

Often students get confused with the many different types of tests they have to complete. One test-taking strategy described by Strichart and Mangrum (2010), called DETER, helps students understand which type of objective test they must complete (multiple-choice,

Before writing:

1. Have I chosen a topic appropriate for the assignment? (not too broad, not too narrow) Yes No

2. If I needed to, did I research and gather enough information in order to adequately cover my topic? Yes No

3. Have I organized my thoughts by using an outline, a web, or index cards? Yes No

Note: Please do not go on until you have answered "yes" to each question above. Remember, you must be able to provide evidence for each step.

After writing a first draft:

1. Is my Introduction clear and interesting? (It should catch the reader's attention.) Yes No

2. Does my introduction lead to a thesis that is stated completely, clearly, and correctly? Yes No

3. Are my supporting paragraphs logically organized? Yes No

4. Does the information in each body paragraph support the thesis? Yes No

5. Have I started each supporting paragraph with a topic sentence? Yes No

6. Have I ended each supporting paragraph with a concluding sentence? Yes No

7. Have I used good transitions (e.g., "however," "therefore," "in addition")? Yes No

8. Do I have enough supporting details in each body paragraph? Yes No

9. Does my concluding paragraph summarize the content of the paper? Yes No

10. In the conclusion, have I restated the thesis in different words? Yes No

11. Have I explained the significance of my topic in the conclusion? Yes No

12. Have I used complete sentences throughout my paper? Yes No

13. Have I used correct tenses? Yes No

14. Have I used proper spelling, capitalization, and punctuation? Yes No

15. Have I asked at least one other person to read my paper and make comments? Yes No

16. Have I met my teacher's specific requirements for this assignment? Yes No

If you have answered "yes" to every question, you are now ready to type your final draft.

FIGURE 9.5 ● Writing Checklist

Source: D. P. Hallahan, W. J. Lloyd, J. M. Kauffman, M. P. Weiss, & E. A. Martinez (2005). Learning disabilities: Foundations, characteristics, and effective teaching. Used with permission.

true–false, matching, or completion) and develop a plan for its completion. The steps in the DETER strategy include the following (Strichart & Mangrum, 2010):

D—Read the **directions** and ask the teacher to explain anything unclear.

E—**Examine** the entire test to determine the extent of the test.

T—Decide how much **time** you have for each question.

E—Answer the **easiest** questions first.

R—**Review** your answers to ensure they are your best answers and that you have answered all of the questions.

Many teachers use multiple-choice tests in class. Using this type of test means that students have to choose the correct answer from several options, usually four or five. There are some general strategies that could be taught to students to help them answer multiple-choice questions. These are described by Strichart and Mangrum (2010, p. 159):

- Circle or underline important words in the item.
- Read all the answer choices before selecting one.
- Cross out any answer choices you are certain are incorrect.
- Look for answer choices that contain absolute terms such as *all, always,* and *never.*
- Look for two answer choices that are the opposite of each other.
- When answering an item, look for hints about the correct answer in other items on the test.
- Look for answer choices that contain language used by your teacher or found in your textbook.
- Select "All of the above" as an answer choice only if you are certain that all other answer choices are correct.
- Select "None of the above" as an answer choice only if you are certain that all other answer choices are incorrect.
- Do not change your answer unless you are sure that a different answer choice is better.
- Answer all items unless there is a penalty for incorrect answers.

Preparing to take a test requires much more than studying the day before. In order to be as ready as possible for tests, students need to prepare for tests throughout the learning process. This includes taking good notes, reviewing notes immediately after class and again before the next class, and having a longer review at the end of the week. In final preparation for the test, the review should include (Study Guides, 2009):

- Estimating time necessary to review materials
- Testing yourself over the materials
- Completing your study for the test a day early

Obviously, prior to test day, students need to review their materials for the test. There are many different ways students can complete this review. Some suggestions include creating study checklists, creating notes and maps, recording notes, and creating flashcards. Checklists help students prepare for the test by listing notes, formulas, ideas, text assignments, and other requirements that could be included on the test. Summary notes and maps help students write and summarize lists and hierarchies of ideas. When recording notes aloud, students are actually reviewing the material. Finally, creating flashcards for definitions, formulas, or lists helps students memorize the content (Study Guides, 2009).

ANSWER Strategy.   Therrien, Hughes, Kapelski, and Mokhtari (2009) described a test-taking strategy that was used effectively for students with learning disabilities in middle school. The strategy, ANSWER, includes six steps (p. 17):

Analyze the action words in the question. In this step, students read the question and underline or highlight key words in the question.
Notice the requirements of the question. After reading the question and noting key words, students reword the question using their own words while understanding the specific requirements of the question.
Set up an outline. Students outline the main ideas of their response.
Work in detail. In this step, students go through their outlined response and add more detail.
Engineer your answer. At this step, students follow their outline and write the essay, making sure to focus on an introduction and explanation of each of the main ideas.
Review your answer. Finally, students edit their essays and make sure that all parts of the outline have been addressed.

Therrien and colleagues (2009) used this model with 61 students who exhibited learning disabilities, in the seventh and eighth grades. Following an instructional period that included six lessons, students using the ANSWER strategy performed significantly better than a control group of students without learning disabilities on a posttest essay. Findings also showed "when students use most of the strategy, their ratings are similar to students without LD on the overall rubric" (Therrien et al., 2009, p. 22).

Homework Completion Strategy.   Successfully completing homework assignments can play a large role in a student's success in middle and high school content classes. Unfortunately, as noted by Hughes, Ruhl, Schumaker, and Deshler (2002), many students with learning disabilities have difficulties even understanding homework assignments, much less completing them correctly. This is often due to difficulties in listening, reading, organization, and memory. This inability puts this group of students at a significant disadvantage in successfully completing the assignment. Unfortunately, when homework is not completed successfully, the chances for the student having success in the class can be greatly diminished.

Hughes and others (2002) devised a homework completion strategy aimed at providing students with a process that could improve their success with homework. The strategy, called PROJECT, focuses on teaching students a particular sequence of behaviors that could improve the likelihood of successful homework completion. The steps include:

Prepare your forms. During this step the student completes a monthly planner that includes special events and assignment due dates. Next, the student completes a weekly study schedule. This schedule blocks out when work cannot be done (because of class or other reasons), and shows when various homework assignments can be worked on. Figure 9.6 shows a sample weekly study schedule.

Record and ask. As soon as a teacher gives an assignment, the student immediately records it on an assignment sheet, giving the due date and any specific details about the assignment. If the assignment is for a subsequent week, then the student makes a note of it on the monthly planner. The monthly planner should be checked daily to remind the student of upcoming assignments.

Organize. During this step, which occurs near the end of the school day, the student (1) breaks down assignments into various steps; (2) estimates how much time will be involved in completing the assignment; (3) schedules times to work on the assignment (which are recorded on the weekly study schedule); and (4) makes sure the appropriate materials for working on the assignment are taken home.

Jump to it. During this step, students engage in the task, as it prevents them from avoiding the task. By getting out the proper materials and engaging in the task, the student can begin focusing on what needs to be accomplished.

Engage in the work. During this step, the student actually completes the work necessary to finish the assignment.

Check your work. At this step the student checks the completed assignment to ensure neatness, completeness, and accuracy. Too often students submit work without proper checking.

Turn in your work. Finally, students submit their assignments.

The PROJECT strategy was put into effect in a middle school with a student population of approximately 500 students. After implementing the strategy, findings revealed that the majority of students with learning disabilities improved in their quarterly grades and teacher ratings after approximately 7 hours of instruction in how to use the strategy. More importantly, findings confirmed that most of these gains were maintained after the instruction was completed (Hughes et al., 2002).

WEEKLY STUDY SCHEDULE

Study Schedule for Week of _____ Ap. 12–18 _____

DATE	12	13	14	15	16	17	18
TIME	SATURDAY	SUNDAY	MONDAY	TUESDAY	WEDNESDAY	THURSDAY	FRIDAY
6:30–7:00							
7:00–7:30							
7:30–8:00							
8:00–8:30							
8:30–9:00							
9:00–9:30							
9:30–10:00							
10:00–10:30							
10:30–11:00	BK RPRT						
11:00–11:30	BK RPRT						
11:30–12:00							
12:00–12:30							
12:30–1:00							
1:00–1:30							
1:30–2:00		HIST TEST					
2:00–2:30		HIST TEST					
2:30–3:00							
3:00–3:30							
3:30–4:00			MATH				
4:00–4:30			BK RPRT				
4:30–5:00			BK RPRT			BK RPRT	
5:00–5:30						BK RPRT	
5:30–6:00						MATH	
6:00–6:30							
6:30–7:00							
7:00–7:30				BK RPRT			
7:30–8:00				BK RPRT	HEALTH		
8:00–8:30				MATH	BK RPRT		
8:30–9:00					BK RPRT		
9:00–9:30							
9:30–10:00							
10:00–10:30							

FIGURE 9.6 ● Weekly Study Schedule

Reprinted with permission from Hughes et al (2002). "Effects of Instruction in an Assignment Completion Strategy on the Homework Performance of Students with Learning Disabilities in General Education Classes." *Learning Disabilities Research & Practice, 17(1)*, p. 6. Copyright © 2002 John Wiley & Sons.

SUMMARY

This chapter focuses on learning strategies—tools that students can learn to use that will enable them to be independent, successful learners. The realities associated with today's schools (e.g., No Child Left Behind, access to the general curriculum, and inclusion) mandate that students be taught skills that facilitate their academic success. As students matriculate through the grades it becomes increasingly more important to teach them how to learn rather than teaching them facts and information.

Research has shown that students can learn to use learning strategies effectively. In order for students to have these strategies in their repertoire of skills, teachers must first teach the strategy, and then give students opportunities for using the strategies. A three-part teaching model can be effective in teaching students how to use strategies. These include *watch me* (modeling), *let's do it together* (guided instruction), and *you do it* (independent practice).

Learning strategies fall into three major areas—strategies to assist in acquiring information; strategies to assist in storing and retrieving information; and strategies to assist in expressing information. Acquiring information includes reading and listening. As students move from elementary school to middle school to high school, being able to acquire information through reading and listening becomes increasingly important. Specific strategies, dealing with decoding, vocabulary, fluency, and comprehension, have been shown to be effective for many students with disabilities.

Students also secure a great deal of information through listening. When information is acquired through listening, students must be able to take coherent notes for later study. Unfortunately, many students with disabilities do not have good note-taking skills, requiring teachers to teach note-taking strategies. With good strategies, students are able to take effective notes from both oral presentations and written materials.

Strategies can also be used to help students store and retrieve information. The most common ways to do so focus on mnemonics. Several different types of mnemonics have been shown to be very effective for students. Finally, following acquiring, storing, and retrieving information, students must be able to successfully express what they have learned. This means they must be able to write effectively and take tests effectively. Again, several strategies have shown success with students in these areas.

Learning strategies are an excellent way for students with disabilities to achieve independence and to become successful learners. School personnel must teach these strategies, give students opportunities to try out the strategies, and reinforce students for using the strategies.

ACTIVITIES

1. Discuss the use of strategies with several secondary students, including students with and without disabilities. Explain different strategies and determine how frequently they are used by both groups of students, and the effectiveness of using these strategies.

2. Teach one student with a disability how to use any of the strategies presented in this chapter. After teaching the strategy, have the student use the strategy for 5 days. At the end of the five-day period, discuss with the student the use of the strategy and its effectiveness, and the likelihood the student will continue using the strategy.

3. Think of the strategies you use when studying. Describe those strategies and compare them to some of the strategies presented in this chapter.

REFERENCES

Archer, A. L., Gleason, M. M., & Vachon, V. L. (2003). Decoding and fluency: Foundation skills for struggling older readers. *Learning Disability Quarterly, 26*, 14–22.

Baxendell, B. W. (2003). Consistent, coherent, creative: The 3 C's of graphic organizers. *Teaching Exceptional Children, 35*, 46–53.

Boyle, J. R., & Weishaar, M. (2001). "The Affects of Strategic Notetaking on the Recall and Comprehension of Lecture Information for High School Students with Learning Disabilities. *Learning Disabilities Research & Practice, 16*, 131–142.

Bulgren, J. A., Marquis, J. G., Deshler, D. D., Schumaker, J. B., Lenz, B. K., Davis, B., & Grossen, B. (2006). The instructional context of inclusive secondary general education classes: Teachers' instructional roles and practices, curricular demands, and research-based practices and standards. *Learning Disabilities: A Contemporary Journal, 4*, 39–65.

Carter, N., Prater, M. A., & Dyches, T. T. (2009). *Making accommodations and adaptations for students with mild disabilities.* Upper Saddle River, NJ: Pearson.

Center for Research on Learning (2009). Learning strategies. www.kucrl.org/sim/strategies.shtml Retrieved 9/29/2010

Deshler, D. D. (2005). Adolescents with learning disabilities: Unique challenges and reasons for hope. *Learning Disability Quarterly, 28*, 122–124.

Deschler, D., & Schumaker, J. (1988). An instructional model for teaching students how to learn. In J. L. Graden, J. E. Zins, & M. L. Curtis (Eds.), Alternative education delivery systems: Enhancing instructional options for all students (pp. 391–411). Washington, D.C.: National Association of School Psychologists.

Ellis, E., Deshler, D., Lenz, K., Schumaker, J., & Clark, F. (1991). An instructional model for teaching learning strategies. *Focus on Exceptional Children, 23*, 1–23.

Faber, S. H. (2006). *How to teach reading when you're not a reading teacher.* Nashville: Incentive Publications.

Faggella-Luby, M., Schumaker, J. S., & Deshler, D. D. (2007). Embedded learning strategy instruction: Story-structure pedagogy in heterogeneous secondary literature classes. *Learning Disability Quarterly, 30*, 131–147.

Grant, R. (1993). Strategic training for using text headings to improve students' processing of content. *Journal of Reading, 36*, 482–488.

Gore, M. C. (2004). Successful inclusion strategies for secondary and middle school teachers: Keys to help struggling learners access the curriculum. Thousand Oaks, CA: Corwin Press.

Hallahan, D. P., Lloyd, J. W., Kauffman, J. M., Weiss, M. P., & Martinez, E. A. (2005). *Learning disabilities: Foundations, characteristics, and effective teaching.* Boston: Allyn & Bacon.

Hardcastle, B., & Justice, K. (2006). *RTI and the classroom teaching: A guide for fostering teacher buy-in and supporting the intervention process.* West Palm Beach, FL: LRP Publications.

Horowitz, S. H. (2009). Strategic Instruction Model (SIM)—How to teach—How to learn. www.ncld.org/content/view/841 Retrieved 9/28/10

Hughes, C. A., Ruhl, K. L., Schumaker, J. B., & Deshler, D. D. (2002). Effects of instruction in an assignment completion strategy on the homework performance of students with learning disabilities in general education classes. *Learning Disabilities Research and Practice, 17*, 1–18.

Land, S. (2009). The strategic instruction model— Helping all students succeed. Training and technical assistance center at the college of William and Mary. Web.wm.edu/ttac/articles/teaching/strategic_instruction_model.htm?svr=www Retrieved 9/28/10

Lebzelter, S., & Nowacek, E. J. (1999). Reading strategies for secondary students with mild disabilities. *Intervention in School and Clinic, 34*, 212–219.

Lenz, B. K., & Deshler, D. D. (2004). Teaching content to all. Boston: Allyn & Bacon.

Lenz, B. K., & Hughes, C. A. (1990). A word identification strategy for adolescents with learning disabilities. *Journal of Learning Disabilities, 23*, 149–158.

Lovett, M. W., Borden, S. L., DeLuca, T., Lacerenza, L., Benson, N. J., & Blackstone, D. (1994). Treating the core deficits of developmental dyslexia: Evidence of transfer of learning after phonological and strategy-based reading training programs. *Developmental Psychology, 30*, 805–822.

Meese, R. L. (2001). *Teaching learners with mild disabilities: Integrating research and practice.* Stamford, CT: Wadsworth.

Mercer, C. D., & Pullen, P. C. (2009). *Students with learning disabilities* (7th ed.). Upper Saddle River, NJ: Merrill/Pearson.

Sabornie, E. J., & deBetencourt, L. U. (2004). *Teaching students with mild and high-incidence disabilities at the secondary level* (2nd ed.). Upper Saddle River, NJ: Merrill/Pearson.

Salend, S. J. (2008). Creating inclusive classrooms: Effective and reflective practices. (6th ed.). Upper Saddle River, NJ: Pearson.

Schumaker, J. B., & Deshler, D. D. (2003). Can students with LD become competent writers? *Learning Disability Quarterly, 26*, 129–141.

Schumaker, J. B., Deshler, D. D., Woodruff, S. K., Hock, M. F., Bulgren, J. A., & Lenz, B. K. (2006). Reading strategy interventions: Can literacy outcomes be enhanced for at-risk adolescents? *Teaching Exceptional Children, 38*, 64–68.

Smith, T. E. C., Polloway, E. A., Patton, J. R., & Dowdy, C. A. (2008). *Teaching students with special needs in inclusive settings.* Boston: Allyn & Bacon.

Strichart, S. S., & Mangrum, C. T. (2010). *Study skills for learning disabled and struggling students* (4th ed.). Upper Saddle River, NJ: Pearson. Study guides and strategies. SQ3R Reading Strategy. http://www.studygs.net.texred2.htm Retrieved 9/22/10

Study guides & strategies (2009). www.studygs.net Retrieved 11/13/2009

Swanson, H. L., & Deshler, D. (2003). Instructing adolescents with learning disabilities: Converting a meta-analysis to practice. *Journal of Learning Disabilities, 36*, 124–134.

Therrien, W. J., Hughes, C., Kapelski, C., & Mokhtari, K. (2009). Effectiveness of a test-taking strategy on achievement in essay tests for students with learning disabilities. *Journal of Learning Disabilities, 42*, 14–23.

10

Strategies for Teaching Content to Adolescents with Disabilities: Reading and Language Arts

Study Questions

1. Why is literacy important for adolescents?

2. What are the components of literacy?

3. What are the five components of reading and what do they mean?

4. What are ways that phonics and phonemic awareness can be taught?

INTRODUCTION

As students matriculate into the middle and secondary grades, teachers assume that they have learned basic reading and literacy skills, including the ability to read fluently, comprehend written material, and effectively express themselves in writing (Vacca & Vacca, 2005). Unfortunately this is not the case for many students. According to the Organization for Economic Cooperation and Development (OECD), 15-year-olds in the United States ranked 15th in reading literacy compared to their peers in other comparable countries (Duplass, 2006; Shanahan & Shanahan, 2008). In 2005, the National Assessment of Educational Progress (NAEP) reported that 36% of fourth graders and 27% of eighth graders performed below basic level in reading comprehension and 26% of 17-year-old students could not demonstrate effective writing skills. The importance of reading and literacy in our society, in conjunction with the fact that many students are performing less than adequately, means that reading ability and success at the middle and secondary levels continues to be a concern (Ruddell, 2008). In today's world, "students need to develop advanced literacy skills to comprehend, analyze, and synthesize large quantities of information" (Alliance for Excellent Education, n.d., p. 1). To become literate in a content area, students must understand how to use reading and writing, as well as oral language in order to learn (Vacca & Vacca, 2005).

Literacy is a broad term that includes the ability to use written language; it includes reading as well as writing (Roe, Stoodt-Hill, & Burns, 2007). Schools refer to this as "academic literacy" and focus its application on understanding content area textbooks and literature (Torgeson et al., 2007). In order to become literate, that is, skilled in reading and writing, students need to progress through three levels of literacy—basic, intermediate, and disciplinary literacy. These three levels correspond to the elementary grades (basic reading skill development), upper elementary/middle grades (intermediate reading skill development), and middle and secondary grades (Shanahan and Shanahan, 2008). By the time students reach middle and then high school, they should have developed the basic and intermediate skills necessary to access information from content textbooks, trade books, magazines, and newspapers. Once students reach high school, the focus shifts to their learning the specialized or disciplinary reading skills that are more sophisticated (Shanahan & Shanahan, 2008).

As noted, literacy deals with effective use of the written language. There are two major areas included in literacy—reading and writing. Each is comprised of numerous subareas. For example, reading includes phonics, phonemic awareness, fluency, vocabulary, and comprehension (National Reading Panel Report, 2000). Writing includes the mechanics of writing, spelling, and written expression (Polloway, Miller, & Smith, 2011). As the information age continues to explode, literacy skills take on added importance in employment and in the quality of people's lives. Indeed, adults in today's society need to be literate to compete in employment and social challenges. To be successful in postsecondary employment, "students must acquire a sophisticated array of literacy skills" (Faggella-Luby & Deshler, 2008, p. 70). Similarly, successful social inclusion requires a certain level of literacy.

INSTRUCTION IN READING

Reading has been at the forefront of educational reforms for years. Several federal initiatives, including Reading First and No Child Left Behind, have resulted in improved reading performances by students in elementary grades. Unfortunately, similar success has not been realized for many adolescents. The number of secondary students reading at the proficient level has remained virtually the same over the past several years, while scores for elementary students have improved (Malmgren & Trezek, 2009).

For students with disabilities, reading is even more problematic since many of these students have reading deficits as part of their disability. Unfortunately, this deficit generally increases as students get older and often results in their inability to access the general education curriculum—a requirement of IDEA and important for postsecondary success. As a result, many students with disabilities are unable to meet high school graduation requirements (Schumaker et al., 2006). The most recent report from the NAEP reveals that eighth-grade students with disabilities perform substantially lower than their nondisabled peers in reading. More than 60% of this group of students scored below basic on their reading assessment, compared to 27% of students without disabilities (U.S. Department of Education, 2009). Figure 10.1 compares reading scores of students with and without disabilities in the eighth grade. Therefore, reading instruction is important for these students even in middle school and high school. The National Joint Committee on Learning Disabilities (2008) noted "the overall picture of adolescent literacy in the United States in not promising" (p. 212), and is even less promising for students with learning disabilities.

Some students, especially those who had poor reading instruction, can overcome their reading problems when provided targeted instruction (Torgesen, 2005). For other older students, however, whose reading difficulties are caused by learning disabilities or some other disability, reading problems are generally found in more than one reading component, which results in greater challenges for teachers (Roberts, Torgesen, Boardman, & Scammacca, 2008).

Although reading instruction is needed at the secondary level, it is often not a component of the school curriculum. This lack of reading instruction is due to several issues,

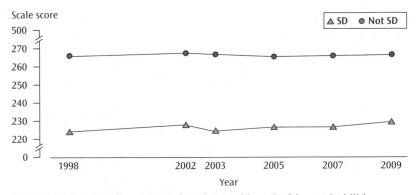

FIGURE 10.1 ● Reading Scores of Students With and Without Disabilities

Note: The NAEP Reading scale ranges from 0 to 500. Some apparent differences between estimates may not be statistically significant.
Source: U.S. Department of Education, Institute of Education Sciences, National Center for Education Statistics, National Assessment of Educational Progress (NAEP), 1998, 2002, 2003, 2005, 2007, and 2009 Reading Assessments.

including the following myths associated with teaching reading in secondary schools (Roe et al., 2007):

- Teaching reading is a concern only in the elementary school.
- Teaching reading in the content areas is separate and distinct from teaching subject matter.
- Reading needs in the secondary school can be met through remedial work alone.
- A reading specialist or an English teacher should be responsible for the teaching of reading.
- The teaching of reading and the teaching of literature are one and the same.

These myths may preclude many middle and high school teachers from providing reading instruction.

Another myth resulting in limited literacy instruction for adolescents is that by the time students reach middle and high school it is too late to teach them reading skills. Some educators believe that reading is a skill that should only be taught during a particular developmental period, typically during the early childhood and childhood years. In fact, research has shown that adolescents can improve their reading skills when teachers focus on specific deficit areas (Faggella-Luby & Deshler, 2008; Malmgren & Trezek, 2009). As a result of the need for reading instruction, and the fact that adolescents are capable of improving their reading skills when provided instruction, middle and high school teachers should be involved in teaching reading to students who have problems with this critical skill.

Teaching reading for students in middle school and high school is the responsibility of many different school staff, "including content area teachers, reading teachers, reading consultants, principals and other administrators, and librarians or media center specialists" (Roe et al., 2007, p. 11). Some secondary teachers continue to consider instruction in reading as an area outside their realm of responsibility. This mindset is extremely unfortunate.

The National Reading Panel Report (2000) identified five major components of reading—phonics, phonemic awareness, vocabulary, fluency, and comprehension. Since this report was issued, most reading instructional programs have used these five components as the basis for their content.

Phonics and Phonemic Awareness

Phonics is the association of sounds with letters, while *phonemic awareness* is understanding that spoken words are comprised of individual units of sounds called phonemes. As students learn to read, they apply their knowledge of phonics and phonemic awareness when decoding words. Adolescents who are good readers consciously understand how phonemes are manipulated to form words. Unfortunately, some adolescents do not have this understanding, due to either poor instruction or the presence of disabilities that interfere with this understanding (National Institute for Literacy, 2007).

Some students have been exposed to an effective reading program for phonics and phonemic awareness and may not need interventions at this level. For many of these students, instruction in advanced word study, including decoding multisyllable words and morphemic analysis, may be beneficial (Roberts et al., 2008). For students whose reading problems include poor phonics and phonemic awareness skills, instruction in these areas may be an important consideration in their intervention programs. Research has shown that effective instruction in phonics and phonemic awareness can be beneficial for adolescents who are struggling with their reading (Malmgren & Trezek, 2009).

The National Institute for Literacy (2007, pp. 6–8) has identified several research-based approaches to teaching phonics and phonemic awareness to adolescents. These include:

- Model phonemic awareness skills when introducing new vocabulary.
- Provide instruction in phonics strategies to help students articulate and identify multisyllabic words.

- Use direct, explicit, and systematic instruction to teach phonics and phonemic awareness.
- Provide extra time for phonemic awareness and phonics instruction and opportunities for students to practice using new skills when reading.

One decoding strategy that has merit with older students is a mini-course in decoding. In this model, students who are reading below grade level are taught how to use various decoding strategies, such as the word identification strategy developed by Lenz and Hughes (1990). Students are excused from their language arts classes during the mini-course until they improve their decoding skills (Schumaker et al., 2006).

Advanced Word Study. Many adolescents who have difficulty in reading can decode single-syllable words but have difficulties with multisyllable words. In order for students to improve their reading skills, they need to be able to decode multisyllable words easily. Word study approaches focus on "morphology, or analysis of the meaningful parts of words (i.e., prefixes, suffixes, inflectional endings, and roots), and orthography, the letter patterns and structural features that are associated with predictable speech patterns" (Roberts et al., 2008, p. 64). When using advanced word study, students are taught how to break words into smaller segments, and use the meaning of the known units and other semantic features to decode the multisyllable word (Roberts et al., 2008).

Vocabulary

Vocabulary includes the words used in speech and writing for communication purposes (National Institute for Literacy, 2007). Students who are good readers and read proficiently typically have a good vocabulary. This results in increased fluency. Good readers usually have large vocabularies that have been built on reading a wide range of material (Roberts et al., 2008). On the other hand, students who do not have a good vocabulary lack fluency in reading. They must spend time finding the meaning of words that are unfamiliar or simply read the words without knowing their meaning, which negatively affects their comprehension.

Students who are not familiar with the vocabulary in a reading passage are not able to focus on the meaning of the passage. Therefore, teachers need to attend to vocabulary development. There are several strategies that have been shown effective for building vocabulary in secondary students. Some of these include direct instruction of new vocabulary words and indirect instruction, such as improving word consciousness which helps students see similarities and overlap in different words (Malmgren & Trezek, 2009). To get the most out of vocabulary instruction, teachers should focus on words across a wide range of material rather than narrowly used words. Of course, teachers in content courses must ensure that students know the vocabulary necessary to understand the specific words used in the content. For example, students in a science class would need different vocabulary than they would in a political science class.

Fluency

Fluency is the ability to read quickly and is related to being able to recognize most of the words in a passage without having to spend time decoding (Malmgren & Trezek, 2009). "While fluency does not directly cause comprehension, it does play a facilitative role" (Roberts et al., 2008, p. 65). Fluent readers do not have to spend time decoding words, which can interfere with their attending to content. Because it is important to comprehension, teachers should spend time to increase students' level of fluency. There are numerous strategies that can help students become more fluent readers. These include repeated readings, increasing sight word recognition, improving vocabulary, and increased general reading time. Repeated readings should not be used without systematic instruction in fluency with students who have reading disorders (Roberts et al., 2008). The National Institute for Literacy (2007) suggests the following:

- Provide models of fluent reading.
- Engage students in repeated oral reading of texts.
- Engage students in guided oral reading.
- Engage students in partner reading.

Comprehension

Comprehension, or getting meaning from reading, is the goal for reading (Malmgren & Trezek, 2009). Without understanding what is read there is little purpose in reading. Faggella-Luby and Deshler (2008, pp. 71–72) summarized the findings of several literature reviews on comprehension and adolescents, as follows:

1. Reading comprehension for both students with LD and those at risk for failure was improved with targeted instruction of what good readers do. Specifically, comprehension improved when readers learned to identify narrative and expository text structures, discover word meaning, tap prior knowledge, and use cognitive strategies. Results demonstrated moderate to large effect sizes.
2. The content of reading comprehension instruction focused on teaching students with LD cognitive strategies (e.g., self-monitoring and self-questioning), narrative and expository text structures, cooperative learning to increase task engagement, and blended components of each of these elements to improve reading comprehension.
3. Cognitive strategies that tended to be remembered best and used most in post-instructional situations included self-monitoring, summarizing, and story grammar self-questioning.
4. Reading comprehension improvement for students with LD was demonstrated for both elementary and secondary learners.
5. Explicit instruction improved the reading comprehension of students with LD, students at risk for failure, and typically achieving students.
6. Strategy instruction that is overt and explicit provides the most accurate prediction of magnitude of treatment outcomes.

There are many strategies that help students develop more effective comprehension skills. Comprehending textbooks is an important area for many students since textbooks are a primary source of information in many classes. Not being able to comprehend material read in a textbook places students at a significant disadvantage. Students with reading deficits must learn strategies to help them gain meaning from texts. One successful strategy is simply to teach students how to ask and answer questions related to the text while they are reading (Faggella-Luby & Deshler, 2008). Others include using graphic organizers, comprehension-monitoring strategies, and cooperative learning discussion groups (Roberts et al., 2008).

In order to help students who have difficulty comprehending textbooks, teachers must use strategies that will enable students with reading deficits gain useful information from textbooks. One thing teachers can do relates to textbook selection. Teachers need to match textbooks to their students' interests, reading abilities, and past experiences. These factors are critical in students' motivation, confidence, and comprehension (Morgan & Moni, 2008). Teachers should use a formal process when selecting textbooks or reading materials for their classroom. Figure 10.2 provides an example of the steps that should be included in the process.

Often teachers cannot select textbooks that match their students' abilities. In this situation they must adapt textbooks or create their own reading materials from textbooks. One way of

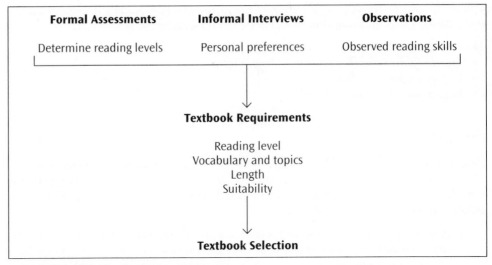

FIGURE 10.2 ● Steps in Textbook Selection

Source: From "Meeting the Challenge of Limited Literacy Resources for Adolescents and Adults with Intellectual Disabilities," by M. F. Morgan and K. B. Moni, 2008, *British Journal of Special Education, 35*, pp. 92–101.

The Day I Split My Pants (Wilson, 1979)	Text adaptation: *The Day My Jeans Split*
I bent down to pick up a block and my shorts split. RIP!	At Uni I dropped a book on the floor. I bent down to pick it up and RIP! My favourite jeans split!

FIGURE 10.3 ● Adapting Early Childhood Concepts in Basal Readers

Source: From "Meeting the Challenge of Limited Literacy Resources for Adolescents and Adults with Intellectual Disabilities," by M. Morgan and K. B. Moni, 2008, *British Journal of Special Education, 35*(2), pp. 92–101. Copyright 2008 John Wiley and Sons.

adapting reading materials is to take a story or passage from a basal reader for lower grades and modify it using more appropriate concepts for adolescents. Using this strategy, teachers adapt language patterns, structures, and vocabulary from basal texts to appropriate interest levels for older students (Morgan & Moni, 2008). Figure 10.3 shows how an early childhood passage can be adapted to reading materials for older students.

Some teachers choose to create their own texts and reading materials. Morgan and Moni (2008) noted that "teachers can create texts for individuals or small groups with similar interests, by using target vocabulary with familiar interest words that are drawn from knowledge of the interests of the learners" (p. 96). This is a time-consuming process and is therefore used sparingly.

Motivation

Although not one of the components of reading identified by the National Reading Panel, Morgan and Moni (2008) recognized that motivation is strongly associated with reading success and reading improvement. Roberts and others (2008) have actually revised the components to include motivation, and pointed out that being an unmotivated reader "limits opportunities to build vocabulary, improve comprehension, and develop effective reading strategies" (p. 67). Although an important component for all levels, motivation is even more important for older students who have a history of struggling with literacy.

The National Institute for Literacy (2007) noted that motivated adolescents are self determined, self-regulated, and engaged. Teachers should therefore focus on these traits when motivating students. There are numerous ways teachers can motivate students to read. Some of these include making sure that:

- Reading materials are interesting to students.
- Reading materials are on students' reading levels.
- Social opportunities are inherent in reading activities.

Comprehensive Reading Programs

While teachers can implement a wide variety of strategies to teach adolescents reading skills, the use of comprehensive models addresses all five components. The Florida Center for Reading Research (2006) conducted an extensive review of comprehensive reading programs. Table 10.1 is a summary of programs that were rated with a + (few aspects), + + (most aspects), or + + + (all aspects). Several programs included all aspects for each of the five components of reading.

TABLE 10.1 ● Summary of Comprehensive Reading Intervention Program Ratings

Program	Phonemic Awareness	Phonics	Fluency	Vocabulary	Comprehension
100 Book Challenge	n/a	n/a	n/a	n/a	+
Accelerated Reader	n/a	n/a	n/a	n/a	+
Barton Reading & Spelling System	+++	+++	+++	n/a	n/a
Building Vocabulary Skills	n/a	n/a	n/a	+++	n/a
Comprehension Plus	n/a	+	n/a	+	+++
Critical Reading Series	n/a	n/a	n/a	n/a	+
Discover Intensive Phonics for Yourself	+	+++	n/a	+	n/a
Elements of Reading, Comprehension	n/a	n/a	n/a	n/a	++
Elements of Reading, Fluency	n/a	n/a	+++	n/a	n/a
Elements of Reading, Phonics and Phonemic Awareness	+++	+++	n/a	n/a	n/a
Elements of Reading, Vocabulary	n/a	n/a	n/a	+++	n/a
Failure Free Reading	n/a	n/a	++	++	+
Fast Forword Language	+++	n/a	n/a	+	+
Fluency First!	n/a	n/a	++	n/a	n/a
Fluency Formula	n/a	n/a	++	n/a	n/a
Great Leaps	n/a	+	+++	n/a	n/a

(continued)

TABLE 10.1 ● *(continued)*

Program	Phonemic Awareness	Phonics	Fluency	Vocabulary	Comprehension
Jamestown Education's Five-Star Stories and Six-Way Paragraphs	n/a	n/a	n/a	n/a	+
KidBiz3000 and TeenBiz3000	n/a	n/a	+	+	++
Kindergarten Peer-Assisted Literacy Strategies (K-PALS)	+++	+	n/a	n/a	n/a
Language First!	+	n/a	n/a	++	+
Language for Thinking	n/a	n/a	n/a	+++	n/a
LIPS	+++	+++	n/a	n/a	n/a
The Literacy Center	+++	+++	n/a	n/a	n/a
Making Connections	n/a	n/a	+	++	+++
My Reading Coach	n/a	+++	+	n/a	+
Phonetics First-Focus on Sounds	++	+++	++	n/a	n/a
Phonics First Foundations	n/a	++	n/a	n/a	n/a
Phonics and Friends	+	++	n/a	n/a	n/a
Phonics for Reading	n/a	+++	n/a	n/a	n/a
Phono-Graphix	+++	+++	++	n/a	n/a
QuickReads	n/a	+	++	++	++
Questioning the Author	n/a	n/a	n/a	n/a	+++
Read Naturally	n/a	n/a	+++	n/a	n/a
Read On!	n/a	+	+	+++	++
Read XL	n/a	+	+	++	++
ReadAbout	n/a	n/a	n.a	+++	+++
Reading Advantage	n/a	++	++	+++	++
Reading Fluency	n/a	n/a	+	n/a	n/a
REWARDS Intermediate and REWARDS Secondary	n/a	+++	+++	++	+
Rewards Plus	n/a	+++	+++	+++	++
Road to the Code	+++	+++	n/a	n/a	n/a
Scientific Learning Reading Assistant	n/a	n/a	+++	+++	+++
Scott Foresman Early Reading Intervention	+++	+++	+++	+++	n/a
Seeing Stars	+++	+++	n/a	n/a	n/a
SIM - Strategic Instruction Model	n/a	++	n/a	++	+++
Six Minute Solution	n/a	n/a	+++	n/a	n/a
Smart Tutor: Reading	++	++	n/a	++	++
Smart Way Reading and Spelling	n/a	+++	n/a	n/a	n/a

TABLE 10.1 ● *(continued)*

Program	Phonemic Awareness	Phonics	Fluency	Vocabulary	Comprehension
Soar to Success	n/a	+	+++	++	+++
Sound Partners	+++	+++	+++	n/a	+
SRA Early Interventions In Reading Level 1	+++	+++	+++	n/a	+++
Text Talk	n/a	n/a	n/a	+++	n/a
Thinking Reader	n/a	n/a	n/a	n/a	+++
Timed Readings	n/a	n/a	+	n/a	+
Tune in to Reading	n/a	n/a	++	n/a	n/a
Visualizing and Verbalizing	n/a	n/a	n/a	n/a	+++
Voyager Passport E, F, & G	n/a	+	++	++	++
Wilson Fluency / Basic	n/a	n/a	+++	n/a	n/a

+ = few aspects of this component taught and/or practiced

++ = most aspects of this component taught and/or practiced

+++ = all aspects of this component taught and/or practiced

n/a = Not Addressed in this program and/or not a goal of this program.

Source: Florida Center for Reading Research. fcrr.org (2010).

INSTRUCTION IN WRITING

Writing is a key process for communicating. It provides a means for self-expression and increases an individual's capacity to learn (National Institute for Literacy, 2007). As noted previously, writing includes the mechanics of writing, spelling, and written expression.

Mechanics of Writing

Similar to phonics and phonemic awareness, most students will have mastered the mechanics of handwriting prior to reaching middle school and high school. For students who have difficulties with the mechanics of writing, including those with physical or sensory imitations, alternative means of expression should be used. This could include computer keyboarding or dictating, using a tape recorder or voice-input computer. Regardless of the medium, teachers should ensure that limited mechanics of writing do not impede students' abilities to express themselves in writing.

Spelling

In order for students to express themselves in writing effectively they need to have mastery of basic spelling skills. Moats (1995) described spelling as complex, with all the sounds, syllables, word parts, and letters associated with the sounds. With today's technology, spelling is not as much a problem as in the past. By the time students reach middle school and high school, there may be minimal remediation in spelling that is effective. Some strategies associated with reading could also be beneficial with students' spelling. Students should be taught how to use spell-check technology to review and correct their written materials prior to submission.

The two approaches typically used for teaching spelling are rule based and whole word. Using a rule-based approach focuses on connecting letters to their sounds (phonics). However, there are numerous irregularities in spelling that result in situations where a whole word approach is necessary (Polloway, Miller, & Smith, 2011). For example, the word *read* does not follow a rule-based spelling approach; students must know how to spell irregular words through a whole word learning approach.

Written Expression

Similar to reading comprehension being the critical component of reading, written expression is the critical component in written language. The purpose of reading is to gain understanding and meaning from the material that is read; the purpose of writing is to communicate and express ideas using written language. Therefore, students need to improve their abilities in the area of written expression, something that is difficult without instruction (National Institute for Literacy, 2007). As reported earlier, the National Assessment of Educational Progress reported in 2005 that 26% of 17-year-old students could not demonstrate effective writing skills. Just as reading is critical for success after formal education, being able to express oneself in writing is also important for many employment opportunities and social interactions.

Written expression is based on speaking, listening, and reading. It includes writing simple sentences to complex essays. Unfortunately, formal instruction in writing is not common in many secondary schools. Many students exit high school with minimal writing skills. All teachers in middle and high schools should engage students in the writing process, with the goal of such instruction being composition writing. Students need to build up to this level of writing, moving from sentence development, to paragraph development, and finally to composition writing (Polloway, Patton, & Serna, 2008).

The National Institute for Literacy (2007, pp. 32–34) lists the following research-based instructional approaches to improve writing skills:

- Use direct, explicit, and systematic instruction to teach writing.
- Teach students the importance of prewriting.
- Provide a supportive instructional environment for students.
- Use rubrics to assess writing.
- Address the needs of diverse learners.

GUIDING PRINCIPLES FOR LITERACY INSTRUCTION

Literacy instruction is a critical component in public schools, including secondary schools. Students in middle school and high school who have deficits in literacy are at a major disadvantage for academic success and postsecondary vocational and social success. Therefore, teachers must provide instruction in these areas. The National Joint Committee on Learning Disabilities (2008) recommended teachers to consider the following factors when developing instructional programs in literacy:

- Focus instructional activities on areas that are critical for effective and efficient reading and writing.
- Use a variety of instructional strategies, including strategy instruction, skill-based instruction, and remediation.

- Teach students literacy as part of their content instruction.
- Make sure that instruction is sequenced in a way that leads to students becoming independent learners.
- Provide opportunities for students to practice their literacy skills.
- Use technology and universal design to incorporate instruction in general education settings.

STRATEGIES TO ENHANCE CONTENT LITERACY

Although some middle and high school content teachers do not believe that teaching reading is their responsibility, or that they are qualified to do so (National Institute for Literacy, 2007), Zwier (2004) noted that these teachers "are uniquely qualified to teach students how to actively think about the texts in their particular classes" (p. v), as they are the ones who know the specific vocabulary and concepts that are essential for students to learn. Teachers often do not recognize that students must learn different sources in each content area taught in middle and secondary schools. For some students this is not a problem, but for others it is. Research (Vacca & Vacca, 2005) has shown that there are a variety of different factors in middle and secondary school classrooms that impact on the students' ability to be literate in the varied content fields. These include (p. 9):

- The learner's prior knowledge of, attitude toward, and interest in the subject
- The learner's purpose for engaging in reading, writing, and discussion
- The language and conceptual difficulty of the text material
- The assumptions that the text writers make about their audience of readers
- The text structures that writers use to organize ideas and information
- The teacher's beliefs about and attitude toward the use of texts in learning situations

Middle and secondary level teachers should address each of these challenges in order for students to become literate in their content area classrooms and to achieve success.

In the past several decades, researchers have developed strategies based on cognitive psychology that can be used by middle and high school teachers to assist in student comprehension of content specific materials (Grady, 2002; Little, 2008). In the following sections, selected evidence-based strategies will be discussed. These evidence-based strategies are used to address the issues students may have with basic skills in reading, including decoding (phonics and phonemic awareness), fluency, vocabulary, and comprehension (National Institute for Literacy, 2007).

Improving students' reading comprehension and vocabulary skills is critical for secondary students to be successful in content classes. To help students improve in these areas, teachers must be able to identify and incorporate direct instructional strategies into their content area lessons. "A growing research base on adolescent literacy supports an emphasis on direct instruction in the reading and writing skills needed to perform these more complex literacy tasks" (National Institute for Literacy, 2007, p. 1). Teachers can assist their students in improving their reading skills while at the same time increasing their knowledge and skills in the content areas they are teaching. The following section includes several evidence-based strategies that teachers can use to do just that. These strategies can be used to expand student comprehension of discipline specific, textual material, to increase discipline specific vocabulary, and to improve student literacy.

Phonics and Phonemic Awareness

As noted, many students in middle and high schools do not need instruction in phonics and phonemic awareness; however, instruction in these areas can be beneficial and should be provided for students who need this level of instruction. This instruction can be provided by all middle and secondary teachers. There are several strategies that teachers can use to help students improve their phonics and phonemic awareness. These include the word identification strategy called DISSECT (Ellis, Deshler, Lenz, Shumaker, & Clark, 1991) and the word identification strategy training (WIST) (Lebzelter & Nowacek, 1999). See Chapter 9 for a discussion of both strategies.

Vocabulary

Vocabulary is critical for students to comprehend their reading materials. In fact, students' vocabularies are directly related to their fluency and comprehension. Therefore, vocabulary development and instruction is critical for middle and high school students. There are several ways teachers can help students improve their vocabulary. One method is using a word wall, where teachers post words associated with a particular lesson on charts around the room. Teachers can also use games where students guess words after teachers provide them with clues, or a game called Wordo in which students use a bingolike card to cover different words as the teacher provides a definition (Faber, 2006). Still another way is through morphemic analysis, where students break words into parts, then analyze the parts to determine the word's meaning. Weekly vocabulary lists provide another means of introducing and teaching specific, content-related vocabulary.

Comprehension

As noted, the ultimate goal of reading is comprehension—gaining meaning from reading. Reading a passage, orally or silently, is ineffective if the student does not understand what has been read. Fluency is directly related to comprehension, so the more fluent a reader is, the more likely comprehension will occur. Following are strategies that can benefit students' fluency and comprehension.

Directed Reading-Thinking Activity (DR-TA). DR-TA is a four-part method that can be used to prepare students to develop higher level thinking skills and comprehend content area materials (Ruddell, 2008). The four steps of this activity are brainstorm, predict, read, and discuss. The first step, *brainstorm,* provides the students with the opportunity to identify as many words as they can that they associate with the subject being studied. This brainstorming step is followed by a teacher-directed examination of the textual material that the students will read. This direction may occur verbally, through a question–answer worksheet, or through a group search of the materials. The result of the examination is a set of *predictions* that the individual student or group of students prepares. Once the first two steps are completed, the students are expected to *read* the textual material. The final step is a postreading *discussion* that can occur in directed small groups or as a whole class experience. Student predictions are revisited and accepted or revised based on the information that students were able to glean from the text. DR-TA supports and extends each student's ability to read and think about the discipline specific content (Allen, 2004) and assists in the development of metacognitive skills (Unrau, 2008).

Directed Reading Activity (DRA). According to Ruddell (2008), DRA is a frequently used method developed in the 1940s by Betts for "increasing students' comprehension of text by removing barriers to comprehension, encouraging guided silent reading of text, and embedding skill development into lessons focusing on conceptual understanding" (p. 124). It is sometimes known as a directed reading lesson (DRL) (Roe et al., 2007). This reading method is commonly used in elementary grades but can be easily transformed to fit the standard secondary curriculum. The five steps of DRA are reading preparation, guided silent reading, comprehension development, skill development, and extension and follow-up activities.

In the first step, reading preparation, discipline specific vocabulary words are introduced and activities to enhance their learning are used. Second, the teacher introduces activities such as DR-TA or one of the concept cluster strategies to guide the students' reading of the text. Third, comprehension development is expanded by the use of postreading strategies such as GMA or ReQuest (described in the following sections). The fourth and fifth steps are based on specific student needs after postreading has occurred. Students may be asked to work in groups to expand their knowledge of vocabulary or specific concepts, or work individually on extension activities to assist in their learning the required materials.

ReQuest. An individual or group form of text material questioning, ReQuest uses a combination of student reading of the textual materials with reciprocal questioning—that is, teacher–student questioning (Ruddell, 2008). The first step in this method is to have the students and the teacher *read* a selected passage in the textual materials. This is followed by an open period when the *questions* that were generated by students during the reading are orally submitted to the teacher. The teacher also has questions prepared from the reading, thus providing the teacher with the *opportunity to model* appropriate question development. According to Unrau (2008) this method assists students in developing appropriate questions, both literal and inferential, if an individual student question is followed by a teacher question, and so on.

List-Group-Label. The list-group-label strategy uses brainstorming before students read the content area materials in order to "activate and build background knowledge prior to beginning a unit of study" (Allen, 2004). In this method students list an assigned number of words they know that they believe are related to the topic, and then through small group discussions combine their individual word lists into a single word list. This discussion of words and categories where they should be placed activates and builds background knowledge for the specific content area. In essence, students identify words that both expand their knowledge of the concept as well as those that will be used in the content area. This activity is sometimes used with cluster strategies as a form of semantic mapping.

Question-Answer-Relationship (QAR). A method developed by Raphael (1986), QAR is used to assist students in identifying ways to find answers to questions about the textual material. According to Allen (2008), students need to learn three types of question development strategies in order to analyze written material: (1) textually explicit questions which are usually stated in the assigned reading; (2) textually implicit questions which are suggested from the material; and (3) scriptally implicit questions which are derived from students' knowledge of the content.

Cluster Strategies. Unrau (2008) defines cluster strategies as "visual arrangements of terms, events, people, or ideas." The use of cluster strategies is considered an alternative to linear descriptions of content, such as chapter outlining. Clustering methods assist students in understanding both the relationships between concepts and discipline specific vocabulary (Roe et al., 2007). These visual arrangements of content information, such as content maps, may use words or pictures to clarify clusters of concepts and relationships. One form of cluster strategy is the *semantic map*. Semantic maps usually refer to any graphic organizer that shows relationships between words. Semantic maps are sometimes called word maps or question maps.

Semantic maps may also be expanded to include a theme or concept. This form of semantic map, known as *concept mastery maps*, graphically represents how specific vocabulary relates to the theme or concept being studied. Using concept mastery maps results in the inclusion of "cross-links" which graphically represent "relationships between concepts in different domains" (Maycumber & Weathers, 2006, p. 2). This can greatly assist in students developing meaningful knowledge. Other names for these visual clusters of information/concepts are mind-mapping (Marguiles, 1991), mindscaping, webbing, and brainstorming webs (Hyerle, 1996).

Another form of mapping is the *group mapping activity* (GMA). In this activity, students prepare a visual and/or written representation of material they have just read. Then they show the map to the class, or teacher, and provide an oral explanation (Ruddell, 2008). These maps can then be used as a means of evaluating student understanding of the material or as a guide for further research and reading.

Semantic Feature Analysis (SFA). The SFA activity can be used to assist students in learning vocabulary and major concepts, especially in the content areas of science and social studies (Sencibaugh, n.d.). Using this activity, students are able to link their knowledge about a subject prior to the reading assignment with new information they learn from the reading assignment by showing the relationships among words from a specific topic (Paulsen, 2007). A visual graphic is also used with this strategy, but instead of a concept map, a matrix is used to represent the relationships between vocabulary words and conceptual knowledge. Both cluster strategies and semantic feature analyses use graphic organization concepts based on Ausubel's (1978) theory that students learn best when concepts are organized in an orderly format (Roe et al., 2007). Figures 10.4 and 10.5 depict different forms of visual organizers.

Context-Structure-Sound-Reference (CSSR). Good readers use the CSSR method to identify unknown words, as it does not take away their focus on comprehension of the material. The first step, context, refers to reading an unknown word in a sentence and "guessing" the word meaning based on surrounding information. Students use context clues or contextual information to identify the meaning of the word and subsequently to comprehend the meaning of the sentence or paragraph. Unfortunately, at times, students are unable to derive meaning from the content because the level of information provided is limited. The second step is for students to *analyze the structural features* of the unknown word. In other words, the root of the

Spider Maps

Spider Maps are used to describe a central idea: a thing (a geographic region), process (meiosis), concept (altruism), or proposition with support (experimental drugs should be available to AIDS victims). Key frame questions are: What is the central idea? What are its attributes? What are its functions?

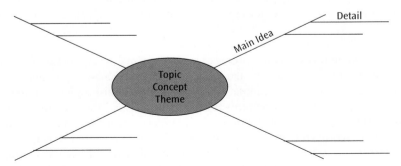

FIGURE 10.4 ● Example of Visual Organizer

Source: From National Institute for Literacy, 2007, *What Content-Area Teachers Should Know About Adolescent Literacy* (p. 50). Washington, DC: National Institute of Child Health and Human Development (NICHD).

Series of Events Chains

Series of Events Chains are used to describe the stages of the steps in a linear procedure (e.g., how to neutralize an acid); a sequence of events (e.g., how feudalism led to the formation of nation states); or the goals, actions, and outcomes of a historical figure or character in a novel (e.g., the rise and fall of Napoleon). Key frame questions include: What is the object, procedure, or initiating event? What are the stages or steps? How do they lead to one another? What is the final outcome?

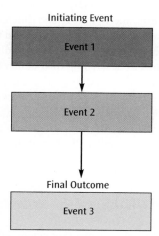

FIGURE 10.5 ● Example of Visual Organizer

Source: From National Institute for Literacy, 2007, *What Content-Area Teachers Should Know About Adolescent Literacy* (p. 50). Washington, DC: National Institute of Child Health and Human Development (NICHD).

word, suffixes or prefixes, plurals, ending, possessives, and so forth, should be analyzed to assist in identifying and understanding the unknown word in the text. The third component, *sound,* relates to a phonics review of the words. Finally, if students are still unsure of the word's meaning, then they should use *reference materials* to clarify the meaning of the vocabulary.

LANGUAGE ARTS AND ENGLISH

As noted by Combs (2004) and Guensberg (2006), the majority of middle and secondary teachers have had little to no training in teaching reading or literacy instruction and usually rely on classroom methods that focus on silent or oral reading of the text, followed by end-of-chapter question completion, and a quiz. For many students, this is not a successful method for learning the content. Selected examples that could be used in middle and secondary classrooms to help students comprehend the material were described earlier. A brief discussion of concerns and classroom strategies that can be used in two content areas (language arts/ English and social studies/history) are provided here.

The content areas where "reading" is most often included are language arts in the elementary and/or middle level grades and English or English education at the secondary level (Duplass, 2006). Skills related to reading, writing, listening, speaking, viewing, visually representing, and thinking are included in this content area. These skills are used with a variety of textual materials, including novels, novellas, short stories, plays, essays, editorials, letters, poetry, biographies, and autobiographies.

For middle and secondary level language arts/English teachers, the challenge is to move students from knowledge that is information based (i.e., content knowledge or facts) to knowledge that is procedural based (i.e., using knowledge to solve problems) (Duplass, 2006). Therefore, teachers must address not only their students' abilities to read and comprehend (Roe et al., 2007), but also their ability to analyze and relate the information to their own lives. Duplass (2006) stated that the challenge for language arts/English teachers is to enhance their students' ability "to read literature and move from literal to interpretive approaches to see different perspectives, to understand temporal contexts, and to understand different genres . . . is crucial to making use of literature" (p. 296). Strategies that use open-ended and follow-up questions such as the QAR method are useful in addressing these challenges. In addition, the use of semantic mapping and SFA can also assist students in developing their ability to read the material, understand what they read, and relate it to their lives. Two other methods that have been used successfully in literature classes are DRA, which "provides students with a purpose for reading using the sharing of previous knowledge to build understanding" (Sadler, 2001, p. 36), and ReQuest, which "encourages students to build on previous knowledge and think about what might be important in the assigned reading" (Sadler, 2001, p. 42).

INSTRUCTION IN SOCIAL STUDIES

The term *social studies* is most often found in elementary grades, whereas in middle and secondary schools this content area is more likely called social sciences or identified by specific course names, such as history, civics, or psychology. The social studies umbrella often includes the disciplines of history, geography, civics, political science, philosophy, sociology, psychology, economics, and even anthropology. Recently, multicultural education has been included within this content area. A major focus in all of these areas is critical thinking, "because understanding cause-and-effect relationships, distinguishing fact from opinion, separating relevant information from irrelevant information, and identifying and evaluating propaganda are essential skills for learning social studies" (Roe et al., 2007, p. 307). As a result, the ability to read and comprehend textual materials in the study of social studies is extremely important (Teaching Today, 2005).

Focusing on critical thinking, while teaching social studies, results in a reconceptualization of teaching and learning, as well as in content literacy having a significant role in secondary education. This approach means that secondary content teachers are not simply providers of information but facilitators of producing or constructing knowledge (Moje, 2006). Therefore, under this view of teaching, content area teachers are not simply "tellers" of knowledge, but individuals who work with students to help them understand their content area (Grady, 2002). In order for middle and secondary teachers to increase the literacy levels of their students, they must understand that reading is different when reading literature, textbooks, newspapers, and governmental forms. This is why teaching students how to improve reading is critical for them to learn and understand subject content (Meltzer & Okashige, 2001).

Teaching social studies also includes moving students from information-based knowledge to procedural-based knowledge. Unfortunately, many textbooks are based on information-based knowledge only and may not be conducive for comprehension problems for many students (Duplass, 2006; Patrick, 1991). When using these types of reading materials, teachers must develop methodologies to include procedural-based knowledge. In addition, social studies teachers must introduce students to a variety of concepts that may pose difficulties when presented in textual format. They teach students not only facts but also how to use critical thinking skills. Duplass (2006, p. 307) noted that social studies teachers should ensure their students can do the following:

- Understand the ideas and viewpoints of others
- Acquire and retain a body of relevant concepts and information
- Think critically and creatively, thus developing new attitudes and values and the ability to make decisions
- Consult a variety of sources to develop more than one perspective regarding a topic
- Read critically about what has happened and why these events occurred

Strategies described above that help students comprehend their reading materials should be used by social studies teachers. These include strategies such as DR-TA or DRA that assist students in learning the vocabulary and interpreting the factual material provided in the text, concept maps, CSSR, and list-group-label methods. These strategies assist students in learning to evaluate and understand the conceptual information, analyze that information, and relate it to their own lives.

Social studies is one of those content classes that students with disabilities can be successful if teachers provide instruction that meets their unique learning needs. Several teaching methodologies discussed in previous chapters are effective when teaching social studies. Cooperative teaching, cooperative learning, peer support systems, differentiated instruction, and universal design for learning are all ways for social studies teachers to make content accessible for their students. Table 10.2 summarizes some techniques for accommodating and adapting social studies instruction. Allowing students to have oral exams, short answer tests, or essay tests also provides them with different options that match individual strengths and weaknesses.

TABLE 10.2 ● Evidence-Based Strategies by Content Area

	Middle School Language Arts and Secondary School English	Middle School Social Studies and Secondary School Social Science
DR-TA	X	X
DRA	X	X
ReQuest	X	
List-Group-Label		X
QAR	X	
Cluster Strategy: Semantic Maps	X	X
Cluster Strategy: Concept Mastery Map	X	X
Cluster Strategy: Group Mapping Activity	X	X
SFA	X	X
CSSR	X	X

SUMMARY

This chapter addresses the broad area of literacy for adolescents, as well as instruction in language arts and social studies. Literacy is a broad term that includes the use of written language, as well as reading and writing. Unfortunately, the adolescent literacy level in the United States falls below comparable countries. In order to address these deficiencies, secondary teachers, including content teachers, must be involved in literacy instruction.

Reading consists of five areas—phonics, phonemic awareness, vocabulary, fluency, and comprehension. Comprehension, gaining meaning from reading, is the ultimate goal of reading. However, in order to comprehend at an appropriate level, students need to have good skills in phonics, phonemic awareness, vocabulary, and fluency. Motivation is another area that is important for adolescents and reading. Often students who have experienced failure in lower grades are not motivated to improve in middle school and high school. Therefore, teachers must develop strategies to motivate students to improve their literacy skills.

Writing includes writing mechanics, spelling, and written expression. Similar to comprehension, written expression is the goal for writing. Too often, writing instruction receives little attention in secondary schools. If students are to improve their writing skills they must have opportunities for writing instruction and practice. Similar to reading, writing instruction should be the responsibility of all middle and secondary teachers, as well as other school staff.

There are numerous strategies useful in teaching reading and writing skills. Many of these strategies (see Chapter 9) are extremely useful with middle and high school students. These strategies, along with reconceptualizing the purposes of teaching language arts and social studies, help students learn how to apply their knowledge of subject matter.

REFERENCES

Allen, J. (2004). *Tools for teaching content literacy*. Portland, ME: Stenhouse.

Allen, J. (2008). More tools for teaching content literacy. Portland, ME: Stenhouse.

Alliance for Excellent Education. (n.d.). *Challenges confronting high schools: Adolescent literacy.* Retrieved November 08, 2008, from http://www.personal.kent.edu/~rfaehnle/adolescents%20literacyPP_002.pdf

Ausubel, D. P. (1978). In defense of advance organizers: A reply to the critics. *Review of Educational Research, 48,* 251–257.

Betts, E. A. (1946). Foundations of reading instruction. New York: American Book Company.

Combs, D. (2004). A framework for scaffolding content area reading strategies. *Middle School Journal, 36*(2), 13–20.

Duplass, J. A. (2006). *Middle and high school teaching: Methods, standards, and best practices*. Boston: Houghton Mifflin.

Ellis, E., Deshler, D., Lenz, K., Schumaker, J., & Clark, F. (1991). An instructional model for teaching learning strategies. *Focus on Exceptional Children, 23,* 1–23.

Faber, S. H. (2006). *How to teach reading when you're not a reading teacher*. Nashville: Incentive Publications.

Faggella-Luby, M. N., & Deshler, D. D. (2008). Reading comprehension in adolescents with LD: What we know; what we need to learn. *Learning Disabilities Research & Practice, 23,* 70–78.

Florida Center for Reading Research (2006). Summary table for FCRR reports. www.fcrr.org/fcrreports/creportscs.aspx?rep=supp Retrieved 10/22/10

Grady, K. (2002). *Adolescent literacy and content area reading*. (ERIC Digest 176.) Retrieved September 10, 2008, from http://www.ericdigests.org/2003-3/area.htm

Guensberg, C. (2006). *Why Johnny (still) can't read: Schools met the challenge of producing teen readers*. Retrieved November 08, 2008, from http://www.edutopia.org/why-johnny-still-cant-read

Hyerle, D. (1996). *Visual tools for constructing knowledge*. Alexandria, VA: Association for Supervision and Development.

Lebzelter, S., & Nowacek, E. J. (1999). Reading strategies for secondary students with mild disabilities. *Intervention in School and Clinic, 34,* 212–219.

Lenz, B. K., & Hughes, C. A. (1990). A word identification strategy for adolescents with learning disabilities. *Journal of Learning Disabilities, 23,* 149–158.

Little, M. E. (2008). Improving content literacy in social studies classrooms: Teachers' voices within comprehensive school reform. *Social Studies Research and Practice, 3*(2), 42–53. Retrieved November 08, 2008, from http://www.socstrp.org

Malmgren, K. W., & Trezek, B. J. (2009). Literacy instruction for secondary students with disabilities. *Focus on Exceptional Children, 41,* 1–12.

Marguiles, N. (1991). *Mapping inner space.* Tucson, AZ: Zephyr Press.

Maycumber, E., & Weathers, J. (2006). *Concept mapping: Learning from Novak.* Retrieved November 08, 2008, from http://www.projectcriss.org/past_public

Meltzer, J., & Okashige, S. (2001). *Supporting adolescent literacy across the content areas. Perspectives on Policy and Practice.* Retrieved September 10, 2008, from http://www.alliance.brown.edu/pubs/perspectives/adlitcontent.pdf

Moats, L. C. (1995). *Spelling: Development, disability, and instruction.* Baltimore, MD: York Press.

Moje, E. B. (2006). *Integrating literacy into the secondary school content areas: An enduring problem in enduring institutions.* Retrieved September 10, 2008, from http://www.umich.edu/~govrel/addes_lit/moje.pdf

Morgan, M. F., & Moni, K. B. (2008). Meeting the challenge of limited literacy resources for adolescents and adults with intellectual disabilities. *British Journal of Special Education, 35,* 92–101.

National Assessment of Educational Progress. (2005). The nation's report card: Reading 2005. Washington, DC: Author.

National Assessment of Educational Progress. (2009). The nation's report card: Reading 2009. Washington, DC: Author.

National Institute for Literacy. (2007). *What content-area teachers should know about adolescent literacy.* Washington, DC: Author

National Joint Committee on Learning Disabilities (2008). Adolescent literacy and older students with learning disabilities. *Learning Disability Quarterly, 31,* 211–218.

National Reading Panel Report (2000). Teaching children to read. Washington, DC: Author

Patrick, J. J. (1991). *Achievement of knowledge by high school students in core subjects of the Social Studies.* (ERIC Digest 329486). Retrieved November 08, 2008, from http://www.ericdigests.org/pre-9219/high.htm

Paulsen, K. (2007). Validated practices: Semantic feature analysis. In D. D. Smith (2007), *Introduction to special education: Making a difference* (6th ed., p. 480). Boston: Allyn & Bacon.

Polloway, E. A., Miller, L., & Smith, T.E.C. (2011). Language instruction for students with disabilities. (4th ed). Denver: Love Publishing.

Polloway, E. A., Patton, J. R., & Serna, L. (2008). Strategies for teaching learners with special needs (9th ed). Upper Saddle River, NJ: Pearson.

Raphael, T. E. (1986). Teaching question-answer relationships, revisited. *The Reading Teacher, 36,* 186–190.

Roberts, G., Torgesen, J. K., Boardman, A., & Scammacca, N. (2008). Evidence-based strategies for reading instruction of older students with learning disabilities. *Learning Disabilities Research & Practice, 23,* 63–69.

Roe, B. D., Stoodt-Hill, B. D., & Burns, P. C. (2007). *Secondary school literacy instruction: The content areas* (9th ed.). Boston: Houghton Mifflin Co.

Ruddell, M. R. (2008). *Teaching content reading & writing* (5th ed.). Danvers, MA: John Wiley & Sons.

Sadler, C. R. (2001). *Comprehension strategies for middle grade learners: A handbook for content area teachers.* Newark, DE: International Reading Association.

Schumaker, J. B., Deshler, D. D., Woodruff, S. K., Hock, M. F., Bulgren, J. A., & Lenz, B. K. (2006). Reading strategy interventions: Can literacy outcomes be enhanced for at-risk adolescents? *Teaching Exceptional Children, 38,* 64–68.

Sencibaugh, J. M. (n.d.). *A synthesis of content enhancement strategies for teaching students with reading difficulties at the middle and secondary level.* Retrieved September 10, 2008, from http://www.redorbit.com/

Shanahan, T., & Shanahan, C. (2008). Teaching disciplinary literacy to adolescents: Rethinking content-area literacy. *Harvard Educational Review, 78*(1), 40–59.

Teaching Today. (2005). *Subject-specific resources: Improving reading skills in the social studies classroom.* Retrieved November 08, 2008, from http://www.glencoe.com/sec/teachingtoday/subject/improving_reading.phtml

Torgeson, J. K. (2005). The prevention of reading difficulties. *Journal of School Psychology, 40,* 7–26.

Torgesen, J. K., Houston, D. D., Rissman, L. M., Decker, S. M., Roberts, G., Vaughn, S., Wexler, J., Francis, D. J., Rivera, M. O., & Lesaux, N. (2007). *Academic literacy instruction for adolescents: A guidance document from the Center on Instruction.* Portsmouth, NH: RMC Research Corporation, Center for Instruction. Retrieved September 15, 2008, from http://www.centeroninstruction.org

Unrau, N. (2008). *Content area reading and writing: Fostering literacies in middle and high school cultures* (2nd ed.). Upper Saddle River, NJ: Pearson.

U.S. Department of Education (2009). National Assessment of Educational Progress (NAEP), 1998, 2002, 2003, 2005, 2007, and 2009 Reading Assessments. Washington, D.C.: Author

Vacca, R. T., & Vacca, J. L. (2005). *Content area reading: Literacy and learning across the curriculum* (8th ed.). Boston: Pearson/Allyn & Bacon.

Zwier, J. (2004). *Building reading comprehension habits in grades 6–12: A toolkit of classroom activities.* Newark, DE: International Reading Association.

11

Strategies for Teaching Content to Adolescents with Disabilities: Math and Science

Study Questions

1. How are the National Council of Teachers of Mathematics standards used for students with disabilities?

2. What are the five components of math instruction that should be available for all students, including those with disabilities?

3. What are cognitive strategies and how can they be used to instruct students with disabilities?

4. Define *curriculum-based measurement* and describe how it can be used.

INTRODUCTION

As a result of the No Child Left Behind (NCLB) legislation and the Individuals with Disabilities Education Act (IDEA), the majority of students with disabilities spend most of their time in general education classrooms, taught by general education teachers. This includes math and science classrooms in middle and secondary schools. Math and science education in the United States has been criticized for many years and has become highly politicized. Frequently one can read about how children in the United States rank lower than many other countries in math and science education. The National Center for Education Statistics (2008) reported that while eighth graders in the United States scored above the average performances of other countries, their scores ranked 9th in math and 11th in science. Rigorous standards for all students, including those with disabilities, are critical if American students are going to improve in their overall math and science skills (Maccini & Gagnon, 2002).

Standards-based education has become the basis for much of public education in the United States. Fueled by the NCLB Act of 2001 and IDEA 2004, students with disabilities are now, more than ever, exposed to the general education curriculum and its standards-based orientation. There are several positive consequences to this development, including higher academic achievement, more access to the general education curriculum, and high school diplomas that are more meaningful. There are also some negative consequences to this reality, including higher dropout rates, too much emphasis on testing, and inappropriate interpretation and use of test scores (National Center on Secondary Education and Transition Capacity Building Institute, 2002). Regardless of consequences, students with disabilities are currently in general classrooms more and more, including math and science classes, and are held to the same standards as students without disabilities.

Prior to No Child Left Behind and IDEA, many students with disabilities, including mild disabilities, received math and science coursework in special education classrooms, provided by special education teachers. Two components of NCLB resulted in changes to this model. First, NCLB requires that all students, including those with disabilities, meet minimal proficiency standards in reading and math (Lenz & Deshler, 2004). As a result of the legislation, "the focal question is *not* whether students with special needs will participate in a standard-based system but more appropriately concerns how well students with special needs will do in this new system" (Polloway, Patton, & Serna, 2008, p. 6). The law requires that students with disabilities are assessed in math and other areas similar to nondisabled children. While alternative assessments can be used for students with disabilities, the assessments must still be aligned with state content standards to ensure that students with disabilities have access to the general curriculum (Browder, Spooner, Ahlgrim-Delzell, Harris, & Wakeman, 2008).

The second component of NCLB impacting students with disabilities in content classes is the requirement that all teachers be "highly qualified." This means that all students must be taught by teachers who are competent in core content areas (Mercer & Pullen, 2009). Prior to NCLB, many secondary special education teachers taught math and science to students in resource room settings. As a result of their not being viewed as "competent" in these content areas, the "highly qualified" requirement eliminates many of these classes taught by special education teachers.

In addition to No Child Left Behind, IDEA also makes it more likely that students with disabilities will be placed in general education math and science classes. IDEA requires that all students with disabilities have access to the general education curriculum (Browder et al., 2007). This mandate, in conjunction with the movement to include students with disabilities in all classes with their nondisabled peers, to the maximum extent appropriate, has resulted in students with disabilities being placed in general math and science classrooms with expectations very similar to those for students without disabilities. The trend, therefore, as a result of legislation and the philosophy of inclusion, is for students with disabilities to receive their math and science instruction in general education classrooms, and to be held accountable for the same identified standards as students without disabilities (De La Paz & MacArthur, 2003).

Unfortunately, the philosophy of inclusion and the legal mandates of NCLB do not guarantee success for students with disabilities in inclusive classes. Many students with disabilities, including those with high incidence or mild disabilities, experience significant problems in math and science classes. For example, students with learning disabilities often have difficulties in problem application (Maccini & Gagnon, 2002) and algebra (Kortering, deBettencourt, & Braziel, 2005). In a recent study, 83% of adolescents classified as emotionally and behaviorally disordered were below the mean on broad math scores as measured by the Woodcock-Johnson-III (Nelson, Benner, Lane, & Smith, 2004). Students with other disabilities, such as attention deficits, sensory impairments, and behavioral problems, also experienced problems with secondary content classes (Smith, Polloway, Patton, & Dowdy, 2008).

There are many characteristics manifested by students with disabilities that make it difficult for them to be successful in math, science, and other content classes. These include problems with attention, distractibility, cognition, reading, and written expression. Deficits in these areas make it very challenging for some students to be successful in math and science classes. While many of these students may have the intellectual capacity to be successful, difficulties associated with their disability create barriers to this success. Many may not have the literacy skills, cognitive skills, or organizational skills to overcome problems presented by their disabilities. Regardless of these problems, legislation has resulted in the inclusion of these students in content classes, meaning that general classroom teachers and special education teachers need to work together to ensure that students with disabilities have an opportunity for success.

TEACHING MATH TO STUDENTS WITH DISABILITIES

Students with disabilities are currently included in math classes in middle and secondary schools. The nature of these classes will depend on the individual needs of students. Because the majority of students with disabilities are classified as having mild disabilities, most will be involved in the same math classes as students without disabilities, namely general math, algebra, trigonometry, geometry, and calculus. Similar to their nondisabled peers, the specific classes taken by students with disabilities will depend on their needs after high school. Those planning on attending postsecondary educational programs will likely take advanced math classes while those planning on attending a vocational-technical school or entering the labor market after high school may only take basic math classes. While most students with disabilities will be included in general education math classes, a few students with more severe disabilities may complete a more functional math program (Polloway et al., 2008). In order to meet the needs of these students, there will likely be a continuing need for some math classes specifically designed for this group, with a focus on a more functional purpose (Cawley, Foley, & Miller, 2003). However, the number of students with disabilities needing a functional program is extremely small compared to the number of students with disabilities included in general math classes.

Math Standards

The National Council of Teachers of Mathematics (NCTM) "is a public voice of mathematics education, providing vision, leadership and professional development to support teachers in ensuring equitable mathematics learning of the highest quality for all students" (www.nctm .org, 2009). As such, NCTM has established standards for K–12 education. Throughout the NCTM standards are references stating that all students should perform well in all math areas. The assertion that the standards should apply to all students—in conjunction with the focus of IDEA 2004 and NCLB that students with disabilities should have access to the general curriculum and meet the same accountability standards as nondisabled students—suggests that the NCTM standards should be the overlay of math instruction for all students, including those with disabilities (Cawley, & Foley, 2002).

The NCTM standards (2009) are not differentiated for different groups of students but are the same for all students. They are guided by five goals that focus on students (1) becoming better problem solvers, (2) learning to reason mathematically, (3) learning to value mathematics, (4) becoming more confident in their mathematical ability, and (5) learning to communicate mathematically. The NCTM standards are organized into 10 areas:

- Number and operations
- Algebra
- Geometry
- Measurement
- Data analysis and probability
- Problem solving
- Reasoning and proof
- Communication
- Connections
- Representation

Within each of these standards are several subcategories, with expectations listed for different grade levels. Table 11.1 describes the subcategories within each standard.

In addition to providing the standards, NCTM also provides numerous examples for meeting these standards. For example, Figure 11.1 depicts expectations for grades 6–8 for the geometry standard. The NCTM website (http://standards.nctm.org) can be used to obtain this information for all standards within each grade level.

Although current legislative mandates require students with disabilities to have access to general math classes, and NCTM standards are for all students, the reality is that many students with disabilities continue to experience lower academic success in math than their nondisabled peers (Stodden, Galloway, & Stodden, 2003). Cawley, Parmar, Foley, Salmon, and Roy (2001) compared math skills of students with disabilities to students without disabilities. Findings indicated that students with disabilities in grades 6–8 performed lower than their nondisabled peers in math vocabulary, computation, and verbal problem solving. Computational fluency, skills involved in answering math problems at various levels of difficulty within a set time frame, are significantly lower for secondary students with math disabilities than their

TABLE 11.1 ● NCTM Standards

1. Number and Operations Standard
   - Understand numbers, ways of representing numbers, relationships among numbers, and number systems.
   - Understand meanings of operations and how they relate to one another.
   - Compute fluently and make reasonable estimates.
2. Algebra Standard
   - Understand patterns, relations, and functions.
   - Represent and analyze mathematical situations and structures using algebraic symbols.
   - Use mathematical models to represent and understand quantitative relationships.
   - Analyze change in various contexts.
3. Geometry Standard
   - Analyze characteristics and properties of two- and three-dimensional geometric shapes and develop mathematical arguments about geometric relationships.
   - Specify locations and describe spatial relationships using coordinate geometry and other representational systems.
   - Apply transformations and use symmetry to analyze mathematical situations.
   - Use visualization, spatial reasoning, and geometric modeling to solve problems.
4. Measurement Standard
   - Understand measurable attributes of objects and the units, systems, and processes of measurement.
   - Apply appropriate techniques, tools, and formulas to determine measurements.
5. Data Analysis and Probability Standard
   - Formulate questions that can be addressed with data and collect, organize, and display relevant data to answer them.
   - Select and use appropriate statistical methods to analyze data.
   - Develop and evaluate inferences and predictions that are based on data.
   - Understand and apply basic concepts of probability.
6. Problem Solving
7. Reasoning and Proof
8. Communication
9. Connections
10. Representation

nondisabled peers. Calhoon, Emerson, Flores, and Houchins (2007) found that the computational fluency for this group was at the third-grade level. Unfortunately, computational fluency is critical for many math activities.

Poor computational fluency can result in significant problems for students in all areas of math. It has been suggested that poor computational fluency may interfere with mathematical comprehension in much the same way that poor decoding skills interfere with reading comprehension (Garnett, 1992). Therefore, just as educators must address decoding skills when improving students' reading skills, they must also address computational fluency when addressing math skills. Without improvement in computational fluency, students with disabilities will likely have significant problems in many secondary math classes.

Regardless of overall lower performance in math, many students with disabilities can be successful in general math classes. However, while students have been found to respond favorably to activities, lessons, and strategies that incorporate recommendations in the NCTM standards, many teachers are unfamiliar with the standards and/or lack appropriate materials for using them (Maccini & Gagnon, 2002). Many special education teachers, who are either responsible for teaching math to students with disabilities or assisting math teachers in general classrooms, are also unprepared to teach math content related to the NCTM standards

Instructional programs from prekindergarten through grade 12 should enable all students to—	**Expectations**
	In grades 6–8 all students should—
Analyze characteristics and properties of two- and three-dimensional geometric shapes and develop mathematical arguments about geometric relationships	• precisely describe, classify, and understand relationships among types of two- and three-dimensional objects using their defining properties; • understand relationships among the angles, side lengths, perimeters, areas, and volumes of similar objects; • create and critique inductive and deductive arguments concerning geometric ideas and relationships, such as congruence, similarity, and the Pythagorean relationship.
Specify locations and describe spatial relationships using coordinate geometry and other representational systems	• use coordinate geometry to represent and examine the properties of geometric shapes; • use coordinate geometry to examine special geometric shapes, such as regular polygons or those with pairs of parallel or perpendicular sides.
Apply transformations and use symmetry to analyze mathematical situations	• describe sizes, positions, and orientations of shapes under informal transformations such as flips, turns, slides, and scaling; • examine the congruence, similarity, and line or rotational symmetry of objects using transformations.
Use visualization, spatial reasoning, and geometric modeling to solve problems	• draw geometric objects with specified properties, such as side lengths or angle measures; • use two-dimensional representations of three-dimensional objects to visualize and solve problems such as those involving surface area and volume; • use visual tools such as networks to represent and solve problems; • use geometric models to represent and explain numerical and algebraic relationships; • recognize and apply geometric ideas and relationships in areas outside the mathematics classroom, such as art, science, and everyday life.

FIGURE 11.1 ● Geometry Standard for Grades 6–8

(Browder et al., 2008). All teachers, general education math teachers and special education teachers, must become more cognizant of the NCTM standards.

As a result of low performance in math by students, mathematics educators and other professionals have identified five components of math instruction that should be available for all students, including those with disabilities. These include (Browder et al., 2008, p. 408):

- *Number and operations*—the ability to understand and represent numbers, relationships among numbers, and number systems (e.g., the number 24 is 2 tens and 4 ones)
- *Measurement*—the ability to understand measurable attributes of objects (e.g., time and money)
- *Data analysis and probability*—the ability to collect, organize, and display relevant data to answer questions with appropriate statistical methods (e.g., graphing)
- *Geometry*—the ability to analyze characteristics and properties of two- and three-dimensional shapes, apply transformation, and use symmetry to analyze mathematical situations (e.g., length, width, area, and volume)
- *Algebra*—the ability to understand patterns, relations, and functions of numbers, and use mathematical models to represent and understand quantitative relations (e.g., $x + 4 = 7$, solve for x)

Math Instructional Ideas

Of the varied ways to teach math, many of these instructional strategies and models work effectively with students with disabilities. There is no one way to effectively teach math to this group of students. Students with disabilities in math classes are just as heterogeneous as their nondisabled peers. Therefore, math teachers must utilize a wide array of instructional methods in an attempt to meet the needs of ever-increasing diverse math classes. Following are suggestions for math instruction that could be effective with students with disabilities.

Cognitive Strategies. Recently, cognitive strategy instruction in math has become a popular instructional technique. Montague and Dietz (2009) contended that this method of instruction can be effective with students with disabilities, especially many with learning disabilities, who often have difficulties problem solving or selecting appropriate strategies when answering math problems. The primary purpose of using cognitive strategies in math is "to teach students how to think and behave like proficient problem solvers and strategic learners" (Montague & Dietz, 2009, p. 286).

Montague's (1992) cognitive strategy for math includes seven steps:

Step 1 Read the problem for understanding.
Step 2 Put the problem into your own words.
Step 3 Visualize the problem by drawing a schematic representation.
Step 4 Hypothesize or develop a plan for solving the problem.
Step 5 Predict the answer.
Step 6 Complete the necessary calculations.
Step 7 Check the answer.

Montague and Dietz (2009) evaluated the evidence for cognitive strategy instruction and mathematical problem solving by reviewing seven studies. They found that while the results from these studies did not meet the methodological criteria to support cognitive strategy instruction as an evidenced-based practice, they did show promise for improving problem-solving skills among students with disabilities.

Using a strategy similar to Montague's, van Garderen (2007) used diagrams to help students with learning disabilities solve mathematical word problems. Van Garderen's method focused on (1) reading the problem for understanding, (2) visualizing the problem, (3) planning on how to solve the problem, (4) computing the answer, and (5) checking the answer. A diagram is drawn to help the student visualize the problem. Figure 11.2 shows an example of a student using this process to answer a mathematics word problem.

Coteaching. As discussed previously in this text, coteaching can be used effectively in many different classes, including middle and high school math classes. It is an excellent model for teaching secondary math because of the specialized content that must be taught. In cotaught secondary math classes, the math teachers provide the specific content while their special education partners utilize their skills in instructional processes, modifications, and accommodations that are effective with students with disabilities (Magiera, Smith, Zigmond, & Gebauer, 2005).

In a cotaught math class, the most common roles played by both teachers include providing instruction and monitoring student performance. In these roles, both teachers provide instruction and check student work, including homework and work completed in class. While special education teachers do provide instruction, the math teacher is typically the primary instructor of math content. The second most common role played by the special education teacher is to assist individual students (Magiera et al., 2005). This can be accomplished with one-on-one or small group activities. In this model, the special education teacher and general

Becky goes to the mall. If she spent $33.00 for a new shirt, $15.00 for a skirt and $8.00 for new socks, how much change will she receive from a $100 bill?

First, I am to **Read** the problem for understanding. So I will say to myself, "Read the problem." (*Read the problem.*) Now I will ask myself, "Have I read and understood the problem?" Well, I understand the problem because I have to find out how much change Becky will get back from a $100.00 bill.

Second, I am to **Visualize** the problem.

Step 1. I am to DRAW a diagram of the problem. First, I will ask myself "What type of a diagram can I draw?" (Remember, if you are not sure what diagram is best, don't worry. Just start by drawing a diagram of the parts of the word problem.) For this problem, it seems as though I will be grouping things together to find a missing amount. A part/whole type of diagram might be best. Now I will draw a diagram of what I know and do not know from the problem. I know that there is one person in this problem, Becky. I know that she bought a shirt, a skirt, and some socks. I also know she spent $33.00 for the shirt, $15.00 for the skirt, and $8.00 for the socks. I also know she gave $100.00 to pay for the clothing. (*Draw diagram.*) One thing I do not know is how much change she got from the $100.00. That will be my final answer. (*Add "FA" beside this unknown.*) Now I am going to check that the information in my diagram is correct. (*Check diagram against word problem.*)

Step 2. I have to ask myself, "Does my diagram show how the parts of the problem are related?" To find out how much change she got, I have to figure out how much she spent altogether. So, I have another unknown. (*Add to diagram to show second unknown.*) This is not the final

answer, but will be the partial answer. (*Add "PA."*) Now I am going to check that the information in my diagram is correct. (*Check diagram against word problem.*)

Third, I am going to set up a **Plan** to solve my problem. I have to ask myself, "What operations and how many steps are needed to solve the problem?" From the diagram I drew, I know that I have to find out how much Becky spent altogether. Then I have to find out how much change she got back from the $100.00. I have two calculations to do to solve this problem, so it will take two steps. To get the partial answer I will have to add. To get the final answer I will have to subtract.

With that information, I can write my first equation that I am going to use to solve the problem. (*Write equation.*) Before I compute the answer, I need to check that my equation is correct. I can use my diagram to do that. Did I use the right numbers? (*Check.*)

Fourth, I am going to **Compute** this answer. (*Compute the answer.*) Now I will say to myself, "Have I correctly computed the answer?" (*Re-calculate equation.*)

Now that I know the partial answer, I can write the second equation to get the final answer. (*Write equation, check numbers are correct, and compute answer.*) I will also need to check that I correctly computed the answer. (*Re-calculate equation.*)

Now I will check that all the operations were done in the right order. (*Check.*)

Finally, I will **Check** my answer to make sure the answer makes sense. Using my diagram, I will ask myself, "Does my answer make sense?" (*Using the diagram, check that the answer makes sense for what we do not know.*) "Are the decimals or money signs in the right order?" (*Check.*) Do I need help? No.

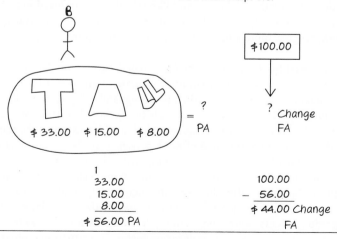

FIGURE 11.2 ● Script and Diagram for Solving a Two-Step Word Problem

Source: From "Teaching Students with LD to Use Diagrams to Solve Mathematical Word Problems," by D. van Garderen, 2007, *Journal of Learning Disabilities, 40*, p. 547. Used with permission.

classroom teacher must communicate and coordinate activities in order to maximize their strengths with diverse student groups.

Magiera and colleagues (2005) observed several cotaught secondary math classes and made numerous observations of the activities and interactions of both teachers. An example of their observations, from a ninth-grade algebra class, follows (p. 21): "General education teacher continued the lesson using the overhead. General education teacher asked the class to name the numbered pairs. Several students answered. General education teacher used a large grid on the overhead for further explanation for finding slope. Special education teacher got up and observed from the side of the room. General education teacher passed out handout." In this example, the general education teacher is leading the classroom presentation while the special education teacher is providing support to individual students.

Curriculum-Based Measurement (CBM). This means of assessing students' performance is related to a specific curriculum. CBM is often used for screening students to determine academic problems, identifying appropriate educational placements, evaluating instructional programs and student responses, and providing information for a wide variety of other educational decisions. CBM allows teachers to set a daily objective and then measure whether or not the objective was achieved. It also provides a way for teachers to track students' performances and make decisions to change instructional materials or strategies if those performances suggest such a change is needed (Hallahan, Lloyd, Kauffman, Weiss, & Martinez, 2005). Often students' performances are graphed so that teachers and students can track the improvement (Sileo & van Garderen, 2007).

In the area of math, CBM can assess a narrow set of skills or a very broad range of skills (Christ, Scullin, Tolbize, & Jiban, 2008). Evidence suggests that using CBM in math classes can have a positive impact on student achievement: "There is considerable and growing evidence that when teachers use CBM to monitor their students' progress and to adjust their instruction accordingly, students make gains at much more rapid rates than when CBM is not used" (Vaughn & Bos, 2009, p. 468).

Calhoon (2008) reviewed the literature on the use of CBM with secondary students in math classes. Her findings support the use of this strategy. Citing a study by Fuchs, Hamlett, and Fuchs (1990) that investigated the use of curriculum-based measurement with students with math disabilities (MD), Calhoon "found that the high school students with MD were motivated by the CBM data and liked the graphs produced monthly to indicate their growth" (p. 237). The graphs served as a visual reinforcement for the students, making it easy to see their progress and motivating them to continue to improve.

Anchored Instruction. A problem-based learning model, anchored instruction occurs when students use a real-life situation or scenario as an anchor for learning. The anchor provides a context or focus for goal setting, planning, and using math tools to solve problems (Woolfolk, 2004). While much of the research on anchored instruction has focused on younger children, Bottge, Heinrichs, Chan, and Serline (2001) studied the use of anchored instruction on adolescents' understanding of math concepts. In their study, eighth-grade students, with and without math deficiencies, were compared following traditional and anchor-based instruction. Results indicated that students in remedial math classes performed as well as other students in prealgebra classes after they were instructed using an anchor-based model.

In another study conducted by Bottge, Rueda, Serlin, Hung, & Kwon (2007), 128 seventh-grade students, with and without learning disabilities, were provided instruction over a 7-month period using two different anchored instructional programs. These programs, *Kim's Komet* and *Fraction of the Cost*, used video anchors that required students to perform various math functions. *Kim's Komet* helped "students develop their informal understanding of pre-algebra concepts, such as linear function, line of best fit, variables, rate of change (slope), and reliability and measurement error" (Bottge et al., 2007, p. 35). *Fraction of the Cost* required students to solve problems that required them "to (a) calculate money in a savings account and sales tax on a purchase, (b) read a tape measure, (c) convert feet to inches, (d) decipher building plans, (e) construct a table of materials, (f) compute whole numbers and mixed fractions, (g) estimate and compute combinations, and (h) calculate total cost" (Bottge et al., 2007, p. 35). Findings from the study indicated that all students in the study, including those with and without disabilities, benefited from the anchored instructional programs (Bottge et al., 2007).

Peer-Assisted Instruction.   Peer support systems for students with disabilities have received widespread recognition as a positive means of assisting students with educational and social goals (Smith et al., 2008). Peer supports can take several forms, including (1) partner learning, when students work in pairs; (2) peer tutoring, a more structured approach where students have regularly scheduled opportunities for correction and feedback; and (3) cooperative learning, where groups of students participate in projects (Walther-Thomas, Korinek, McLaughlin, & Williams, 2000).

Calhoon and Fuchs (2003) studied the use of peer-assisted learning strategies (PALS) and curriculum-based measurement with high school students with math deficiencies. After 8 weeks, students receiving peer-assisted learning who had learned how to complete weekly curriculum-based measurements (PALS/CBM group) performed significantly better than the control group on computation scores. Students in the PALS/CBM group did not perform significantly better than the control group in the area of concepts/applications skills. Still, the findings support previous research on peer supports and suggest that these programs can have a positive impact on students' math skills.

Kroeger and Kouche (2006) described the results of using peer-assisted learning strategies in a middle school math class. Students were paired for various math activities, where one student would solve the problem and the other would guide and check the other student's process and success. After using this model for several months, Kroeger and Kouche (2006) found it to be a highly motivating method for teaching math.

Differentiated Instruction and Math.   As discussed in Chapter 7, differentiated instruction can be very effective in math classes. Because math is quite difficult for many students, including those with disabilities, it presents an excellent opportunity for differentiation. As noted by Tomlinson (2002), "the goal of a differentiated classroom is to plan actively and consistently to help each learner move as far and as fast as possible along a learning continuum" (p. 2). In order to assist students with disabilities to "move as far as possible" in math, differentiated instruction is an excellent tool.

Differentiated instruction requires teachers to deal with three areas: content, process, and products. Teachers must ask what is the goal of their instruction, how they plan on getting to the goal, and how they will know when they achieve the goal (Gartin, Murdick, Imbeau, & Perner, 2002). For math classes, the goal of the instruction is likely determined, in part, by the curriculum frameworks or state standards. Aside from this component, however, teachers are able to determine how they will assist students in achieving this goal. Since students with a wide range of abilities are in math classes, teachers first must determine the learning goals for students. In doing this, they may ask themselves what all students need to know, what some students need to know, and finally, what a very few students need to know. This process will assist teachers in differentiating their math classes.

Algebra is a basic math class that most students complete; however, even though in some states passing algebra is a requirement for high school graduation, all students do not need to develop the same skills in an algebra class. Tomlinson (2002) provided an excellent example of using differentiated instruction to teach students how to solve an algebra problem. Tomlinson's example shows how some students can learn how to solve an algebraic problem differently from others.

Concrete-to-Representational-to-Abstract (CRA) Model. Some students are able to learn math when they have access to concrete manipulatives, but have difficulties moving from these manipulatives to abstractness. The concrete-to-representational-to-abstract (CRA) model for teaching math is an instructional sequence that includes three levels.

C represents learning through concrete or hands-on instruction using manipulatives.
R is learning through pictorial representations of manipulatives previously used.
A is learning through abstract notation.

This particular model provides numerous benefits for the learner. First, it provides multiple learning opportunities for students using different learning modalities. Second, it provides opportunities for students with particular learning needs to engage in a variety of activities. Third, the model enables students to use concrete manipulatives to develop more abstract understandings. Fourth, CRA gives students the opportunity to learn and understand math facts other than simply using rote memorization and drill (Witzel, Riccomini, & Schneider, 2008).

Witzel and others (2008) adapted the CRA model to one that is effective with students with disabilities. This model, called the CRAMATH model, uses the following seven steps for math instruction (p. 273):

1. *Choose* the math topic to be taught.
2. *Review* procedures to solve the problem.
3. *Adjust* the steps to eliminate notation or calculation tricks.
4. *Match* the abstract steps with an appropriate concrete manipulative.
5. *Arrange* concrete and representational lessons.
6. *Teach* each concrete, representational, and abstract lesson to student mastery.
7. *Help* students generalize what they learn through word problems.

This model does not guarantee success for students with disabilities; however, its use of a specific sequence and multisensory learning opportunities provides teachers with different options for teaching students with disabilities (Witzel et al., 2008).

RQWQC Strategy to Solve Math Word Problems. Many students are able to calculate but have difficulties with math word problems. They are simply unable to take a written problem and translate it into one represented by numbers and understand the necessary calculations. One strategy students can use to help solve math word problems is the RQWQC strategy (Strichart & Mangrum, 2010). The strategy includes five steps:

1. *Read.* Students read the problem to learn what it is about.
2. *Question.* Students find the question to be answered.
3. *Write.* Students write the information needed to answer the question.
4. *Question.* Students ask themselves what computations must be done.
5. *Compute.* Students set up the problem on paper and perform the necessary computations.

The following is an example of how students can apply this strategy to a math word problem (Strichart & Mangrum, 2010). The problems is:

The paper factory in town has 156 full-time employees. Each employee works 40 hours a week. The factory manufactured more than 100,000 reams of paper last year. What is the total number of hours worked by the employees in one week?

Read: Students read the problem to find out what it is about.   During this step, students learn the problem is about the number of hours worked by employees at the paper factory.

Question: Identify the question asked.   Students find out that the question to be answered is, "What is the total number of hours worked by the employees in one week?"

Write: Write the information needed to answer the question.   After leaving out or crossing out information that is not needed, the student writes:

> There are 156 full-time employees.
> Each employee works 40 hours a week.

Question: Students determine what computations are needed to answer the question.   The student will need to multiply 40 times 156.

Compute: Do the necessary computations. $156 \times 40 = 6,240$

This strategy lays out a process for students to use that will help them translate a word problem into one that is represented with numbers. Once this is accomplished, they are able to complete the computations necessary to solve the problem.

Student Ideas for Instruction

While there has been more and more research on improving math instruction for students with disabilities, few studies have actually asked students what they think would be helpful. Kortering and colleagues (2005) interviewed more than 400 students in grades 9–11 about their experiences in algebra classes. Forty-six of the students had been classified as having learning disabilities. Of the respondents with learning disabilities, 14% indicated that math was their favorite high school class, while 55% indicated that it was their least favorite class. Reasons given by students for math being their least favorite included "It's hard," "It's over my head," "I can't read," and "I just don't get it."

Students were also asked what was the most difficult part of algebra class and what teachers could do to help them do better in math. Forty-one percent of the students indicated that the work was the most difficult part, while another 16% indicated that tests were too hard. Ways teachers could help ranged from providing more help to using more group activities. Table 11.2 summarizes students' quotes for how teachers could help more in algebra class.

Using Games

Many students, especially students in middle and high schools who have had years of failure in math classes, are simply afraid of math; they are not motivated for success. One way of teaching math in secondary grades that may address these issues is through games. Using games to teach math enables students to try out different problem-solving strategies and use trial-and-error approaches without the stress of making a bad grade or getting a wrong answer (Shaftel, Pass, & Schnabel, 2005). Games can be fun and motivating. One game described by Shaftel and others (2005) is "That's Life–A Math Game About Real-Life Expenses." In this game, students learn how to use math to understand the cost of living on their own. Players have a specific amount of money in a checkbook, and they must deal with expected and unexpected costs. Teachers should be creative when using games for math instruction. Many games that are played by students can be easily used for math instruction. Teachers should develop ways to use more games in this manner.

TABLE 11.2 ● Ways Teachers Could Help Students with Algebra

Theme	Supporting Quotes
More Help (16 responses)	Help students out more; Help each student when needed; Take time with a student that may be having difficulty, and please try to be patient; Tutoring with a peer or a teacher; Help out some more; Tutoring; Help students out with the test and quizzes; Teach us how to work out tests; First make sure students know how to do problems; Help students to understand better and go slower; Encourage us more; More one-on-one help; Study with me and make sure I get the lesson; More one-on-one time with the students; More help one-on-one; Help students who need help.
Teaching Style (8 responses)	Take longer time in teaching a subject; Teach more slowly; Not be so rushed for time; Really depends on how the teacher teaches; Give me a different teacher; Make teachers take downers so they will not come to school in a bad mood; Better instruction; Explain the problems more.
Group Work (5 responses)	Let us work in groups more than once a month; More group work and some encouragement from the teacher; You could at least make us have group work; Let us work with partners more; Group work.
More Interesting (5 responses)	Make algebra fun and exciting; Get teachers that make the class fun and not boring; Tell the teacher to lighten up some and stop being so boring; Make more interesting; Make class more fun.
Fewer Distractions (2 responses)	The distractions from students who don't want to learn; Make class less distracting.
Other (7 responses)	Give us a part-time free time to study or whatever; Make it more mature for some students; Teach us how to take tests; Have more tests; Do stuff with the students; Less work; Help me learn to read.

Source: From "Improving Performance in High School Algebra: What Students with Learning Disabilities Are Saying," by L. J. Kortering, L. U. deBettencourt, and P. M. Braziel, 2005, *Learning Disability Quarterly, 28*, p. 200. Used with permission.

General Math Accommodations

There are numerous accommodations that math teachers use to facilitate the successful inclusion of students with disabilities. These range from allowing students to use calculators to using cue cards to assist students in following the appropriate steps in problem solving. Maccini and Gagnon (2006) surveyed 179 secondary general education math and special education teachers to determine the instructional practices they used with students with disabilities. Results indicated that 40% of the general secondary math teachers allowed the use of calculators during math class. Other instructional practices included the following: individualized instruction (32%), additional practice (17%), reduced class work (19%), extended time on assignments (34%), reduced homework problems (17%), color coding (5%), peer or cross-age tutoring (27%), problems read to students (22%), cue cards of strategy steps (4%), use of concrete objects (21%), individualized attention by class aide (12%), graphic organizers (86%), and mnemonics (11%).

Numerous strategies for teaching math to students with disabilities, especially those with math disabilities, have been described. There appears to be several strategies that have merit. Witzel, Smith, and Brownell (2001, p. 104) summarized some recommendations for teaching algebra:

1. Continue to instruct secondary math students with LD in basic arithmetic.
2. Use think-aloud techniques for modeling steps to solve equations.

3. Provide guided practice before independent practice so that students can first understand what to do for each step and then understand why.
4. Provide a physical and pictorial model, such as diagrams or hands-on materials, to aid the processes for solving equations.
5. Relate algebra problems to real-life events that match the students' age and interests.

Furner, Yahya, and Duffy (2005) identified 20 ways to teach mathematics that are useful for all students, as shown in Table 11.3. Note: Many of the suggestions in Table 11.3 are based on previous sections in this chapter.

Assessing Math Skills

Creating opportunities for students with disabilities to access the general curriculum can result in significant gains for students in the area of math. However, without making accommodations in the assessment of these students, the test results for many will be substantially below desired performance levels. There are numerous accommodations that can be used in math assessment. Examples include:

- Read story problems for students with literacy issues.
- Test in short time frames for students with attention deficits.
- Provide manipulatives and other concrete materials when permissible.
- Allow students to take assessments in quiet areas.
- Allow students the use of calculators when permissible.

TABLE 11.3 ● Strategies to Reach All Students When in Math Instruction

1. Teach vocabulary using real objects and demonstration.
2. Relate math problems and vocabulary to prior knowledge and background.
3. Apply problems to daily life situations.
4. Use manipulatives to make problems concrete.
5. Encourage drawings to translate and visualize word problems.
6. Have ELL/special education students pair with typical students for computer/cooperative activities.
7. Encourage children to think aloud when solving word problems, and have students give oral explanations of their thinking, leading to solutions.
8. Have students write original word problems to exchange with classmates.
9. Explain directions clearly, and repeat key terms.
10. Encourage students to follow the four-step problem-solving process.
11. Realize that not all math notations are necessarily universal.
12. Group students heterogeneously during cooperative learning.
13. Make interdisciplinary connections to what students are learning in math.
14. Make cultural connections for students when teaching mathematics.
15. Rewrite word problems in simple terms.
16. Concretize math concepts with total physical response.
17. Create word bank charts and hang them in the classroom for viewing.
18. Take Internet field trips and use mathematics software.
19. Use children's literature to teach mathematics and develop the language.
20. Using auditory, visual, and kinesthetic teaching approaches for different learning styles enables teachers to reach more students than the traditional direct-instruction or paper and pencil drill and practice forms of instruction.

Source: From "Teach Mathematics: Strategies to Reach All Students," by J. M. Furner, N. Yahya, and M. L. Duffy, 2005, *Intervention in School and Clinic, 41,* 16–23.

Elbaum (2007) studied the effects of oral testing accommodations on the math performance of 643 students in grades 6–10. These students were classified as having learning disabilities. Results of the study revealed that the use of oral testing accommodations, namely a read-aloud test, "resulted in improved performance for students both with and without disabilities" (p. 225).

TEACHING SCIENCE TO STUDENTS WITH DISABILITIES

Students with disabilities accessing the general curriculum, which as a result of No Child Left Behind and IDEA make up most students with disabilities, will enroll in many of the same science classes as nondisabled students. The exact nature of the science program for these students will depend on the focus of the program. This means that they will likely take courses in the areas of life science/biology, physical science, chemistry, physics, and earth science. Similar to math, specific courses will be selected based on each student's future academic demands. Few students with disabilities would be enrolled in more functional programs (Polloway et al., 2008). With this reality unlikely changing, instruction for students with disabilities in science that takes into consideration their overall developmental patterns of achievement is important (Cawley, Foley, & Miller, 2003).

Since most students with disabilities will enroll in general science classes, taught by regular classroom teachers, it is imperative that these teachers understand the needs of students with disabilities. Kirch, Bargerhuff, Cowan, and Wheatly (2007) conducted a qualitative study of 14 current secondary science teachers to determine their perceived confidence levels in teaching students with disabilities. Findings indicated that while these teachers believed that students with disabilities could be successful in inclusive science classrooms, many did not feel confident in teaching this group of students. Asked about which categories they felt comfortable teaching, teachers indicated that the only group of students with disabilities they felt completely comfortable teaching were those with attention deficit disorders and learning disabilities. All 14 teachers noted that science methods courses in their teacher preparation programs did not cover, or only minimally covered, methods for teaching science to students with disabilities.

Traditional Science Teaching Approaches

Science has been a subject in American secondary schools for several decades. Basic science classes, such as biology, chemistry, and physics, have been available in the comprehensive high school model adopted in the early 20th century. As a result, all students take some science classes. Over the past several years, the availability of advanced science classes has increased. Science typically has been taught using one of two basic approaches—textbook and hands-on/activity-based.

Textbook Approach.   Focusing on textbook delivery of science has long been the traditional approach. Polloway and colleagues (2008) noted that the majority of teachers teaching science use textbooks as the basis for their class content and activities. Science textbooks can be used in a variety of ways, including students reading and discussing the content and students using textbooks as reference materials (Polloway et al., 2008).

Using textbooks as the basis for science classes has advantages and disadvantages (Polloway et al., 2008). Advantages include:

- Excellent teacher resource
- Excellent for beginning teachers

- Assist in organizing science content
- Durable
- Should be aligned with state standards

Along with these advantages are numerous disadvantages. Textbooks "require complex literacy and study skills competence, are often abstract, typically have readability levels above the reading levels of students, may be the only source of science information, become outdated, and may not be in concert with the curricular needs or goals of some students" (Polloway et al., 2008, p. 321). Cawley and others (2003) noted that the use of textbooks as the primary source for science education creates difficulties for many students with disabilities because of the significant demand for reading and writing skills.

Hands-On Approach.   The hands-on/activity-based approach stresses the use of inquiry skills. Using a hands-on approach to science instruction reduces the dependency on literacy skills, which is one of the major problems associated with a textbook approach. These programs (Cawley et al., 2003, p. 162):

1. Provide the teacher with an opportunity to make on-the-spot adjustments
2. Allow students to raise and answer questions using different sources
3. Enhance conceptualization through the use of alternative representations
4. Offer the teacher an opportunity to pace the lessons according to the rates of student learning
5. Present an opportunity for students to demonstrate selected principles at high levels of generalization

The hands-on/activity-based approach lends itself to most topics in science. Students are able to engage in hands-on laboratory activities that can provide instruction as well as reinforce information learned in classrooms. Using this approach, students "actively explore science concepts by processing science by observing, measuring, classifying, comparing, predicting, and inferring" (McCarthy, 2005, p. 249). These activities can also be extremely motivating for students, and teachers become more learning facilitators than simply conveyers of information (Polloway et al., 2008).

McCarthy (2005) studied the effects of thematic-based, hands-on science teaching versus a textbook approach for 18 junior-high students classified as having emotional disturbance. Students receiving instruction from the textbook approach spent approximately 5 to 10 minutes of review, 10 minutes for teacher demonstration, 15 to 20 minutes of textbook reading and discussion, and 10 minutes of independent practice. The hands-on group spent about 5 to 10 minutes in review, 30 to 40 minutes conducting experiments in small groups under the teacher's guidance, and 5 to 10 minutes to review concepts and results. Findings indicated that the students receiving instruction using the hands-on, thematic approach scored significantly better than the textbook group on two out of three measures. The study supported the use of the hands-on, thematic approach for students with disabilities, and noted that these methods "tend to ameliorate language expectations of traditional classrooms, which rely heavily on the text" (p. 257).

Other Science Teaching Methods

Similar to teaching math, social studies, English, and other content areas at the secondary level, there is no one best way to teach science. Students with disabilities included in general science classes are a very heterogeneous group of students. Some have above average intellectual abilities but significant deficits in literacy, organizational skills, or attention; others may have mild impairments in cognitive areas. The result is that science teachers must develop a broad array of instructional strategies to meet the needs of a diverse student population.

Students with disabilities in content classes, regardless of which content class, are likely to have difficulties. This may be due to a variety of factors, including their literacy skills, math skills, social skills, and memory skills. Regardless of the specific class, there are numerous instructional strategies that teachers can use to facilitate student success. While some of these will be discussed more significantly in other chapters, a brief overview of some of the principles that may be effective with students with disabilities will be provided.

Peer-Assisted Learning Activities. The peer assisted learning activities have been shown to be very successful for students with disabilities, especially in content classes. When teaching science using a hands-on orientation, using peer-assisted learning can be quite effective. In McCarthy's (2005) study, the group of students with emotional disturbance receiving instruction using a hands-on, thematic approach worked with peers during their lab time. As noted, results supported the hands-on approach when peer-assisted learning was utilized.

Mastropieri and others (2006) studied 13 eighth-grade science classrooms, comparing differentiated hands-on activities, with peer-assisted opportunities, and teacher-directed instruction for students with mild disabilities. Of the 213 students in these classrooms, 44 were classified as having disabilities, with another 35 English language learners. In the teacher-directed classrooms, teachers directed all instruction, including reviewing previous lessons, presenting new instruction, providing opportunities for guided and independent practice, and leading lab activities. Students were then required to complete worksheet activities associated with chapters in the book.

The group receiving a differentiated, hands-on approach had the same instruction as the teacher-directed group, but instead of completing worksheet activities on the chapters, these students engaged in peer-assisted learning with differentiated science activities. Findings indicated that students receiving the differentiated hands-on instruction, with peer partners, performed better on high stakes and end-of-year tests than students receiving a more traditional, teacher-directed instruction program (Mastropieri et al., 2006).

Universal Design. As a result of our growing diversity, and the requirement of No Child Left Behind to have all children achieve at a minimal academic level, teachers now must teach a wide variety of students with different abilities and skills. The use of universal design is one approach for ensuring that all students have access—not only to the general curriculum, but also to classes in which they can succeed.

The components of universal design can be used effectively in science classes. These components include (Kurtts, Mathews, & Smallwood, 2009, p. 152):

- Providing content in different modes—visual, graphic, or auditory, for example—so that all students have diverse ways to access information
- Providing students with many opportunities to demonstrate what they have learned
- Providing a variety of ways to involve students in learning

By implementing these components, and various accommodations that could be beneficial to all students, teachers are prepared to effectively deal with students with disabilities who may need access to the class at a future date. The following list includes strategies that could be implemented in a science lab as a part of universal design efforts that would benefit students with disabilities, as well as other students who may need some accommodations or modifications:

- Provide both written and verbal instructions.
- Give verbal and visual descriptions of demonstrations and visual aids.
- Use plastic instead of glass.
- Allow extra time for setup and completion of lab work.

- Address safety procedures for students with a variety of sensory and mobility abilities, including the provision of visual lab warning signals.
- Make laboratory signs and equipment labels in large print, with high contrast.
- Ensure that field sites are wheelchair accessible.
- Maintain wide aisles and keep the lab uncluttered.
- Incorporate an adjustable height work surface for at least one workstation.

Tables 11.4 through 11.8 depict a model lesson from a secondary physical science class that demonstrates universal design components. Similar lessons could be built around the universal design model for math, as well as other content classes. Using these components enables students to access the general education curriculum through differentiated instruction and assessments.

Cooperative Teaching.   Another excellent way to provide appropriate instruction to students with disabilities in middle and high school content classes, including science, is through cooperative teaching. Similar to math, science includes a large amount of specialized content.

TABLE 11.4 ● Universally Designed Lesson Plan Model: Goals

Lesson Components	UDL Instructional Supports	Example: Physical Science Lesson on Solubility
Goals	Aligned with national standards	*National Science Education Standards:* *Content Standard A:* A-1 Abilities necessary to scientific inquiry A-2 Understandings about scientific inquiry *Content Standard B:* B-2 Structure and properties of matter B-6 Interactions of energy and matter
	Aligned with state and/or district competencies, standards, or frameworks	*Unifying Concepts and Processes—UPC:* Systems, order, and organization Evidence, models, and explanation Change, consistency, and measurement Form and function *North Carolina Standard Course of Study:* 6.04 Measure and analyze indicators of chemical change; investigate and analyze properties and composition of solutions

Note: UDL = universal design for learning.

Source: From "(Dis)solving the Differences: A Physical Science Lesson Using Universal Design," by S. A. Kurtts, C. E. Matthews, and T. Smallwood, 2009, *Intervention in School and Clinic, 44*, p. 154. Used with permission.

TABLE 11.5 ● Universally Designed Lesson Plan Model: Instructional Objectives

Lesson Components	UDL Instructional Supports	Example: Physical Science Lesson on Solubility
Instructional objectives	Use planning pyramid (Schumm, Vaughn, & Harris, 1997) as its basis	All students will define solubility and list three types of solutions; Most students will identify how to express the concentration of solutions; Some students will describe the effects of pressure and temperature on the solubility of gases.

Note: UDL = universal design for learning.

Source: From "(Dis)solving the Differences: A Physical Science Lesson Using Universal Design," by S. A. Kurtts, C. E. Matthews, and T. Smallwood, 2009, *Intervention in School and Clinic, 44*, p. 153. Used with permission.

TABLE 11.6 ● Universally Designed Lesson Plan Model: Lesson Description

Lesson Components	UDL Instructional Supports	Example: Physical Science Lesson on Solubility
Lesson description	*Resources* UDL principles	Textbook handouts: milk carton, bottle of concentrated acid, computers and printer paper, color pencils or crayons, graph paper, computer, e-handouts (hard copy and digital text), digital photographs, textbook on audiotapes, Web, CD, print Computer and Internet
		Web sites www.dewasa.com/about/facilities.cfm wastewatertreatment www.graphicorganizers.com http://negpscience.com/self check quiz http://nsdt.org
	Strategies Differentiating instruction	Compacting or chunking of important key information throughout lesson Questions for varied ability levels Flexible grouping arrangements K-W-L chart and other graphic organizers

Note: UDL = universal design for learning.

Source: From "(Dis)solving the Differences: A Physical Science Lesson Using Universal Design," by S. A. Kurtts, C. E. Matthews, and T. Smallwood, 2009, *Intervention in School and Clinic, 44*, p. 154. Used with permission.

TABLE 11.7 ● Universally Designed Lesson Plan Model: Instructional Sequence

Lesson Components	UDL Instructional Supports	Example: Physical Science Lesson on Solubility
Instructional sequence using UDL	*Representation:* Includes various ways content will be presented in different ways to meet the needs of all students	*Representation:* teacher Lecture notes: by lecture, print, and audiotape, teaching vocabulary and major concepts Science journal: students will imagine they have a crystal and a solution of zinc chloride. They will explain how to use the crystal to tell whether the solution is saturated, unsaturated, or supersaturated Demonstration: open can of soda. Point out that when soda is sealed, pressure keeps the gas in solution. Once opened, pressure is reduced and bubbles become visible Explicit instruction: On the board draw three identical large beakers. Draw the same number of small circles in each beaker (representing particles of solute). Ask students to copy drawings and color in circles to represent saturated, unsaturated, or supersaturated solutions Assessment: journal entry, open-ended questions

TABLE 11.7 ● (continued)

Lesson Components	UDL Instructional Supports	Example: Physical Science Lesson on Solubility

	Expression:
	Includes various methods students will use to demonstrate what they have learned
	Activity giving students opportunity to attain intended learning outcomes
		Expression: student
		Oral:
		    Vocabulary (matching definitions game)
		    Talking word processor for definitions
		    Online atlas for definitions of terms
		    K-W-L chart created
		Written:
		    E-text vocabulary handout/written handout
		    Electronic virtual lab
		    Completed worksheet printed or handwritten worksheet
		    Highlighting feature of word processing program
		Artistic:
		    Create multimedia product using online resources

	Engagement:
	Includes various pathways in which students will learn the concepts presented
	Pacing to sustain interest and facilitate learning
	A balance between teacher-directed and student-centered activity
		Engagement: teacher/student curriculum
		Partner activity to plot a solubility curve graph from data on e-worksheet using multicolors and/or plot graph Excel spreadsheet
		Virtual investigations, virtual lab-solution chemistry
		Foldables solubility and concentration
		Web site activities
		    Online, search for wastewater facility and find out what is dissolved in the water
		    Create a graph that shows solutes and their quantities in water
		    Virtual investigations rubric, foldables rubric, task analysis, self-check form, open-ended questions, computer printout worksheet

Note: UDL = universal design for learning.

Source: From "(Dis)solving the Differences: A Physical Science Lesson Using Universal Design," by S. A. Kurtts, C. E. Matthews, and T. Smallwood, 2009, *Intervention in School and Clinic, 44*, p. 154. Used with permission.

TABLE 11.8 ● Universally Designed Lesson Plan Model: Assess Learning Outcomes

Lesson Components	UDL Instructional Supports	Example: Physical Science Lesson on Solubility

Assess learning outcomes	How teacher and students will assess what has been learned	Construct a graph of the amount and types of contaminants released in the effluent at a wastewater facility
		Create a final product that demonstrates understanding of scientific terms
		Self-assessment: textbook, quiz or http://nc.gpscience.com/self_check_quiz
		Review of journal entries:
		    Check for understanding in whole class discussion
		    Creation of foldable

Note: UDL = universal design for learning.

Source: From "(Dis)solving the Differences: A Physical Science Lesson Using Universal Design," by S. A. Kurtts, C. E. Matthews, and T. Smallwood, 2009, *Intervention in School and Clinic, 44*, p. 155. Used with permission.

As a result, science classes lend themselves well for science teachers who focus on content while special education teachers focus on the different learning needs of students with disabilities and those with other diverse learning needs.

There are several strategies for successful coteaching at the secondary level. Rice, Drame, Owens, and Frattura (2007) described six strategies that can greatly facilitate the success of coteaching: (1) focus on professionalism; (2) articulate and model instruction to meet students' needs; (3) accurately assess student progress; (4) analyze teaching and teaching styles; (5) work with a wide range of students; and (6) employ teachers who are knowledgeable of the subject matter.

While cooperative teaching has been shown to be an effective model for teaching students with disabilities in inclusive classrooms, there are often not enough special education teachers to coteach many content classes, which may result in a large number of students with disabilities being included in the same class. This not only violates the purpose of inclusion, but also may result in the role of the special education teacher primarily being that of an aide. One way of avoiding this development is through collaborative cooperative teaching. Using a collaborative model for coteaching enables special education teachers to work in a larger number of classrooms. This can be implemented in three different models, including:

Model 1—the special education teacher spends parts of periods in more than one general classroom, focusing on specific activities during those times.

Model 2—the special education teacher goes to specific classrooms on different days.

Model 3—the special education teacher's schedule in general classrooms changes on a weekly basis, determined by the nature of the instructional activities.

These collaborative coteaching models result in better use of the special education teacher's time and make it more likely that students with disabilities will be included in classes in more typical numbers (Walsh & Jones, 2004).

Differentiated Instruction.   One of the most promising strategies for teachers to use for all students, including those with disabilities, is differentiated instruction. Differentiated instruction can be defined as a philosophy where curriculum and instruction are driven by the needs of students (Gartin et al., 2002). Its focus is to provide instruction to students, taking into consideration their ability levels, readiness, motivation, and other factors that could impact their learning. Differentiated instruction can be used effectively in science classes at the secondary level. When using differentiated instruction in science, teachers need to keep in mind any discrepancy that may exist between the instructional demands of the classroom and the ability of students to be successful with the tasks, and appropriately modify the lesson content and teaching methods to meet the needs of students. "Science teachers can use numerous instructional strategies to differentiate instruction without 'watering down' the curriculum" (Watson & Houtz, 2002, p. 269).

Watson and Houtz (2002) utilized the planning pyramid to show how a lesson can be organized around the three levels: what all students should learn, what most students will learn, and what some students will learn. This model demonstrates the assumption that "all students are able to learn although *not all students* will learn *all the information* presented in a lesson" (p. 269). Figure 11.3 shows the planning pyramid.

General Accommodations and Principles

There are numerous accommodations and modifications that science teachers can make to facilitate the success of students with disabilities (Steele, 2008). Steele (2008) provided a list of modifications that can be made for students with learning disabilities. These are arranged into

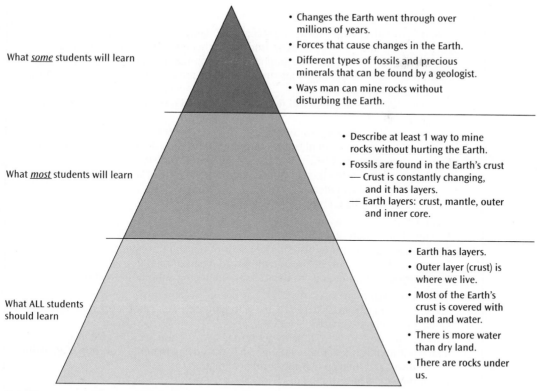

What *some* students will learn

- Changes the Earth went through over millions of years.
- Forces that cause changes in the Earth.
- Different types of fossils and precious minerals that can be found by a geologist.
- Ways man can mine rocks without disturbing the Earth.

What *most* students will learn

- Describe at least 1 way to mine rocks without hurting the Earth.
- Fossils are found in the Earth's crust
  — Crust is constantly changing, and it has layers.
  — Earth layers: crust, mantle, outer and inner core.

What ALL students should learn

- Earth has layers.
- Outer layer (crust) is where we live.
- Most of the Earth's crust is covered with land and water.
- There is more water than dry land.
- There are rocks under us.

FIGURE 11.3 ● Planning Pyramid

Source: From "Teaching Science: Meeting the Academic Needs of Culturally and Linguistically Diverse Students," by S. M. R. Watson and L. E. Houtz, 2002, *Intervention in School and Clinic, 37,* pp. 267–278.

modifications related to lecture and class time, textbook readings, homework assignments, and assessment. Figure 11.4 lists these accommodations. While specifically suggested for students with learning disabilities, many of these modifications would be effective for students with other learning problems and disabilities.

Grumbine and Alden (2006) identified several principles that can greatly assist science teachers in secondary schools teaching students with disabilities. These principles were developed following the Biology Success! project, a National Science Foundation (NSF) grant program that developed strategies for teaching students with diverse abilities. The principles include the following:

Principle 1: Learning is enhanced when teachers recognize and teach to diverse learning styles and strengths. Teachers need to teach to the entire spectrum of diversity found among today's students.

Principle 2: Content learning supported by explicit instruction in skills and strategies includes teaching and modeling reading and study strategies; teaching ways to organize, revise, and review notes; and providing models and templates for writing lab reports.

Principle 3: Learning is facilitated when instruction and assessment are clearly organized. In order to implement this principle, teachers can post and review daily activities related to a lesson; establish a routine for class activities; and use a standard format for assignments.

Lecture and class time

Collaborate with special education teachers for planning and instruction

Focus lectures and class activities around major themes and their relationships

Use advance organizers, such as graphic displays or discussion of key concepts

Incorporate explicit, structured instruction, such as prompts and organizational cues, into science lessons

Clarify vocabulary at the beginning of the lesson on PowerPoint slides, handouts, or on the board

Use everyday life examples to connect new science content to student experiences

Use visual displays of content, such as graphs, charts, illustrations, and concept maps

Provide study strategy instruction on note taking or provide teacher-made notes

Incorporate group activities and projects during class time to supplement instruction and focus on main ideas

Review notes; model revising and studying notes

Textbook readings

Provide chapter notes for students to study

Teach organization of text including key parts of book and chapters

Summarize key concepts before and after reading assignments

Encourage use of mnemonic strategies for memorizing critical information

Homework assignments

Ask special education teachers to assist with homework for extra support on an individual or small group basis

Provide class time to help students get started on assignments with guidance

Teach self-management interventions, such as studying material, covering it up, writing it down, and then comparing to original material

Clarify directions for assignments

Monitor progress, drafts, and deadlines for specific assignments

Break down assignments and check progress on each part

Teach study skills related to assignments and provide guidance as needed

Assessment

Encourage students to organize study time on a regular basis

Use class time to model the review and study process

Encourage students to preview the entire test before they begin so they can plan their time for all sections

Encourage students to read directions carefully, emphasizing key vocabulary words and focusing on examples of typical directions for different formats

Encourage students to record formulas, mnemonics, or lists they have memorized so they will be available during the test

Teach students to mark items that are difficult and to try responding to them near the end of the test time

Practice with specific strategies for each type of question (e.g., multiple choice, essay, true-false)

Remind students to save time to review responses and edit essays

FIGURE 11.4 ● Summary of Science Modifications for Students with LD

Source: From "Helping Students with Learning Disabilities Succeed," by M. M. Steele, 2008, *The Science Teacher, 75*, p. 40. Used with permission.

Principle 4: Learning is maximized when instruction and assessment are based on explicit objectives. Teachers need to directly link classroom activities and learning objectives; provide rubrics for assessment of projects; and provide study guides for test preparation.

Principle 5: Learning is improved when teachers provide consistent feedback. This principle can be implemented by teaching that uses more frequent and shorter evaluations and provides direct feedback to students about their progress.

Principle 6: Learning is sustained when students develop self-knowledge. For students to develop self-knowledge, teachers need to discuss their strengths and weaknesses with students and provide opportunities for students to reflect on their performances during assignments.

Watanabe, Nunes, Mebane, Scalise, and Claesgens (2007) conducted two case studies to determine effective methods of teaching science for a wide range of students, not just students who were intellectually capable of success in chemistry classes. Throughout a 2-year period, information was collected from students and teachers in two schools that had been "detracked," meaning that students were no longer placed in classes based on their ability level. This resulted in a significantly more heterogeneous student population in chemistry classes.

Results of the study found that four different characteristics of classrooms resulted in positive gains from students. These included (p. 705):

(1) teachers' true belief in a developmental, as opposed to fixed conception of ability and intelligence, as reflected in teachers providing multiple entry points to chemistry concepts and making outside-of-the-classroom support available for students; (2) a focus on an inquiry-based pedagogical approach to chemistry foregrounding real-world contexts, which helps to draw on students' existing knowledge of the subject and to build student confidence in the content area; (3) a focus on teaching students study skills such as reading science texts, taking notes and studying for tests; (4) a strong sense of community in the classroom, where students are held responsible for their own and each other's learning.

RIDD Strategy.   Many students with disabilities at the secondary level have significant difficulties because of their limited literacy skills. Therefore, some strategies to assist low-level readers can have a very positive impact in all academic content areas. One strategy that has been used effectively in secondary schools is RIDD, which stands for *read, imagine, decide,* and *do*. Using RIDD enables students to counteract common characteristics associated with poor reading skills. These characteristics include stopping reading at the end of a line rather than at the end of a sentence and scanning for specific words without really understanding what to do when the words are found. RIDD assists students in overcoming these common characteristics. Steps in RIDD are as follows (Jackson, 2002):

Step 1 Read the passage without stopping.
Step 2 Imagine or make a mental picture of what you have read.
Step 3 Decide what to do.
Step 4 Do the work.

Commercial Programs.   Although not extensive, there are a few science programs specifically designed for students with disabilities. These are primarily focused on limited reading requirements and would therefore be more appropriate for students with more severe disabilities. Two of these programs with a secondary focus include (Polloway et al., 2008):

- Science Activities for the Visually Impaired (SAVI) and Science Enrichment for Learners with Physical Handicaps (SELPH)—involve major adaptations for students with vision and physical problems that need a hands-on curriculum
- Applications in Biology/Chemistry (ABC)—provides program for secondary students who are in the middle 50% in academic areas; contains a real-life focus

Accessibility and Science Labs.   When teaching students with disabilities in science class, one of the major considerations is how to make labs accessible. Science labs are an integral part of science classes. Regardless of the instructional format used, effective science classes include laboratory time. For many students with disabilities, accommodations in labs are critical if they are going to be able to participate in lab work. Therefore, it is imperative that accommodations for students with disabilities in labs are in place.

The nature of the accommodation for labs is directly related to the type and degree of disability exhibited by the student. Table 11.9 provides examples of lab accommodations that could be useful for students with specific disabilities.

TABLE 11.9 ● General Accommodations for Science Labs

ACCOMMODATIONS

Following are examples of accommodations that might benefit a student with a disability.
- Use wheelchair-accessible labs and field sites.
- Talk to a student about special learning needs and accommodation alternatives.
- Provide a lab partner.
- Use plastic instead of glass.
- Allow extra time for setup and completion of lab work.
- Address safety procedures for students with a variety of sensory and mobility abilities.
- Use institutional resources for students with disabilities.

Typical science lab accommodations for students with specific disabilities include those in the following lists.

Blindness
- Verbal descriptions of demonstrations and visual aids
- Braille text and raised line images
- Braille or tactile ruler, compass, angles, protractor
- Braille equipment labels, notches, staples, fabric paint, and Braille at regular increments on tactile ruler, glassware, syringe, beam balance, stove, other science equipment
- Different textures (e.g., sandpaper) to label areas on items

Low Vision
- Verbal descriptions of demonstrations and visual aids
- Preferential seating to assure visual access to demonstrations
- Large-print, high-contrast instructions and illustrations
- Raised line drawings or tactile models for illustrations
- Large-print laboratory signs and equipment labels
- Video camera, computer or TV monitor to enlarge microscope images
- Handheld magnifier, binoculars
- Large-print calculator

Mobility Impairments
- Wheelchair-accessible field site
- Uncluttered lab; clear, wide aisles

TABLE 11.9 ● *(continued)*

- Preferential seating to avoid physical barriers and assure visual access to demonstrations
- Mirrors above the instructor giving a demonstration
- Enlarged screen
- Wheelchair-accessible, adjustable-height work surface
- Slip stop mat
- Utility and equipment controls within easy reach from seated position
- Electric stirrer, container filler
- Support stand, beaker and object clamp; test tube rack
- Handles on beakers, objects, and equipment
- Surgical gloves to handle wet or slippery items
- Modified procedures to use larger weights and volumes
- Extended eyepieces so students who use wheelchairs can use microscopes
- Flexible connections to electrical, water, and gas lines
- Single-action lever controls in place of knobs
- Alternate lab storage methods (e.g.,"Lazy Susan," storage cabinet on casters)

Deaf and Hard of Hearing

- Preferential seating to view demos and watch instructor captioning for video presentations
- Written instructions prior to lab
- Visual lab warning signals

Learning and Attention Disabilities

- Combination of written, verbal, and pictorial instructions with scaffolding
- Repeated demonstration of procedure and support practice
- Frequent brief breaks
- Preferential seating to avoid distractions and minimize extraneous stimuli
- Scanning and speaking "pen"

Health Impairments

- Avoid chemical materials to which student is allergic or provide alternate assignment
- Flexible schedule and time allocation
- Install a mirror above the location where demonstrations are typically given.
- Use lever controls instead of knobs.
- Install flexible connections to water, gas, and electricity.
- Buy lab products that can be used by students with a variety of abilities (e.g., plastic lab products instead of glass, tactile models, large print diagrams, non-slip mats, support stands, beaker and object clamps, handles on beakers and equipment, surgical gloves to handle slippery items, video camera with computer or TV monitor to enlarge microscope image).
- Ensure that utility and equipment controls are within easy reach from a standing or seated position.
- Provide surgical gloves for handling wet or slippery items.

Source: From S. Burgstahler, www.washington.edu/doit/Brochures/Academics/science_lab.html, retrieved April 21, 2009.

CONNECTING MATH AND SCIENCE INSTRUCTION

While math and science have some unique content, and some methods and activities definitely work better with one subject than the other, there are some methods and strategies teachers can use to connect math and science. NCTM (2009) has noted that connecting math and instruction can help students understand connections both among different math ideas and between math and other subject areas. Connecting math and science is ideal because of the relationship between these two subject areas.

Cawley and Foley (2002) proposed the use of problem-solving programs that "take advantage of the structure and sequence of math curricula and inject science topics into the lessons" (p. 14). They provided an example of a lesson combining math and science for seventh and eighth graders that focused on using proportions and science problems. In their example, teachers do the following activities (p. 17):

1. Introduce proportions with different activities involving weight/distance relationships.
2. Provide students with objects of different masses and have students use a balance to sort the objects based on similar and different masses.
3. Have students place objects of similar mass on each side of the scale, then remove one of them and replace it with an object of different mass to tilt the balance.
4. Have students show how they could use objects of different mass to create balance by placing the objects different distances along the balance.
5. Students create a chart showing the different combinations of mass and distance used for balance.
6. Finally, students place different combinations of mass and distance on the balance and explain the principle that "changing either the distance or the mass does not disturb the balance, as long as both sides are changing the same way."

Successfully connecting math and science requires effective teaching, which is critical for improving academic success for students with disabilities. In one study of the impact of effective teaching on students representing a wide variety of learning abilities, Johnson, Kahle, and Fargo (2006) found that the use of effective teaching strategies, with a goal of helping middle school students make connections between science and math, resulted in improved academic achievement. The degree of effective teaching was rated using five different levels. Level 1, classified as ineffective instruction, represented passive learning or learning activities simply for the sake of the activity. The highest degree of teaching, level 5, classified as exemplary instruction, focused on a highly engaging classroom environment. Table 11.10 describes each of these levels. After 3 years, students receiving the highest level of effective instruction performed better on the discovery inquiry test than students not receiving this degree of instruction.

Integrated Curriculum

Extending the connectiveness between math and science into other curricular areas would require an integrated curriculum. The objective of this approach is to link and integrate science with other subject areas. As noted, the relationship between math and science is relatively obvious; however, using an integrated curriculum approach takes advantage of the relationships between science and other content areas (Polloway et al., 2008).

Table 11.11 describes an integrated model for teaching a unit on marine biology. While using science as the basis of the lesson, other areas are integrated into the lesson with a variety of activities. When using such a model, teachers are able to work with students on a wide variety of areas through a unit on science that is likely very motivating.

Bryan and Warger (1998) described an integrated curricular approach called Amazing Discoveries. This framework integrates social science and science by emphasizing thinking skills such as analytic, critical, creative, original, synthesizing, predicting, and drawing inferences. The program includes 28 different hands-on experiments and demonstrations

TABLE 11.10 ● Levels of Effective Instruction

LEVEL 1: INEFFECTIVE INSTRUCTION

Limited or no evidence of student thinking or engagement; instruction highly unlikely to enhance student's understanding. Characterized by passive learning or performing an activity simply for the sake of performing the activity.

LEVEL 2: ELEMENTS OF EFFECTIVE INSTRUCTION

Contains some elements of effective practice; serious design problems remain in design, implementation, content, and/or appropriateness of many students. Instruction limited in likelihood to enhance students' understanding.

LEVEL 3: BEGINNING STATES OF EFFECTIVE INSTRUCTION

Instruction is purposeful and has several elements of effective practice. Students are often engaged in meaningful activities; however, some weaknesses remain in design, implementation, or content. Instruction somewhat limited in enhancing students' understanding.

LEVEL 4: ACCOMPLISHED, EFFECTIVE INSTRUCTION

Purposeful instruction for most students. Students actively engaged in meaningful work. Instruction well designed and delivered. Quite likely that students' understanding will be enhanced.

LEVEL 5: EXEMPLARY INSTRUCTION

All students are purposefully engaged in meaningful work. Lessons are well designed and delivered. Highly likely that most students' understanding will be enhanced.

Source: From "Effective Teaching Results in Increased Science Achievement for All Students," by C. C. Johnson, J. B. Kahle, and J. D. Fargo, 2006, *Science Education, 91*, 371–382.

TABLE 11.11 ● Integrated Lesson on Marine Biology

Disciplines				
Reading	**Research**	**Written Expression**	**Oral Expression**	**Spelling**
Research to gain/locate information on individual marine animals Teacher-made handouts specific to area of study: narratives poetry In-class story (story combining "It was a hot summer day . . .") Class poetry book	Brainstorming questions of interest Classifying questions into five categories Outlining Note taking Drafts Table of contents Referencing (APA style) Intro/body/conclusion About the author	Whale short story Note taking Outlining Research paper drafts editing Poetry traditional cinquain, limerick, acrostic	Magic Circle (daily group counseling) Group discussions Brainstorming Oral reading of stories/ poetry Oral presentations (public speaking skills) Responses to teacher inquiries Oral sharing of observations	Functional spelling Dictionary/thesaurus skills New vocabulary

(continued)

TABLE 11.11 ● (*continued*)

		Disciplines		
Math Application	**Science**	**Social Studies/Issues**	**Visual Arts, Music, Performing Arts**	**Computer Skills**
Averaging hermit crab race times	Inquiry skills	Careers related to marine biology	Rap song	Word processing
Graphing shell preferences of hermit crabs	Observation of hermit crabs	Endangered species	Individual lyrics	Marine organism database information sheet (10 categories)
Animal measurement	Comparisons		Class song	
Counting of syllables/ words for poetry	Classifications of species		Rhythm	Printout of database
Problem solving	Hypothesizing		Performance	Information on marine animals
	Collecting/recording data		Seaweed pressing	Graphics (cross section of shoreline and ocean)
	Description		Fish printing	
	Inferencing		Rubber stamp art	Word processing and graphics for title page of research paper
	Experimenting		Illustration/diagrams to accompany poetry/research project/short stories	
	Dissection		Marine animal world/ picture art	
	Research		Cross section of shoreline and ocean	
	Database entries		True coloration of student-selected Hawaiian reef fish	
	Fieldwork			

Source: From E. A. Polloway, J. R. Patton, and L. Serna, 2008, *Strategies for Teaching Learners with Special Needs* (9th ed., p. 325). Upper Saddle River, NJ: Merrill/Pearson. Used with permission.

for grades 4 through 10. The experiments and demonstrations are organized around four areas:

1. Basic principles when conducting scientific experiments, such as objectivity and reliability
2. How thinking influences behavior
3. How other individuals influence behavior
4. How human interactions affect behavior

SUMMARY

This chapter focuses on teaching math and science to students with disabilities included in general math and science classes. As a result of the No Child Left Behind legislation and IDEA, most students with disabilities spend the majority of their school days in general education classes. At this secondary level, this includes science and math classes. As a result of these legislative acts, students with disabilities are now held accountable to the same standards in math and science as students without disabilities. This means it is imperative that general education teachers and special education teachers work together to ensure that all students achieve at proficient levels. When teaching students with disabilities in math, teachers should attend to the national standards established by the National Council of Teachers of Mathematics (NCTM). All students, including those with disabilities, should be exposed to five components of math instruction, including number and operations, measurement, data analysis and probability, geometry, and algebra. When teaching students with disabilities in math classes, some of the strategies that have been shown effective include cognitive-based instruction, coteaching anchored instruction, and peer-assisted instruction. Using games and math accommodations has also been effective.

Similar to math, science also presents unique challenges to students with disabilities included in science content courses. While the traditional textbook approach is still used in many science classrooms, using a hands-on approach is likely more beneficial to many students, including many with disabilities. Some of the same strategies useful when teaching math are effective in science classrooms. These include peer-assisted learning and coteaching. Differentiated instruction, an excellent approach for teachers to use in all classes because of the increasing diversity of the student population, is an important tool for teachers working with students with disabilities. Finally, math and science instruction can and should be linked during instructional activities. When using problem-solving and other strategies, teachers can enhance learning opportunities by integrating math and science instruction.

ACTIVITIES

1. Describe the No Child Left Behind Act and interview several school principals to determine their views on the impact of this law on children with disabilities and special education. Make sure you discuss the impact of requiring all students to pass certain tests as part of the school making annual yearly progress.

2. Review the educational standards prescribed by the National Council of Teachers of Mathematics for secondary students. What impact do these standards have on students with disabilities in secondary classes, and is this impact good or bad, and why?

3. Interview teachers who coteach a content subject area. Find out from these teachers their views on coteaching. What are good things and what are bad things that result from coteaching? Finally, have these teachers describe the personal characteristics they view as beneficial for coteachers to be successful.

REFERENCES

Bottge, B. A., Heinrichs, M., Chan, S., & Serline, R. C. (2001). Anchoring adolescents' understanding of math concepts in rich problem-solving environments. *Remedial and Special Education, 22*, 299–314.

Bottge, B. A., Rueda, E., Serlin, R. C., Hung, Y., & Kwon, J. M. (2007). Shrinking achievement differences with anchored math problems: Challenges and possibilities. *Journal of Special Education, 41*, 31–49.

Browder, D. M., Spooner, F., Ahlgrim-Delzell, L., Harris, A. A., & Wakeman, S. (2008). A meta-analysis on teaching mathematics to students with significant cognitive disabilities. *Exceptional Children, 74*, 407–432.

Browder, D. M., Wakeman, S. Y., Flowers, C., Rickelman, R. J., Pugalee, D., & Karvonen, M. (2007). Creating access to the general curriculum with links to grade-level content for students with significant cognitive disabilities: An explication of the concept. *Journal of Special Education, 41*, 2–16.

Bryan, T., & Warger, C. L. (1998). Teaching science as social science: A curriculum focus for adolescents with mild disabilities. *Focus on Exceptional Children, 30*, 1–14.

Calhoon, M. B. (2008). Curriculum-based measurement for mathematics at the high school level. *Assessment for Effective Intervention, 33*, 234–239.

Calhoon, M. B., & Fuchs, L. S. (2003). The effects of peer-assisted learning strategies and curriculum-based measurement on the mathematics performance of secondary students with disabilities. *Remedial and Special Education, 24*, 235–245.

Calhoon, M. B., Emerson, R. W., Flores, M., & Houchins, D. E. (2007). Computational fluency performance profile of high school students with mathematics disabilities. *Remedial and Special Education, 28*, 292–303.

Cawley, J. F., & Foley, T. E. (2002). Connecting math and science for all students. *Teaching Exceptional Children, 34*, 14–19.

Cawley, J. F., Foley, T. E., & Miller, J. (2003). Science and students with mild disabilities: Principles of universal design. *Intervention in School and Clinic, 38*, 160–171.

Cawley, J. F., Parmar, R., Foley, T. E., Salmon, S., & Roy, S. (2001). Arithmetic performance of students: Implications for standards and programming. *Exceptional Children, 67*, 311–328.

Christ, T. J., Scullin, S., Tolbize, A., & Jiban, C. L. (2008). Implications of recent research: Curriculum-based measurement of math computation. *Assessment for Effective Intervention, 33*, 198–205.

De La Paz, S., & MacArthur, C. (2003). Knowing the how and why of history: Expectations for secondary students with and without learning disabilities. *Learning Disability Quarterly, 26*, 142–156.

Elbaum, B. (2007). Effects of an oral testing accommodation on the mathematics performance of secondary students with and without learning disabilities. *Journal of Special Education, 40*, 218–229.

Fuchs, L. S., Hamlett, C. L., & Fuchs, D. (1990). Monitoring basic skills progress: Basic math (Computer software). Austin, TX: Pro-Ed.

Furner, J. M., Yahya, N., & Duffy, M. L. (2005). Teach mathematics: Strategies to reach all students. *Intervention in School and Clinic, 41*, 16–23.

Garnett, K. (1992). Developing fluency with basic number facts: Intervention for students with learning disabilities. *Learning Disabilities Research & Practice, 7*, 210–216.

Gartin, B., Murdick, N., Imbeau, M., & Perner, D. (2002). Differentiated instruction. Reston, VA: Division on Autism and Developmental Disabilities, Council for Exceptional Children.

Grumbine, R., & Alden, P. B. (2006). Teaching science to students with learning disabilities. *The Science Teacher*, 26–31.

Guerra, N. S. (2009). LIBRE stick figure tool: A graphic organizer to foster self-regulated social cognitive problem solving. *Intervention in School and Clinic, 44*, 229–233.

Hallahan, D. P., Lloyd, J. W., Kauffman, J. M., Weiss, M. P., & Martinez, E. A. (2005). *Learning disabilities: Foundations, characteristics, and effective teaching*. (3rd ed.). Boston: Allyn & Bacon.

Jackson, F. B. (2002). Crossing content: A strategy for students with learning disabilities. *Intervention in School and Clinic, 37*, 279–282.

Johnson, C. C., Kahle, J. B., & Fargo, J. D. (2006). Effective teaching results in increased science achievement for all students. *Science Education, 91*, 371–382.

Kirch, S. A., Bargerhuff, M. E., Cowan, H., & Wheatly, M. (2007). Reflections of educators in pursuit of inclusive science classrooms. *Journal of Science Teacher Education, 18*, 663–692.

Kortering, L. J., deBettencourt, L. U., & Braziel, P. M. (2005). Improving performance in high school algebra: What students with learning disabilities are saying. *Learning Disability Quarterly, 28*, 191–203.

Kroeger, S. D., & Kouche, B. (2006). Using peer-assisted learning strategies to increase response to intervention in inclusive middle math settings. *Teaching Exceptional Children, 38*, 6–13.

Kurtts, S. A., Matthews, C. E., & Smallwood, T. (2009). (Dis)solving the differences: A physical science lesson using universal design. *Intervention in School and Clinic, 44*, 151–159.

Lenz, B. K., & Deshler, D. D. (2004). Teaching content to all. Boston: Allyn & Bacon.

Maccini, P., & Gagnon, J. C. (2002). Perceptions and application of NCTM standards by special and general education teachers. *Exceptional Children, 68*, 325–344.

Maccini, P., & Gagnon, J. C. (2006). Mathematics instructional practices and assessment accommodations by secondary special and general educators. *Exceptional Children, 72*, 217–234.

Mastropieri, M. A., Scruggs, T. E., Norland, J. J., Berkeley, S., McDuffie, K., Tornquist, E. H., & Connors, N. (2006). Differentiated curriculum enhancement in inclusive middle school science: Effects on classroom and high-stakes tests. *Journal of Special Education, 40*, 130–137.

Magiera, K., Smith, C., Zigmond, N., & Gebauer, K. (2005). Benefits of co-teaching in secondary mathematics classes. *Teaching Exceptional Children, 37*, 20–24.

McCarthy, C. B. (2005). Effects of thematic-based, hands-on science teaching versus a textbook approach for students with disabilities. *Journal of Research in Science Teaching, 42*, 245–263.

Mercer, C. D., & Pullen, P. C. (2009). *Students with learning disabilities* (7th ed.). Upper Saddle River, NJ: Merrill/Pearson.

Montague, M. (1992). The effects of cognitive and metacognitive strategy instruction on the mathematical problem solving of middle school students with learning disabilities. *Journal of Learning Disabilities, 25*, 230–248.

Montague, M., & Dietz, S. (2009). Evaluating the evidence base for cognitive strategy instruction and mathematical problem solving. *Exceptional Children, 75*, 285–302.

National Center for Educational Statistics (2008). Digest of Educational Statistics. Washington, DC: Author.

National Center on Secondary Education and Transition Capacity Building Institute. (2002). Retrieved March 7,

2009, from http://www.ncset.hawaii.edu/Institutes/Pdfs/proceedings _ july_2001.pdf.

National Council of Teachers of Mathematics. (2009). About NCTM. www.nctm.org. retrieved 9/28/10

Nelson, J. R., Benner, G. J., Lane, K., & Smith, B. W. (2004). Academic achievement of K–12 students with emotional and behavior disorders. *Exceptional Children, 71*, 59–73.

Polloway, E. A., Patton, J. R., & Serna, L. (2008). *Strategies for teaching learners with special needs* (9th ed.). Upper Saddle River, NJ: Merrill/Pearson.

Rice, N., Drame, E., Owens, L., & Frattura, E. M. (2007). Co-instructing at the secondary level: Strategies for success. *Teaching Exceptional Children, 39*, 12–18.

Shaftel, J., Pass, L., & Schnabel, S. (2005). Math games for adolescents. *Teaching Exceptional Children, 37*, 25–30.

Sileo, J. M., & van Garderen, D. (2007). Creating optimal opportunities to learn mathematics. *Teaching Exceptional Children, 39*, 14–18.

Smith, T. E. C., Polloway, E. A., Patton, J. R., & Dowdy, C. A. (2008). *Teaching students with special needs in inclusive settings*. Boston: Allyn & Bacon.

Steele, M. M. (2008). Helping students with learning disabilities succeed. *The Science Teacher, 75*, 38–42.

Stodden, R. A., Galloway, L. M., & Stodden, N. J. (2003). Secondary school curricula issues: Impact on postsecondary students with disabilities. *Exceptional Children, 70*, 9–25.

Strichart, S. S., & Mangrum, C. T. (2010). *Study skills for learning disabled and struggling students, grades 6–12*. Upper Saddle River, NJ: Merrill/Pearson.

Tomlinson, C. A. (2002). Invitations to learn. *Educational Leadership, 60*, 6–11.

Van Garderen, D. (2007). Teaching students with LD to use diagrams to solve mathematical word problems. *Journal of Learning Disabilities, 40*, 540–553.

Vaughn, S., & Bos, C. S. (2009). Teaching students with learning and behavior problems (7th ed.). Upper Saddle River, NJ: Pearson.

Walsh, J. M., & Jones, B. (2004). New models of cooperative teaching. *Teaching Exceptional Children, 36*, 14–20.

Walther-Thomas, C., Korinek, L., McLaughlin, V. L., & Williams, B. T. (2000). Collaboration for inclusive education. Boston: Allyn & Bacon.

Watanabe, M., Nunes, N., Mebane, S., Scalise, K., & Claesgens, J. (2007). "Chemistry for all, instead of chemistry just for the elite": Lessons learned from detracked chemistry classrooms. *Science Education, 91*, 683–709.

Watson, S. M. R., & Houtz, L. E. (2002). Teaching science: Meeting the academic needs of culturally and linguistically diverse students. *Intervention in School and Clinic, 37*, 267–278.

Witzel, B. S., Riccomini, P. J., & Schneider, E. (2008). Implementing CRA with secondary students with learning disabilities in mathematics. *Intervention in School and Clinic, 43*, 270–276.

Witzel, B. S., Smith, S. W., & Brownell, M. T. (2001). How can I help students with learning disabilities in algebra? *Intervention in School and Clinic, 37*, 101–104.

Woolfolk, A. (2004). *Educational Psychology* (8th ed). Upper Saddle River, NJ: Pearson.

12

Strategies for Teaching Social Skills to Adolescents with Disabilities

Study Questions

1. Define *social skills*.

2. Why are social skills so important for students in educational settings?

3. Why are social skills even more important for students with disabilities?

4. What are some ways that social skills can be taught?

5. How are social skills impacted by culture?

6. What are the various levels of social skills instruction?

INTRODUCTION

Humans are social beings. We interact with each other during school, work, and leisure time activities. Often, we simply go to *social* functions, which could be described as events where individuals get together to talk and interact. Indeed, social skills, skills required to be successful in these situations, play a critical role in our society. They are necessary for success in many settings, including family, school, employment, and community. It has often been said that individuals with good social skills can be very successful, even if they lack other skills. Similarly, individuals who do not possess good social skills often find themselves at a distinct disadvantage in many endeavors.

School is a very social place. Students interact regularly with each other and teachers. Students form cliques, friendships, and learn how to get along with others. This is important at all levels, but even more so in secondary schools. Social skills are also important in many job settings. Individuals who choose not to interact with other workers, or who do not have skills to successfully interact with others, are often at a disadvantage for promotions, raises, and other employment benefits. Social skills also play a role in how individuals live in their communities. Neighborhood, church, and recreation areas are a few examples of where social skills are important. In all endeavors of our society, individuals with good social skills have an advantage, whereas those with poor social skills are at a distinct disadvantage.

The development of social skills begins in the early months of a child's life. Infants learn to interact and react to others in their environments. Erikson developed a stage theory of personal and social development. In his theory, children move through various social developmental levels, beginning with stage one, which he classifies as trust versus mistrust. This stage, typically between birth and age 1 year, emphasizes the development of trust with others. When babies cry, they are often picked up and fed. This helps them develop a sense of trust with those in their environments; this is a time when babies actually begin interacting with other individuals. Erikson's stages move through different age levels until stage five, which is between the ages of 12 and 18 years. During this final stage of social development, individuals turn more away from parents toward peer groups for their identity (Slavin, 2009).

Table 12.1 summarizes Erikson's stages of development.

Social skills are not one skill, but a myriad of different skills. They include knowing how to act and interact with other individuals; how to get along with others; how to make and

TABLE 12.1 ● Erikson's Stages of Development

Stage 1 Infancy	Birth to 1 day	Trust versus mistrust
Stage 2 Early childhood	1 day to 3 years	Autonomy versus shame/doubt
Stage 3 Play age	3–5 years	Initiative versus guilt
Stage 4 School age	5–12 years	Industry versus inferiority
Stage 5 Adolescence	12–18 years	Identity and repudiation versus identity confusion
Stage 6 Young adult	18–25 years	Intimacy and solidarity versus isolation
Stage 7 Adulthood	25–65 years	Generativity versus stagnation
Stage 8 Maturity	65+ years	Integrity versus despair

Source: From E. Erickson, 1963, *Childhood and Society* (2nd ed.). New York: W. W. Norton & Company.

maintain friendships; what and when to say certain things; what not to say in certain situations; and how to act in certain situations. We all know people who are very social. In fact, sometimes we identify individuals using descriptors related to their social skills. We may say that an individual is very social, or is not very social. When individuals are described using these phrases, their social skill levels are usually understood by others.

IMPORTANCE OF SOCIAL SKILLS

To say that social skills are important in our society is an understatement. "Common social interaction, appropriate language, and development of a variety of interests are fundamental skills critical for life success" (Welton, Vakil, & Carasea, 2004, p. 40). In fact, it may be very difficult for individuals to be successful without these skills. This is especially true in secondary schools. A big part of social skills includes friendships and getting along with others. Friendship is something that we need; it is something most of us strive to establish and maintain (Boutot, 2007). While we may say we don't care if we have friends, most of us desperately seek friendships. For most individuals, the importance of friends and social groups grows as they get older. During lower elementary grades, friendships often are same-sex and in the same age range. However, as children get older their friendships and social groups grow to include a wider range of ages and both males and females (Slavin, 2009). At the secondary level, social activities and involvement are often the predominant theme among high school students.

Friendship, which is a "natural and essential part of human existence . . . involves a series of complicated social interactions" (Morris, 2002, p. 67). It is not always easy to establish and maintain friendships. To look at the importance of friendships, one only has to look at children as they grow up and mature. For the most part, children prefer to be around other children who are similar to them in the way they dress, talk, and act. They also prefer to be with students who are successful and who are liked by the teacher (Boutot, 2007). Because students with disabilities are frequently not successful in school, the result may be that nondisabled students may not want to be their friends even though they are accepted in the classroom and liked by their teachers.

In school settings, social skills are very important. In fact, "[s]chool success may be minimal for students who have difficulties building social relationships and ultimately fail at developing social competence" (Smith & Gilles, 2003, p. 30). This is even more critical at the secondary level. While schools are typically thought of as institutions where academic skills are necessary for success, and where academic skills are learned, in addition to academics, schools are also places where social skills are very necessary, and where many social skills are learned (Morris, 2002). One concern when dealing with students with disabilities is that teachers and other professionals focus on determining a student's academic strengths and weaknesses, and often overlook the entire composite of the child, a feature that definitely includes social skills (Welton et al., 2004). With social skills being so important in the success of individuals, this can be a major oversight.

While social skills are important for all children, they take on a more important role as children move into adolescence. This is a period that is a very social time. Think about your own high school experiences. It is likely that social involvement was one of the most important parts of your school experiences. Research has shown that popular students typically have good social skills, whereas unpopular students often have poor social skills (Boutot, 2007). School clubs, athletic events, dances, parties, and daily interacting with other students are examples of the important social activities of students in secondary schools.

SOCIAL SKILLS AND INDIVIDUALS WITH DISABILITIES

Social skills are critically important for student success, and most students develop social skills as a natural part of the maturation process. Unfortunately, many students with disabilities have deficits in this area. In fact, "historically, social competence has been a fundamental criterion used to define and classify students with high-incidence disabilities" (Gresham, Sugai, & Horner, 2001, p. 332). By virtue of their disability, many of these students display social skills deficits. Hallahan, Lloyd, Kauffman, Weiss, and Martinez (2005) noted that whereas some individuals with learning disabilities display good social skills, some students with this disability display very poor social skills. Nowicki (2003) conducted a meta-analysis of studies related to social skills and students with learning disabilities. Findings indicated that "children with learning disabilities and children designated as low in academic achievement are at a greater risk for social difficulties than are average- to high-achieving children and children with learning disabilities and their low-achieving classmates do not appear to have accurate self-perceptions of social acceptance" (p. 171). In another study focusing on students with learning disabilities, Estell and colleagues (2008) found that this group of students are lower in best friend nominations, are less popular, and have lower social status than their nondisabled peers. The conclusion from the study was "students with LD lack the social skills and abilities to achieve average levels of social acceptance among students without LD" (p. 11). Other studies of social skills and individuals with learning disabilities indicate that 33% of students with learning disabilities (Morris, 2002) and up to 75% of students with learning disabilities (Kavale & Forness, 1996) demonstrate social skills problems. Since learning disabilities account for more than 50% of all students in special education programs, the deficits in social skills for this group means that it is a major problem for special education.

In addition to students with learning disabilities exhibiting deficits in social skills, students with other disabilities also display these problems. For example, by definition, individuals with autism display deficits in social skills (Morris, 2002; Welton et al., 2004). Also, students with mental retardation (Taylor, Richards, & Brady, 2005), visual and hearing impairments, emotional problems, and health and physical impairments (Hardman, Drew, & Egan, 2008) exhibit deficits in social skills.

There are several reasons why students with disabilities often have difficulties with social skills. Some of these include limited opportunities to model appropriate social skills, limited cognitive abilities, limited attention to environment, high levels of distractibility, and emotional issues related to disabilities. In speaking about children with cerebral palsy, Best and Bigge (2005) noted that one of the reasons why some of these students display social skills deficits is they are often isolated from other students to avoid their being ridiculed or made fun of and that this often results in deficits because they have not had the opportunity to interact like nondisabled students. This could also be a factor in students with other disabilities having similar problems.

One factor associated with social skills is acceptance. Many students with disabilities often have a difficult time being accepted. Boutot (2007) lists several factors associated with being accepted compared to those associated with nonacceptance. For example, students who are perceived as being part of the class are much more acceptable than students who are frequently not in the class, for whatever reason. Since students with disabilities are often pulled from the class for special interventions, or possibly due to repeated behavioral issues, not being part of the class for part of each day could be a factor in their level of acceptance. Table 12.2 describes other factors that could be related to acceptability.

TABLE 12.2 ● Factors Associated with Acceptance versus Non-Acceptance of Students with Disabilities

Acceptance	Non-Acceptance
Perceived as being part of the class	Frequent removal from classroom
Peer tutors and/or independence	Presence of a one-on-one adult assistant
Limited self-abuse, aggression, or loud behaviors	Extreme or disruptive behaviors
Overall classroom culture of acceptance and tolerance	Negative attitude or treatment by teacher
Knowledge of the disability or differences as well as similarities	Lack of understanding of disability or differences
Specific training	Unusual or "scary" equipment or behaviors

Source: From "Fitting In: Tips for Promoting Acceptance and Friendships for Students with Autism Spectrum Disorders in Inclusive Classrooms," by E. A. Boutot, 2007, *Intervention in School and Clinic, 42,* p. 157. Used with permission.

Social Skills Deficits

Along with the myriad social skills are several different types of social skills deficits. Sargent (1998) described the following types of deficits in social skills (p. 13):

1. Skill deficits occur when the students simply do not have the skills in their behavioral repertoire.
2. Inadequate skill performance deficits occur when students perform social skills, but leave out some critical component.
3. Performance deficits mean that the students possess the skills but simply do not use them with sufficient frequency.
4. Self-control deficits occur in two types. First, there are obtrusive behaviors that interfere with other students or the conduct of a teacher's lesson. There are also excessive behaviors that may subject a youngster to social ridicule.

Students with disabilities may exhibit any of these types of deficits. An obvious key in teaching social skills, therefore, is to determine what type of deficit is present.

Importance of Social Skills for Students with Disabilities

The level of social competence of individuals is important to their success. This can be even more critical for individuals with disabilities than for individuals without disabilities, because individuals tend to focus on a person's negative characteristics more than the positive. For the most part, disabilities are viewed negatively, and it is often difficult for individuals with disabilities to get others to focus on their "positive" abilities rather than their disabilities. The practice of using person-first language is an attempt to have individuals with disabilities viewed first as individuals. The disabilities experienced by these individuals are simply characteristics that must be addressed, not the defining factors of who they are as individuals.

The more socially competent an individual, the better chance that individual has for success. Marc Gold, a leading proponent of services for individuals with severe disabilities in the 1970s, spoke of a competence-deviance hypothesis. In this hypothesis, it is posited that the more competent an individual is, the more deviance society will accept in that individual. It was Gold's perspective that as a result of having disabilities, individuals must be very competent to overcome the perceived deviance presented by the disability. Unfortunately, as pointed out, students with disabilities frequently lack adequate social skills. The fact that they are already hampered by particular manifestations of the disability (e.g., academic deficiencies, motor problems, cognitive issues) makes it crucial that these individuals possess strong social skills. While incredibly bright, successful students might be able to get by with minimal social skills, individuals with disabilities and academic challenges need to display good social skills to help overcome other deficits.

Social skills are just as critical for success for adults as they are for adolescents. Being successful in postsecondary educational settings, employment settings, and community living are all somewhat dependent on social skills. For example, social skills are important for success in many work settings. Gold's competence-deviance hypothesis applies to adults in employment settings just like it applies to students. Employers are much more likely to tolerate good workers with poor social skills than bad workers with poor social skills. Likewise, in social settings, individuals with disabilities are much more likely to be part of a social group with friendships if they have good social skills than if they display poor social skills. Adults with disabilities, similar to adolescents with disabilities, often display deficits in social skills. As a result, goals related to social skills should be part of many students' transition plans to help prepare them for postsecondary settings.

SOCIAL SKILLS INSTRUCTION

Providing academic supports and instruction for students with disabilities is the core of special education, and indeed, is the focus of secondary education for all students. Even when the social competence of students with disabilities is a consideration, too often it is assumed that merely placing students with disabilities in inclusive settings is sufficient for them to develop good social skills (Coster & Haltiwanger, 2004). After all, one of the primary reasons to include students with disabilities in general education settings is to enhance their social skills (Smith, Polloway, Patton, & Dowdy, 2012). Merely placing students in inclusive settings, however, is not sufficient to help them develop adequate social skills. In fact, placing students with disabilities in inclusive settings without appropriate social supports and interventions can result in even more social isolation. Therefore, proactive interventions must be implemented to assist students with disabilities to develop their social skills.

While many students without disabilities, and some with disabilities, develop adequate social skills as they grow and mature, many students, especially those with disabilities, need direct interventions and supports in order to develop these skills. For this group of students, social skills instruction and supports are often necessary. Unfortunately, many teachers and IEP team members do not see the need to overtly support and teach these skills. It is often assumed that merely giving students with disabilities the opportunity to interact with other students and observe good social skills will result in their social skill development. As previously noted, this is not the case; students with these deficits must frequently be given an opportunity to develop or be taught social skills in order for them to achieve an adequate level of social competence.

There is no single method for supporting or teaching these skills, but myriad strategies and techniques. Specific methods used will depend on several variables, including the student's age, cognitive ability, ability to communicate, and opportunities for practice (Sargent, 1998; Vaughn et al., 2003). In addition, the student's cultural background and unique characteristics are critical in determining the appropriate intervention strategies to use. The most important thing to remember is that all students are capable of learning social skills; it is up to educators to determine what skills are needed and how to teach those needed skills (Chadsey & Gun Han, 2005).

Assessment of Social Skills

Several studies have revealed the importance of linking social skills instruction to the student's current social skills abilities. Just as assessment is necessary to determine appropriate academic interventions for students with learning deficits, assessment of social skills is also critical. Teachers would never develop an IEP without assessment information on the nature of the student's academic problems. Similarly, social skills interventions should not be implemented without having an understanding of the student's current abilities in this area. Social skills assessment enables teachers to determine the current level of social skills and how best to support and teach needed social skills. It is inefficient to teach skills that may not be needed, or to use a strategy that will likely have limited effect on the student's skills.

There are many different ways to assess social skills. Church, Gottschalk, and Leddy (2003) suggested the use of observations, interviews, rating scales, and checklists. No one method is best; educators should maximize the use of all forms of assessment information to determine the most accurate picture of the level of social skills possessed by students. In order to gather appropriate assessment information, some specific observation tools need to be developed (Murdock, Cost, & Tieso, 2007). Casual observations, while useful, are insufficient to obtain comprehensive information on students' social skill levels. This form of observation will be described below.

Social skills are frequently assessed using some form of a behavior rating scale. These scales usually consist of written questionnaires that include a list of behaviors that are rated by the individual completing the assessment. Frequently Likert scales are used to measure the presence and strength of a particular behavior. These scales are usually in a checklist format and can be completed in about 20 minutes (Venn, 2007). Some behavior scales that are frequently used to measure various behaviors, including social skills, are described in Table 12.3.

Taylor (2008) described the social skills rating system (SSRS), developed by Gresham and Elliott (1990). This assessment system is norm-referenced, for grades 3 to 6 and 7 to 12, and uses multiraters to determine behaviors that could impact teacher–student relations, peer acceptance, and academic performance. "According to the authors, the SSRS can be used for a variety of purposes, including (1) identifying students at risk for social behavior problems, (2) differentiating mildly handicapped students from non-handicapped students, (3) categorizing behavior difficulties, (4) selecting behaviors for school and home interventions, and (5) guiding the selection of intervention strategies" (p. 412). Since there are three forms of the SSRS—teacher, parent, and student—Venn (2007) noted that this rating system can provide a comprehensive assessment of an individual's social skills across school, home, and community settings.

Probably the best way to assess social skills is through teacher observations. Teachers, more than any other professionals, spend more time with students with disabilities and can observe them in natural environments (e.g., in classrooms, during extracurricular activities, in the lunchroom). These observations can be informal or formal. Venn (2007) noted that informal observations consist of casual, unsystematic observations, after which the teacher typically makes notes of the behaviors observed. In addition to the specific observations, teachers may also include subjective judgments of the behaviors in their assessment. Although very useful information can be collected using informal observations, the following potential pitfalls to this form of data collection may result:

- Biased observer
- Inaccurate recollections
- Inaccurate subjective judgments
- Missed important behaviors

TABLE 12.3 ● Behavior Rating Scales

ADJUSTMENT SCALES FOR CHILDREN AND ADOLESCENTS (MCDERMOTT, 1993)

Norm-referenced, 1,400 children, ages 5–17

20 minutes to administer

97 problem behavior pinpoints and 26 positive behavior indicators

BEHAVIOR ASSESSMENT SYSTEM FOR CHILDREN, 2ND EDITION (REYNOLDS & KAMPHAUS, 2004)

Norm-referenced, 2–21 years

Measures behaviors, thoughts, and emotions

Uses teacher rating scale, parent rating scale, self-report scale

BEHAVIOR AND EMOTIONAL RATING SCALE, 2ND EDITION (EPSTEIN, 2004)

Norm-referenced, ages 5–18

Uses child, parent, and teacher rating scales

Good as a prereferral rating scale

BEHAVIOR RATING PROFILE–2 (BROWN & HAMMILL, 1990)

Norm-referenced, ages 6–18

Student, parent, and teacher completed scales

Sociogram completed by students' classmates measures social acceptance

CHILD BEHAVIOR CHECKLIST FOR AGES 6–18 (ACHENBACH, 2001)

Norm-referenced, ages 6–18

Uses parents' reports on child's activities; includes teacher and self-report

COMPREHENSIVE BEHAVIOR RATING SCALE FOR CHILDREN (NEEPER, LEHEY, & FRICK, 1990)

Norm-referenced, ages 6–14

10–15 minutes to complete; 70-item scale

DRAW A PERSON: SCREENING PROCEDURE FOR EMOTIONAL DISTURBANCE (NAGLIERI, MCNEISH, & ACHILLES, 1991)

Norm-referenced screening, ages 6–17

Helps identify children and adolescents with potential emotional problems

Source: From J. J. Venn, 2007, *Assessing Students with Special Needs* (4th ed.). Upper Saddle River, NJ: Merrill/Pearson.

While these pitfalls can lead to inaccurate information, informal observations can still provide useful information. One outcome of informal observations is a recognized need for more formal observational efforts.

Formal observations are better than informal observations because the observer sets out to observe specific behaviors in controlled situations. The process used for formal observations includes (Venn, 2007, p. 285):

- Identifying an observable target behavior
- Selecting a procedure for measuring the target behavior, including setting up a data collection system

- Observing the target behavior and collecting data
- Recording the results on a graph
- Interpreting and applying the results

By structuring the observations, it is more likely that valid, useful information will be collected on a particular skill. This is an excellent means for assessing social skills of students in a classroom or other setting.

Another way to assess social skills is through a functional behavior assessment. Since inappropriate social skills are typically manifested through inappropriate behaviors, determining the function of the behavior may assist in determining social skills deficits. A functional behavior assessment is a means of determining what may be causing and reinforcing a particular behavior and is an excellent way of determining what targeted interventions may be helpful for a particular student. A more thorough discussion of this form of assessment will be included in a later section.

Regardless of which assessment system is used to determine social skills, it is important for school personnel to have a general understanding of students' levels of social skills prior to developing and implementing social skills interventions. Sargent (1998, p. 7) suggested that any assessment of social skills answer the following questions:

1. Is the skill deficient or inadequate?
2. Does the student have the cognitive ability to learn the skill?
3. Will the student have an opportunity to practice the skill?
4. Does changing the student's behavior have importance to significant others in the student's life?
5. Is the skill needed in current or future environments?
6. Is acquisition of the skill essential to remain in the current environment?

These questions relate to the different types of social skills deficits and are necessary to obtain information useful for intervention purposes.

Social Skills and Culture

When determining the level of social skills and making decisions about interventions, educators must remember the cultural nature of social skills (Church et al., 2003). Just like different social skills are expected at different age levels, different skills are also expected with different cultures. Trying to apply socials skills and expectations of the majority culture on students from other cultures without taking into consideration the expectations of those cultures is highly inappropriate.

One prime example of cultural differences and social skills is eye contact. In the majority culture, making eye contact with individuals while speaking is considered appropriate. However, in some cultures, such eye contact is viewed as disrespectful; looking away is considered the appropriate behavior. There are many differences among cultures. Educators must recognize those differences and incorporate cultural and linguistic diversity in their daily educational activities. "Modifying instruction to accommodate culturally and linguistically diverse students is crucial for their academic success" (Sparks, 2008, p. 138). It is also critical for their social success.

There are certain components that should be present to ensure that social skills instruction is culturally relevant. These include (Cartledge & Kourea, 2008):

1. Social skills instruction should reflect the lifestyle and experiences of the culturally diverse student.
2. Social skills instruction should include heterogeneous groups with socially competent representatives from socially diverse cultures.
3. Social skills instruction should incorporate the language of culturally diverse learners.

STRATEGIES TO TEACH SOCIAL SKILLS

Schools are an ideal place to teach social skills. Throughout the school day there are numerous opportunities for students to interact with each other and with their teachers in a variety of settings and activities, and also many opportunities for modeling and direct instruction in social skills. However, there are also barriers to social skills instruction. These include a lack of time, resources, and training (Bellini, Peters, Benner, & Hope, 2007). Often, teachers may lack knowledge of the importance of social skills. Many think that merely placing students in inclusive settings will result in adequate social skills development. Also, teachers may simply not know how to teach social skills. Teacher preparation programs are packed with helping prospective teachers know how to teach literacy, math, and content subjects; however, many of these programs contain little if any information on how to teach social skills. With the current emphasis on literacy and other academic areas, schools may also simply ignore the need to teach these skills or do not have the time to include this focus during the school day.

Regardless of the barriers, schools must take a proactive role in social skills development. These skills are simply too important for schools to ignore. There are many ways to increase the level of socials skills in individuals with disabilities. Meadan and Monda-Amaya (2008) suggested a three-level system to promote the development of social skills:

Level I—Structuring a classroom community
Level II—Specific strategies and curriculum for promoting social competence
Level III—Targeted individual interventions

In this system, the first level is the least intrusive and most natural, and the third level is the most intrusive. The goal is to increase social interactions and social skills as much as possible with the least intrusive means. For most students, the first level is sufficient to support the development of social skills. Table 12.4 summarizes each of the levels of intervention described. These levels will be used to organize various interventions to enhance social skills.

Level I—Structuring a Classroom Community

The first level, structuring a classroom community, is the simplest, most natural way to facilitate the development of social skills. At this level, teachers merely create a positive environment where all students, including those with disabilities, have an opportunity for social interactions. In this environment, all students feel like they belong in the classroom and that their involvement is important. Smith and others (2012) described inclusion as students with disabilities *belonging* with their chronological-age peers. They indicate that "students with special needs are truly included in their classroom communities only when they are appreciated by their teachers and socially accepted by their classmates" (p. 41). This is critical at all educational levels, but with the increased importance of social skills for adolescents, it is even more critical in secondary schools.

In order for all students, including those with disabilities, to feel a part of the classroom community, teachers must establish a climate for interactions among students. Indeed, they set the tone for positive collaboration and interactions (Meadan & Monda-Amaya, 2008). Creating such a classroom that is accepting of all students uses noninstructional strategies that can improve social skills through natural social interactions, similar to those that nondisabled students have with other students (Hughes, Carter, Hughes, Bradford, & Copeland, 2002). Teachers are critical in the creation of this environment; without their support it is highly unlikely that such an accepting environment can be present. An open, accepting classroom environment where all students are valued goes a long way in providing social supports for students with disabilities.

TABLE 12.4 ● Levels of Social Support System

Structure	Activities
Level I: Structuring a Classroom Community	
Creating an accepting classroom environment	• Establish clear and positive classroom rules and expectations • Promote disability awareness and acceptance • Create culturally responsive classrooms • Welcome collaborating partners (i.e., family members, support staff, paraprofessionals)
Creating a "place/voice" for each student in the classroom	• Set up classroom jobs and responsibilities • Promote individual talents and interests • Promote classroom membership and belonging
Creating opportunities for social interaction	• Structure in-class activities (e.g., centers, flexible grouping) • Use cooperative learning and peer tutoring • Structure out-of-class interactions (e.g., groups, games, recess) • Encourage collaboration (e.g., group/pairs projects)
Level II: Specific Strategies and Curriculum for Promoting Social Competence	
Using strategies for teaching social skills in large or small group contexts (role-playing, games, and vignettes)	• Teach problem-solving skills • Teach effective communication and group interaction • Teach conflict-resolution skills • Provide character education • Use strategies to deal with frustration, anger, and other emotions (children's books and social stories)
Using social skills or character education curricula	• Use published or teacher-developed curricula
Level III: Targeted Individual Interventions	

Teaching specific social skills corresponding with student needs	• Conduct functional assessments
	• Develop targeted intervention to match student needs
	  • Acquisition deficit: teaching new skills that do not exist in the student's repertoire
	  • Competing behavior: teaching replacement behavior (socially acceptable behavior instead of problem behavior)
	  • Fluency deficit: providing practice and generalization of target behavior

Teaching students specific strategies for recognizing and enhancing their social support networks	• Help student establish support networks • Teach how to provide support to others
Teaching self-management strategies	• Teach strategies for self-monitoring, self-evaluating, self-reinforcement, self-instruction
Enhancing and promoting student's self-determination	• Enhance self-knowledge of student's strengths and abilities • Valuing oneself (acceptance, responsibilities) • Teach strategies to promote self-determination and self-advocacy

Source: From "Collaboration to Promote Social Competence for Students with Mild Disabilities in the General Classroom: A Structure for Providing Social Support," by H. Meadan and L. Monda-Amaya, 2008, *Intervention in School and Clinic, 43*, p. 162. Used with permission.

For this to happen, there must be a belief among teachers and students that a community that empowers students can exist. All members of the class need to understand the importance of building a classroom community. After this is accomplished, students need to understand the many commonalities, as well as the differences, they have with their classmates. This can be done in several ways. One suggestion is for students to develop an actual map of their class-room, noting where people and things are located in the classroom and describing each person and thing. Other suggestions include conducting classroom meetings, giving students choices, and using group contingency management systems that promote students working together for class goals (Obenchain & Abernathy, 2003).

The teacher in this type of classroom needs to share, or at least understand, the notion of social inclusion—that all students *belong* in the classroom. One way teachers can support indi-viduals with disabilities is to interact with them in the same way they interact with nondisabled students. This will likely influence how other students in the room interact with this group of students because students tend to model their teachers' actions and attitudes (Boutot, 2007).

Morris (2002) noted the following strategies teachers can implement in their classrooms to make a more positive environment:

- *Notice children.* Teachers should make an effort to mention every child's name regularly, but at a minimum daily.
- *Provide a forum.* Teachers should pose problems during group or circle time and facilitate a discussion about potential solutions.
- *Get personal.* Teachers can promote appropriate social skills by anticipating problems before they develop and discussing them with the group.
- *Jump-start social skills.* Group discussions help students develop social skills that they will be able to use independently in the future.
- *Provide positive reinforcement.* Students' display of good social skills must be positively reinforced.

The following describes some specific ways teachers can create and maintain an open classroom conducive for social interactions and learning.

Rules and Expectations.   One way for promoting a positive classroom environment is to have clear rules and expectations for all students. Students need to know what is expected of them. As part of a positive classroom environment, teachers need to establish clear and positive classroom rules and expectations. All students need to feel they are valued members of the class; this is easier to accomplish if teachers hold all students accountable to high expectations. When teachers communicate positive expectations to all students, including those with disabilities, and reinforce appropriate behaviors and actions, they maintain a positive classroom environment (Emmer, Evertson, & Worsham, 2003).

Physical Arrangement of the Classroom.   Something as simple as the way a classroom is arranged is important for promoting an open classroom. When determining the physical ar-rangement of the classroom, teachers should consider the amount of interaction they want for their students. For example, if social interaction among students is a goal for the class, then arranging desks in clusters may be desired. "In clusters, students can work together on activities, share materials, have small-group discussions, and help each other with assignments" (Weinstein, 2007, p. 35). This sort of arrangement is ideal for cooperative learning activities, whereas an arrangement with desks in rows may impede such activities. Rather than opting for a permanent arrangement, teachers may choose to arrange the layout of the classroom depend-ing on the activity and the degree of interactions desired.

Facilitate Friendships.   Social relationships and friendships are critical for all students, in-cluding those with disabilities. Since students tend to congregate and socialize with students who are similar to them, students with disabilities may be left out of these groups. Therefore, for students with disabilities to have social relationships and friendships with nondisabled peers, it is often necessary for school personnel and family members to facilitate the development of these relationships (Demchak, 2008). In the school setting, it is imperative that teachers play a significant role in promoting these relationships (Hughes et al., 2002). Boutot (2007) listed several strategies that can facilitate the development of friendships and acceptance: (1) selecting the classroom wisely; (2) scheduling wisely; (3) selecting supports wisely; (4) preparing the classroom teacher; (5) preparing the general education students; (6) preparing students with disabilities; and (7) securing and maintaining family support.

Model Positive Interactions. As noted, students often model the behaviors and attitudes of their teachers. Therefore, it is crucial that teachers and other professionals make it a point to display positive attitudes toward students with disabilities. "The manner in which an adult (e.g., a teacher or paraprofessional) interacts with a student with disabilities can subsequently influence how peers view and interact with that student" (Demchak, 2008, p. 296).

Therefore, the way teachers interact and speak with students with disabilities can go a long way in creating an open classroom (Demchak, 2008). In modeling verbal positive interactions, teachers need to realize that they should not answer for students with disabilities; this gives other students the impression that students with the disabilities cannot communicate their own thoughts and ideas. Teachers often want to help students by answering for them, whereas in reality, this could be doing them harm socially.

Facilitate Conversations. Being able to engage in a conversation is a critical component to social skills. Sometimes students with disabilities simply do not know how to initiate and engage in conversations. Teachers can enhance conversational skills by merely engaging in conversations with all students, including those with disabilities, as well as subtly encouraging these students to initiate conversations with other students (Demchak, 2008). Ways that teachers can encourage students with disabilities to initiate conversations include the following:

1. Ask the student with a disability to ask another student a particular question.
2. Have a student with a disability lead a cooperative learning group on a topic he or she is very familiar with.
3. Pair a student with a disability with a nondisabled student and have them share what they did over the weekend and then report to the group what their partner did.
4. Ask the student with a disability to go to another teacher's room and ask for a particular item.
5. Send the student with a disability to the office to ask the principal a question about the assembly and then come back and tell the class what was learned.

Use Games. In-class games can be very useful in promoting social interactions among students. They can provide a fun, relaxed activity for students that encourages interactions. Forgan and Gonzalez-DeHass (2004) described the use of Mancala, an African term that describes strategy games, and Sungka, a Malaysian game of riddles, that can easily be used to teach problem-solving and, indirectly, social skills. Other group games could be tied to academic activities, such as spelling bees and other games where students team up to deal with academic challenges. These games, and many others useful for this purpose, can be found on the Internet.

Implement Peer Strategies. One of the most important times for social skills to be used effectively is in unstructured settings with peers. While teachers and family members may not be present to support students during these times, it is possible for understanding peers to provide a great deal of support and appropriate modeling. Students often deal with students with disabilities the way their peers do. Therefore, having peer buddies, or peers who are positive toward students with disabilities, can go a long way in helping students be accepted by other students. Peer support groups, including groups that focus on academics and social skills, can be very effective in promoting both academic and social growth in inclusive settings (Welton et al., 2004).

Demchak (2008) noted that peer support programs can be used with any age group and can provide an opportunity for students with disabilities to interact with nondisabled peers in a variety of different activities. Implementing peer support programs goes an important step beyond simply placing students with disabilities in inclusive classrooms; it provides a structure for interaction between students with and without disabilities that would not likely occur naturally (Welton et al., 2004).

Peer support programs have been shown to be very effective in facilitating the social inclusion of students with disabilities. Copeland and colleagues (2004) studied seven high schools that used a peer support program to provide social and academic support and friendships to students. Participants were volunteers who received 0.5 elective credit for their participation. Using a focus group methodology, the authors found that the peer buddies:

1. Increased the interactions of students with disabilities with their nondisabled peers
2. Viewed themselves as role models for other nondisabled students regarding their interactions with students with disabilities
3. Increased their own knowledge and skills regarding facilitating social and academic success of students with disabilities
4. Increased their advocacy for students with disabilities
5. Noted participation in the program had positively changed their attitudes toward students with disabilities

In another study, Hughes and others (2001) found that high school students felt their involvement in the peer buddy program with students with severe disabilities had both helped them to better understand students with disabilities and helped the students with disabilities become more socially integrated in the school. The conclusion of the study was that peer buddy programs appear "to be effective as a service learning experience and a means for promoting social interaction and friendships among general education high school students" (p. 356).

Peer support systems can focus on academics or social activities. While both have been shown to be effective, Salend (2008) noted that noninstructional activities with peer buddies can actually lead to more quality social interactions than peer instructional activities. As a result, it is recommended that teachers arrange for numerous opportunities during the school day for such interactions. To ensure that the arrangement is successful, teachers should also meet with the peer partner occasionally.

Develop Friendship Circles.   Similar to peer support systems, friendship circles, also called circle of friends, circles of support, peer networks, and peer-supported committees, offer an excellent means of providing students with disabilities with positive peer supports (Demchak, 2008). These social organizations enable students to develop a better understanding of friendships and relationships (Salend, 2008). There are several different ways of developing friendship circles; however, regardless of how this approach is implemented, it has been shown to be an effective way of encouraging friendships and improving social skills. When using this approach, it is important for adults to facilitate the activities and provide ongoing support and follow-up to ensure long-term success (Demchak, 2008).

Service Learning.   Service learning can also be used to promote social skills. Kleinert and others (2004) described how four high schools used a service-learning project to facilitate social skills among students with and without disabilities. In the project, members of the Key

Clubs of the four high schools teamed with students with disabilities to plan and cook a dinner, and plan an evening of entertainment for a senior citizens group. The project resulted in very positive reactions from the students with disabilities as well as those without disabilities. The authors concluded that the service-learning project provided an opportunity for students to engage in sustained social interactions and develop cooperative group skills. The project, therefore, not only provided a service opportunity for students, but also a social skills development opportunity for students with disabilities.

Cooperative Learning. Cooperative learning provides an opportunity for students to develop and practice social skills while engaged in academic pursuits (Obenchain & Abernathy, 2003). Cooperative learning can be described as having a group of students work together to achieve a common academic goal. Students engaged in cooperative learning activities are not only responsible for their own work, but also for the work of the group. This approach provides an opportunity for friendships to develop, as well as supporting group problem solving (Salend, 2008).

There are several different formats for cooperative learning, including peer tutoring and class-wide peer tutoring, jigsaw, and learning together. Peer tutoring was previously described. Using the jigsaw format, students assigned to a group have a particular part of the group's task to complete that is necessary for the group to achieve its goal. Each member of the group must contribute to the group effort for success. The learning together approach requires group members to determine how to achieve a goal. The group can divide tasks or have the entire team complete the task (Salend, 2008). Both jigsaw and learning together approaches require students to work together to achieve a common goal. The development and practice of social skills is a key outcome for using this instructional method.

By providing students opportunities to work in cooperative learning groups, it helps to "break the cycle of students feeling isolated by structuring academic assignments that encourage students to interact with their classmates" (Church et al., 2003, p. 308). When using cooperative groups, it is imperative that each group member has an opportunity to do different things, otherwise students with disabilities may find themselves in the common role of not really being involved (Church et al., 2003).

The first level of the three-level system to promote the development of social skills includes a large number of things teachers can do to make their classrooms more open and conducive for social skills development and reinforcement. The following summarizes a few of these actions (Church et al., 2003, pp. 308–310):

1. Engage in behaviors and use language that fosters the belief that *all* students are valued and accepted members of the class.
2. Employ social skills instructional programs to promote positive interactions with others.
3. Use videos to explore appropriate social interactions and promote friendships.
4. Offer rewards that foster positive interpersonal strategies and encourage social interaction.
5. Create a classroom environment that promotes social interaction among students.
6. Teach students simple, noncompetitive, enjoyable games that do not require a great deal of skill or language.
7. Help students recognize nonverbal language in social situations, and introduce them to the conversational patterns that may occur in a particular setting.
8. Help students read the clues in social situations, and teach them about the unwritten rules that guide social interaction.
9. Make the rules of social situations simple and clear.
10. Set social behavior goals and acknowledge and comment specifically on displays of appropriate social behavior without making comparisons.

11. Teach students to reflect on the positive and negative outcomes of situations and evaluate the effectiveness of their strategies.
12. Encourage students to develop outside interests as a way to interact with other classmates.
13. Teach students learning strategies to cope with problematic social situations.
14. Encourage students to share peer-related concerns.
15. Involve family, students' peers, and community members.

Level II—Specific Strategies and Curriculum for Promoting Social Competence

For most students, creating an environment that is supportive of social skill development and use is sufficient for their developing adequate levels of these skills; however, there are other students who need more structured interventions and supports. For this group, specific strategies and curricula must be identified and implemented; merely placing them in classrooms that are open and conducive for social skills development is insufficient for their development of adequacy in this area (Meadan & Monda-Amaya, 2008).

Second-level strategies can be implemented in many ways, including large or small group activities and implementing a social skills or character education curricula. There is no one best way to teach social skills at this level (Morris, 2002). Regardless of the particular method used, Sargent (1998) offered a six-step process for teaching these skills:

1. Establish the need
2. Identify the skill components
3. Model the skill
4. Role-play the skill
5. Practice the skill
6. Generalize the skill

Efficacy of Social Skills Training.   While instruction in social skills is necessary for some students, several studies have raised questions about the efficacy of such interventions. In a study to determine the effects of social skills interventions for children with autism spectrum disorders, it was found that school-based interventions for this population were only minimally effective (Bellini et al., 2007). In a meta-analysis of the literature related to social skills training, Gresham and colleagues (2001) found that such training does not produce significant changes in students with high-incidence disabilities. They found that the training did not result in "large, socially important, long-term, or generalized changes in social competence" (p. 331). After reviewing six narrative reviews of studies, they summarized the following conclusions: (1) Modeling, coaching, and reinforcement procedures appear to be most effective; (2) evidence for cognitive-based strategies is weaker; (3) demonstration of consistent, durable gains is difficult; (4) cognitive-based strategies use outcomes measures that lack social validity; (5) the amount of intervention appears to be related to success; and (6) interventions based on assessments are best.

Their recommendations were not to discontinue such training, but to take into consideration several recommendations when contemplating such training. These recommendations include the following (Gresham et al., 2001):

1. Social skills training needs to be more frequent and intense.
2. Treatment should be targeted to specific deficits.
3. Functional assessment-based planning to tie interventions to current deficits works well.
4. Inappropriate behaviors that compete with social skills must be addressed.

Rather than a hit-or-miss, casual approach to social skills instruction, teachers should therefore use a well-planned program, based on specific social skills deficits, and provide the program over a period of time that allows students to learn and practice the skill.

Teach Problem-Solving Skills. One focus for large or small group training is problem solving. Rather than providing solutions to problems, teachers should facilitate students' problem solving, which can create an excellent opportunity for social interactions and the development of social skills. A simple problem-solving strategy that could be used includes (1) identifying the problem; (2) finding possible solutions to the problem; (3) identifying pros and cons for different solutions; and (4) choosing a solution (Hughes et al., 2002).

Burden and Byrd (2006) described an inquiry problem-solving lesson that can be used to enhance social skills. This five-step process includes the following:

Step 1 Students are presented with a problem that is important to them. The problem needs to be authentic and something that would motivate students to develop solutions.

Step 2 Students describe the problem and what prevents an easy solution to the problem.

Step 3 Students identify possible solutions to the problem. This could result from a group discussion into possible solutions to the problem.

Step 4 Students try solutions to the problem and gather information to determine the effectiveness of the solutions.

Step 5 Students analyze the results of their solutions and make a report about the problem-solving process.

By working through each of these steps, students involved in the problem-solving activity are required to use social skills.

Technology can also be used to assist students with problem-based learning (Cote, 2007). While the use of technology to teach problem solving can be used by students independently, lessons can be organized requiring students to work together using the technology for problem solving. Problem-solving software is available that can be used to assist students in developing these skills. These programs are available that "provide practice in solving problems by modeling general critical thinking steps, by focusing on specific subject area issues, or by creating an open environment in which students can discover their own strategies" (Bitter & Pierson, 2005, p. 141).

Effective Communication and Group Interactions. Poor communication among individuals can lead to many misconceptions and misunderstandings. For students trying to "fit in" socially, being able to communicate effectively is critically important. Miscommunications among students can destroy personal and social relationships. Such miscommunications can occur as a result of several situations, including not understanding what others are saying, even though their speech is comprehendible, and not making oneself understood clearly (Oliva, 2005). Pragmatics is described as the functional use of language, and is a primary concern for adolescents. "If students are unable to express themselves in a functional manner, making their wishes, needs, feelings, and responses understood, their oral language efforts may be wasted" (Polloway, Miller, & Smith, 2004, p. 502). This is obviously critical for adolescents in relation to their social inclusion.

In order to facilitate social skills development, students must be able to communicate effectively—that is, they must have good functional language. Therefore, interventions focusing on helping students communicate might be appropriate for some students. One way to support effective communication is through a positive classroom environment, as previously mentioned. Students must feel comfortable expressing themselves, which can result from such a positive classroom. However, for some students, interventions need to be more direct.

To assist students with their functional language, consider the following tips for teaching adolescents (Polloway & Patton, 1997, p. 220):

- Initiate and close conversations appropriately.
- Select appropriate topics of conversation.
- Make contributions to the conversation truthful.
- Make contributions to the conversation relevant.
- Match oral and nonverbal messages.
- Detect and display emotion through facial expression.
- Maintain a socially acceptable distance.
- Maintain appropriate eye contact.

Another way of helping students develop better pragmatics is to have them practice conversational situations. For example, Mercer and Mercer (1993) suggested having students listen to questions and indicate if an answer is required or if the question is simply a statement. Examples of questions are as follows:

1. Can you stop and think about what you just did?
2. What did you just do?
3. Will you ever be able to drive a car?
4. When will you learn to drive a car?

Students need to understand the meaning of language in order to communicate effectively with their peers, which will have a definite relationship with their social skills.

Conflict-Resolution Skills.   Students will invariably get into conflicts with each other and with adults, as it is a normal part of growing up. For students trying to develop social skills, being able to resolve these conflicts is essential because conflicts impede the development of social relationships. One method of conflict resolution uses peer mediators. In this model, students with conflicts meet to discuss and resolve problems with the assistance of a trained peer mediator (Salend, 2008). Daunic, Smith, Robinson, Miller, and Landry (2000) described the use of schoolwide conflict resolution and a peer mediation program implemented at three middle schools. The program focused on ensuring a safe environment and facilitating appropriate social interactions. The peer-mediated conflict resolution program provided a structured method for dealing with conflicts. Daunic and colleagues found that such a program, with administrative support, can be successful and can greatly reduce conflicts.

Character/Values Education.   Teaching values is another way of facilitating the development of social skills. One method of teaching values is through role playing. In role playing, students can work together to explore their feelings, attitudes, values, and problem-solving strategies. Role playing "attempts to help individuals find personal meaning within their social worlds and to resolve personal dilemmas with the assistance of the social group" (Joyce, Weil, & Calhoun, 2004, p. 233). Using role playing, students are able to work together in a group to analyze situations and arrive at solutions to problems. When using this model, teachers initiate activities and provide guidance; however, students select their own discussion topics and enactments (Joyce et al., 2004).

Character education programs have become popular in some states. These programs can help students learn problem-solving skills and conflict resolution (Sadker & Sadker, 2003). An issue with character education programs is the determination of which values to include. While there are some generic values that most would accept, there are others that could be controversial; parents may disagree with some of these values and oppose the character education program. Still, character education, which focuses on group interactions, can be a good tool for teaching social skills.

Literature-Based Strategies. Social stories have been shown to be an effective way of teaching social skills to students with disabilities. Social stories provide students with a story that describes expected behaviors, how to achieve those behaviors, and rewards earned as a result of those expected behavior (Welton et al., 2004). Social stories can be described as an "individualized cognitive intervention that describes the salient social cues and appropriate responses associated with a particular social situation" (Smith-Myles, Hubbard, Muellner, & Hider, 2008, p. 87).

In one study, Crozier and Tincani (2005) utilized a social story as an intervention with a student with autism who was displaying disruptive behaviors. The results of this research concluded that social stories can be used effectively to reduce disruptive behaviors. Other studies have substantiated the usefulness of social stories in reducing inappropriate social behaviors (Adams, Gouvousis, VanLue, & Waldron, 2004). Using storytime to provide direct instruction for social skills has also been shown to be effective. Students typically enjoy reading books together in a group, either by the teacher or by other students. Many stories have social lessons that can provide excellent opportunities for talking about social issues (Moris, 2002).

Forgan and Gonzalez-DeHass (2004) supported the use of literacy instruction as a means for improving social skills. They note that "literature instruction is an enjoyable academic activity, and it offers an ideal opportunity to teach social skills" (p. 25). Using literature for social skills instruction provides a natural way for teaching these skills. Anderson (2000) described a way to use *Romeo and Juliet* for social skills instruction. In using this play, as well as other literature, it is important to select specific scenes that relate to particular social skills. Once scenes have been selected, it is important to develop a social skills literature strategy lesson plan (Anderson, 2000).

Learning Strategies. Learning strategies have been used to help students with disabilities in academics for many years. They can also be used to help students improve their social skills. One strategy, described by Smith-Myles and others (2008), is called SODA. The strategy SODA, developed by Bock (2003), stands for *stop, observe, deliberate,* and *act.* These skills, learned through direct instruction or coaching, include the following steps:

1. *Stop:* The student determines what is going on in the environment.
2. *Observe:* Various aspects of the environment are observed, which could include what individuals are doing and saying.
3. *Deliberate:* The student would develop an action plan of what to do or say.
4. *Act:* The student implements the plan developed during the deliberate stage.

Teachers can develop their own strategies for helping students cope with different social situations. Strategies can be very useful to students because they provide a practical means for handling issues.

Videotherapy. Dole and McMahan (2005) described the use of videotherapy as a means for helping high school students deal with social and emotional problems. Using this technique, students watch a video, followed by a teacher-facilitated discussion. The discussion provides an opportunity for students to identify with the character and connect their own lives to the events in the movie. Strategies for solving problems, similar to ones presented in the movie, are shared among students (Dole & McMahan, 2005). Table 12.5 provides examples of videos that can be used for videotherapy, with a synopsis and associated themes.

TABLE 12.5 ● Examples of Videos to Use for Videotherapy

Video	Synopsis	Themes
Breaking Away (1979) 20th Century Fox PG	Semiautobiographical story of four 19-year-old young men who don't know what to do with their lives in the small town where they live. One develops a passion for bicycling, much to the bewilderment of his father.	• Setting goals • Meeting challenges • Following a passion
Finding Forrester (2000) Columbia PG-13	The story of a Black student at a Bronx high school who is a basketball player and gifted writer. His talents are nurtured by an odd, reclusive White writer who lives in the neighborhood.	• Mentoring • Intergenerational and intercultural friendship • Stereotypes • Peer pressure
Hoosiers (1986) MGM PG	The story of an underdog basketball team in the 1950s from a small Indiana high school that makes it all the way to the state championship.	• Rising above limitations • Committing to a goal
The Loretta Claiborne Story (2000) Walt Disney PG	The true story of a mentally challenged young woman who, through the inspiration and friendship of her social worker, becomes a champion athlete.	• Perseverance • Intergenerational • Friendship • Dealing with rejection
The Mighty (1998) Miramax Films PG-13	The story of a friendship between two adolescent boys, both with problems that label them as outcasts. They successfully combine their strengths to overcome their individual limitations.	• Building on strengths • Friendship
Mulan (1998) Walt Disney PG	Animated film based on a Chinese fable about a young girl who impersonates herself as a man in the army in order to save her family's honor.	• Sociocultural expectations • Gender roles • Conquering fears
October Sky (1999) Universal Pictures PG	Based on Homer Hickham, Jr.'s 1950's memoir, this is the story of four high school boys' determination to build a rocket. Homer's coal-mining father sternly disapproves of his son's pursuit of science and urges him to carry on in the family tradition of coal mining.	• Goal setting • Family conflict • Overcoming odds • Determination
The Other Sister (1999) Buena Vista Pictures PG-13	The story of the relationship between two young people who are mentally challenged. The very capable young woman has trouble gaining her independence from her overly protective mother.	• Independence • Family conflict • Goal setting
Simon Birch (1998) Buena Vista Pictures PG	Adapted from John Irving's novel, *A Prayer for Owen Meany*, this is the story of the friendship of two boys labeled as misfits.	• Purpose in life • Friendship • Faith
Smoke Signals (1998) Miramax PG-13	Adapted from Sherman Alexie's short stories in *The Lone Ranger* and *Tonto Fistfight in Heaven*, this Native American-made movie depicts the bus trip of Victor and Thomas to pick up the ashes of Victor's deceased father. The two young men have very different memories of Victor's father.	• Coming of age • Fathers and sons • Friendship
Remember the Titans (2000) Walt Disney PG	Based on the true story of the integration of a high school football squad by Black coach Herman Boone in 1971, who succeeded in breaking down walls and uniting the team.	• Breaking down barriers • Overcoming obstacles • Teamwork
Wild Hearts Can't Be Broken (1991) Walt Disney PG	Story of real-life Sonora Webster, a spunky teenager who becomes a diving girl in a traveling show in the 1930s and is challenged by a series of tragedies.	• Following your dreams • Adjusting to life's circumstances

Source: S. Dole & J. McMahan (2005). Using videotherapy to help adolescents cope with social and emotional problems. *Intervention in School and Clinic, 40*, p. 153. Used with permission.

Social Skills Curricula. Teachers may elect to use a published or self-developed curricula for large or small group instruction for social skills. Most teachers opt to teach social skills using ideas presented previously. Social skills curricula are not used nearly as frequently as teacher-initiated activities; however, some teachers prefer a comprehensive curriculum that focuses on social skills development. The Division on Autism and Developmental Disabilities, Council for Exceptional Children, has developed an extensive compilation of social skills intervention programs for use at all grade levels. Table 12.6 provides an example one of these strategies.

TABLE 12.6 ● Strategies for Increasing Positive Social Interactions

Social Skills Lesson–Senior High, Dealing with Failure

Objective: The students will refrain from responding to failure in a negative manner.

Performance Criteria: This skill will be performed adequately when the student:

1. Decides or recognizes that they have failed (e.g., interpersonal, academic, or athletic).
2. Considers reasons for failure (e.g., bad luck, lack of skill, lack of effort, etc.).
3. Refrains from verbally or physically expressing anger in an aggressive manner.
4. Considers what can be done to avoid failure another time (e.g., practice, make more effort, get help, etc.).
5. Decides whether or not to try again.
6. Tries again or chooses to try something else.

Materials: Chalkboard, general homework form.

Procedures:

Step #1. Establishing the Need

a. Ask students if they have ever failed at anything. Elicit that they had.
b. Ask if they had ever gotten angry when they failed. Elicit that they probably had in some instances.
c. Ask students if they thought it had done any good to get angry. Elicit that it had not.
d. If possible, procure a film which shows the negative consequences of becoming angry. There are some driver training films which depict that type of situation. After showing the film, discuss the consequences of dealing with failure poorly.
e. If no films are available, discuss the following story:

When Lou Howe turned 16, he went right down to the Motor Vehicle Office to take a test for a drivers' license. He thought he knew all the traffic laws, but when the test was graded, he had failed. He was so angry that he tore up the test and yelled at the lady behind the counter. He then demanded to take the test again. The lady told him to leave and that if he came back again, she would refuse to wait on him.

Cliff Brown wanted to get a date with Barbara. He waited until after school to walk her home. He asked her out, but she turned him down saying that she was already busy. Cliff didn't say much, but he didn't ask Barbara or any other girls out for a date again.

f. Ask students to respond differently than the individuals in the story. Through discussion elicit from the students that it is important to contain expressions of anger for failing and that it is important to try again.

Step #2. Identify the Skill Components

Tell students that you are going to list some helpful suggestions for dealing with failure. Discuss each step.

1. Decide that you failed, you were turned down, received failing grade, made a bad play, lost a game, etc.
2. Think about why you failed, discuss bad luck, lack of effort, lack of skill, etc.
3. Hold your anger or frustrations inside.
4. Think about what you can do to avoid failure next time (discuss practice, try harder, do something different, etc.).
5. Decide to try again or try something new.

TABLE 12.6 ● (continued)

Have students write the list on a general homework form.

Step #3. Model the Skill

a. Create a hypothetical situation where failure occurs. Model dealing with failure through use of the think aloud procedure.
b. Have student recall the steps you went through and discuss a second situation where those steps might be followed.

Step #4. Role Play

a. Have students select a failure situation which could possibly occur in their lives (e.g., failing a test, failing to get a job, etc.).
b. Have students think aloud as they demonstrate the skill.
c. Have classmates provide feedback.
d. Have students evaluate their own performance.

Step #5. Practice

a. Have students fill out the general homework form and practice the skill at home.
b. Challenge students with bogus failures on class work. Give students feedback and have them evaluate their own performance.
c. Review the steps of the skill during skill review sessions.

Step #6. Generalization

a. Ask regular classroom teachers to provide feedback to the students with disabilities in cases where failure is evident.
b. Ask students to report on how they handled failure experience. Praise self-reporting.

Source: From L. R. Sargent, 1998, Social Skills for School and Community. Reston, VA: Division on Autism and Developmental Disabilities. Used with permission.

Level III—Targeted Individual Interventions

Most students develop appropriate social skills naturally, as part of their normal maturation. For many, first-level supports are all that are necessary for appropriate social skills development. For a few others, second-level interventions provided by large and small group strategies are necessary. A few students, however, require even more individualized interventions and supports. This third level is used only if the first two levels do not produce the desired results. For this group of students, teachers must develop individual, targeted interventions. As with the first two levels, there is no one specific method that will be effective for all students at the third level; interventions are based on the individual student's needs, which are determined using a functional behavior assessment (Meadan & Monda-Amaya, 2008).

A functional behavior assessment is a process that uses interviews and observations to identify targeted behaviors and antecedents, and consequences related to those behaviors. The assessment should provide an understanding of what may be causing and reinforcing the behaviors in question (Wheeler & Richey, 2008). Functional behavior assessment is based on the belief that behaviors do not occur in a vacuum; rather, they are a function of different factors. The purpose of the assessment is to determine what those factors are so that appropriate interventions can be developed.

Three questions (factors) that can be answered by a functional behavior assessment include:

1. The function of the behavior (i.e., Is the function of a problem attention-seeking or avoidance?)
2. The type of deficits (i.e., Does the student know how to perform the behavior correctly?)
3. The social validity of the target behavior (i.e., Is the behavior important?)

Through such a functional analysis, specific interventions can be developed that target the inappropriate behaviors. Examples of individual interventions include the following (Meadan & Monda-Amaya, 2008):

- Teach specific new skills that the student does not possess.
- Teach a competing behavior to replace a socially inappropriate behavior.
- Provide practice and generalization for newly learned skills.
- Help students establish support networks.
- Teach self-monitoring, self-evaluating, self-reinforcement, and self-instruction strategies.
- Teach acceptance and responsibilities.
- Teach strategies to promote self-determination and self-advocacy.

PLANNING AND IMPLEMENTING SOCIAL SKILLS INTERVENTIONS

Most individuals learn social skills naturally. For those who need interventions and supports to assist them in developing appropriate social skills, comprehensive planning is necessary. Educators and family members need to have an understanding of the nature of social skills deficits before implementing a plan for improvement. Regardless of whether needs are determined with casual observations or a functional behavior assessment and analysis, the important thing to remember is that there needs to be an understanding of the level of social skills before implementing a program to improve them.

SUMMARY

This chapter focuses on social skills instruction for adolescents with disabilities. By nature, humans are social beings. Social skills are important in many different endeavors, including school, employment, and participating in the community. Individuals with good social skills have a much easier time with success than individuals with poor social skills. Unfortunately, many individuals with disabilities have poor social skills.

The various ways of assessing social skills include informal and formal observations and rating scales. The most important thing about assessing social skills is to obtain a good understanding of the level of social skills prior to developing interventions and supports. Not understanding an individual's needs in the area of social skills often results in ineffective programs.

Among the wide range of interventions for social skill development, those presented in this chapter are organized around levels. Level I, the least intrusive, focuses on creating an environment where social skills can be learned and reinforced naturally. At level II, large and small group activities provide social skills interventions. At level III, the most intrusive level, individual targeted interventions, developed following a functional behavior assessment, prove useful.

ACTIVITIES

1. Observe a group of adolescents in a variety of settings, such as school, church, leisure time, and so forth. Make notes about the social skills that students use when they are together in groups. What impact would not having these social skills have on students?

2. Think about your own social skills and those exhibited by your friends. Do you think you would be successful in school and social settings if you had fewer social skills? More social skills? Why?

3. As students transition from secondary school to postschool environments, including postsecondary education, employment, and community activities, social skills are critical. Think about individuals you know who have been very successful in these settings, because of social skills; and those who have experienced failures because of a lack of socal skills.

REFERENCES

Achenbach, T. M. (2001). *Child behavior checklist for ages 6–18*. Burlington, VT: ASEBA.

Adams, L., Gouvousis, A., VanLue, M., & Waldron, C. (2004). Social story intervention: Improving communication skills in a child with autism spectrum disorder. *Focus on Autism and Other Developmental Disabilities, 19*, 87–94.

Anderson, P. L. (2000). Using literature to teach social skills to adolescents with LD. *Intervention in School and Clinic, 35,* 268–273.

Bellini, S., Peters, J. K., Benner, L., & Hope, A. (2007). A meta-analysis of school-based social skills interventions for children with autism spectrum disorders. *Remedial and Special Education, 28*, 153–162.

Best, S. J. (2005). Health impairments and infectious diseases. In S. J. Best, K. W. Heller, & J. L. Biggee (Eds.). Teaching individuals with physical and multiple disabilities (5th ed). Upper Saddle River, NJ: Pearson, pp 59–82.

Best, S. J., & Bigge, J. L. (2005). Cerebral palsy. In S. J. Best, K. W. Heller, & J. L. Biggee (Eds.). Teaching individuals with physical and multiple disabilities (5th ed). Upper Saddle River, NJ: Pearson, pp 87–107.

Bitter, G. G., & Pierson, M. E. (2005). *Using technology in the classroom* (6th ed.). Boston: Allyn & Bacon.

Bock, M. A. (2003). SODA Strategy: enhancing interaction skills of youngsters with Asperger syndrome. *Focus on Autism and Other Developmental Disabilities, 17,* 132–137.

Boutot, E. A. (2007). Fitting in: Tips for promoting acceptance and friendships for students with autism spectrum disorders in inclusive classrooms. *Intervention in School and Clinic, 42,* 156–161.

Brown, L. L., & Hammill, D. D. (1990). *Behavior rating profile – 2*. Austin, TX: Pro-Ed.

Burden, P. R., & Byrd, D. M. (2006). *Methods for effective teaching* (3rd ed.). Boston: Allyn & Bacon.

Cartledge, G., & Kourea, L. (2008). Culturally responsive classrooms for culturally diverse students with and at risk for disabilities. *Exceptional Children, 74,* 351–371.

Chadsey, J., & Gun Han, K. (2005). Friendship-facilitation strategies: What do students in middle school tell us? *Teaching Exceptional Children, 38,* 52–57.

Church, K., Gottschalk, C. M., & Leddy, J. N. (2003). 20 ways to enhance social and friendship skills. *Intervention in School and Clinic, 38,* 307–310.

Copeland, S. R., Hughes, C., Carter, E. W., Guth, C., Presley, J. A., Williams, C. R., & Fowler, S. E. (2004). Increasing access to general education: Perspectives of participants in a high school peer support program. *Remedial and Special Education, 25,* 342–352.

Coster, W. J., & Haltiwanger, J. T. (2004). Social-behavioral skills of elementary students with physical disabilities included in general education classrooms. *Remedial and Special Education, 25,* 95–103.

Cote, D. (2007). Problem-based learning software for students with disabilities. *Intervention in School and Clinic, 43,* 29–37.

Crozier, S., & Tincani, M. J. (2005). Using a modified social story to decrease disruptive behavior of a child with autism. *Focus on Autism and Other Developmental Disabilities, 20,* 150–157.

Daunic, A. P., Smith, S. W., Robinson, T. R., Miller, M. D., & Landry, K. L. (2000). School-wide conflict resolution and peer mediation programs: Experiences in three middle schools. *Intervention in School and Clinic, 36,* 94–100.

Demchak, M. A. (2008). Facilitating social relationships and friendships in school settings. In H. P. Parette & G. R. Peterson-Karlan (Eds.), *Research-based practices in developmental disabilities* (2nd ed., pp. 293–308). Austin, TX: Pro-Ed.

Dole, S., & McMahan, J. (2005). Using videotherapy to help adolescents cope with social and emotional problems. *Intervention in School and Clinic, 40,* 151–155.

Emmer, E. T., Evertson, C. M., & Worsham, M. E. (2003). *Classroom management for secondary teachers* (6th ed.). Boston: Allyn & Bacon.

Epstein, M. H. (2004). *Behavior and emotional rating scale* (2nd ed.). Austin, TX: Pro-Ed.

Estell, D. B., Jones, M. H., Pearl, R., Van Acker, R., Farmer, T. W., & Rodkin, P. C. (2008). Peer groups, popularity, and social preference. *Journal of Learning Disabilities, 41,* 5–14.

Forgan, J. W., & Gonzalez-DeHass, A. (2004). How to infuse social skills training into literacy instruction. *Teaching Exceptional Children, 36,* 24–30.

Gold, M. (1980). Did I say that? New York: Research Publications.

Gresham, F. M., & Elliott, S. N. (1990). Social skills rating system. Bloomington, MN: Pearson Assessments.

Gresham, F. M., Sugai, G., & Horner, R. H. (2001). Reference: Trajectories for social functioning among students with and without learning. Interpreting outcomes of social skills training for students with high-incidence disabilities. *Exceptional Children, 67,* 331–344.

Hallahan, D. P., Lloyd, J. W., Kauffman, J. M., Weiss, M. P., & Martinez, E. A. (2005). *Learning disabilities: Foundations, characteristics, and effective teaching* (3rd ed.). Boston: Allyn & Bacon.

Hardman, M. L., Drew, C. J., & Egan, M. W. (2008). *Human exceptionality: School, community, and family* (9th ed). Boston: Houghton Mifflin Company.

Hughes, C., Carter, E., Hughes, T., Bradford, E., & Copeland, S. R. (2002). Effects of instructional versus noninstructional roles on the social interactions of high school students. *Education and Training in Mental Retardation and Developmental Disabilities, 37,* 146–162.

Hughes, C., Copeland, S. R., Guth, C., Rung, L. L., Hwang, B., Kleeb, G., & Strong, M. (2001). General education students' perspectives on their involvement in a high school peer buddy program. *Education and Training in Mental Retardation and Developmental Disabilities, 36,* 343–356.

Hughes, L. (2002). *Paving pathways: Child and adolescent development.* Belmont, CA: Wadsworth.

Joyce, B., Weil, M., & Calhoun, E. (2004). *Models of teaching* (7th ed.). Boston: Allyn & Bacon.

Kavale, K. A., & Forness, S. T. (1996). Social skills deficits and LD: A meta-analysis. *Journal of Learning Disabilities, 29,* 226–237.

Kleinert, H., McGregor, V., Durbin, M., Blandford, T., Jones, K., Owens, J., Harrison, B., & Miracle, S. (2004). Service-learning opportunities that include students with moderate and severe disabilities. *Teaching Exceptional Children, 37,* 28–34.

McDermott, P. (1993). *Adjustment scales for children and adolescents.* Philadelphia, PA: Edumetric and Clinical Science.

Meadan, H., & Monda-Amaya, L. (2008). Collaboration to promote social competence for students with mild disabilities in the general classroom: A structure for providing support. *Intervention in School and Clinic, 43,* 158–167.

Mercer, C. D., & Mercer, A. R. (1993). *Students with learning disabilities* (4th ed.). Upper Saddle River, NJ.

Moris, S. (2002). Promoting social skills among students with nonverbal learning disabilities. *Teaching Exceptional Children, 34,* 66–70.

Murdock, L. C., Cost, H. C., & Tieso, C. (2007). Measurement of social communication skills of children with autism spectrum disorders during interactions with typical peers. *Focus on Autism and Other Developmental Disabilities, 22,* 160–172.

Naglieri, J., McNeish, T., & Achilles, B. (1991). *Draw a person: Screening procedure for emotional disturbance.* Austin, TX: Pro-Ed.

Neeper, R., Lahey, B. B., & Frick, P. J. (1990). *Comprehensive behavior rating scale for children.* San Antonio, TX: Psychological Corp.

Nowicki, E. A. (2003). A meta-analysis of the social competence of children with learning disabilities compared to classmates of low and average to high achievement. *Learning Disability Quarterly, 26,* 171–188.

Obenchain, K. M., & Abernathy, T. V. (2003). 20 ways to build community and empower students. *Intervention in School and Clinic, 39,* 55–60.

Oliva, P. F. (2005). *Developing the curriculum* (6th ed.). Boston: Allyn & Bacon.

Polloway, E. A., & Patton, J. R. (1997). *Strategies for teaching learners with special needs* (6th ed.). Upper Saddle River, NJ: Merrill/Pearson.

Polloway, E. A., Miller, L., & Smith, T. E. C. (2004). *Language instruction for students with disabilities* (3rd ed.). Denver: Love.

Reynolds, C. R., & Kamphaus, R. W. (1998). *BASC monitor for ADHD.* Circle Pines, MN: American Guidance Service.

Sadker, M. P., & Sadker, D. M. (2003). *Teachers, schools, and society* (6th ed.). Boston: McGraw-Hill.

Salend, S. J. (2008). *Creating inclusive classrooms: Effective and reflective practices* (6th ed.). Upper Saddle River, NJ: Merrill/Pearson.

Sargent, L. R. (1998). *Social skills for school and community.* Arlington, VA: Division on Mental Retardation. Council for Exceptional Children.

Slavin, R. E. (2009). *Educational psychology: Theory and practice* (9th ed.). Upper Saddle River, NJ: Pearson.

Smith, S. W., & Gilles, D. L. (2003). Using key instructional elements to systematically promote social skills generalization for students with challenging behavior. *Intervention in School and Clinic, 39,* 30–37.

Smith, T. E. C., Polloway, E. A., Patton, J. R., Dowdy, C. A. (2012). *Teaching students with special needs in inclusive settings* (6th ed.). Upper Saddle River, NJ: Pearson.

Smith-Myles, B., Hubbard, A., Muellner, K., & Hider, A. S. (2008). Autism spectrum disorders. In H. P. Parette & G.R. Peterson-Karlan (Eds.). Research-based practices in developmental disabilities. Austin: Pro-Ed. (75–98).

Sparks, S. (2008). Culturally and linguistically diverse learners with developmental disabilities. In H. P. Parette & G.R. Peterson-Karlan (Eds.). Research-based practices in developmental disabilities. Austin: Pro-Ed. (125–141).

Taylor, R. L. (2008). *Assessment of exceptional students.* Boston: Allyn & Bacon.

Taylor, R. L., Richards, S. B., & Brady, M. P. (2005). *Mental retardation: Historical perspectives, current practices, and future directions.* Boston: Allyn & Bacon.

Vaughn, S., Kim, A., Sloan, C. V. M., Hughes, M. T., Elbaum, B., & Sridhar, D. (2003). Social skills interventions for young children with disabilities. *Remedial and Special Education, 24,* 2–15.

Venn, J. J. (2007). *Assessing students with special needs* (4th ed.). Upper Saddle River, NJ: Merrill/Pearson

Weinstein, C. S. (2007*). Middle and secondary classroom management* (3rd ed.). Boston: McGraw Hill.

Welton, E., Vakil, S., & Carasea, C. (2004). Strategies for increasing positive social interactions in children with autism: A case study. *Teaching Exceptional Children, 37,* 40–46.

Wheeler, J. J., & Richey, D. D. (2008). Behavior support strategies for learners with developmental disabilities. In H. P. Parette & G. R. Peterson-Karlan (Eds.), *Research-based practices in developmental disabilities* (2nd ed.). Austin, TX: Pro-Ed.

13 Strategies for Teaching Self-Determination Skills to Adolescents with Disabilities

Study Questions

1. What are self-determination skills?

2. Why are self-determination skills important for students with disabilities?

3. What are some strategies for teaching self-determination skills?

4. Describe some commercial programs to teach self-determination skills.

5. What does IDEA have to say about self-determination skills?

6. How can students become more involved in their IEPs?

INTRODUCTION

Being self-determined is a goal for all individuals in our society. We all like to be in charge of our own lives; we all like to make our own decisions; we all like to set our own goals and determine how to achieve those goals; we all like to make our own choices. Indeed, wanting to be self-determined begins early in life and often results in conflicts with parents and other caregivers who are not ready to give up control. Seeking self-determination is a natural process that is actually expected of children as they mature.

Although most adolescents develop a level of self-determination through the maturation process, students with disabilities often need assistance in developing their self-determination skills; many students with disabilities will not develop self-determination skills without direct interventions. Becoming self-determined is a critically important developmental task that is necessary for independence (Eisenman, 2007). In fact, "[p]romoting self-determination (SD), or teaching students to take control of their life, is becoming a hallmark of providing full and complete special education services" (Karvonen, Test, Wood, Browder, & Algozzine, 2004, p. 23).

Goals and objectives for students with disabilities must be determined individually, because of the legal requirements of the IEP and best practices. While the goals and objectives for students with disabilities vary widely from one student to the next, one common focus for all students should be self-determination. IEP committees must determine the extent of self-determination skills in students and the interventions needed to further develop these skills.

The inclusion model of serving students with disabilities can be traced to the so-called "normalization" movement that was advocated by Nirje as early as 1969. Wolfensberger (1972) defined normalization as the "utilization of means which are as culturally normative as possible, in order to establish and/or maintain personal behaviors and characteristics which are as culturally normative as possible" (p. 28). In other words, normalization means facilitating individuals with disabilities to live as normal a life as possible. In public schools, this philosophy has evolved into the inclusion of students with disabilities in general classrooms, extracurricular activities, and all other aspects of public education. Unlike the mainstreaming or integration era, where students with disabilities *belonged* in a special education classroom and were included with nondisabled peers occasionally, inclusion *assumes* that students with disabilities actually *belong* with their nondisabled peers (Smith, Polloway, Patton, & Dowdy, 2008).

As adults, inclusion means being included in employment, living, and social situations. Once again, the basis for inclusion of adults is the normalization principle. Young and older adults with disabilities should not be relegated to living in congregate care facilities, working in sheltered employment settings, and interacting only with other individuals with disabilities, unless these interventions are absolutely necessary. They should be included in all aspects of life as much as possible. These individuals should have some control over their own lives and not be totally dependent on the decisions of others related to where they want to live and work, and with whom they want to socialize.

Self-determination is linked to feelings of competence. Individuals who feel competent are more likely to display self-determination than individuals who feel less than competent (Eisenman, 2007). Think of instances where you have felt less than competent. In those situations it is highly likely that you did not feel as if you were in total control of what was happening. In situations where we do not feel competent we are more likely to depend on others to lead and direct us. Helping individuals with disabilities feel more competent will invariably help them feel more in control of their lives.

When students face situations where they do not feel competent, they depend on others for supports. While there is nothing wrong with needing supports, in order to become as independent as possible, students need to learn to be successful with the least amount of assistance. Therefore, they need to have a good understanding of their strengths and weaknesses and the minimal supports that are needed to assist them to be successful.

SELF-DETERMINATION

Self-determination can be defined in varied ways. Basically, it means being responsible for oneself. Wehmeyer, Abery, Mithaug, and Stancliffe (2003) defined self-determined behavior as "acting as the primary causal agent in one's life and making choices and decisions regarding one's quality of life free from undue external influence or interference" (p. 177). In other words, being self-determined is the equivalent of being in charge of your own life.

Self-determination is not a single trait; rather, it involves numerous components. Some of the themes commonly associated with self-determination include self-awareness, goal setting, problem solving, self-evaluation, self-advocacy, choice, decision making, and goal attainment (Eisenman, 2007; Trainor, 2005). Field, Hoffman, and Spezia (1998, p. 2) summarized the following definitions of self-determination:

- The attitudes, abilities, and skills that lead people to define goals for themselves and to take the initiative to reach these goals (Ward, 1988, p. s)
- The capacity to choose and to have those choices be the determinants of one's actions (Deci & Ryan, 1985, p. 38)
- Determination of one's own fate or course of action without compulsion; free will (*American Heritage Dictionary*, 1992)
- One's ability to define and achieve goals based on a foundation of knowing and valuing oneself (Field & Hoffman, 1994, p. 164)

Field and colleagues (1998) added that words such as *control, choice, confidence*, and *self-esteem* are often found in descriptions of self-determination. As one can determine, there are many common themes in each of these definitions.

It is important not only to view self-determination from a professional perspective but also from the eyes of individuals with disabilities. The website "Self-Advocates Becoming Empowered," at http://thechp.syr.edu/HumanPolicyPress/SABE.html, defines self-determination as

> "speaking for our rights and responsibilities and empowering ourselves to stand up for what we believe in. This means being able to choose where we work, live, and our friends; to educate ourselves and others; to work as a team to obtain common goals; and to develop the skills that enable us to fight for our beliefs, to advocate for our needs, and to obtain the level of independence that we desire" (Wehmeyer, Bersani, & Gagne, 2000, p. 331).

Individuals with disabilities thus see self-determination as a major goal for independence.

Self-determination has been the subject of research since the 1990s to promote a way that individuals with disabilities can achieve self-sufficiency and independence. A common misunderstanding about self-determination is it involves only making complex decisions and acting independently or totally controlling one's own life. While this may be the goal of self-determination for all individuals, including those with disabilities, it must be remembered that individuals with significant cognitive disabilities may never be able to totally control their own lives (Wehmeyer, Martin, & Sands, 2008). This in no way means that individuals with significant disabilities cannot achieve some level of self-determination. Self-determination, therefore, is maximizing individual potential for controlling one's life. For an individual with severe mental retardation, being able to make simple choices such as what to eat for a snack is a reflection of self-determination, compared to an individual with a learning disability who makes choices about what college major to choose and where to live.

Self-determination, therefore, does not mean the same thing for all individuals. The degree of self-determination achieved by individuals will depend on several factors, including age, gender, type and degree of disability, support system, and culture and value system. This is no different from individuals without disabilities. Nondisabled adults vary in their own degree of self-determined behaviors. The key is that supports and interventions are implemented that enable all individuals with disabilities, regardless of type and severity, to achieve a maximum level of self-determination.

COMPONENTS OF SELF-DETERMINATION

Self-determination includes myriad components, not a single overarching skill. Wehmeyer and colleagues (2008) identified 12 specific elements of self-determined behaviors. The following discussion describes 10 of these elements, which are summarized in Table 13.1.

TABLE 13.1 ● Component Elements of Self-Determined Behavior

Choice-making skills

Decision-making skills

Problem-solving skills

Goal-setting and attainment skills

Independence, risk-taking, and safety skills

Self-observation, evaluation, and reinforcement skills

Self-instruction skills

Self-advocacy and leadership skills

Internal locus of control

Positive attributions of efficacy and outcome expectancy

Self-awareness

Self-knowledge

Source: Wehmeyer, M. L., Martin, J. E., & Sands, D. J. (2008). Self-determination and students with developmental disabilities. In H. P. Parette and G. R. Peterson-Karlan (Eds.). *Research-Based Practices in Developmental Disabilities*, 2nd ed. Austin: Pro-Ed., p. 102.

Choice-Making Skills

Choice making can occur in every conceivable situation. We make hundreds of choices every day, such as what to wear, what to eat, who to socialize with, and when to go to bed. Often individuals with disabilities are not given choices for even these simple things. Choice making includes all levels of choices, even things like what reinforcement to receive in a behavior management program (Peterson, Caniglia, & Royster, 2001).

Decision-Making Skills

Decision-making skills can be manifested in all different types of situations. Wehmeyer and others (2008) noted that "decision making involves coming to a judgment about which of a number of potential options is best at a given time" (p. 105). They further pointed out that students need to have opportunities for decision making in their classrooms where teachers can facilitate their decision making with real-life issues. For example, students could be given several options for completing an in-class assignment and allowed to decide which option to select; or, they could be given the option of taking an oral test or a written test. Practice in decision making results in those skills being used more in real-life situations than they would be without practice.

Problem-Solving Skills

When confronted with problem situations, individuals with disabilities need to be able to analyze the problem and develop responses to the problem. Wehmeyer and others (2008) defined a problem as "an activity for which a solution is not known or readily apparent" (p. 105). When confronted with problems, individuals must first realize a problem exists, and then develop solutions to the problem. Being able to solve problems is critical for independence because of situations developing that may not have been anticipated.

All individuals, including those with disabilities, often find themselves in a situation where there is no set solution or answer. For example, if a student is confronted by a bully, the student would need to know how to seek a solution to the problem. This might include who to go to for assistance or how to deal directly with the bully. If an adult with a disability gets a letter indicating that the water will be shut off because of lack of payment, the individual needs to know how to solve the problem or run the risk of going without water.

Goal-Setting and Attainment Skills

Goal setting is a very important skill in self-determination. "The process of promoting goal-setting skills involves working with students to help them learn to: (a) identify and define a goal clearly and concretely, (b) develop a series of objectives or tasks to achieve the goal, and (c) specify the actions necessary to achieve the desired outcome" (Wehmeyer et al., 2008, p. 104). Being able to set goals is important for individuals to achieve success. How often do we ask young people, "What are your goals?" Without goals, individuals often waste their efforts and do not achieve up to their potential.

For individuals with disabilities, goal setting is very critical. Because these individuals have to overcome the impact of their disability, they do not have the luxury of wasting efforts that are not goal oriented.

Independence, Risk-Taking, and Safety Skills

While not listed as frequently as some other components of self-determination, being independent and able to take risks is part of self-determination. While the risks taken do not need to be life threatening, they do need to place individuals in situations where they challenge themselves. Not ever taking any risks may result in individuals not achieving at levels they could if they would simply try something different.

Self-Observation, Evaluation, and Reinforcement Skills

While in educational settings, students with disabilities are observed, evaluated, and reinforced by teachers and others in their environments, including family members. However, when individuals exit school and transition into their postschool environments, they need to be able to self-evaluate and self-reinforce. Many young adults are unsuccessful in college and employment because they lack these skills. Without a parent, teacher, or other significant other to provide this evaluation and self-reinforcement, they may not be successful. Being able to determine one's own level of success, and reinforcing that success, can lead to success.

Self-Instruction Skills

Just like individuals need to be able to self-evaluate and self-reinforce, they also must be able to self-instruct. After formal education, much of what individuals learn is self-taught. Realizing that certain skills are lacking and taking steps to learn those skills greatly facilitates the level of self-determination an individual exhibits.

Self-Advocacy and Leadership Skills

Being able to advocate for one's self is a vital part of gaining independence. "Self-advocacy is the process whereby individuals literally advocate for themselves" (Smith, Palloway, Patton, & Dowdy, 2008, p. 66). Individuals, with and without disabilities, who cannot self-advocate often find themselves in situations where they are not in control of their own lives. During most of the school years, parents and school personnel advocate for students with disabilities. However, once these individuals exit school this support system for advocacy may not be present. For example, if a young adult is mistreated by his supervisor, he needs to know how to advocate for his own rights. School personnel will not be available to advocate for him, and it is unlikely his parents will advocate for him. The individual must know how to advocate for himself.

One way to prepare adults to self-advocate is to teach them how to advocate during their educational programs. Students must understand their rights in the educational process and be encouraged to express their desires. Wehmeyer and colleagues (2008) suggested that teaching students to be self-advocates includes teaching them how to be assertive, communicate their perspectives, negotiate and compromise, and deal with bureaucracies, such as school districts and adult service agencies.

Internal Locus of Control

Locus of control is the perception individuals have about their ability to exert some control of their own life. Individuals who feel they have this control are said to have an internal locus of control; individuals who perceive they do not have this control are described as having an external locus of control (Wehmeyer et al., 2008).

Self-Awareness

Self-awareness includes a basic understanding of one's strengths, needs, and abilities (Price, Wolensky, & Mulligan, 2002). While individuals need to be self-confident, they also need to have a realistic understanding of their abilities. Constantly trying to achieve an unachievable goal can result in repeated failure and eventually giving up. There is a fine line between self-confidence and overconfidence. Educators and family members need to help individuals with disabilities develop an appropriate self-awareness of their ability levels.

NEED FOR SELF-DETERMINATION SKILLS

Self-determination skills are important for all individuals in order for them to become as independent as possible. Most individuals develop sufficient self-determination skills as they mature. In fact, the development of self-determination skills could be viewed as part of the maturation process, often causing conflicts between the individual and his or her parents and school personnel.

Self-determination can be seen as early as infancy. Babies who continue to cry until someone picks them up or feed them are examples of the beginning of self-determination. This increases with physical and mental development. Toddlers, elementary-aged students, and adolescents all display different levels of self-determination.

While most individuals develop self-determination naturally, there are some individuals who need assistance in the development of these skills. Individuals with disabilities often find themselves lacking many of the components of self-determination. Whether this failure to develop self-determination naturally is a result of the disability, caregivers, or a combination is irrelevant for teachers trying to promote self-determination skills. The fact remains that "increased independence and the ability to manage one's own behavior and task performance continue to be areas of concern when working with persons with disabilities" (Mechling, 2007, p. 252).

As noted, the lack of self-determination skills among individuals with disabilities could be the result of the nature of the disability, or even as a result of learned helplessness. For example, the disability could directly impact some of the components of self-determination. Individuals with cognitive deficits might not be able to understand their rights and therefore have difficulties with self-assertiveness. Individuals with learning disabilities often have deficits in social skills, which could lead to a lack of self-confidence and assertiveness. Individuals with physical impairments might lack assertiveness because of their physical limitations.

In addition to the nature of the disability impacting self-determination, some individuals actually learn to be helpless, which directly impacts self-determination. Indeed, special educators, family members, and others have been guilty of facilitating learned helplessness, strictly from trying to provide supports needed by individuals with disabilities (Smith, Polloway, Smith, & Patton, 2007). The nature of special education and other support services is to provide students with disabilities the supports and services they need. Any individual can learn to depend on these services. If individuals with disabilities are provided services without learning how to do things independently, their development of self-determination may be negatively impacted. Regardless of the intent, individuals with disabilities who have learned to be helpless are at a significant disadvantage when it comes to independence and self-determination. Parents and school personnel will not be present forever to provide needed supports. Therefore, individuals need to develop self-determination so they can advocate for themselves when necessary.

Self-determined individuals are simply in a better position to live as independently as possible. "Students who can articulate and explain their disabilities, their presenting characteristics, and what their accommodations or modifications should be in the classroom are much more apt to succeed than students who cannot" (Barrie & McDonald, 2002, p. 118). Students who are unaware of their specific learning problems do not know what kind of assistance they need, and are unaware of where to get needed assistance; these students often become frustrated and discouraged (Hong, Ivy, Gonzalez, & Ehrensberger, 2007). Adults with disabilities have many more positive outcomes if they are self-determined than those without self-determination (Zhang, Wehmeyer, & Chen, 2005). For example, Fowler, Konrad, Walker, Test, and Wood (2007) noted that individuals with mental retardation have a much better chance for success after leaving school if they have a certain level of self-determination. Young adults experience more success in employment, postsecondary education, social situations, and living arrangements if they are self-determined.

As more and more students with disabilities enter postsecondary educational settings, the need for self-determination becomes even more critical (Hong et al., 2007). While the vast majority of postsecondary educational programs must comply with Section 504 and/or the Americans with Disabilities Act (ADA) to provide supports, the responsibility for indicating a need for accommodations lies with the individual with the disability. Unlike Section 504 for school-age children, and the Individuals with Disabilities Education Act (IDEA), where school personnel are responsible for referring students who may be eligible for services and protections and developing intervention programs, in postsecondary settings individuals must self-refer and provide documents to support their needs. They must understand their disability and know how to request services. Adults with disabilities must also advocate for themselves in employment settings, living arrangements, and social settings. As adults, it is unlikely that other individuals will be looking out for their needs. They must learn to look out for themselves. Self-determined individuals are much more likely to indicate a need for services and request such services than individuals who are not as self-determined.

As a result of many students with disabilities not naturally developing self-determination skills, educators should incorporate training opportunities in students' educational programs. "The proposition that self-determination is an important outcome if youth with disabilities are to achieve more positive adult outcomes assumes that students with disabilities are not self-determined, and that self-determination and positive adult outcomes are causally linked" (Wehmeyer et al., 2008, p. 103).

Self-determination can result in numerous positive benefits for individuals. These include improved academic achievement, prevention of school dropouts (Eisenman, 2007), increased self-esteem and self-confidence, increased likely success in employment, increased likely success in postsecondary education, and increased likely inclusion in the community. Self-determination is critical for all individuals; for individuals with disabilities it is just as critical but it also may need to be taught.

A review of the literature confirms many implications related to self-determination and individuals with disabilities. These include the following (Malian & Nevin, 2002):

- Self-determination is a developmental phenomenon that changes over an individual's development.
- Self-determination is impacted by the individual's interactions within the environment.
- Self-determination is a teachable skill.
- Self-determination is desirable and valuable for individuals.
- Self-determination is characterized by autonomy and self-regulation.
- Self-determination is enhanced by other individuals.

The bottom line is, "students who feel competent see themselves as able to accomplish optimally challenging tasks and have the tools to initiate and regulate their behaviors" (Eisenman, 2007, p. 3).

TEACHING SELF-DETERMINATION SKILLS

As noted, most individuals develop self-determination skills naturally as part of the developmental process; however, certain individuals, including those with disabilities, do not develop such skills without assistance. As a result of the importance of self-determination skills for successful independence, and the fact that many students need instruction in this area, school personnel must take an active role in helping students develop self-determination skills (Hughes, Wood, Konrad, & Test, 2006). Numerous research studies have found positive results from training in self-determination for students with a wide variety of disabilities, including learning disabilities, mental retardation, emotional disturbance, autism, down syndrome, and cerebral palsy (Malian & Nevin, 2002). Therefore, it is not a question of whether or not instruction can facilitate the development of self-determination skills, but a matter of teachers implementing such instruction.

The teaching of self-determination skills is an ethical responsibility, as determined by criteria of this nature established by Bredberg and Davidson (1999). Their criteria included justice, respect for autonomy, beneficence, and no malfeasance. In analyzing the ethical responsibility of teachers to teach self-determination, Smith and others (2007) noted that (1) it would be inappropriate to not help students become self-determined; (2) teaching self-determination skills helps students become more autonomous; (3) students benefit from being self-determined; and (4) teachers could be doing harm to students by not teaching self-determination skills. As a result of this analysis using these four criteria, Smith and colleagues (2007) determined that it is indeed an ethical responsibility for schools to teach these skills to students who need to possess self-determination in order to transition effectively into adulthood.

There is no single way to teach self-determination skills. These skills can be taught by teachers using a variety of strategies and/or the use of commercial programs. Regardless of the approach used, teachers play a critical role in the development of self-determination skills by students. Unfortunately, many teachers do not feel competent in teaching these skills. In a study of 500 special education teachers, 75% indicated that they were familiar with the term *self-determination*, but only 33% indicated that they were adequately prepared to deliver self-determination training. When asked if they were familiar with the leading commercial programs used to teach self-determination skills, more than 90% of the respondents indicated that they had not heard of any of the programs (Thoma, Nathanson, Baker, & Tamura, 2002). Although many teachers may not feel comfortable teaching self-determination skills, or they may not be familiar with some of the programs available, most teachers indicate that they teach these skills in some form (Thoma et al., 2002), and feel that teaching them is worthwhile (Jones, 2006). Table 13.2 reflects the number of teachers indicating they can and do teach specific skills.

While self-determination skills can be taught to anyone at anytime in just about any setting (Eisenman, 2007; Price et al., 2002), it is important to consider the students' ages, grade levels, cultural backgrounds, and family involvement. Depending on some of these characteristics, teachers may decide to teach self-determination skills in one of the following ways:

- Target one skill or a series of more complex skills (Eisenman, 2007)
- Use children's literature (Konrad, Helf, & Itoi, 2007)
- Use literature circles (Blum, Lispett, & Yocom, 2002)
- Use direct instruction (Test, Browder, Karvonen, Wood, & Algozzine, 2002)
- Use technology (Mechling, 2007)
- Use teaching strategies
- Use commercial programs

TABLE 13.2 ● Teaching Core Component Skills to Students

Skills	Can Teach/ Do Teach (%)	Can Teach/ Not Priority (%)	Can't Teach/ Priority (%)	Can't Teach/ Not Sure (%)	Can't Teach/ Not Priority (%)
Choice making	86.0	9.3	2.3	2.3	0.0
Decision making	79.1	11.6	9.3	2.3	0.0
Problem solving	83.7	4.7	9.3	0.0	0.0
Goal setting & attainment	60.5	23.3	14.0	0.0	0.0
Self-advocacy & leadership skills	62.8	18.6	16.3	0.0	0.0
Self-management & self-regulation	65.1	20.9	9.3	2.3	0.0
Self-awareness & self-knowledge	65.1	18.6	9.3	2.3	2.3

Source: Thoma, C. A., Nathanson, R., Baker, S. R., & Tamura, R. (2002). Self-determination: What do special educators know and where do they learn it? *Remedial and Special Education, 23,* p. 246.

There are numerous actions teachers can take to facilitate the development of self-determination skills. These include (Price et al., 2002, p. 114):

- Encourage self-directed learning in the classroom versus only expert-driven learning and teaching methods. Encourage decision making with both student and teacher input.
- Tap into older students' life experiences and accept individual differences, to promote autonomy.
- Structure teaching and learning to be more problem centered instead of topic centered. Employ cooperative learning groups and community-based instruction.
- Use future adult roles and responsibilities when possible to trigger learning in both general and special education settings. Observational learning occurs through role modeling and team teaching. Validate students.
- Encourage mutual responsibility and goal setting for both teachers and students. View education as a partnership. Ask yourself, "What can we do to achieve this goal?" Participants in this process are both the students and the teachers.
- When possible, stress internal, intrinsically based motivation versus external, extrinsic rewards. Self-awareness of strengths and needs is important. Provide safe risks and opportunities for dialogue.
- As a general rule, infuse choice anywhere and everywhere. Listen and learn all the time!

One way of assisting students in developing self-determination skills is through autonomy-supportive instruction—that is, using instructional strategies that facilitate the development of self-determination. This model can be implemented by providing students with opportunities to make choices in the classroom. Figure 13.1 includes examples of teacher behaviors that should be present in an autonomy-supportive classroom (Eisenman, 2007, p. 5).

A good way of determining how schools implement self-determination training is to look at the methods used in particular schools. Karvonen and others (2004) studied six schools that were considered exemplary in their implementation of self-determination strategies. The primary approaches used included (1) direct instruction, (2) student-led support groups, (3) self-advocacy strategy, (4) integrated instructional philosophy, (5) case manager approach, and (6) person-centered planning. Table 13.3 describes each of these approaches and the school staff member responsible for their implementation.

Another way that teachers can positively influence the development of self-determination skills is through collaboration with families. IDEA requires schools to involve families in all aspects of special education. As a result, they are involved in referral, assessment, IEP

- Help students to identify what they already know and what they want to learn about a topic.
- Provide safe opportunities for students to discuss their personal interests and goals.
- Allow students to select a topic of study that matches their personal interests.
- Explain how particular knowledge, skills, and experiences will help students to achieve personal goals.
- Allow students to choose among learning activities or arrange the sequence of activities.
- Teach students how to determine an optimally challenging performance good for specific tasks.
- Allow students to select their personal performance goal for a task.
- Develop individual performance contracts with students.
- Suggest resources, activities, and people who can help students reach their goals.
- Explicitly teach problem-solving and goal attainment strategies.
- Have students record their performance results and monitor their progress toward goals.
- Acknowledge students' efforts to reach their goals.
- Help students' identify what they did well and where they need improvement.
- Express the belief that students can meet challenges; offer support when needed.
- Celebrate successes.

FIGURE 13.1 ● Examples of Autonomy-Supportive Teacher Behaviors in the General Education Classroom.

Source: Eisenman, L. T. (2007). Self-determination interventions: Building a foundation for school completion. *Remedial and Special Education, 28,* p. 5.

TABLE 13.3 ● Summary Information of Self-Determination Practices, Staff Roles, and University Links

	Site					
	A	**B**	**C**	**D**	**E**	**F**
Primary approach	Classroom instruction on self-determination skills, integrating self-determination into general curriculum, coaching on IEP participation and planning. One 4th grade teacher working on student self-awareness.	Student-led support group, public speaking, self-advocacy and leadership training, communication skills. Some mentoring of middle school students by group members.	Self-advocacy strategy and other learning strategies to develop self-awareness and set goals in middle and high school. Person-centered planning and community-based activities for older students (ages 18–21).	Integrated instructional philosophy, "counseling" approach. Some infusion of self-determination instruction in general curriculum classes.	Teaching goal setting, job skills, and how to recruit help. "Case manager" approach to teaching families how to navigate the adult services system.	Person-centered planning, preference assessment, and "tryouts" to explore vocational and other postsecondary options.
Who intervenes	Special education teachers	One special education teacher and guidance counselor	Special education teachers, transition coordinators	Special education teachers and teacher assistants	Case managers via federal grant project	Transition specialist, parent partners, special education teachers

Source: Karvonen, M., Test, D. W., Wood, W. M., Browder, D., & Algozzine, B. (2004). Putting self-determination into practice. *Exceptional Children, 71,* p. 29.

development, and program review. Schools also need to realize that parents can be valuable in teaching self-determination skills (Smith et al., 2007). Because a major part of skill determination is practicing self-determination skills, parents can greatly facilitate the process by teaching and promoting self-determination at home.

As with many skills, "efforts to promote self-determination are more likely to be successful when there is collaboration between parents and teachers" (Lee, Palmer, Turnbull, & Wehmeyer, 2006, p. 37). Most children learn how to set goals, solve problems, and make decisions at home. As a result, involving parents in helping children develop self-determination skills is a logical strategy. Following are ways that family members can help their children develop self-determination skills (Lee et al., 2006):

- Encourage decision making and problem solving
- Help students understand available choices
- Help students with goal setting and evaluation
- Help students realize and acknowledge their strengths and weaknesses

Table 13.4 offers tips for parents in helping their children develop self-determination. School personnel must encourage parents to support the development of self-determination skills in their children and realize the important role they can play in this endeavor.

Self-Determination Preparation Programs

In addition to teaching self-determination skills through the general curriculum, there are several commercial programs that can be used by teachers. These include (Malian & Nevin, 2002; Trainor, 2005):

TABLE 13.4 ● Tips for Parents

- Encourage children to make choices, set priorities, and make decisions about everyday activities such as what to wear, what foods to eat during snacks, after-school activities, etc.
- Illustrate that choices have results or consequences that need to be considered. For example, "If I choose a candy bar at every snack, I will not be eating in a healthy way," or "If I choose the same shirt to wear daily, it will be dirty most days."
- Help children to identify interests, strengths, and needs. For students with severe disabilities, infer preferences or interests based on observation of their behavior, and consider a wide range of communication efforts including verbal, gesture, computer, and micro-switch technology as a means to determine preferences (Hughes, Pitkin, & Lorden, 1998).
- Explain to children that a goal is something that you want to achieve, and that barriers are things that may get in the way of achieving goals. Encourage the child to assess whether he or she needs to learn something new, change something in the environment, or both to surmount the barriers.
- Place students at the center of goal setting, action planning, and progress monitoring activities, even if children require extensive support to complete the activities. Let the child decide on a schedule and action plan, as well as monitor his or her own progress.
- Support a child's need to rethink a goal, if progress is slow or minimal. Encourage adjusting or reworking the action plan, if the child wants to pursue the goal.
- At the end of the process, be sure to ask how the child felt about the goal and what he or she learned.

Source: Lee, S. H., Palmer, S. B., Turnbull, A. P., & Wehmeyer, M. L. (2006). A model for parent-teacher collaboration to promote self-determination in young children with disabilities. *Teaching Exceptional Children, 38,* p. 37.

- ChoiceMaker (Martin & Huber-Marshall, 1995)
- Steps to Self-Determination (Field & Hoffman, 1994)
- Whose Future Is It Anyway? (Wehmeyer, 1995)

Other commercial programs available include:

- Get a Life (Hughes et al., 2006)
- LEAD (Pocock et al., 2002)
- Classroom Competency-Building Modules (Avery et al., 1995)
- I PLAN (Van Reusen & Bos, 1990)
- Learning Life Management in the Classroom (Kaiser & Abell, 1997)
- Learning with Purposes (Serna & Lau-Smith, 1995)
- Life-Centered Career Education (Brolin, 1993)

In the Get a Life program (Hughes et al., 2006), students are directly involved in activities that "encourage self-determination skills—including making choices, setting goals, making decisions, solving problems, and self managing" (p. 57). They have an opportunity to practice self-determination activities, practice academic skills, and be involved in community-based experiences (Hughes et al., 2006). Table 13.5 describes the four phases of the *Get a Life* curriculum.

Learning and Education About Disabilities (LEAD) is a program that can be used in secondary schools to help students develop self-advocacy and other self-determination skills. The program, based upon student ownership, consists of four specific components. The first component, self-awareness and disability knowledge, facilitates students' understanding of themselves, educationally. Students actually use their cumulative folders and IEPs as their textbooks

TABLE 13.5 ● Instructional Phases and Units

Instructional Phase	Instructional Units
Phase 1: Establishing an occupation and income	Applying for a job Interviewing for a job
Phase 2: Setting up and managing a budget	Managing checking and savings accounts Budgeting and managing expenses Making decisions about life and money: • Where to live and how to select a roommate • How to obtain renter's insurance. • What to eat • How to get around town • How to shop for car insurance (collision, liability, deductibles) • How much to pay for fun (recreation and leisure activities) • What to wear • How to plan for medical expenses • How to obtain health and dental insurance • How to make decisions about savings, investments, and retirement
Phase 3: Payroll	Getting paid for work: • Gross and net pay • Income tax • Social Security
Phase 4: Dealing with the unexpected	Learning from good and bad decisions

Source: Hughes, W., Wood, W. M., Konrad, M., & Test, D. W. (2006). Get a life: Students practice being self-determined. *Teaching Exceptional Children, 38,* p. 58.

in gaining a better understanding of their disability and its educational impact. The second component, support group, provides an opportunity for students to support each other and cope with their disabilities. Students have an opportunity to present information about their disability and discuss it with their peers. In the third component, students make community presentations to parents, students, teachers, and others about their disabilities in an attempt to help others understand the impact of disabilities. Being able to help others understand their disability can also help those with the disability understand their own disability better. In the final component, mentoring, students work with elementary and middle school students, sharing their own experiences with other students who are also experiencing disabilities. Research has shown the LEAD program to be successful in helping students develop self-awareness, self-advocacy, and leadership skills (Pocock et al., 2002). Table 13.6 describes several other curricular programs for self-determination.

STUDENT INVOLVEMENT IN THE EDUCATIONAL PROCESS

One aspect of self-determination that has been gaining in popularity is for students with disabilities to become more involved in their own educational programming. This provides them with an opportunity to take an active role in planning and implementing their educational program and practice self-determination skills. Who better than the student to participate in program development and implementation? Allowing students to participate in this process provides the perfect laboratory setting to learn and practice self-determination skills. Practicing self-determination skills is an excellent way to improve self-determination skills.

Not only does including students in their IEP meetings represent best practice, it is also required by IDEA. IDEA 2004 requires students to be involved in their IEP meetings when transition components are being discussed. That means that when students reach 16 years of age they must be included in the IEP meeting. The idea underlying this requirement is that students often know more than any other person what they want to do after leaving high school. While personal goals may be inappropriate, if self-determination preparation has been successful in previous years they are likely to have a good understanding of their strengths and weaknesses and can provide meaningful input into the planning process.

Inviting students to participate in their IEP meetings by no means results in their active involvement in the process (Mason, McGahee-Kovac, & Johnson, 2004). Students attending their own IEP meetings often simply lack the opportunity to make meaningful contributions to the process (Myers & Eisenman, 2005). Trainor (2005) used focus groups to interview students, aged 16–19, regarding their involvement in transition planning. Across all age and cultural groups, participants indicated that they were not actual "discussants" at these meetings. Rather, they noted that they were present but not involved. Teachers interacted with family members much more extensively than with the students.

Recent studies have shown a growing trend in this direction. Martin, Marshall, and Sale (2004) found that while 70% of students in junior high, middle school, and high school actually attended their IEP meetings, there was limited, meaningful participation. For example, students talked significantly less than other team members, even in the area of determining their own interests. This lack of involvement could be the result of teachers simply not understanding self-determination or the need for students to develop self-determination skills through the IEP process (Konrad, 2008). It could also reflect that many students do not know how to be more involved in the process.

Unfortunately, having students present at IEP meetings but not taking actions to facilitate their real involvement could have a negative impact. They might get the opinion that their ideas were not really wanted by others in the group. Having them sit passively in meetings could result in their developing the idea that their role is to be seen and not heard, which would be the opposite of the goal for self-determination. In other words, this could actually negate self-determination skills that could have been learned to this point.

When students are involved in discussing and selecting IEP and transition goals, they are more likely to consider themselves as active planners in their own life and are more likely to work toward the attainment of their goals (Arndt, Konrad, & Test, 2006). Think of yourself; if others plan things for you without your active involvement you are less likely to be enthusiastic about the activity than if you had been involved. It reflects common sense to involve adolescents in planning their program that will have a direct impact on their life as young adults.

Involvement in the IEP process also provides students with an opportunity to practice self-determination skills, skills that are critically important as adults (Konrad, 2008). Without opportunities for practice, students need support and preparation in order to actualize self-determination opportunities. Trainor (2005) noted, "Frequent opportunities to include students in transition-related conversations and activities are essential" (p. 244).

There are at least three different levels of student involvement in the IEP meetings. The first level is when students simply present information about plans for the future. Students might discuss what they would like to be doing after they exit from school. For example, they might say they want to go to college, or they might say they want to go to work for the local factory. At the second level, students explain their disability, strengths, weaknesses, and accommodations and services needed. This is a very important component of self-determination. As previously noted, students need to have a good understanding of their disability in order to adequately self-advocate. At the third and most comprehensive level, students actually lead the conference (Mason et al., 2004).

Student-led IEPs offer an excellent opportunity for students to become more actively involved in determining their futures and practicing self-determination. Unfortunately, as has been noted, student involvement in the IEP process is often not meaningful, and even though many teachers agree with the concept, they may not feel competent to facilitate this level of participation. Myers and Eisenman (2005) were involved in a project where six teachers engaged in student-led IEP conferences. Their efforts revealed several concerns and common approaches. For example, they expressed concerns about knowing where to start with the student in the IEP meeting; how to talk with students about their disabilities; and how to help students set goals. They noted that a common approach to dealing with their concerns was to use transition planning as the vehicle for discussing goals, strengths, and weaknesses (Myers & Eisenman, 2005). Other approaches, such as using role play and learning how to seek feedback from other IEP committee members, were also used. Table 13.6 summarizes the concerns and common approaches.

After their involvement with student-led IEPs, the six teachers noted "the most important outcome of the process was that students had a chance to have more say about their lives and, in turn, become more self-determined" (p. 56). Even with difficulties they encountered, all six teachers felt that their efforts were worthwhile and that the student-led IEP is a very useful tool (Myers & Eisenman, 2005).

Several positive outcomes can result from student-led IEP meetings. Results from a study of more than 100 students with mild disabilities who had been involved in leading their own IEPs showed the following (Mason et al., 2004, p. 20):

- Students were involved and did contribute to meetings.
- Students knew about their disability rights and their accommodations.
- Students gained increased self-confidence and were able to advocate for themselves.
- Parental participation increased.

TABLE 13.6 ● Six Teachers' First Experiences with Student-Led IEPs

---

Concerns

- Knowing where to start and with what.
- Becoming familiar with new curricula, materials, instructional tasks, and meeting roles.
- Talking sensitively with students about their disabilities.
- Helping students identify and set personally meaningful goals.
- Finding time for additional conversations and instruction with students.
- Integrating activities into the general curriculum.
- Adapting materials for students with significant cognitive disabilities.
- Working with younger students who are in middle school.
- Preparing other professionals to share information in student and family friendly ways.
- Discussing such complex issues as a change of placement.

Common Approaches

- Use transition planning as framework for discussion of goals, strengths, weaknesses.
- Break IEP meeting into smaller tasks (e.g., introductions, goal-presentation, asking for input) and allow student to lead the parts with which she or he is most comfortable.
- Take advantage of existing curricula and materials and adapt as needed.
- Review and explain IEP document components.
- Involve students in gathering information about their strengths and weaknesses.
- Demystify diagnoses and labels by explaining them in functional terms relative to the student's strengths and weaknesses.
- Encourage students and their families to discuss goals, interests, and preferences.
- Collaborate early and often with families, colleagues, students' peers, and administrators.
- Facilitate access to guidance from other caring adults.
- Work with the student to create a script for the meeting.
- Role-play with peers.
- Seek feedback from IEP meeting participants.

Source: Myers, A., & Eisenman, L. (2005). Student-led IEPs: Take the first step. *Teaching Exceptional Children, 37,* p. 55.

The study also found that students interacted more positively with adults, had greater knowledge of their rights, assumed more responsibility for themselves, and were more aware of their limitations than before leading their IEP meetings. Involving students in their IEP development is not only the legal requirement but has been shown to have positive results.

While student involvement in their IEP meetings may not be as meaningful as it could be, significant gains have been made. Prior to IDEA requiring student participation in transition planning, student presence at IEP meetings was rare. As a result of this change, students are much more likely to be present. While getting students to their IEP meetings is an important accomplishment, making them meaningful contributors is still the ultimate goal. Unfortunately, most students do not know how to participate effectively. They are used to adults making most of the decisions affecting their lives and being in control of their IEP meetings. Therefore, instructing students in how to become more involved in the IEP process is important in order to maximize their involvement (Martin et al., 2004). This instruction can be accomplished using teacher-made activities or commercial programs. Konrad (2008) provided 20 different ways to involve students in the IEP process:

1. Use your resources.
2. Develop an IEP scavenger hunt that requires students to find things in their own IEPs.
3. Assign students the task of evaluating their IEPs to make sure they contain all the requirements of the law.

4. Have students read fiction books featuring characters with disabilities and identify strengths and weaknesses of the characters.
5. Work with students to help them develop vision statements for themselves.
6. Get students involved in the assessment process.
7. Have students write letters inviting meeting participants to attend.
8. Use commercial programs such as The Self-Advocacy Strategy to help students identify potential needs, goals, and services.
9. Involve students in preparing the meeting.
10. Have students write paragraphs about their strengths and needs.
11. Have students take each need statement and turn it into an "I will" statement.
12. Require students to meet with their parents before their IEP meeting to review the draft.
13. Keep in mind that there is a range of options for involving students in IEP meetings.
14. Use published curricula such as The Self-Directed IEP.
15. Provide students with several opportunities to rehearse for their meeting.
16. Have each student create a fact sheet that summarizes his or her IEP for general education teachers.
17. Teach students self-advocacy and self-recruitment skills.
18. Provide students with access to their IEP files.
19. Teach students to self-monitor and self-evaluate their progress.
20. Have students develop first-person progress reports to share with their parents and the IEP team.

One program to help students learn how to become more involved in their IEP meetings is the Self-Directed IEP (Martin, Marshall, Maxson, & Jerman, 1996). In a study of the effectiveness of the Self-Directed IEP, Arndt and colleagues (2006) found that the program was effective in teaching self-determination skills and increasing students' knowledge and participation in their IEP meetings. One important finding of the study was that students were able to generalize their skills from the training session to the actual IEP meetings. Since many students with disabilities have problems with generalization, this finding was very important in promoting direct training programs to increase student involvement in their IEP meetings.

Torgerson, Miner, and Shen (2004) reported on another training model for preparing students to lead their IEP meetings. The program includes four sessions. In the first session, students develop a workbook entitled *It's My Life* (Bates et al., 2001). The workbook enables students to focus on their strengths, needs, and priorities. The second session involves a videotape of a simulated student-led IEP meeting. After watching the videotape, students complete the 10-step guide to the self-directed IEP (Bates et al., 2001) that was adapted from the *Self-Directed IEP Student Workboo*k (Martin et al., 1996). In the third session, students discuss social skills needed in the IEP meeting and practice them with a partner. The fourth session involves another videotape activity where students participate in a simulated IEP meeting, assuming various roles represented in the meeting. Students then review the tapes and discuss the taped session.

Mason and colleagues (2004) described another model to help students develop necessary skills for leading their IEP meetings. This program consists of five sessions:

Session 1: Students learn information on the law and students' rights.
Session 2: Students discuss assessment information and its meaning.
Session 3: Students solicit opinions of their family and teachers related to goals.
Sessions 4 and 5: Students use the draft IEP to practice presentation; other students who have led their IEP meetings may model behaviors.

Participating in and leading their own IEP meetings is a major step toward self-determination. While there is no one program that will prepare students to assume a more active role in their IEP meetings, it is incumbent on the school to implement strategies that will assist students in their increased role. This is a critical responsibility for schools. For school personnel to say that the student is present at the IEP meeting but does not choose to become actively involved in the process is failing to meet its responsibility.

AGE OF MAJORITY

IDEA requires that students, at the age of majority, assume the responsibility to make their own educational decisions, "unless the student is determined to be incompetent by State law, or has not been determined incompetent by State law, but considered unable to provide informed consent with respect to educational programming" (Millar, 2007, p. 119). This means that upon reaching the age of majority, most students must be allowed to make decisions that were previously made by parents and other family members. In most states, the age of majority is 18 years. Obviously, many students are not prepared to assume this role even though they may be legally old enough to do so. Because parents and school personnel have been making all these decisions, often with little or no involvement of the student, suddenly expecting them to be able to assume this role may be unrealistic. To assist students in this role, schools are obligated by law to provide training to help them develop skills necessary to assume responsibility for their educational program. Therefore, an appropriate component of the IEP of a student who is nearing the age of majority should focus on preparation to assume this new role.

Millar (2007) studied the issues of self-determination and guardianship with focus groups of students with disabilities, their parents, and teachers, to obtain the perspectives of these groups on the issues of guardianship and self-determination. Participants felt that teaching self-determination skills was vitally critical to facilitate the transition of students from school to adulthood; however, they had not realized that their efforts to obtain guardianship over some of these students negatively impacted this effort.

The Millar (2007) study supports a concern that teachers, while advocating for self-determination for their students, are in a difficult situation because of their role in developing individualized educational programs for students throughout the students' educational career. During most of the school years teachers are advocates for these students. They lead in the development, implementation, and evaluation of the IEP. For the most part, these teachers view themselves, along with the child's parents, as the leading advocate for the child. Turning this role over to students themselves sometimes is a difficult thing to do. How, if the goal for these students is maximized self-determination, then part of the school's role is to prepare them for this important step.

Self-Determination Supports in Postsecondary Educational Settings

With more students with disabilities attending postsecondary education programs, the need for their being self-determined is more important than ever. Unlike the requirements of grades P–12, where schools are responsible for initiating referrals, conducting evaluations, and being proactive about a child's educational program, in postsecondary educational settings the responsibility for referral, identification, and request for accommodations rests with the individual student. For example, students in postsecondary educational settings must self-refer. They must go to the appropriate office, usually a disability support office, and indicate that they have a particular disability and need certain accommodations. To substantiate their request, students must provide the necessary documentation. If students do not possess the self-determination skills to do this they may not receive the accommodations and modifications they need to be successful. Students in postsecondary education must be proactive.

TABLE 13.7 ● Recommended Practices to Support Self-Determination in Postsecondary Educational Settings

Environmental Characteristic	Examples of Recommended Practices
Self-determined role models are available	• Staff demonstrates self-determination in professional practices. • Support for staff self-determination is addressed in hiring, orientation, and staff development.
Instruction and support for the development of knowledge, skills, and beliefs that lead to self-determination	• Staff are familiar with curriculum and instructional strategies to foster self-determination competencies. • Instruction that leads to self-determination knowledge, skills, and beliefs is infused throughout postsecondary coursework. • Instruction, counseling, and supports that lead to the development of self-determination knowledge, skills, and beliefs are available through student affairs and disability services.
Opportunities for choice	• Students are provided with opportunities to make decisions and be responsible for their decisions. • Students have opportunities to select courses.
Positive communication patterns	• Staff use assertive communication and active listening techniques in their communication with students. • Students know specific times that staff are available for individual questions and discussion. • Administrators designate specific opportunities for students and staff to express opinions on key issues affecting the school.
Availability of student supports	• Universal design practices are used. • Accommodations are determined collaboratively by students, faculty, and disability services. • Personnel are available to meet with students to discuss individualized needs.

Source: Field, S., Sarver, M. D., & Shaw, S. F. (2003). Self-determination: A key to success in postsecondary education for students with learning disabilities. *Remedial and Special Education, 24,* p. 342.

Since many secondary education programs do not adequately prepare individuals with disabilities with self-determination skills, it may be important for postsecondary educational programs to provide supports in self-determination. This could be provided by the disability support office. Field, Sarver, and Shaw (2003) provided a list of practices that would support self-determination in postsecondary educational settings, shown in Table 13.7. While these are provided as examples for the settings, many would also apply to secondary programs.

SUMMARY

This chapter covers the broad area of self-determination for adolescents with disabilities. Most important, the goal for all individuals in our society is to be self-determined. Being self-determined means that individuals get to make choices. It means being responsible for oneself—making choices and decisions, setting goals, evaluating attainment of goals, and being as independent as possible. Adolescents, in general, struggle to gain self-determination. On one hand, they want to be self-determined, but on the other, they still depend on their families for basic needs. Attempts

of adolescents to become self-determined often lead to conflict within the family.

Adolescents with disabilities have a difficult time with self-determination. This may be due to their disability, but is often the result of their being overprotected by family members and often school personnel. Teachers, and sometimes family members, actually teach individuals with disabilities to be somewhat helpless. While wanting to provide supports and protections for this group of individuals, doing so without giving them the opportunity to become self-determined is detrimental in the long run. All individuals, including those with disabilities, need to be as independent as possible. For individuals with severe disabilities, being fully independent may not be possible. However, this does not mean that this group cannot become somewhat independent and make choices for themselves.

Teaching adolescents with disabilities to be self-determined is an important component of their educational program. This can be done with direct instruction, commercial programs, or simply giving students opportunities during their school day and at home to make decisions, choices, and set goals for themselves. One excellent way of helping adolescents with disabilities become more self-determined is to encourage them to participate, and eventually lead, their IEP meetings. Regardless of how this develops for each student, schools and families must work together to encourage the development of self-determination skills for this group of individuals.

ACTIVITIES

1. On a scale of 1 to 10, with 10 being the highest, rate yourself on self-determination skills. Why do you think some of your self-determination skills are better than others?

2. Discuss the importance of self-determination skills for adolescents with disabilities with regular and special education secondary teachers. Did all teachers have a common understanding of the importance of self-determination skills or was there variability?

3. Think about some of your peers who went to college and were successful, and others who went to college and had significant difficulties. Do you think the levels of self-determination skills present had any impact on this success or lack of success? What specific self-determination skills seemed to be most related to success?

REFERENCES

American Heritage Dictionary (1992). (3rd ed.). Boston: Houghton-Mifflin.

Arndt, S. A., Konrad, M., & Test, D. W. (2006). Effects of the self-directed IEP on student participation in planning meetings. *Remedial and Special Education, 27,* 194–207.

Avery, B., Rudrud, L., Arndt, K., Schauben, L., & Eggebeen, A. (1995). Evaluating a multicomponent program for enhancing the self-determination of youth with disabilities. *Intervention in School and Clinic, 30,* 170–179.

Barrie, W., & McDonald, J. (2002). Administrative support for student-led individualized education programs. *Remedial and Special Education, 23,* 116–121.

Bates, P. E., Miner, C., Heckenkamp, D., & Walter, S. (2001). *The self-directed IEP: An interactive workshop format.* Springfield: Illinois State Board of Education.

Blum, H. T., Lipsett, L. R., & Yocom, D. (2002). Literature circles: A tool for self-determination in one middle school inclusive classroom. *Remedial and Special Education, 23,* 99–104.

Bredberg, E., & Davidson, I. (1999). Ethical reasoning used by teachers of children with severe and profound intellectual disabilities: A preliminary investigation. *International Journal of Disability, Development, and Education, 46,* 88–107.

Brolin, D. (1993). Life centered career education: A competency based approach. *The Council for Exceptional Children.* Reston, VA.

Deci, E. L., & Ryan, R. M. (1985). *Intrinsic motivation and self-determination in human behavior.* New York: Plenum.

Eisenman, L.T. (2007). Self-determination interventions: Building a foundation for school completion. *Remedial and Special Education, 28,* 2–8.

Field, S., & Hoffman, A. (1994). *Steps to self-determination: A curriculum to help adolescents learn to achieve their goals.* Austin, TX: Pro-Ed.

Field, S., Hoffman, A., & Spezia, S. (1998). *Self-determination strategies for adolescents in transition.* Austin, TX: Pro-Ed.

Field, S., Sarver, M. D., & Shaw, S. F. (2003). Self-determination: A key to success is postsecondary education for students with learning disabilities. *Remedial and Special Education, 24,* 339–349.

Fowler, C. H., Konrad, M., Walker, A. R., Test, D. W., & Wood, W. M. (2007). Self-determination interventions' effects on the academic performance of students with developmental disabilities. *Education and Training in Developmental Disabilities, 42,* 270–285.

Hong, B. S. S., Ivy, W. F., Gonzalez, H. R., & Ehrensberger, W. (2007). Preparing students for postsecondary education. *Teaching Exceptional Children, 40,* 21–38.

Hughes, C., Pitkin, S., & Lorden, S. (1998). Assessing preferences and choices of persons with severe and profound mental retardation. *Education and Training in Mental Retardation and Developmental Disabilities, 33,* 299–316.

Hughes, W., Wood, W. M., Konrad, M., & Test, D. W. (2006). Get a Life: Students practice being self-determined. *Teaching Exceptional Children, 38,* 57–63.

Jones, M. (2006). Teaching self-determination: Empowered teachers, empowered students. *Teaching Exceptional Children, 39,* 12–17.

Kaiser, D., & Abell, M. (1997). Learning life management in the classroom. *Teaching Exceptional Children, 30,* 70–75.

Karvonen, M., Test, D. W., Wood, W. M., Browder, D., & Algozzine, B. (2004). Putting self-determination into practice. *Exceptional Children, 71,* 23–41.

Konrad, M. (2008). Involve students in the IEP process. *Intervention in School and Clinic, 43,* 236–239.

Konrad, M., Helf, S., & Itoi, M. (2007). More bang for the book: Using children's literature to promote self-determination and literacy skills. *Teaching Exceptional Children, 40,* 64–71.

Lee, S. H., Palmer, S. B., Turnbull, A. P., & Wehmeyer, M. L. (2006). A model for parent-teacher collaboration to promote self-determination in young children with disabilities. *Teaching Exceptional Children, 38,* 36–41.

Malian, I., & Nevin, A. (2002). A review of self-determination literature. *Remedial and Special Education, 23,* 68–74.

Martin, J. E., & Huber-Marshall, L. H. (1995). Choice-Maker: A comprehensive self-determination transition program. *Intervention in School and Clinic, 30,* 147–156.

Martin, J. E., Marshall, L. H., Maxson, L. M., & Jerman, P. L. (1996). *The self-directed IEP.* Longmont, CO: Sporis West.

Martin, J. E., Marshall, L. H., & Sale, P. (2004). A 3-year study of middle, junior high, and high school IEP meetings. *Exceptional Children, 70,* 285–297.

Mason, C. Y., McGahee-Kovac, M., & Johnson, L. (2004). How to help students lead their IEP meetings. *Teaching Exceptional Children, 36,* 18–24.

Mechling, L. C. (2007). Assistive technology as a self-management tool for prompting students with intellectual disabilities to initiate and complete daily tasks: A literature review. *Education and Training in Developmental Disabilities, 42,* 252–269.

Millar, D. S. (2007). "I never put it together": The disconnect between self-determination and guardianship—implications for practice. *Education and Training in Developmental Disabilities, 42,* 119–129.

Myers, A., & Eisenman, L. (2005). Student-led IEPs: Take the first step. *Teaching Exceptional Children, 37,* 58.

Nirje, B. (1969). The normalization principal and its human management implications. In R. Kugel & W. Wolfensberger (Eds.), *Changing patterns in residential services for the mentally retarded.* Washington, DC: President's Committee on Mental Retardation.

Peterson, S. M. P., Caniglia, C., & Royster, A. J. (2001). Application of choice-making intervention for a student with multiply maintained problem behavior. *Focus on Autism and Other Developmental Disabilities, 16,* 240–246.

Pocock, A., Lambros, S., Karvonen, M., Test, D. W., Algozzine, B., Wood, W., & Martin, J. E. (2002). Successful strategies for promoting self-advocacy among students with LD: The LEAD group. *Intervention in School and Clinic, 37,* 209–216.

Price, L. A., Wolensky, D., & Mulligan, R. (2002). Self-determination in action in the classroom. *Remedial and Special Education, 23,* 109–115.

Serna, L., & Lau-Smith, J. (1995). Learning with purpose: Self-determination skills for students who are at risk for school and community failure. *Intervention in School and Clinic, 30,* 142–146.

Smith, T. E. C., Gartin, B. A., & Murdick, N. (2006). *Families and children with special needs.* Upper Saddle River, NJ: Merrill/Pearson.

Smith, T. E. C., Polloway, E. A., Patton, J. R., & Dowdy, C. A. (2008). *Teaching students with special needs in inclusive settings.* Boston: Allyn & Bacon.

Smith, T. L., Polloway, E. A., Smith, J. D., & Patton, J. R. (2007). Self-determination for persons with developmental disabilities: Ethical considerations for teachers. *Education and Training in Developmental Disabilities, 42,* 144–151.

Test, D. W., Browder, D. M., Karvonen, M., Wood, W., & Algozzine, B. (2002). Writing lesson plans for promoting self-determination. *Teaching Exceptional Children, 35,* 8–14.

Test, D. W., Fowler, C. H., Wood, W. M., Brewer, D. M., & Eddy, S. (2005). A conceptual framework of self-advocacy for students with disabilities. *Remedial and Special Education, 26*, 43–54.

Thoma, C. A., Nathanson, R., Baker, S. R., & Tamura, R. (2002). Self-determination: What do special educators know and where do they learn it? *Remedial and Special Education, 23*, 242–247.

Torgerson, C., Miner, C. A., & Shen, H. (2004). Developing student competence in self-directed IEPs. *Intervention in School and Clinic, 39*, 162–167.

Trainor, A. A. (2005). Self-determination perceptions and behaviors of diverse students with LD during the transition planning process. *Journal of Learning Disabilities, 38*, 233–249.

Van Reusen, A. K., & Bos, C. S. (1990). I PLAN: Helping students communicate in planning conferences. *Teaching Exceptional Children, 22*, 30–32.

Ward, M. J. (1988). *The many facets of self-determination.* National Information Center for Children and Youth with Handicaps Transition Summary, S, 2–3.

Wehmeyer, M. (1995). A career education approach: Self-determination for youth with mild cognitive disabilities. *Intervention in School and Clinic, 30*, 157–163.

Wehmeyer, M. L., Abery, B., Mithaug, D. E., & Stancliffe, R. J. (2003). *Theory in self-determination: Foundations for educational practice.* Springfield, IL: Thomas.

Wehmeyer, M. L., Bersani, H., & Gagne, R. (2000). Riding the third wave: Self-determination and self-advocacy in the 21st century. *Focus on Autism and Other Developmental Disabilities, 15*, 106–115.

Wehmeyer, M. L., Martin, J. E., & Sands, D. J. (2008). Self-determination and students with developmental disabilities. In H. P. Parette & G. R. Peterson-Karlan (Eds.), *Research-based practices in developmental disabilities* (2nd ed., pp. 99–122). Austin, TX: Pro-Ed.

Wolfensberger, W. (1972). *Normalization: The principle of normalization in human services.* Toronto: National Institute on Mental Retardation.

Zhang, D., Wehmeyer, M. L., & Chen, L. J. (2005). Parent and teacher engagement in fostering the self-determination of students with disabilities: A comparison between the United States and the Republic of China. *Remedial and Special Education, 26*, 55–63.

14

Vocational/Technical Education for Adolescents with Disabilities

Study Questions

1. What was the impact of federal legislation on protecting the right of "equal access" for students with disabilities?

2. How does the definition of disability and eligibility criteria differ between IDEA 2004 and ADA?

3. What consists of an appropriate vocational assessment for students with disabilities whose vocational goals include postsecondary education?

4. Why is the high school program of study and choice of diploma critical to students with disabilities?

5. What knowledge should secondary teachers ensure that students acquire to assist in their transition to postsecondary education?

INTRODUCTION

In the opinion of numerous educators, advocates, and parents of persons with disabilities, many students with disabilities need a functional emphasis in their educational program if they are to transition successfully to adult life. As part of their schooling, they need the opportunity to develop skills necessary in the personal, community, and vocational sectors of their lives. The nation addressed this need by enacting legislation in the 1970s and 1980s in areas of access to public facilities, employment, and education to ensure the right for persons with disabilities to equal opportunities.

LEGISLATION

There were numerous legislative acts passed during this period with a focus on equal opportunities and civil rights. Prior to the passage of these laws many individuals with disabilities were discriminated against in employment, education, and community living areas. Legislation passed during this period can be grouped in five categories: (1) vocational rehabilitation, (2) special education, (3) developmental disabilities, (4) employment services, and (5) civil rights. A brief discussion of each will follow.

Vocational Rehabilitation

Repeatedly persons with disabilities refer to the Rehabilitation Act of 1973 as their civil rights legislation. Within this law, Sections 503 and 504 have the greatest significance to schools. Section 503 requires all employers to comply with "affirmative action" regulations in any personnel actions. In addition, Section 503 requires that school personnel and vocational rehabilitation personnel develop and implement a collaborative process for developing an individualized work rehabilitation plan (IWRP). The IWRP outlines the job goal and preparation, training, and supports that schools and vocational rehabilitation personnel will provide the student.

Section 504 is primarily civil rights legislation for individuals with disabilities. It impacts entities that receive federal funds. Because virtually all public schools are recipients of federal funds, they must comply with Section 504. Section 504 mandates equal opportunities in education and training for students with disabilities. Students with disabilities include those identified for special education services as well as those who do not qualify for special education but demonstrate disability-related learning and behavioral issues that affect their ability to be successful without the provision of services.

The definition of *disability* in Section 504 is broader than the one used in IDEA. Section 504 says that an individual is considered to have a disability if that person has a mental or physical impairment that substantially limits a major life activity. The law does not require a person to have a particular disability, similar to IDEA, but covers a broad range of disabilities. Also, unlike IDEA, learning does not have to be impacted for a person to be eligible under Section 504. Under Section 504, a person's impairment must substantially limit a major life activity, which includes learning, walking, talking, hearing, seeing, working, and performing manual tasks.

Unfortunately, Section 504 has no funding attached to it and is often not utilized efficiently by schools. It does, however, require that students who qualify for services be provided a plan developed by teachers, school officials, the student with disabilities, and parents of the student. The Section 504 plan must include modifications that are essential for the student to have equal access to schools and schooling (Smith, Polloway, Patton, & Dowdy, 2012).

Special Education

The bill of rights for children with disabilities is the Education for All Handicapped Children Act of 1975 (now known as IDEA). Prior to its enactment, children with disabilities were rarely educated in public schools. Under the legislative definition in IDEA, the term "children" includes ages 3–21. The regulations direct that a committee including school personnel, community providers, the student, and the student's parents develop an individualized educational program (IEP); and that the IEP from age 16 until exit from the program includes an individualized transition plan (ITP). The IEP is to be an outcomes-based document that addresses the educational, community, and vocational goals of the student. Fortunately, IDEA provides some funding although full funding never has occurred.

One of the key requirements of IDEA is that students with disabilities should have access to the general curriculum. For students in elementary grades this is nearly automatic since more students with disabilities today are educated in general classroom settings than more restrictive settings. For students in middle and high schools, the requirement to ensure access to the general education curriculum for students with disabilities can be more problematic. General classroom teachers, in content classes, must facilitate the placement of students with disabilities in their classroom. And, with No Child Left Behind legislation, these students are also expected to meet certain academic outcomes (Smith et al., 2008).

Developmental Disabilities

The Developmental Disabilities Assistance and Bill of Rights Act of 2000 authorized grants related to the pursuit of competitive employment goals to support the planning, coordination, and delivery of specialized services to persons with developmental disabilities. The law mandates the development of plans and programs to assist students with severe disabilities to transition, and the development of an interagency committee to plan and coordinate such activities. This legislation also requires each state to implement a statewide protection and advocacy (P&A) system for all persons with developmental disabilities. Funding for these mandated services is to each state through grants for services (Murdick, Gartin, & Crabtree, 2007).

Employment Services

In 1973, the Comprehensive Employment and Training Act (CETA) was passed in order to provide job training and employment opportunities for economically disadvantaged, unemployed, and underemployed persons. Although persons with disabilities often were present in these categories, the legislation did not specifically mention "disability" as a category. This changed in 1978 when amendments to the act specify "individuals with disabilities" as a distinct group of persons covered. In 1982, Congress replaced CETA with the Job Training and Partnership Act (JTPA), which again did not specifically mention individuals with disabilities as an eligibility category. In 1990, Congress again ensured access to vocational education for persons with disabilities with the passing of the Carl D. Perkins Vocational and Applied Technology Amendments, which was amended again in 1998. In subsequent years, Congress has continued to pass legislation to ensure equal access to persons with disabilities in all programs receiving federal funding or oversight.

Civil Rights

The first legislation guaranteeing the civil right of access was limited to programs receiving federal funding. For example, Section 504 of the Rehabilitation Act of 1973 comprised the civil rights legislation covering preschool, elementary, secondary, adult education programs, and colleges and universities that received any form of federal financial aid for over 20 years. It was not until the 1990s that Congress broadened the civil rights protections for persons with disabilities by passing the Americans with Disabilities Act (ADA) of 1990. ADA extends antidiscrimination requirements to public and private colleges, testing centers, the employment sector, and telecommunications. Unlike Section 504, the ADA applies to a wide range of entities and is not restricted to those who receive federal funding. This means that the ADA protects the employment of individuals with disabilities in both the public and the private sectors.

There are distinct differences in these laws that protect against discrimination (Section 504 and ADA), and IDEA (1990, 1997, 2004), which is an entitlement law that assures a free public education to any student with disabilities needing special education within the public K–12 system. It is important that students with disabilities recognize that upon graduation they leave behind the entitlement of IDEA protection and enter the civil rights coverage of Section 504 and ADA. Once they are under Section 504 and ADA, individuals with disabilities are assured equal access and nondiscriminatory treatment by meeting the criteria of proving to (a) have a disability or impairment and (2) be "otherwise qualified."

In 2009, the Americans with Disabilities Act Amendments Act (ADAAA) of 2008 went into effect. The definition of disability or impairment remains the same, but states that the definition of disability will be construed in favor of a broad coverage of individuals. An inexhaustible list of "major life activities" was developed and "episodic conditions" were clarified to be considered active even during their inactive periods. For example, even though individuals with epilepsy do not display seizure activities constantly, they are still considered disabled and protected under the ADA because when they have episodes of seizures they are definitely considered disabled. A second important change resulting from the ADAAA deals with "mitigating measures" such as medication. The reauthorized ADA notes that mitigating measures should not be a consideration when determining eligibility. In other words, if a student with ADHD does well in school while medicated, but would have substantial limitations in learning if he or she were not medicated, he would be considered eligible under the ADA. Prior to the amendments this individual would not have been considered eligible. The impact of these amendments was to greatly increase the number of persons under its protection. Table 14.1 provides a list of web resources related to federal legislation.

Students with disabilities planning to enter postsecondary education need to be aware of the differences between IDEA and services and protections provided under Section 504 and the ADA. These differences are as follows:

- Under IDEA, the school is responsible for initiating a referral; under 504 and the ADA, the individual with a disability must self-refer.

TABLE 14.1 ● Web Resources: Federal Legislation

Federal Legislation	Web Resource
Rehabilitation Act of 1973, Section 504	http://ed.gov/policy/speced/reg/narrative.html
Individuals with Disabilities Education Act (IDEA)	http://idea.ed.gov/
Developmental Disabilities Assistance and Bill of Rights Act	www.acf.hhs.gov
Comprehensive Employment and Training Act (CETA)	www.answers.com/.../comprehensive-employment-and-training-act
Carl D. Perkins Vocational and Applied Technology Amendments	http://ed.gov/policy/sectech/leg/perkins/index.html
Americans with Disabilities Act (ADA)	www.ada.gov/
No Child Left Behind Act (NCLB)	www2.ed.gov/nclb/overview/intro/edpicks.jhtml

- Under IDEA, the school is responsible for assessment to determine eligibility; under 504 and the ADA, the individual with a disability is responsible for providing assessment information to justify eligibility.
- Under IDEA, the school is responsible for initiating the determination of appropriate services; under 504 and the ADA, the individual with a disability must request specific services.
- Under IDEA, public schools receive a great deal of federal funding to assist in carrying out its provisions; there are no federal funds to support Section 504 and the ADA.

Preparing for these changes will ensure that eligible students and their families will have adequate documentation for the transition to postsecondary settings and ensure that appropriate accommodations are requested and received. The preparation should also include preparing students to be self-determined so they can advocate for themselves in postsecondary educational and employment settings.

ASSESSING VOCATIONAL NEEDS OF ADOLESCENTS WITH DISABILITIES

By age 16, IDEA mandates the development of an individualized transition plan (ITP) for all students as part of their IEP. To develop an appropriate ITP, school personnel need to perform a vocational assessment that will lead to the establishment of appropriate transition goals and objectives. A vocational evaluation is used to identify information on the student's strengths, needs, and preferences; personal, social, and educational goals; hobbies, activities, and social interests; ability to live independently and to function within the community; vocational interests, employment skills, and job skills. Therefore, vocational assessments are broad in scope and include both formal and informal procedures.

Although there are specialists in vocational assessment, often classroom teachers are responsible for conducting these assessments as well as providing any vocational training needed by these students. Some middle school curriculum includes opportunities for students to explore topics and content related to potential vocational goals. Many states even require a semester or more of career awareness or vocational information during the middle school years.

By the time students enter high school they should be expected to make choices concerning their high school program of study. Therefore, middle and high school teachers need to be knowledgeable concerning any vocational issues that potentially could impact their students, particularly students with disabilities. It is therefore essential that teachers have a general knowledge of the evaluation procedures and assessment instruments that might be used in a vocational evaluation and assessment process.

Vocational Assessment: Data Gathering

According to Sitlington, Neubert, and Clark (2010), "Transition assessment is an on-going process that focuses on an individual's current and future roles as a family and community member, lifelong learner, and worker" (p. 86). The process requires the evaluator to gather and utilize information from (a) background information, (b) interviews with the student and others, (c) standardized tests, (d) curriculum-based assessments, (e) performance sampling, and (f) situational assessments. The task for teachers is to determine what information will be most helpful in determining how to assist students in making a successful transition to future environments. Understanding the sources and types of information available will assist teachers in ensuring the success of this process.

Background Information.   When conducting a comprehensive evaluation, the first item that should be reviewed is any existing records of the individual. Existing records always include the school cumulative folder, but other records are typically available for students with disabilities. These are likely to include formal assessment information, previous IEPs, and consent forms completed by parents. Teachers and school support personnel often retain records of student test results, class observations, and any behavioral incidents. Possibly, there may be other official records available, such as those from mental health, juvenile justice, or youth and family services. For some of these items, teachers may have to sign a release before viewing their content. When teachers review this information, they should look for trends and patterns of student behaviors, likes and dislikes, and interests. Teachers need to always remember that (1) students may have changed, perhaps matured, and (2) students may react differently in different situations.

Interviews.   Interviews with students, their friends and family, former teachers and support personnel, and employers may be excellent sources of information on student functioning. Interviews can also provide essential information on students' school, work, social skills, and living preferences. When interviewing students, teachers need to know the information they are seeking. Teachers should not only ask about students' past, but also about the present and their desired futures. Questions should be short, but allow for a determination of communications skills. At regular intervals and at the conclusion of interviews, teachers should summarize what has been said and provide an opportunity for students to correct any of their responses.

A second source of informal interview-type information results from the use of checklists and rating scales. These provide teachers with an opportunity to ask specific questions that can be used for future planning purposes. Teachers may use checklists and rating scales with middle level students as part of an informal assessment of attitudes toward different work situations and preferences for differing types of work. Additionally, school personnel can use the assessment data from these performance-based checklists or rating scales to determine the extent of students' knowledge and level of development of prevocational skills. In interpreting the information gained from checklists and rating scales, teachers should look for similarities and differences in the information that has been gathered. This information can provide teachers with an outline of the students' preferences, knowledge, skills, and aptitudes. The more information school personnel gather, the better understanding they can develop about particular students, resulting in relevant intervention plans for each one of them.

Standardized Testing.   Standardized testing can provide essential information concerning the academic performance of the students, and help teachers determine if students possess the appropriate academic base for successful transition to adult life. In the area of vocational education, standardized testing can provide information on the knowledge level of students related to functional and vocational skills necessary for specific employment areas. However, even though schools can determine if students possess prerequisite skills for particular jobs, they cannot provide information on how well students will apply these skills in real-life situations.

Several vocational interest tests have been standardized to give school personnel, students, and their families ideas about specific interests and aptitudes students may have. Most of these instruments are paper-pencil tests that provide information about students' aptitude skills, such as verbal or mechanical reasoning, and career-occupational interests. The Transition Planning Inventory–2 (Clark & Patton, 2006) provides a different type of assessment. This instrument "provides linkages from assessment to program planning, including linkages with postschool agencies" (Taylor, 2009, p. 392). This type of instrument is a better fit for securing information that could be useful in developing IEPs and transition plans.

Some of the interest and aptitude instruments that are commonly used in public schools include the Differential Aptitude Test (Bennett, Seashore, & Wesman, 1992); Job Observation and Behavior Scale (Rosenberg & Brady, 2000); Occupational Aptitude Survey and Interest Schedule–3 (Parker, 2001); and Wide Range Interest and Occupation Test–2 (Glutting & Wilkinson, 2003). These represent only a small number of different assessment instruments that could be useful in determining students' vocational aptitude and interests (Taylor, 2009).

Curriculum-Based Assessment.   Curriculum-based assessment is an approach that employs assessment instruments that focus on specific content taught. These assessment instruments are typically developed by teachers, and focus only on what is being taught. Data collected from curriculum-based measures can be extremely useful in determining specific skills students learn from a particular class and should therefore be used by teachers to change how their courses may be taught.

Performance Samples.   Performance sampling replicates real-life situations in a structured environment under controlled circumstances. This type of assessment also provides students with opportunities to learn the task. Examples of performance samples include using a school store to simulate the task of selling school supplies or the school kitchen to practice dishwashing on a commercial machine. To develop a performance sample, teachers must conduct an analysis of the actual task in its natural environment. Performance samples generally include:

- A standard set of tasks with written instructions
- Actual materials used in the competitive environment
- Target behaviors to observe

Information gained from performance samples includes appropriate and inappropriate student behaviors, likes and dislikes of the student, task learning time, and quality of the outcome.

Situational Assessment.   Situational assessment is similar to performance sampling in that students are observed doing particular assigned tasks. This type of assessment is also called work samples. Situational assessments are excellent for determining students' skills, interests, work habits, and social skills in a work environment (Taylor, 2009). This form of assessment differs from performance sampling in that students are observed while performing the tasks in real-life environments. The advantage of situational assessment is that teachers can observe the students in real-life environments; the disadvantage is that teachers cannot control what is occurring, which can be done in performance sampling. Table 14.2 provides a summary matrix of different forms of vocational assessments.

Vocational Assessment: Future Environments

When student data have been collected, the assessment process is only halfway complete. Teachers should compare the current assessment data with information about the requirements of the future living, learning, and working environments that students have identified through the person-centered planning strategies that have determined students' preferences for their futures. To learn of the demands within the future environments, teachers may need to directly investigate the environment or find an expert within the setting to explain the demands. This information compared with the demands of future environments can assist school personnel in determining potential educational goals and needs. At this point, teachers need to begin the process of analyzing students' skill levels to determine if supports and accommodations or assistive technologies are necessary to support instruction and skill acquisition. There is also the possibility that the students' goals may be inappropriate and that new goals will need to be developed.

Transition goals need to emerge from student assessment data. Instructional goals must then be developed to relate to the performance of skills required to perform the transition goals. It is critical that those conducting assessments be sensitive to both gender and culture when conducting vocational assessments. For some, the language of the future is unfamiliar. Teachers

TABLE 14.2 ● Summary Matrix of Vocational Assessment

Instrument or Technique	Prereferral: Screening and Initial Identification	Prereferral: Informal Determination of Teaching Programs and Strategies	Postreferral: Determination of Current Performance Level and Educational Need	Postreferral: Decisions about Classification and Program Placement	Postreferral: IEP Goals	Postreferral: IEP Objectives	Postreferral: IEP Evaluation	Mild/Moderate	Severe/Profound	Preschool	Elementary Age	Secondary Age	Adult	Special Consideration	Educational Relevance for Exceptional Students
Checklists and Rating Scales		X						X			X	X		Informal techniques that provide preliminary data but require additional techniques for complete data.	Adequate
Work Samples			X		X	X						X	X	Combination of commercial and locally developed instruments is suggested although cost is a concern.	Useful
Curriculum-Based Vocational Assessment		X	X		X	X	X	X			X	X		Validity of vocational curriculum must be considered.	Very Useful
Direct Observation and Ecological Assessment		X	X		X	X	X	X	X		X	X	X	Probably most adaptable and widely applicable technique.	Very Useful
Portfolio Assessment		X	X		X	X	X	X	X		X	X	X	See Chapter 6; use of a career portfolio is helpful.	Useful
Outcomes Assessment		X	X				X	X	X				X	Emphasizes importance of determining postschool outcomes.	Useful
Differential Aptitude Tests						X		X				X	X	Widely used instrument; time consuming; computerized version available.	Adequate
Job Observation and Behavior Scale					X		X	X				X	X	Actually measures on-the-job performance.	Useful
Occupational Aptitude Survey and Interest Schedule–3						X		X				X		Measures aptitude and interests.	Adequate
Strong-Campbell Interest Inventory						X		X				X	X	A popular instrument that is widely researched.	Adequate
Vocational Preference Inventory–Revised												X	X	Based on Holland's six work typologies.	Limited
Wide Range Interest and Occupation Test–2						X		X			X	X	X	Is a reading-free instrument.	Adequate

Source: From R. L. Taylor, 2009, Assessment of Exceptional Students (8th ed., p. 399). Upper Saddle River, NJ: Pearson. Used with permission.

TABLE 14.3 ● Resources for Developing Vocational Goals

SCHOOL

Follow-up studies of previous graduates
Placement data from vocational programs

COMMUNITY

List of community businesses and industries
Information from the Private Industry Council (PIC)
Chamber of Commerce information
Small Business Association
Social services agencies, especially those related to employment of persons with disabilities
    (i.e., The ARC)
Work adjustment and shelter employment agencies
Telephone book of the area—especially Yellow Pages
Newspapers
Radio/television
Websites

STATE

Department of Labor
Department of Commerce
Employment services
Labor/apprenticeship programs

NATIONAL

Occupational Outlook materials
Occupational reference materials
Materials on analyzing jobs

---

must remember that work beyond the family unit for some is inappropriate. Also school personnel need to be sensitive to both cultural and communication barriers and search for common goals and understandings. Table 14.3 provides guidelines for developing vocational goals.

APPLICATION OF ACADEMIC CONTENT TO REAL-LIFE SITUATIONS

At the secondary level, the responsibility for preparing students with disabilities for successful transitions to postsecondary environments rests on school personnel. Once the team prepares the IEP that contains the transition component, academic content area teachers must address the goals established in the plan. To provide effective transition programs, schools should stress the development of student independence by having teachers develop and teach a functional skills curriculum. In addition, teachers and support staff must foster an environment that encourages self-determined behaviors. There are some students with disabilities who have the necessary skills and motivation to be successful in postsecondary educational environments. For this group of students, IEPs and ITPs should incorporate goals and objectives that will prepare them for these opportunities. There are many other students with disabilities, however, who do not have the prerequisite skills or motivation to pursue postsecondary education. For this group of students, school personnel must focus their efforts on preparing them for independent living and employment opportunities.

Wimmer (1981) defined functional skills as "essential in carrying out everyday social, personal, and on the job tasks" (p. 613). Later, Wehman (2001) described functional skills as those related to (a) domestic living, (b) leisure and recreation, (c) community, and (d) vocation. Wehman's categories can easily be adopted by schools as a basis to provide instruction in the classroom to support the postsecondary transition process.

Domestic living skills include cleaning a home or room, planning and cooking meals, and cleaning and maintaining clothing. In some schema, this area includes personal health such as hygiene and preventative health and wellness issues. Traditionally, teachers of home economics and health courses addressed these skills, while teachers in general math classes have addressed measurement and essential mathematics skills. Although domestic skills might be most appropriate for students who are not planning to attend postsecondary educational opportunities, instruction in these areas could still be beneficial for those who plan to attend postsecondary educational programs. Many students with learning disabilities, attention deficit hyperactivity disorder, and other disabilities that do not necessarily prevent students from attending postsecondary educational programs could still benefit from instruction in this area.

Leisure and recreational skills include constructive use of free time such as participating in exercise activities, jogging, playing on community teams, bowling, playing video games, and going to athletic events, movies, theater, or concerts. Health or physical education classes are excellent arenas for students with disabilities to learn these skills. Teachers need to provide training opportunities in the necessary literacy skills for such activities as reading a movie schedule or finding directions to a desired location. Basic math skills such as money and time as well as the skill of estimation for travel and costs, as they relate to leisure and recreation, can easily be incorporated in math classes.

Social skills for appropriate interactions with members of the community, using restaurants, shopping at grocery stores, buying clothing or other items at department stores, depositing and writing bank checks, and paying bills are examples of community skills. This area can also include civic participation, being a good neighbor, and abiding by local laws. Civics classes provide an excellent opportunity to address these citizenship skills. The natural school environment provides an excellent opportunity to teach and practice social skills within traditional classroom activities. Math teachers can provide instruction and practice in the skills necessary for using money, including developing and staying in a budget. The school environment provides varied opportunities for learning and practicing all of these community skills.

Essential vocational skills include finding and maintaining employment. For years, teachers have used worksites available within the school for work training. The school office provides a training site for word processing, data entry, faxing, photocopying, and physical assembly and distribution of school-related materials. Tasks available in the school library include cataloging books, securing and returning requested materials, and cleaning and maintaining computers and other media equipment. School cafeterias have numerous work tasks including dishwashing, preparing foods, displaying and serving foods, and table and floor cleanup. The physical plant offers both indoor and outdoor training sites. Indoor are traditional janitorial tasks including cleaning and repair of the furniture and building. Outdoor are traditional grounds-keeping activities.

In addition to the training available at worksites, vocational classes can provide essential skills training that will lead to employment opportunities for students beyond entry-level employment. Recently, vocational classes have increased the requirements of academic components in the courses to the point where some students with disabilities might be unable to meet required academic standards for admission. Vocational teachers should work in conjunction with special educators to determine the appropriateness of entrance requirements and, in some cases, implement accommodations and modifications that will allow students with disabilities to engage in the performance aspects of the training. In some cases, a modified curriculum can be implemented so students with disabilities can learn the basic skills related to the occupation as well as general skills essential to all employees. General skills for all workers include regular attendance, arriving on time, cleaning personal workspace, accepting supervision and responding to correction appropriately, and recognizing one's own mistakes and implementing correction. All students need to learn these skills, including those with disabilities. As a result of Section 504 and the ADA, students with disabilities should be eligible to enroll in these courses. School staff need to ensure that they are aware of the requirements of these laws to assure students equal access to the vocational curriculum (Smith et al., 2008).

At some point, training opportunities offered at school sites are mastered and it becomes necessary to offer opportunities for students to generalize the skills they have mastered in community settings. This should result in opportunities for community-based instruction. Community-based instruction is a regularly scheduled opportunity for students to practice previously taught skills within community settings. When using community-based instruction, students should be required to perform targeted behaviors in restaurants, department stores, groceries, shopping malls, athletic events, bowling alleys, and other community sites which they might frequent after leaving school.

Wehman (2001) recommended that a maximum of three students simultaneously train at a particular community site. It is also recommended that students rotate through several worksites in order to provide them with a better understanding of common requirements and necessary employee skills, as well as the opportunity to compare different worksites to determine their own work preferences. Wehman (2001) also recommended that any site used for vocational training should provide students with opportunities to perform a variety of different tasks as a fully integrated member of the workforce interacting with coworkers who do not have disabilities.

While community-based instruction can be extremely valuable for some students, it has potential difficulties associated with it, as follows:

- Community-based instruction requires adequate staffing to ensure proper instruction is occurring. Wehman (2001) recommended a 1:4 (or less) instructor to student ratio in community-based instruction. Additional staff can include paraprofessionals, parents, high school club members, and student teachers.
- Transportation can be a barrier to community-based instruction. Some school districts have vans or special activity buses that are used to transport students to a site.
- The cost of community-based instruction can also be a barrier. It is beneficial to the program when the district includes it as a line item in the budget.
- Liability insurance can be problematic. While all school districts have liability insurance, teachers need to ensure community-based instruction is included under the district's policy since the students will be traveling beyond the school property.
- The inclusion movement and the academic standards movement driven by No Child Left Behind of 2001 have resulted in many students with high-incidence disabilities being included in the general education classrooms. This may be the appropriate placement but it should not prevent students from receiving what they need in terms of community-based instruction, as determined by the IEP team.

VOCATIONAL PROGRAMS FOR ADOLESCENTS WITH DISABILITIES

"Work is a central component of a quality adult life. Employment provides a source of income, enhances self-esteem, provides important social connections, and allows people to fulfill their duties as contributing, tax-paying citizens" (Rogan, Grossi, & Gajewsi, 2002, p. 104). As a result, one of the most important goals in transition planning concerns the future employment of students with disabilities. Most adolescents with disabilities who have received training in high school can obtain and maintain competitive employment. However, many adolescents with disabilities are not offered the opportunity to purse vocational preparation.

School-Based Vocational Training

Work-based learning programs are activities that include work experiences at the high school. The purpose of these activities is to provide students with real-life work experiences and connect those work experiences with classroom learning (National School-to-Work Office, 1996). Work-based learning is an essential component of career and technical education (CTE, sometimes CATE) programs. Students attend vocational classes on campus for one to three periods each day and participate in worksite internships the remainder of the day. Usually high schools offer training options based on the needs of local industries, but not specific to a narrow occupation. CTE utilizes youth apprenticeship programs and Tech Prep to allow students an opportunity to pair academic preparation in actual work situations. Other approaches to work-based learning include cooperative education, internships, apprenticeships, and school-based enterprises.

Tech Prep.   Tech Prep is a model of CTE based on a formal articulation agreement between high school and postsecondary institutions that provides a bridge between the two levels of education. The Tech-Prep program design encompasses grades 11 and 12, with 2 years of post-secondary education. Some programs also incorporate an additional 2 years at a 4-year college.

Cooperative Education.   Cooperative education is "a program which combines academic study with paid, monitored and credit-bearing work" (Ascher, 1994, p. 1). Most often, cooperative education occurs in the areas of marketing, trade and industry, and business. Generally, the program lasts no more than a year with students attending both traditional academic and vocational classes for half day and taking a cooperative education class during the remainder of the day. The cooperative education class consists of a classroom component and an off-campus work placement. On-campus instruction and monitoring is provided by the school coordinator who monitors student progress through student observations and conferences with students and their worksite mentor.

Student Internships.   The National School-to-Work Office (1996) defined student internships as "situations where students work for an employer for a specific period to learn about a particular industry or occupation" (p. 31). Student activities may include a number of different jobs or tasks, or a single job. Student internships are usually short term and vary in the complexity of the targeted knowledge and skills. They are usually unpaid.

Apprenticeships.   Apprenticeships are defined as "relationships between an employer and employee during which the worker, or apprentice, learns an occupation in a structured program sponsored jointly by employers and employee associations" (National School-to-Work Office, 1996, p. 3). Apprentices complete occupational training equivalent to a college degree in other professions. During the apprenticeship, apprentices receive financial compensation for their work.

Supported Employment.   Persons with more severe disabilities are good candidates for supported employment as opposed to individuals with milder disabilities who can be successful in competitive employment. Supported employment is work in integrated worksites of at least 20 hours per week supported by a job coach who helps employees with disabilities learn the skills necessary for success on the job. The job coaches provide support while the person is learning the job and slowly diminish their presence until the person can maintain employment with intermittent or no assistance. This model has proven extremely successful, especially for individuals with severe disabilities.

Although work-based learning has demonstrated its value in terms of preparing students for postsecondary employment, school staff and parents often display hesitancy concerning vocational education. This could be due to the belief that vocational preparation is inferior to academic programs. A regular high school diploma may mean academic competency while vocational education may mean settling for a degree or certificate that carries lower status. Some parents and school staff may also have difficulty believing that properly trained students with disabilities will still be unemployable in competitive employment situations. Often parents of female students are even more reluctant to see the need for vocational training. Finally, school staff and parents may be hesitant because of concern over the lack of appropriate vocational education offerings. Many schools offer only limited choices, many of which may not seem appropriate for today's job market. Cosmetology, welding, and some of the other traditional vocational preparation programs may not be as marketable today as 25 years ago. Despite these concerns, many students with disabilities need the opportunity to receive vocational education that will better prepare them for their futures than a more academic curriculum.

Postsecondary Education

The term *postsecondary education* includes programs that emphasize the educational- or institutional-based vocational and/or technical training. In some cases, it also includes apprenticeships, Tech Prep, and other CTE programs that were discussed previously. However, there are other postsecondary options available, such as 4-year colleges and universities, community colleges, and career-technical colleges. Opportunities in these areas should be addressed in the ITP as well as the development of a plan addressing the student's needs for a successful transition to postsecondary educational environments. Transition plans for college-bound students need to include college preparatory courses and a program of study that leads to a diploma. Today, many schools offer a plethora of diploma options including honors diplomas, standard diplomas, certificates of attendance (or completion), and IEP diplomas. For college-bound students, the selection of an appropriate diploma is essential for their admission to the institution of choice.

Technology. College-bound students also need to be aware of the growing use of technology in postsecondary educational environments. Word-processing technology—spell and grammar checks, dictionary, thesaurus, electronic messaging, math calculators—is routinely used in elementary, middle, and secondary classrooms. Once seen as a tool for accessing information, technology is now an essential element in college classrooms. Computers can be used to assist students with disabilities by compensating for their literacy weaknesses and providing them flexibility and support in written expression. Therefore, middle and high school teachers must encourage the use of computers in their classrooms to prepare these students for using technology in postsecondary educational settings. By using computers in daily learning activities, students will be better prepared for their use in other academic settings.

Teachers should also use a wide range of technologies when teaching. Assistive technology, originally used to provide remedial support to students, has been expanded to provide compensatory support for the functional limitations resulting from disabilities. Some of the specific ways that assistive technologies can be used to support students with disabilities include (Banerjee, 2010, pp. 120–121):

- Circumvent a specific functional limitation.
- Allow students to keep pace with their peers in basic skills areas.
- Create opportunities for equal access and participation.

- Provide a range of accommodations that any eligible student with a disability is legally entitled to receive.

During the students' time in middle and secondary schools, school staff should assist them in learning how to make maximum use of assistive technology. One important area that has become critical for academic success in secondary and postsecondary classrooms is use of the Internet. Internet literacy includes the ability to (1) clearly define a search question or query; (2) navigate links so as to locate information; (3) assess the relevancy of the information in relationship to the query; (4) evaluate the information and choose what information to use; and (5) synthesize and compile the information into an appropriate format. It is imperative that school staff work with all students, including those with disabilities, to assist them in developing skills necessary to take advantage of Internet technology.

In addition to the Internet, some students may need to learn strategies for using audiobooks. The following steps may help students take advantage of this option:

- *Prelistening*—students examine the book, looking for pictures, tables, print variations, and such that will not be noted in the audio of the book.
- *Gist listening*—students listen to a section of the audiobook to get the overview of the information without pausing the recording.
- *Strategic listening*—students stop the recording to take notes or to use self-teaching (talking aloud).
- *Relisten*—students listen to selected portions of the audio to confirm understanding.

Teachers who use some of the strategies discussed in earlier chapters, such as cluster strategies, may want to show students how to use technology when using semantic mapping or semantic feature analysis. Organizational software, which is available online, has built-in templates that can be used by teachers and students alike to provide a visual or text-based outline of the materials to be learned. By modeling its use with the entire class, all students can benefit from learning new study strategies appropriate for postsecondary settings.

During the transition to postsecondary education, students with disabilities face the same adjustment issues as their nondisabled peers. Gartin, Rumrill, and Serebrini (1996) described four difficulties commonly experienced by students with disabilities when they make the transition from high school to postsecondary education: (1) a decrease in teacher/student contact, (2) an increase in academic competition, (3) a change in personal support networks, and (4) a loss of the protective public school environment. Brinckerhoff (1994) identified similar differences between high school and college requirements, but placed them under seven categories:

1. Time in class
2. Class size
3. Preparation time required for each class
4. Frequency of tests
5. Minimum grades necessary for remaining enrolled in school
6. Teaching practices
7. Amount of freedom allowed the student

Getzel and Thoma (2008) identified another group of skills important for students making the transition from secondary to postsecondary programs. Using focus groups of 2- and 4-year college students with disabilities, four major groups of skills for securing the support needed for staying in college were identified. These included the ability to (1) seek services available on campus, (2) form relationships with professors and instructors, (3) develop support systems on campus with friends, support groups, and the disability services offices, and (4) develop self-awareness and an understanding of themselves. Teachers need to address these areas as well as those described above in order to facilitate students' transitions. Many of these skills are related to social skills and self-determination. By focusing on these areas, teachers can prepare many of these students for a successful transition.

In addition to the needs of students are several barriers inherent in the school system that might prevent students with disabilities from making a successful transition to postsecondary education. One of the most important barriers is access, or lack of access, to guidance counselors. At many high schools, guidance counselors serve as gatekeepers for information concerning entrance into postsecondary educational settings. Often, counselors may not believe that students with disabilities are capable of success in postsecondary settings and therefore exclude them from information that could be useful. All students must take the high school coursework required for admission to the targeted postsecondary educational settings. The correct admissions tests need to be taken, perhaps with appropriate accommodations that must be secured by application completed by the guidance counselor. Financial support might be needed and guidance counselors are often the experts on this topic. Also, for students with disabilities, documents verifying the presence of the disability must be provided if accommodations are needed. For all of these reasons, plus the simple support provided by counselors for students making this decision, the role of the counselor is critical.

Students with disabilities and their parents should consult with the guidance counselor for assistance in identifying potential colleges or other postsecondary educational settings that would be appropriate for a particular student. For example, some colleges and universities provide specific supports for students with disabilities. Parents and students may not readily have this information and would therefore depend on a guidance counselor to provide it. Potential programs should have preparation opportunities appropriate for students' vocational goals, as well as programs that match students' interests and abilities. Finally, postsecondary programs must have appropriate support services available that would meet specific needs for students with disabilities.

SUMMARY

Transition planning first emerged in response to the poor postsecondary outcomes exhibited by persons with disabilities. By federal law (e.g., IDEA), transition planning must begin by age 16 and an IEP must be prepared. Students with disabilities need a functional emphasis in their transition plan if they are to transition successfully to adult life. In their educational programs, they require opportunities in schools to develop skills needed in the personal, community, and vocational sectors of their lives. Teachers need to address these goals throughout the secondary years. Vocational goals will determine the type of program the student will need. For some students with disabilities, this preparation may involve multiple school personnel and representatives of community adult service agencies; for others, it may be a guidance counselor or support in only one area. Whatever the needs of the students, secondary schools have the responsibility of addressing the transitional needs of all secondary students with disabilities while working toward ensuring a successful transition to adulthood.

ACTIVITIES

1. Interview a student with disabilities who is attending or has attended the college or university where you are taking this course. Ask about what his or her transition from high school was like. Ask what has been most helpful since that time.

2. What besides content knowledge did your middle and high school teachers teach you that helped to prepare you for your college or university education? Work in a small group sharing your lists. Discover what you have on your lists that are similar.

3. Observe a secondary classroom and list the procedures and skills on which the teacher is focusing that might be useful in a postsecondary setting.

REFERENCES

Americans with Disabilities Act (ADA) of 1990, P. L. 101-336, 42 U.S.C. §§ 12101 *et seq.*

Americans with Disabilities Act Amendments Act (ADAAA) of 2008, P. L. 110-325, 42 U.S.C. §§ 12101 *et seq.*

Ascher, C. (1994, January). Cooperative education as a strategy for school-to-work transition. *Center Focus, 3*, 1–3. (ERIC Document Reproduction Service No. ED365798).

Banerjee, M. (2010). Technology trends and transition for students with disabilities. In S. F. Shaw, J. W. Madaus, & L. L. Dukes, III (Eds.), *Preparing students with disabilities for college success: A practical guide to transition planning* (pp. 115–136). Baltimore: Paul H. Brookes.

Bennett, G. K., Seashore, H. G., & Wesman, A. G. (1992). *The Differential Aptitude Test* (5th ed.). San Antonio, TX: Pearson/The Psychological Corporation.

Brinckerhoff, L. C. (1994). Developing effective self-advocacy skills in college-bound students with learning disabilities. *Intervention in School and Clinic, 29*, 229–237.

Carl D. Perkins Vocational and Applied Technology Act Amendments of 1990, P. L. 101-392, 20 U.S.C. §§ 2301 *et seq.*

Carl D. Perkins Vocational and Applied Technology Act Amendments of 1998, P. L. 105-332, 20 U.S.C. §§ 2301 *et seq.*

Clark, G. M., & Patton, J. R. (2006). *Transition planning inventory-2.* Austin, TX: PRO-ED.

Comprehensive Employment and Training Act (CETA) of 1973, P. L. 93-203, 29 U.S.C. §§ 961 *et seq.*

Comprehensive Employment and Training Act (CETA) of 1978, P. L. 95-524, 29 U.S.C. §§ 961 *et seq.*

The Developmental Disabilities Assistance and Bill of Rights Act of 2000, P. L. 106-402, §§ 151 *et seq.*

Gartin, B. C., Rumrill, P., & Serebrini, R. (1996). The higher education transition model: Guidelines for facilitating college transition among college-bound students with disabilities. *Teaching Exceptional Children, 29*(1), 30–33.

Getzel, E. E., & Thoma, C. A. (2008). Experiences of college students with disabilities and the importance of self-determination in higher education settings. *Career Development for Exceptional Individuals, 31*(2), 77–84.

Glutting, J. J., & Wilkinson, G. S. (2003). *Wide Range Interest and Occupation Test* (2nd ed.). Lutz, FL: Psychological Assessment Resources.

Individuals with Education Act (IDEA) of 1990, P. L. 101-476, 20 U.S.C. §§ 1400 *et seq.*

Individuals with Education Act Amendments (IDEA) of 1997, P. L. 105-17, 20 U.S.C. §§ 1400 *et seq.*

Individuals with Education Improvement Act (IDEA) of 2004, P. L. 108-446, 20 U.S.C. §§ 1400 *et seq.*

Job Training and Partnership Act (JTPA) of 1982, P. L. 97-300, 29 USC §§ 1501 *et seq.*

Murdick, N. L., Gartin, B. C., Crabtree, T. (2007). *Special education law* (2nd ed.). Upper Saddle River, NJ: Pearson.

National School-to-Work Office. (1996). *School-to-work glossary of terms.* Washington, DC: Author.

No Child Left Behind Act of 2001, P. L. 107-100.

Parker, R. M. (2001). *Occupational Aptitude Survey and Interest Schedule* (3rd ed.). Austin, TX: Pro-Ed.

Rehabilitation Act Amendments of 1992, P. L. 102-569, 29 U.S.C. §§ 701 *et seq.*

Rehabilitation Act of 1973, P. L. 93-112, 29 U.S.C. §§ 701 *et seq.*

Rogan, P., Grossi, T. A., & Gajewsi, R. (2002). Vocational and career assessment. In C. L. Sax & C. A. Thoma (Eds.), *Transition assessment: Wise practices for quality lives* (pp. 103–117). Baltimore: Paul H. Brookes.

Rosenberg, H., & Brady, M. (2000). *JOBS: Job Observation and Behavior Scale.* Wood Dale, IL: Stoelting.

Sitlington, P., Neubert, D., & Clark, G. (2010). *Transition education and services for students with disabilities* (5th ed.). Upper Saddle River, NJ: Merrill/Pearson Education.

Smith, T. E. C., Polloway, E. A., Patton, J. R., & Dowdy, C. A. (2012). *Teaching students with special needs in inclusive settings* (6th ed.). Upper Saddle River, NJ: Pearson.

Taylor, R. L. (2009). *Assessment of exceptional students* (8th ed.). Upper Saddle River, NJ: Pearson.

Wehman, P. (Ed.). (2001). *Life beyond the classroom: Transition strategies for young people with disabilities* (3rd ed.). Baltimore: Paul H. Brookes.

Wimmer, D. (1981). Functional learning curricula in the secondary schools. *Exceptional Children, 47*, 610–616.

INDEX